Microsoft® Windows® 98,

Second Edition

Faithe Wempen

Contents
at a Glance

A Division of Macmillan USA
201 W. 103rd Street
Indianapolis, Indiana 46290

i

Practical Microsoft® Windows® 98, Second Edition

International Standard Book Number: 0-7897-2202-X

Library of Congress Catalog Card Number: 99-067437

Printed in the United States of America

First Printing: October 1999

01 00 99   4   3   2   1

Trademarks

Warning and Disclaimer

Publisher
Jim Minatel

Acquisitions Editor
Jill Byus

Development Editors
Valerie Perry
Ben Milstead

Managing Editor
Lisa Wilson

Project Editor
Linda Seifert

Copy Editor
Barbara Hacha

Indexer
Joy Dean Lee

Proofreaders
Bob LaRoche
Megan Wade

Technical Editor
Coletta Witherspoon

Team Coordinator
Vicki Harding

Interior Design
Nathan Clement
Ruth Lewis

Cover Design
Ruth Lewis
Dan Armstrong

Production
Dan Harris
Heather Moseman
Timothy Osborn

Contents

About the Author

Faithe Wempen owns and operates Your Computer Friend, a computer training and troubleshooting business in Indiana that focuses on helping beginning users one-on-one. She is also an A+ certified PC technician and holds a masters degree in English. She is the author of more than 40 books on computer hardware and software, including the best-selling *Microsoft Office 97 Professional 6-in-1* (Que Corporation).

Dedication

To Margaret

Acknowledgments

Many thanks to the wonderful editorial team for this book, whose names appear on the Credits page. Macmillan Publishing truly has some of the best editors in the business!

Tell Us What You Think!

As the reader of this book, *you* are our most important critic and commentator. We value your opinion and want to know what we're doing right, what we could do better, what areas you'd like to see us publish in, and any other words of wisdom you're willing to pass our way.

As a Publisher for Que, I welcome your comments. You can fax, email, or write me directly to let me know what you did or didn't like about this book—as well as what we can do to make our books stronger.

Please note that I cannot help you with technical problems related to the topic of this book, and that due to the high volume of mail I receive, I might not be able to reply to every message.

When you write, please be sure to include this book's title and author as well as your name and phone or fax number. I will carefully review your comments and share them with the author and editors who worked on the book.

Fax: 317–581–4666

Email: opsys@mcp.com

Mail: Publisher
          Que
          201 West 103rd Street
          Indianapolis, IN 46290 USA

introduction

Welcome! Thanks for picking up this book. Before you get started with it, please indulge me and take a few moments to read through this Introduction. In it, I'll explain the concept behind the book and help you figure out where to start in it.

As a writer and computer consultant who specializes in training beginners, I know it can be frustrating when you are faced with a complicated piece of software such as Windows 98. You may have heard that it can do all these wonderful things, but you may not know how to make them happen.

In writing this book, my focus is to provide the answers to questions that I often hear from my clients[md]people *just like you*, who want to use Windows 98 for useful things.

Practical Windows 98 may be the only reference that you ever need for Windows 98. It covers installing Win98, running programs, managing files, and many more basics such as setting up networking components, connecting to the Internet, and troubleshooting device problems. But I promise I'll never throw scary technical jargon at you without explaining it, and I'll never include details that don't have some concrete, practical benefit.

Along the way, I'll also provide tips, tricks, and cautions that I've learned over the years as a consultant. You'll learn things that can make your life easier, such as setting up shortcuts and toolbars to quickly access the programs you use the most. And you'll find out what some of those mysterious utility programs are for that come with Windows, and when you might want to use them.

Where to Start?

This book starts at a very basic, "no experience required" level. If you have never used Windows 98 before or feel like you have missed out on a basic Windows education in the past, start in Part I: "Starting Out with Windows." Here, you'll get a solid grounding in things such as windows, menus, folders, mouse actions, and program use. These are essential skills that every Windows user needs to know.

More experienced Windows users will probably want to jump immediately to a chapter that fits what they want to do. If you're interested in customizing how Windows looks and works, start in Part II: "Modifying Your System." It teaches how to install new programs, change your color scheme, set up new hardware, and more.

Part III: "Sharing Resources," is for those of you who need to work with others. You'll learn how several people can share a single PC (and each has its own chosen colors and other settings!), how you can work with shared files on a network, how you can share one modem among PCs (a new feature in Windows 98 version 2), and how to set up and transfer files from a laptop.

If your main goal in using a computer is to explore the Internet, jump right into Part IV: "Using the Internet." You'll find out how to set up a modem, configure an Internet connection, and get down to business with the Web, email, newsgroups, chatting, and other online communications.

Part V: "Maintenance and Problem-Solving," the final part, teaches you to run your own preventive maintenance and system checks to prevent and solve problems. So many of my clients call me to come look at their computers and fix their problems when 75% of the time they could have fixed the problem themselves with a few simple actions that I'll describe here.

Special Helps

Each chapter starts out with a Roadmap section that lists the topics to be covered. You can skim this Roadmap and skip the chapter if you don't need any of that information at the moment. (You can always come back to it later.)

Extra Help

I'll also provide extra information, such as tips, cautions, and ideas, in boxed notes like this one.

Within a chapter, step-by-step procedures (many with pictures) walk you through important tasks. You'll never have to wonder exactly how something is done; just follow the steps.

I'll use a kind of shorthand for telling you which keys to press. When you see a combination of keys separated by plus signs, such as Alt+F4, you should hold down the first key while you tap the second, then release both keys. In a three-key combo, such as Ctrl+Alt+Delete, you hold down the first two while you tap the last.

Each chapter is also extensively cross-referenced with pointers to the exact pages where related information is covered. For example, if we're talking about creating sound clips, I'll let you know where you can find information about assigning system sounds and changing multimedia system settings.

Let's Get Started!

If you read through this entire introduction—thanks! I really enjoyed writing this book, and I hope you will enjoy reading it. If you'd like to let me know what you thought of the book, email me at `fwempen@iquest.net`.

Happy Computing,

Faithe Wempen

part

I

STARTING OUT WITH WINDOWS

chapter

1

Windows Basics

What Is Microsoft Windows?

Microsoft Windows is the most popular operating system for personal computers (PCs) on the market today. These days you'd be hard-pressed to find a new computer that *didn't* come with it! Windows has become the worldwide standard for which most software and hardware manufacturers design their products.

An *operating system* does just what the name implies: It helps the computer operate on a basic level. Some of the tasks an operating system handles include

- Creating the graphical display on your screen
- Translating your keyboard and mouse actions into commands
- Keeping track of where saved files are stored
- Running programs that enable you to do useful things such as word processing
- Making the PC's memory available to the running programs in the most efficient way
- Directing traffic to and from your computer's processor (its "brain") so no collisions occur

And that's only a few examples. The operating system coordinates all the devices, files, and programs, making them all work together so that you can use your PC productively.

Starting Windows

Black Screen at Startup

It is normal for the screen to go black temporarily as Windows starts up. As long as you can hear the hard disk turning or see the hard disk light flashing, Windows is still loading. If the screen goes black for more than a minute and you do not observe any disk activity, turn the power off and back on again. Then, refer to Chapter 25 for troubleshooting help.

As soon as you press the power button on your PC, Windows begins its loading process, and a minute or so later, Windows is ready to roll.

You may be prompted to enter your Windows username and password, depending on how your system is set up. If you see that prompt, enter the requested information in the boxes provided and click **OK** to continue.

After Windows has started, you may see a Welcome to Windows 98 window on your screen, as shown in Figure 1.1. This window reappears every time you start Windows (until it is disabled by deselecting the checkbox in the bottom-left corner). It provides easy access to several features that beginners find useful, such as a registration form and a tutorial. You will learn more about it in Chapter 2.

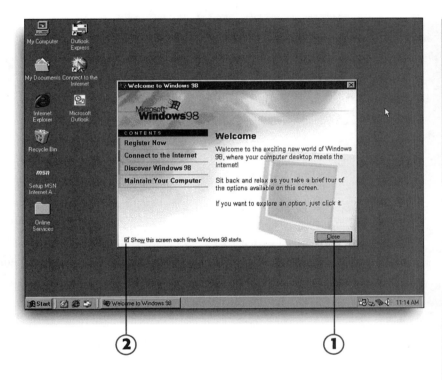

FIGURE 1.1
This Welcome window provides help for new users.

(1) Click here to close the window.

(2) Click here to prevent the window from appearing in the future.

Other Login Names?

In addition to (or instead of) the Windows username and password, you may be prompted to log on to your local area network (LAN) or some other network system. Respond to each logon request with the correct username password for that system. Pay attention to the title of the dialog box so you will know which logon each box is asking for. For example, the Windows logon's dialog box is titled Enter Windows Password.

SEE ALSO

➤ *To troubleshoot startup problems, see page 438.*

➤ *To run the Windows 98 tutorial from the Welcome to Windows 98 screen, see page 34.*

➤ *To register your copy of Windows 98 from the Welcome to Windows 98 screen, see page 35.*

➤ *To change your password, see page 239.*

➤ *To set Windows to start without prompting for a password, see page 231.*

Using Your Mouse

Can't I Stick with the Keyboard?

You can use either the keyboard or the mouse to do most activities in Windows (and in Windows-based programs), but you will find that using the mouse is almost always the easier method. Throughout this book, I'll tell you about keyboard alternatives to many of the mouse operations you will learn about.

You may have used a mouse before in other programs, but in Windows 98 some special mouse features are available that you may not have seen before. Take a moment to review mouse use now.

The following are some of the most common mouse operations:

- **Click.** To press and release the left mouse button once. Clicking something usually selects it.

- **Double-click.** To press and release the left mouse button twice in succession. Double-clicking something usually activates or opens it.

- **Drag.** To point at something and then hold down the left mouse button while you move the mouse. Dragging something moves it.

- **Right-click.** To press and release the right mouse button once. Right-clicking opens a menu of actions for that object.

Other Mouse Features

Some mice have three buttons instead of two, and/or a wheel between the buttons. The middle button and the wheel are not used in Windows 98.

Depending on what's going on at the moment in Windows, the mouse pointer can look different. For example, when Windows is busy and not ready to accept another command, the mouse pointer turns into an hourglass. Table 1.1 shows some different mouse pointers you might see as you work in Windows 98.

Table 1.1 Common mouse pointers

Pointer	Name	Seen When...
⬉	Normal Select (Arrow)	Windows is ready to accept your next command.
⌛	Busy (Hourglass)	Windows is busy and you must wait.
⬉⌛	Working in Background (Hourglass/Arrow)	Windows is busy, but you can continue working.
⬉?	Help Select (What's This? Arrow)	What's This? Help is activated (in some programs).
I	Text Select (I-beam)	The mouse pointer is over a text box where you can type text.

Pointer	Name	Seen When...
⊘	Unavailable	The mouse pointer is over a button or feature that cannot be used right now.
☝	Link Select (Hand)	The mouse pointer is over a hyperlink.
+	Precision Select (Crosshair)	The mouse pointer is ready to draw a new object (in certain programs).
↔	Resize (Double-Headed Arrow)	The mouse pointer is over the border of a window that can be resized by dragging here.
⊕	Move (Four-Headed Arrow)	The mouse pointer is over an object or window that can be moved by dragging here

Windows 98 comes with several alternative sets of mouse pointers that you can choose to use instead of the normal ones shown in Table 1.1. If yours don't look like the ones in Table 1.1, perhaps someone has set up one of those alternative sets.

SEE ALSO

➤ *To change how quickly the pointer moves across the screen when you move the mouse, see page 187.*

➤ *To change the appearance of the mouse pointer, see page 188.*

➤ *To switch the button functions on the mouse (for left-handed operation), see page 186.*

Understanding the Windows Screen

The Windows screen may seem mysterious at first, but it's really fairly simple. Take the time to master its basic controls now, and you'll be zipping around productively in no time.

Figure 1.2 points out some of the parts of the screen.

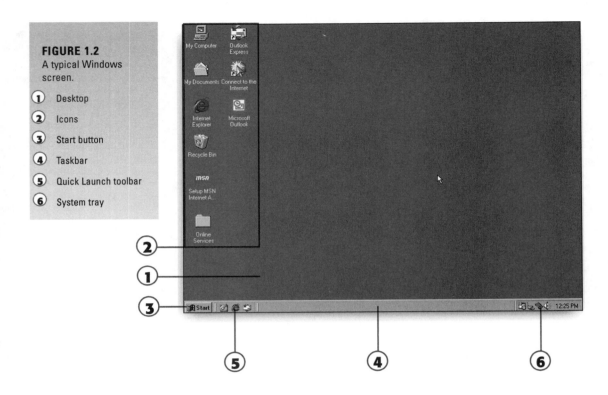

FIGURE 1.2
A typical Windows screen.

① Desktop

② Icons

③ Start button

④ Taskbar

⑤ Quick Launch toolbar

⑥ System tray

- **Desktop.** The colored background on which everything else sits. Just like on a regular desk, the items that you work with appear on it.

- **Icons.** Small pictures (with text beneath them) that appear on the desktop. An icon can represent a program to run, a folder to open, or a data file (such as a document) to edit. To open whatever program, file, or folder the icon represents, double-click it.

- **Shortcuts.** Some icons have a small arrow in the bottom-left corner. This indicates that the icon is a *shortcut*. A shortcut is a pointer to the actual program, folder, or file. The actual file that starts the program is safely stored somewhere else; the shortcut is merely a convenient way to access it. In Figure 1.3, compare the original program file (on the left) to the shortcut (on the right).

FIGURE 1.3
A shortcut can be placed on your desktop without having to place the actual file there.

■ **Start button.** Your gateway to the programs installed on your PC. When you click the **Start** button, the Start menu appears. From there, you can move through the menu levels to find and run a program. See Figure 1.4. You will learn a lot more about the Start menu (as well as other ways to start a program) in Chapter 3, "Running Programs."

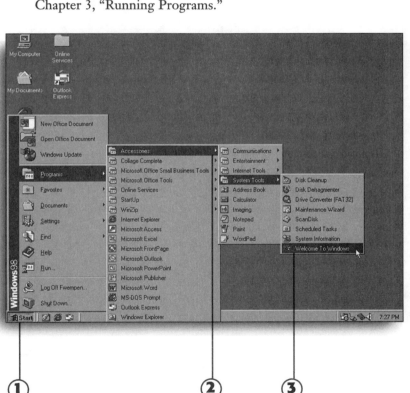

FIGURE 1.4
Most of the programs installed on your system can be run from the Start menu.

① Click the Start button.

② Point to each submenu name to open it.

③ Click the program you want to run when you see it.

Shortcut To...
Sometimes, a shortcut will include the words "Shortcut to" in its text name, but don't rely on this text to tell whether an icon is a shortcut. The Outlook Express icon on the desktop, for example, does not have this wording.

■ **Quick Launch toolbar.** A cluster of small buttons next to the Start buttons. Each of these is a shortcut for launching a program or issuing a command.

What Does That Button Do?

You can find out what program or command a button represents, both on the Quick Launch toolbar and on the desktop itself, by pointing at it. A ScreenTip appears, providing the button's name.

FIGURE 1.5

There is a button on the taskbar for each of the two open windows.

- **Taskbar.** The area to the right of the Quick Launch toolbar. It shows a rectangular button for each open window or running program. (You will learn about windows later in this chapter.) If no windows are open, it is blank. Figure 1.5 shows the taskbar with two open windows: My Documents and My Computer.

  You can use the taskbar to switch among the open windows by clicking the rectangular button for the window you want to work with. You can also close a window from the taskbar, as you will learn later in this chapter in the section "Closing a Window."

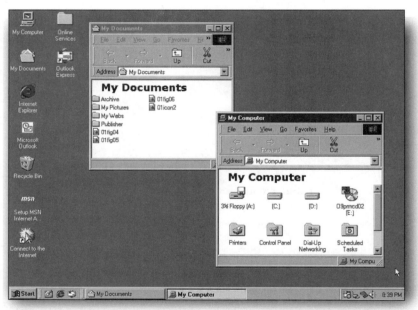

- **System tray.** The area at the far-right end of the taskbar. It contains a digital clock and a cluster of icons. Each of these icons represents a program that is running quietly behind-the-scenes as Windows operates, performing some special function (such as virus protection or speaker volume control).

  You can point to an icon in the System tray to see a ScreenTip with its name or status. You can right-click a System tray icon to see a shortcut menu of actions you can perform on that running program. Depending on what programs are installed on your computer, your System tray may have different icons from the ones shown in Figure 1.6.

FIGURE 1.6
The System tray on a laptop computer; yours will probably contain different icons.

SEE ALSO

➤ *To learn how to change the desktop's appearance, see page 153.*

➤ *To create and delete shortcut icons on the desktop, see page 128.*

➤ *To alter the appearance of the permanent icons on the desktop, see page 174.*

➤ *To run programs from the Start menu, see page 48.*

➤ *To rearrange the programs and submenus on the Start menu, see page 124.*

➤ *To control what buttons appear on the Quick Launch toolbar, see page 132.*

➤ *To use the taskbar to switch between running programs or open windows, see page 61.*

➤ *To customize how the taskbar operates, see page 179.*

➤ *To shut down a program running in the system tray, see page 64.*

Working with Windows

As you might guess from the name "Microsoft Windows," rectangular blocks called *windows* play a big part in this operating system. Every program or folder you open appears in its own window. You can have multiple windows open at once and switch among them freely. Figure 1.7 shows several types of windows.

Almost every window has the following elements, as shown in Figure 1.8:

- **Title bar.** The bar across the top of the window containing the window's title.

- **Minimize button.** Minimizes the window (without closing it) so that it appears only on the taskbar until you need it again.

- **Maximize button.** Enlarges the window to fill the entire screen.

- **Close button.** Closes the window.

- **Control-menu button.** Opens the window's Control menu.

- **Window border.** Can be dragged to resize the window.

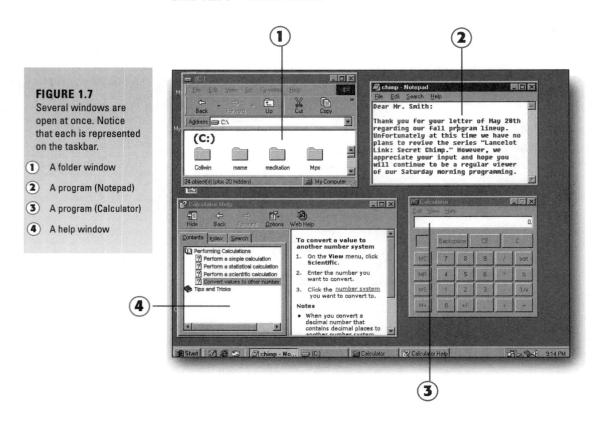

FIGURE 1.7
Several windows are open at once. Notice that each is represented on the taskbar.

① A folder window

② A program (Notepad)

③ A program (Calculator)

④ A help window

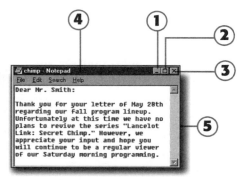

FIGURE 1.8
Almost all windows provide these elements with which to control them.

① Minimize button

② Maximize button

③ Close button

④ Title bar

⑤ Window border

You will review the use of each of these elements in the following sections.

Minimizing, Maximizing, and Restoring Windows

Each window can be in any of three states:

- **Maximized.** Expanded to fill the entire screen. This lets you see as much content as possible onscreen at once in that window. See Figure 1.9.

- **Minimized.** Hidden except for its rectangular button on the taskbar. This is *not* the same as closed; the window is still open but it is not visible at the moment. Minimizing a window gets it out of the way temporarily while you work on something else.

- **Restored.** Visible but not maximized. When several windows are restored, you can arrange them onscreen to see them all at once.

Figure 1.10 shows two windows: one minimized and one restored.

FIGURE 1.9
A maximized window fills the entire screen.

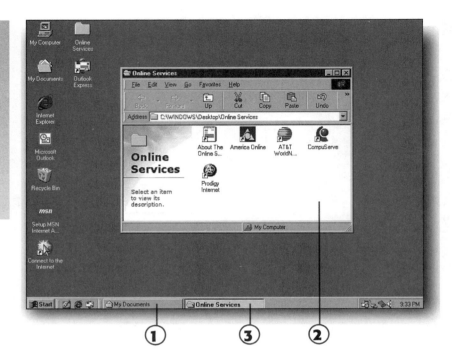

FIGURE 1.10
A restored window floats on the desktop; a minimized window appears only on the taskbar.

(1) Minimized window (on taskbar only)

(2) Restored window on the desktop

(3) Restored window on the taskbar

You can change a window's state by clicking one of the buttons in its upper-right corner:

 To minimize a window, click its Minimize button.

 To maximize a window, click its Maximize button.

 When a window is maximized, the Maximize button changes to a Restore button. Click it to return the window to its premaximized size.

Resizing a Window

A restored window (that is, one that is neither minimized nor maximized) can be resized so that it is any size you want it to be. You might make a window smaller so that another window can also be open without the two overlapping, for example. Or you might make a window larger so you can see more of its content onscreen at once.

To resize a window, position the mouse pointer over the border of the window so that the mouse pointer turns into a Resize pointer (a double-headed arrow).

- To resize in only one dimension (height or width), position the mouse pointer over the top, bottom, right, or left border.
- To resize in both dimensions at once (both height and width), position the mouse pointer over one of the corners.

Then, hold down the left mouse button and drag to change the window size. An outline shows the new size (as in Figure 1.11). When the window is the size you want, release the mouse button.

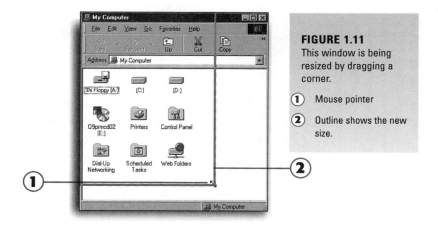

FIGURE 1.11
This window is being resized by dragging a corner.

① Mouse pointer

② Outline shows the new size.

Moving a Window

A restored window can also be moved. (Maximized windows cannot be moved because there is nowhere for them to go—they fill the entire screen.) You might want to move a window out of the way so you can see the icons on the desktop, for example, or move two windows around so that they do not overlap one another. To move a window, drag its title bar, as shown in Figure 1.12.

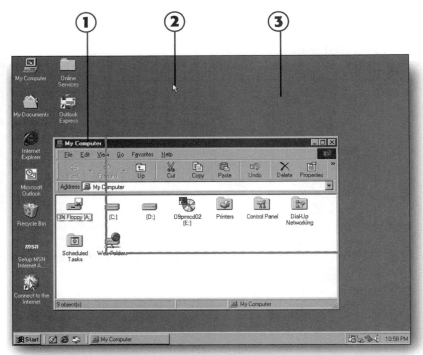

FIGURE 1.12
Move a window by drag-
ging its title bar.

① Title bar

② Mouse pointer
dragging

③ Outline shows new
position.

Arranging Windows Automatically

In addition to moving and resizing windows manually as you learned
in the preceding two sections, you can ask Windows to do the adjust-
ment for you so that all the open windows are arranged in a uniform
way.

You can choose from three preset arrangements:

- **Cascade Windows.** Arranges all windows so that their title bars
  are visible. Each successive window's title bar appears slightly
  below and to the right of the one underneath it, resulting in a
  cascading look. See Figure 1.13.

- **Tile Windows Horizontally.** Arranges all windows so that col-
  lectively they fill the entire screen in horizontal rows, but no
  window overlaps another. See Figure 1.14.

- **Tile Windows Vertically.** The same as Tile Windows
  Horizontally, except the windows are tiled vertically. See
  Figure 1.15.

20

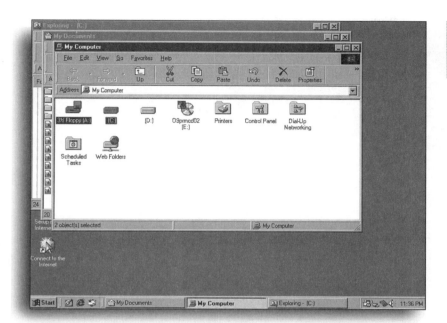

FIGURE 1.13
Cascading windows.

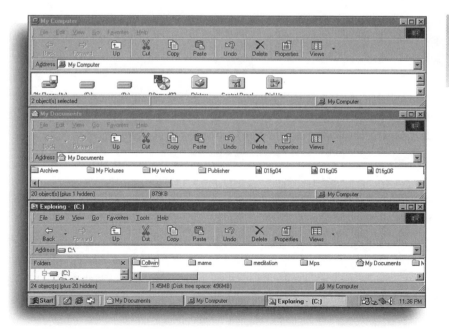

FIGURE 1.14
Tiled windows
(horizontal).

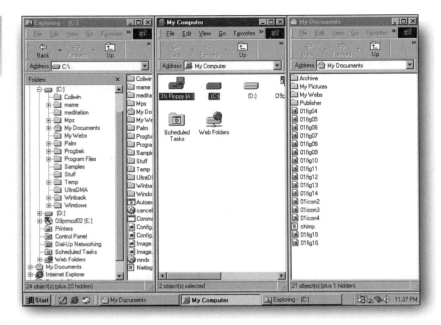

FIGURE 1.15
Tiled windows (vertical).

Undoing the Arrangement

You can undo the last action you have taken with the taskbar's shortcut menu. Simply right-click the taskbar again and choose **Undo {command name}**. The **{command name}** part varies depending on what the last command was. For example, if the last command was Tile Windows Horizontally, the command is **Undo Tile**. Undoing can be handy if you want to temporarily arrange the windows so you can see something, and then put them back the way they were right away.

Arranging Windows

1. Right-click an empty spot on the taskbar. A shortcut menu appears.

2. Click one of the following commands:

   - **Cascade Windows**
   - **Tile Windows Horizontally**
   - **Tile Windows Vertically**

Scrolling a Window's Display

Sometimes, a window has more content than what will fit in the allotted space at once. In such cases, scrollbars appear on the right and/or bottom of the window. The scrollbar provides controls that help you scroll through the window's content, bringing parts of the content that you want to see into view. Figure 1.16 shows a window with both vertical and horizontal scrollbars.

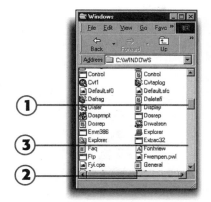

FIGURE 1.16
A typical window with scrollbars.

(1) Scroll box

(2) Scroll arrow

(3) Scrollbar

To scroll through the window, you can do any of the following:

- To scroll slowly, click a scroll arrow. Each time you click a scroll arrow, the display moves one line.

- To scroll quickly, click and hold down the scroll arrow or drag the scroll box.

- To scroll one windowful at a time, click the scrollbar above or below (or to the right or left of) the scroll box.

Closing a Window

You will want to close a window when you are finished working with it so your Windows screen does not become cluttered. Closing a window also conserves your computer's memory so it can be employed in other ways (such as running programs that you want to use).

You can do any of the following to close a window:

- Click the **Close (X) button** in the top-right corner.

- Double-click the **Control menu icon** in the top-left corner.

- Open the **File** menu (if the window has one) and click **Close** or **Exit** (depending on the window).

- Right-click a window's button on the taskbar and choose **Close** from the shortcut menu that appears.

- Click the window's title bar to select it, and then press **Alt+F4**.

Scrollbar Size

Some windows have scroll boxes that change size depending on how much of the window's content is not visible.

For example, in Figure 1.16, the horizontal scroll box occupies about one-half of the scrollbar. That means that about one-half of the content from side-to-side is not visible. The vertical scroll box, on the other hand, is very small (only about one-sixth of the total scrollbar area). That means that there is a great deal of undisplayed content vertically.

Not all scrollbars in all programs work this way; in some programs the scroll box is always the same size regardless of the content.

Figure 1.17 shows some of these methods.

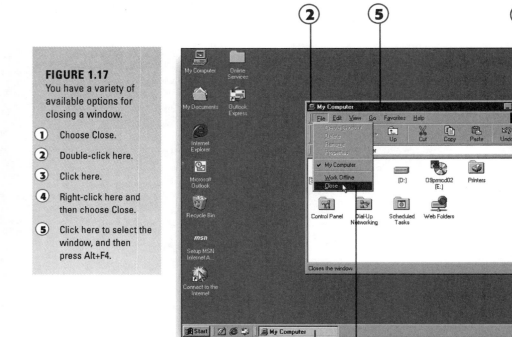

FIGURE 1.17
You have a variety of available options for closing a window.

1. Choose Close.
2. Double-click here.
3. Click here.
4. Right-click here and then choose Close.
5. Click here to select the window, and then press Alt+F4.

Working with Menus

As you learned about windows in the last section, you had the opportunity to try out a few menu commands. In this section you will learn more about the various types of menus that Windows 98 provides for your use.

Drop-Down Menus

For most menus, you click the menu name on a menu bar to open it, and then click the command you want to select.

Most menus have an underlined letter in their names; this is the selection letter. You can press **Alt** plus that letter to open the menu with the keyboard if you prefer that method. Each command on each menu also has a selection letter; you can press the selection letter (without the Alt key) when a menu is open to select the command.

Figure 1.18 shows an open menu in a program called Paint that comes with Windows 98. It illustrates several important features that you will encounter on menus in Windows programs.

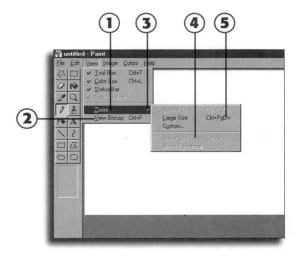

FIGURE 1.18
A typical drop-down menu.

① I clicked this command.

② I could have pressed Alt+V because V is the selection letter for the View menu.

③ Selecting this command makes the submenu fly out to the right.

④ Some commands are unavailable.

⑤ Some commands have keyboard shortcuts.

- **Checkmarks.** Some commands are toggles; each time you select that command, you turn the feature on or off like a light switch. A check mark means the command is currently on.

- **Keyboard shortcuts.** In some programs, there are keyboard alternatives to selecting a particular command from the menu system. These shortcuts are listed next to the equivalent menu command for your reference.

- **Unavailable commands.** Depending on what you are working on, not all commands may be available. Unavailable commands appear dimmed or grayed out.

■ **Submenus.** Selecting a command with a right-pointing arrow next to it opens a submenu with additional commands on it.

Shortcut Menus

One of the handiest features in Windows 98 (and many Windows-based programs) is the shortcut menu. When you right-click virtually any object onscreen, a shortcut menu appears, providing you with easy access to some of the most common actions you can take with that object.

Each object's shortcut menu is different. For example, when you right-click the My Computer icon on your desktop, you see the shortcut menu shown in Figure 1.19. In contrast, when you right-click the desktop itself, you see the shortcut menu in Figure 1.20. Each is appropriate for the chosen object.

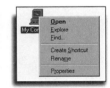

FIGURE 1.19
This shortcut menu appears when you right-click My Computer.

FIGURE 1.20
This shortcut menu appears when you right-click the desktop. (Yours may look slightly different.)

After a shortcut menu is open, you select a command from it by clicking (normally, that is—with the left mouse button) on the command you want. Or, to close the shortcut menu without choosing anything, click away from it.

Working with Toolbars

Many of the windows you will work with will have some sort of toolbar. A *toolbar* is a collection of buttons (usually graphical) that act as shortcuts for common menu commands. For example, in Figure 1.21, the Cut, Copy, and Paste buttons on the toolbar are shortcuts for the commands of the same name on the **E**dit menu. To use a toolbar button, just click it.

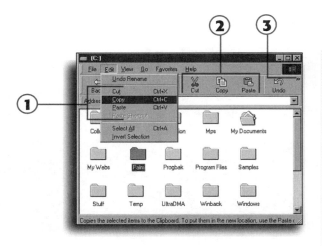

FIGURE 1.21
Toolbar buttons are shortcuts for menu commands.

① These menu commands have toolbar buttons.

② These buttons represent the commands.

③ This symbol means more tools are available than what will fit.

If you see a >> symbol at the right end of a toolbar, it means that more toolbar buttons are available than what will fit in the window at its current size. One way to see the other buttons is to enlarge the window so that they all fit. Another is to click that >> button to display the extra buttons, as shown in Figure 1.22.

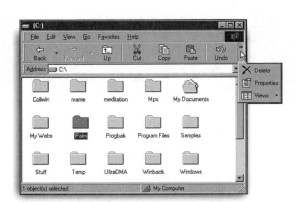

FIGURE 1.22
You can still use the full set of buttons, even if you can't see them all at once in the window.

Turning Off Your PC

You do not have to shut off your computer every time you step away from it for a few hours. It doesn't hurt anything to leave it on while you go do something else. I shut mine off only when I am going to be away from it for more than a day or so.

When you do shut down your PC, *don't* just turn the power switch off. You must tell Windows to shut down first. This closes any open files and deletes temporary files that Windows has been using. If you fail to do this, you can cause errors in your PC's file organization system.

Shutting Down Your PC

1. Click the **Start** button.

2. Click **Shut Down**. The Shut Down Windows dialog box appears. See Figure 1.23.

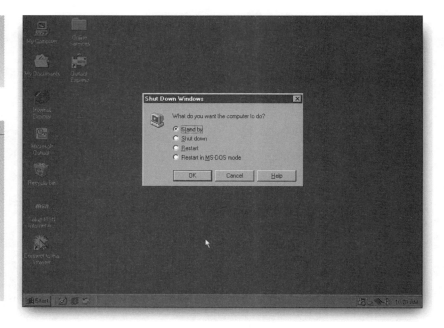

FIGURE 1.23
Choose to shut down the PC from here.

Fixing Your Problems

If you shut your PC down improperly, when you restart it, a program called Scandisk will run automatically, checking for any errors that you might have caused and offering to fix them for you. You will learn how to run Scandisk at other times in Chapter 24.

3. Click **Shut down**.

4. Click **OK**.

5. Wait for the PC to shut down.

It will either turn the power off by itself, or you will see a message onscreen telling you it is safe to turn off the power.

6. If you see the message telling you it is safe to turn off the power, press the computer's Power button to shut it off.

7. Shut off your monitor.

SEE ALSO

➤ *To check a disk for errors that may have been caused by an improper shutdown, see page 406.*

➤ *To shut down a locked-up program without shutting Windows down entirely, see page 460.*

Restarting Windows

Sometimes, Windows starts acting weird. The definition of weird can vary. Perhaps your mouse pointer disappears, or all the folders are suddenly gray instead of yellow. Perhaps a dialog box won't close, or you start a program but the program never appears.

When you start experiencing such anomalies, restarting Windows will often fix the problem.

Restarting Windows

1. Click **Start**.

2. Click **Shut Down**. The Shut Down Windows dialog box opens, as shown earlier in Figure 1.23.

3. Click **Restart**.

4. Click **OK**. Windows restarts.

If you see any warnings or messages after you click **OK** (but before Windows restarts) about programs not responding, click **Shut Down** in the box that appears to shut down the unresponsive program.

Depending on what was causing your PC to act strangely in the first place, your PC may not restart using the preceding steps. After Step 4, when it is supposed to restart, it may lock up (that is, stop doing anything and just sit there with the Windows desktop in the

Shutting Down Without the Mouse

If your mouse pointer has disappeared, you can accomplish the preceding steps using the keyboard. Press the **Windows** key ({insert Windows key symbol}) or press **Ctrl+Esc** to open the Start menu, and then press **U** for Shut Down. Press **R** to select Restart and then press **Enter** to select OK.

background). If that happens, see "Restarting a PC That Won't Restart Normally" in Chapter 25, "Troubleshooting Problems."

SEE ALSO

➤ *To check a disk for errors that may have been caused by an improper shutdown, see page 406.*

chapter

2

Getting Help

Although Windows 98 doesn't come with a printed manual, it does not leave you bereft of assistance. You can get help in many ways as you work; in this chapter, you will learn about them.

Welcome to Windows 98

The Welcome to Windows 98 box (Figure 2.1), which appears when you start the PC unless you have disabled its display, provides some guidance to help ease you into Windows 98 operation. It guides you through four common tasks:

- Registering your copy of Windows
- Connecting to the Internet
- Running the Windows tutorial (Discover Windows 98)
- Setting up a maintenance schedule

FIGURE 2.1
The Welcome to Windows 98 box suggests activities with which to start.

Automatic Welcome

When you first install Windows 98, it sets the Welcome to Windows 98 box to appear automatically each time you start Windows. You can disable its display, however, so if you don't see it automatically, someone may have already disabled it. No matter; the steps below show you how to make it appear.

You will learn about registering and running the Windows tutorial in this chapter. Connecting to the Internet is covered in Chapter 17, "Setting Up Online Connectivity," and scheduling maintenance is covered in Chapter 24.

Displaying the Welcome to Windows 98 Box

1. Start your computer (see Chapter 1, "Windows Basics"). The Welcome to Windows 98 box may automatically appear.

2. If it does not appear automatically, choose **Start, Programs, Accessories, System Tools, Welcome to Windows**. See Figure 2.2.

3. (Optional) To change whether the box appears automatically at startup, select or deselect the **Sho̲w this screen each time Windows 98 starts** check box.

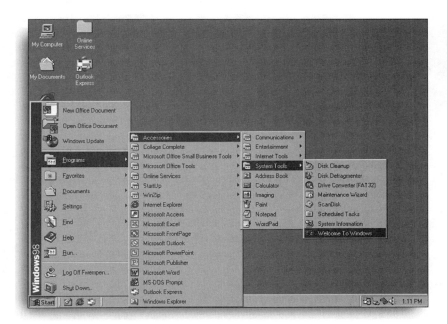

FIGURE 2.2
Here's how to display the Welcome to Windows 98 box if it doesn't appear automatically.

SEE ALSO

➤ *To start or restart your computer, see page 8.*

➤ *To learn more about running programs from the Start menu, see page 48.*

➤ *To run the Windows 98 tutorial, see page 34.*

➤ *To register Windows 98, see page 35.*

➤ *To set up your Internet connection, see page 288.*

➤ *To schedule maintenance tasks for your PC, see page 421.*

Exploring the Discover Windows 98 Tutorial

Although Chapter 1 gave you a firm grounding in Windows fundamentals, you may want to reinforce that knowledge by working through at least part of the Windows 98 tutorial. The tutorial consists of four sections:

- **Computer Essentials.** Helps first-time users learn about computing basics.
- **Windows 98 Overview.** Provides lessons that build your Windows 98 navigation skills.
- **What's New.** Shows off the new and improved features in Windows 98.
- **More Windows 98 Resources.** Provides information about Windows resources produced by Microsoft Press.

To start the tutorial, click **Discover Windows 98** from the Welcome to Windows 98 box. Then, choose which of the four tutorials you want to run. The following steps will get you started with the first one, Computer Essentials.

Run the Computer Essentials Tutorial

1. Click **Discover Windows 98** in the Welcome to Windows dialog box. The Discover Windows 98 Contents screen appears.
2. Click **Computer Essentials**, or press **1** on the keyboard.
3. Read the information that appears, and then follow the onscreen instructions to run the tutorial. A sample screen appears in Figure 2.3.
4. When you return to the Contents screen, run another tutorial by clicking its name,

   or

   Click **Close** to exit the tutorial system and return to the Welcome to Windows 98 box.
5. Click **Close** to close the Welcome to Windows 98 box.

Hear Anything?

Each tutorial includes recorded narration that reinforces the written text onscreen. To hear the narration that goes along with the tutorial, be sure that your speakers are plugged into your PC and that the volume is turned up.

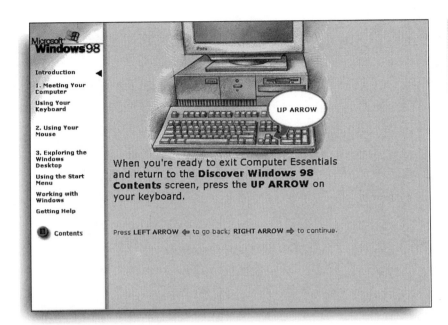

FIGURE 2.3
The Computer Essentials tutorial.

Registering Your Copy of Windows 98

When you buy Windows 98 off the shelf or get it with a new PC you have bought, Microsoft has no way of knowing who you are or how to reach you. If product updates become available or other announcements are made, how will you get them?

That's why registering your copy of Windows 98 is important. By letting Microsoft know your name and address, you make sure that you'll get product notices and upgrade offers in the future.

Registering also has an important additional benefit: After you have registered, you can use the Windows Update service on the Internet. This service scans your system and informs you when you need to download new device drivers or software updates. As a registered user, you also can access Microsoft's online technical support department to get answers to your questions and to troubleshoot problems.

Microsoft provides a Registration Wizard that walks you through the steps of registering. You can run it by clicking **Register Now** in the Welcome to Windows 98 box.

Register Windows

1. Click **Register Now** in the Welcome to Windows box. The Registration Wizard starts.

2. Read the information on the first screen, and then click **Next**.

3. Continue through the wizard, reading the onscreen information and filling in the boxes as requested. See Figure 2.4.

FIGURE 2.4
To register, provide the requested information.

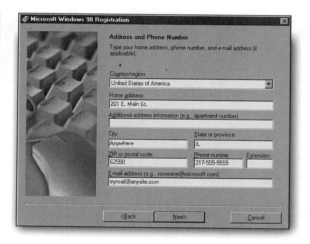

4. When you reach the last screen, click **Register**.

5. What happens next depends on your computer system:

   - If you already were connected to the Internet when you began the registration, the wizard attempts to send your registration over the Internet using that connection.

   - If you were not already connected but you have a modem, it attempts to dial Microsoft's toll-free number to send the information.

   - If neither of the above applies, it provides instructions for sending the registration by mail.

   Follow the prompts that appear to finish sending your information to Microsoft. When the wizard is finished, the Welcome to Windows 98 box reappears.

6. Click **Close** to close the Welcome to Windows 98 box.

Using the Help System

"Where's the manual?" you may have wondered when you got Windows 98. Well, there isn't one. At least not a printed one.

To save paper (and printing costs), Microsoft does not include printed documentation; instead, it provides a Help file with all the information in it that would have gone into a printed manual. You may come to prefer this Help file to a book because it has some benefits that books lack.

Opening the Help System

Choose **Start, Help**. The Windows Help window opens. See Figure 2.5.

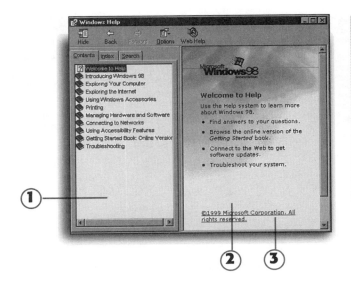

FIGURE 2.5
The Windows Help system.

(1) Look up an article in this pane.

(2) Read the article in this pane.

(3) Click underlined words to see a definition or jump to another article.

After the Help system is open, you can use several ways to look up the topics you want to read about. You can browse the contents by topic, you can look up words in an index, or you can search for a particular word or phrase. We'll look at each of those methods of finding a topic, and then discuss what to do with a topic after you've found it.

SEE ALSO

➤ *To resize or maximize a window, see page 15.*

Maximize Your View

Like any other window, the Windows Help window can be resized and even maximized so that you can see more of its text onscreen at once without scrolling.

37

Browsing the Help Contents

The Contents tab contains a list of broad topics. As shown in Figure 2.5, each one has a book icon next to it. One way to locate information is to narrow it down by topic until you come to the article you want.

For example, suppose you want to know about starting a program. You click **Exploring Your Computer**, and a list of "sub-books" appears under it. Then, you click **Working with Programs**, and a list of articles appears. (Articles have question mark icons next to them rather than book icons.) You can then click the **Start a program** article to display it in the right pane. Figure 2.6 shows the path to the article.

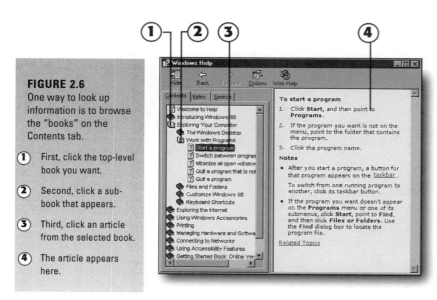

FIGURE 2.6
One way to look up information is to browse the "books" on the Contents tab.

① First, click the top-level book you want.

② Second, click a sub-book that appears.

③ Third, click an article from the selected book.

④ The article appears here.

Browsing the Help System for an Article

1. Click the book you want to open on the Contents tab in Help.
2. Continue clicking books within books until you see the title of the article you want to read.
3. Click the article title. The article appears in the right pane of the Help system.

Looking Up Terms in the Index

Browsing topics can be educational, but it is not the quickest method of finding an answer. If you know the exact term you want to look up (such as Printing or Recycle Bin), you can find that term in the index.

The index is one big alphabetical list of terms. You can scroll through it on the Index tab of the Help window, or you can type the first few letters of a term to jump quickly to that spot in the list. See Figure 2.7.

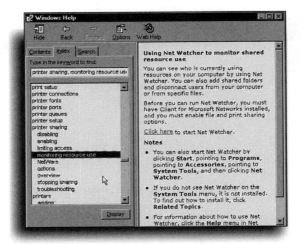

FIGURE 2.7
Look up terms alphabetically in the index.

When you find the term you want, double-click it.

Some of the terms in the index correspond one-to-one with certain articles. If you double-click such a term in the index list, that article appears in the right pane.

Other terms in the index have multiple articles associated with them. If you double-click such a term in the index list, a Topics Found window opens, listing the articles associated with that term (see Figure 2.8). From there, you can select the exact article you want.

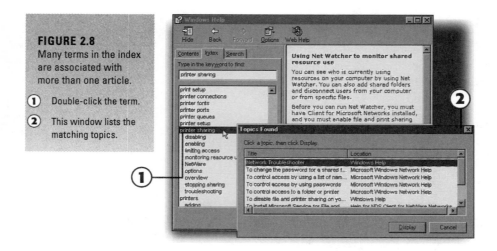

FIGURE 2.8
Many terms in the index are associated with more than one article.

① Double-click the term.

② This window lists the matching topics.

Finding Help Topics Using the Index

1. Click the **Index** tab from Help.

2. Type the first few letters of the term you want to look up. Keep typing until you see the term on the list.

3. Double-click the term.

4. If a Topics Found window appears, click the topic you want, and then click **Display**.

Searching for a Term

My favorite way of using the Help system is to search it. Even if you don't know the name of the article or exactly what an activity is called, you can still find it with Search.

When you search, Windows looks in every article for that term and presents a list of articles in which it is found.

Searching the Help System

1. Click the **Search** tab from **Help**.

2. Type the word you want to find.

3. Click **List Topics**. The matching articles appear on the Select Topic to Display list.

4. Double-click the article you want to read. It appears in the right pane, with the word you searched for highlighted. See Figure 2.9.

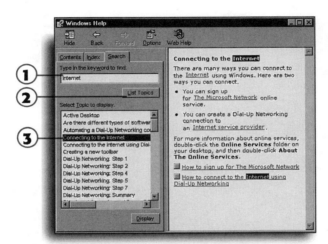

FIGURE 2.9
Search for a certain word across all articles.

(1) Type the term here to search for.

(2) Click List Topics.

(3) Double-click the article you want.

Working with Found Help Topics

The same articles appear no matter which way you retrieve them. After an article that you are interested in is onscreen, you can take advantage of the Help system's many features to work with it.

The following is a list of some of the activities you can do with a Help article:

- See a definition of an underlined term in the article by clicking it. Then, click away from the definition box to close it. See Figure 2.10.

- Jump to other help topics by clicking the underlined hyperlinks. For example, in Figure 2.11, two hyperlinks at the bottom of the article point to more information.

- Return to the previously viewed article by clicking the **Back** button. Then, go forward again by clicking the **Forward** button.

Hyperlinks

Throughout the Windows Help system, you will see underlined words. Clicking some underlined words displays their definitions; clicking other underlined words or phrases jumps to a different article. These underlined words and phrases that take you someplace else when you click them are called *hyperlinks*. You will learn more about hyperlinks in Chapter 18, "Exploring the Web," which discusses Web pages.

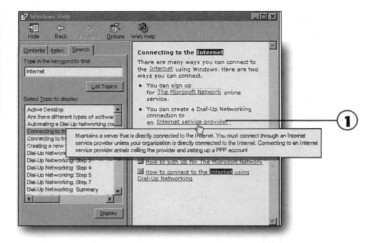

FIGURE 2.10
See definitions of important technical terms by clicking them.

① Underlined term

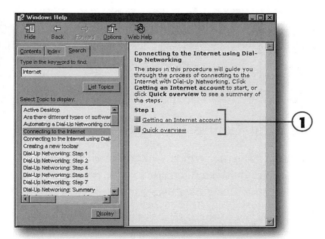

FIGURE 2.11
Jump to related topics by following hyperlinks.

① Hyperlinks to other articles

Print Dialog Box

The Print dialog box that appears when you print a Help topic is the same one that you see when you print in Internet Explorer. You will learn more about it in Chapter 18.

■ Hide the left pane, leaving only the article displayed, by clicking the **Hide** button. (It then becomes a **Show** button, which you can use to return the left pane to view.)

■ Print the article by clicking **Options** and **Print**. This opens a Print dialog box. From there, just click **OK**.

SEE ALSO

➤ To learn more about hyperlinks, see page 305.

➤ To learn more about the Print dialog box, see page 311.

Getting More Help on the Web

If you have an Internet connection, you can use it to connect to Microsoft's Support Online Web site. From there, you can look up additional Help articles and find the latest information on troubleshooting known problems. (If you do not yet have an Internet connection, see Chapter 17, "Setting Up Online Connectivity.")

You can either browse the extra Help information available online, or you can search for specific information. It all depends on your goal in using Web Help. The following procedures explain each activity.

Browsing the Web Help Information

1. Start your Internet connection if it is not already running. (See Chapter 17 for help if needed.)

2. To open the Help system (if it is not already open), choose **Start**, **Help**.

3. Click the **Web Help** button.

4. In the article that appears, click the **Support Online** hyperlink. A Web page with support information appears in your Web browser.

5. Browse the available articles, clicking any hyperlink that looks interesting. See Chapter 18 for details about browsing a Web page.

This procedure is fun and educational if you are not in a hurry and if you don't have a particular problem to solve, but it's not very efficient. Searching Microsoft's Web site is a much more efficient way of finding details.

The following procedure involves using Internet Explorer to view a Web page, and you won't learn that officially in this book until Chapter 17. However, it won't hurt you to try it out now, and if you run into any problems, you can either quit and come back to it later or jump ahead to Chapter 17 for some help.

Searching for Specific Help Information Online

1. Start your Internet connection if it is not already running. (See Chapter 17 for help if needed.)

2. To open the Help system (if it is not already open), choose **Start**, **Help**.

You Must Register

To use Support Online, you must have registered your copy of Windows 98. If you try to use it without having registered, you will be prompted to register online.

Here Today, Gone Tomorrow

Microsoft periodically changes how its Web site is organized, so if the following steps do not work for you, don't assume that you are doing anything wrong; Microsoft may simply have changed the site since this book was published.

3. Click **Web Help**.

4. In the article that appears, click the **Support Online** hyperlink. A Web page with support information appears in your Web browser.

5. Click the **Have a Question About Windows 98?** hyperlink.

6. Type your question into the text box. You can use real language, just as if you were talking to a person. Figure 2.12 shows an example.

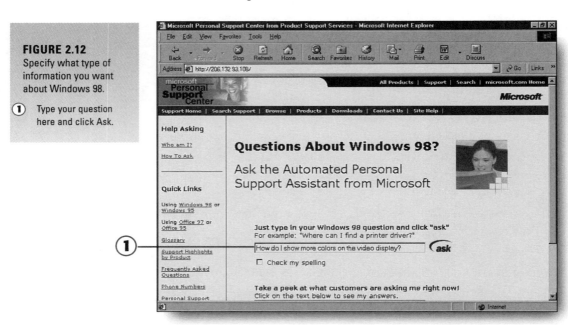

FIGURE 2.12
Specify what type of information you want about Windows 98.

① Type your question here and click Ask.

7. Click **Ask**.

8. Choose the question that most closely matches yours on the next screen, and then click **Ask** next to the one you want. See Figure 2.13.

9. If a list of articles appears, click the one you want to read.

10. Read the article, and then click the **Back** button to return to the list of articles.

11. When you are finished, close Internet Explorer and disconnect from the Internet if needed.

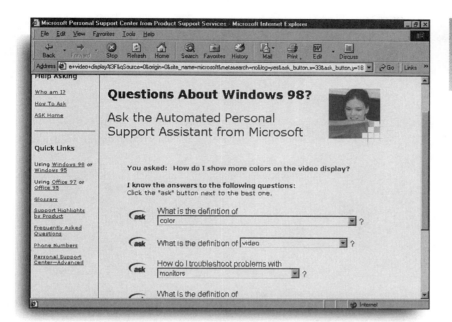

FIGURE 2.13
Choose the information
you want.

chapter

3

Running Programs

Think about it for a minute: What is the purpose of Windows 98? Is it to display pretty colors on your monitor or make interesting sounds? No, of course not. The purpose of Windows is to run useful programs that enable you to accomplish your daily tasks. Those tasks could include word processing, accounting, email communication, or any of dozens of other activities. In this chapter, you'll learn how to make Windows 98 run the programs that you want to use for work or play.

Starting a Program

Starting a program is such an essential and common task that Windows 98 provides several methods for doing it. You can choose which method is most convenient for you in each circumstance. The following sections explain the various methods and give you an opportunity to try them out.

SEE ALSO

➤ *To install a program, see page 142.*

From the Start Menu

You have already seen in Chapters 1 and 2 how to run a program through the **Start/Programs** menu (that is, the **Programs** menu, which is a submenu on the **Start** menu). This is the most common method of starting a program, and it works for almost all Windows-based programs.

To open the **Start** menu, click the **Start** button. Then, point to Programs to see the list of programs. Some programs appear directly on the Programs list; others are in folders (submenus) off it.

If you see the program you want to run, click it. Otherwise, point to the submenu name for that program's category or manufacturer. The submenu opens. Figure 3.1 shows an example. Move through any additional levels of submenus as needed until you find the program's name. Click the program's name to start the program.

First, You Install

To run a certain program on your PC, that program must be installed, of course. Therefore, your first step should be to purchase (or download) and install the program if that has not already been done.

It's Not on the Start Menu?

Some small programs, particularly free or trial programs created by computer hobbyists, may not set themselves up to be run from your **Start** menu when you install them. Try the "From a File List" method described later in this chapter to run such programs.

On the Menu

Most programs made by Microsoft place themselves directly on the **Start** menu when you install them. Most programs made by other companies place themselves in a submenu with the company name (such as Intuit) or the program name (such as WordPerfect).

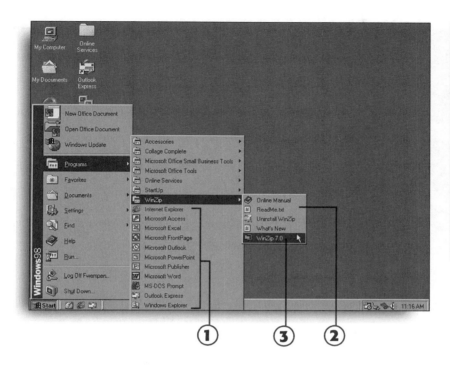

FIGURE 3.1
Move through the submenus by pointing with the mouse to find the program you want to start.

(1) Some programs are on the **Programs** menu directly.

(2) Other programs are on submenus.

(3) Click the name of the program you want to start.

SEE ALSO

➤ *To run a program that doesn't appear on the Start menu, see page 50.*

➤ *To install a program, see page 142.*

➤ *To reorganize the programs and submenus on the Start menu, see page 124.*

From a Desktop Icon

In Chapter 1, you learned about icons that sit on your desktop. You can double-click an icon to activate it. Some icons open folders and display file listings; other icons start programs.

How do those icons get put on the desktop in the first place? Well, many programs place a shortcut for themselves on your desktop when you install them. For example, when you install Microsoft

Office 2000, it places a shortcut for Outlook (a contact management and scheduling program) on your desktop. You can also create shortcut icons on the desktop for any program or file you wish; you'll learn how in Chapter 7, "Organizing Your Programs."

SEE ALSO

➤ *To create shortcut icons on the desktop, see page 129.*

➤ *To remove shortcut icons from the desktop, see page 130.*

➤ *To change the way a particular shortcut works, see page 131.*

From a Toolbar

You learned in Chapter 1 about the Quick Launch toolbar—the row of buttons to the right of the **Start** button. Some of these buttons start programs. For example, the button that looks like an "e" starts Internet Explorer. To start a program with one of these toolbar buttons, simply click the button.

SEE ALSO

➤ *To customize which buttons appear on the Quick Launch toolbar, see page 132.*

➤ *To create more toolbars to hold programs you want to run, see page 134.*

From a File List

As you may already know, all the files on your computer are stored on your hard disk, including the files that run each program. If you can locate the file that starts a particular program, you can start the program by double-clicking it. See Figure 3.2. (The trick, of course, is to locate the right file. You'll learn how to do that in upcoming chapters.)

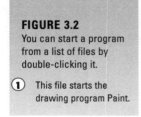

FIGURE 3.2
You can start a program from a list of files by double-clicking it.

① This file starts the drawing program Paint.

You can also start a program by double-clicking a data file from that program in a file listing. For example, suppose you created a letter that you saved under the name Chimp using the Notepad program that comes with Windows. You could locate that saved letter in a file listing and double-click it to open it in the program that created it. See Figure 3.3.

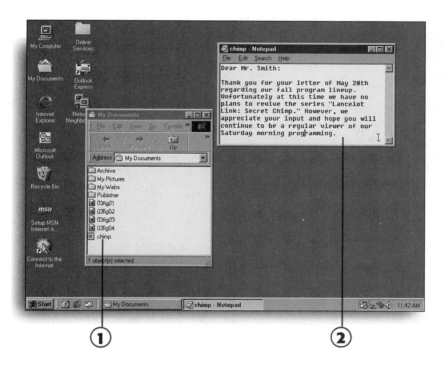

FIGURE 3.3
Double-clicking the data file opens it in its native program.

① Double-clicking this file...

② ...Opens it in the program that created it.

From the Documents Menu

While we're on the subject of data files, here's a wonderful shortcut. Windows 98 keeps track of the previous 15 data files you worked with in your various programs. That includes word processing documents, spreadsheets, databases, text files (such as Chimp in Figure 3.3), and all kinds of other saved work. You can reopen any of those files, along with the program that created them, with the following procedure:

Concerned About Privacy?

To clear the Documents menu, right-click the taskbar and choose **Properties**. Then, choose the **Start Menu Programs** tab and click the **Clear** button. Click **OK** to close the dialog box when you're done.

Start a Program from the Documents Menu

1. Click **Start**.

2. Point to **Documents**. The **Documents** menu appears, with the previous 15 files you have worked with listed. Figure 3.4 shows an example.

3. Click the file you want to reopen. The program used to create it opens, and the file appears in it ready for editing.

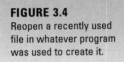

FIGURE 3.4
Reopen a recently used file in whatever program was used to create it.

With the Run Command

The **Run** command is a rather "techie" way of starting a program. It's not very convenient, and you will probably not use it very often. However, it does offer one great benefit: It lets you set command-line options for how the program will run.

What does that mean? Well, the answer involves a bit of history. Back in the old days of MS-DOS, you ran programs by typing the program name on a command line. Some programs had several modes in which they could operate, and you chose a mode by typing a slash and some extra characters (a *switch*) after the command name.

For example, you could open the program DRAWIT in black-and-white video mode by typing **DRAWIT /B**.

In contrast, when you run a program in Windows by choosing it from the **Start** menu, no opportunity occurs to enter any special instructions. (Most Windows programs don't require any, so it's not a great loss.) However, you may occasionally need to run a program for which you want to use a switch. The **Run** command allows you to enter extra instructions when you run a program.

Starting a Program with the Run Command

1. Click **Start**, **Run**. The Run dialog box opens.

2. Click **Browse**. The Browse dialog box opens.

3. Locate the program file you want to run, and click it. Then, click **Open**.

   The command for starting the program appears in the Run dialog box. See Figure 3.5.

4. (Optional) Type additional commands, filenames, or switches after the command, as desired.

5. Click **OK**. The program runs.

FIGURE 3.5
The Run dialog box enables you to edit and add to the command that runs the program before you issue it.

SEE ALSO

➤ *To learn more about locating files in a Browse dialog box, see page 59.*

➤ *To set up DOS programs to run in Windows, see page 461.*

Navigating in a Program

Every program works a little differently, of course, but most Windows-based programs have much in common. Most of them open, save, and print your work in the same way, for example.

The figures in the following sections use WordPad as an example. (Start it with **Start, Programs, Accessories, WordPad** if you want to follow along.) WordPad is a simple text editor that comes with Windows. The basic steps work in nearly all programs, however. You can transfer these skills to almost any other Windows program that you use.

Starting a New File

Programs usually store your work in data files. You can have separate files for each document, spreadsheet, or other item that you create.

Most programs start a new file automatically when you start the program. That way, you can start creating immediately, without having to issue any special command.

Most programs also have a **File, New** command (that is, a command called **New** on the **File** menu) that starts a new file anytime you want. Some programs (such as Microsoft Word) also have a **New** button on the toolbar.

Starting a New Data File

1. Choose **File, New** or click the **New** button [new button] on the program's toolbar if it has one.

2. Depending on the program, a New dialog box may appear, asking what kind of file you want to create. The one for WordPad appears in Figure 3.6. Make your selection, and click **OK**.

3. Depending on the program, a box may appear asking whether you want to save your changes to the existing file before starting a new one. Choose **Yes** or **No** as needed.

FIGURE 3.6
Some programs, such as WordPad shown here, enable you to choose the format of the new file or the template on which it is based.

Typing and Editing Text

If you're a typical home or business user, the majority of your work will probably involve typing and editing text.

Text appears at the *insertion point* (the flashing vertical line) as you type. The insertion point moves over as you enter more text. To move the insertion point, use the arrow keys or click with the mouse where you want it. When the mouse pointer is over an area in which you can type, it changes to an I-beam (see Figure 3.7). Click to place the insertion point at the I-beam position.

In some programs, the Insert key toggles between two text editing modes: Insert and Overtype. Insert mode is the default; when you position the insertion point and type, the text to the right moves over to make room. In Overtype mode, text to the right of the insertion point is replaced by whatever you type.

Editing Text

1. Click to position the insertion point where you want it.

2. Do one of the following as needed to remove unwanted text:

   ■ Press **Backspace** to remove one character to the left of the insertion point.

   ■ Press **Delete** to remove one character to the right of the insertion point.

3. Type new text to replace it.

Multiple Files Open?
Some programs can have multiple files open at once; in such programs, starting a new file does not close the open file (as it does in WordPad).

No Return
Unlike on a typewriter, you don't have to press **Enter** (or Return) at the end of each line. Your words wrap to the next line automatically when they reach the end of a line. This feature is called *word wrap*. It is turned on by default in almost every program. Notepad is an exception, however; to turn on word wrap in Notepad, you must choose **Edit**, **Word Wrap**.

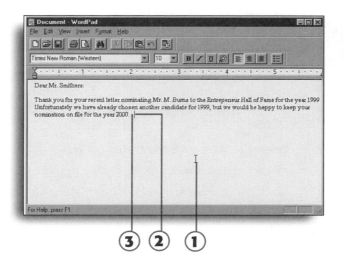

FIGURE 3.7
Typed text in WordPad.

① I-beam mouse pointer

② Insertion point

③ The next character I type will appear here.

Selecting Text

You can also work with a block of text by selecting it. For example, you could select an entire sentence and then press **Delete** once to remove it all at once. Figure 3.8 shows some text selected in WordPad.

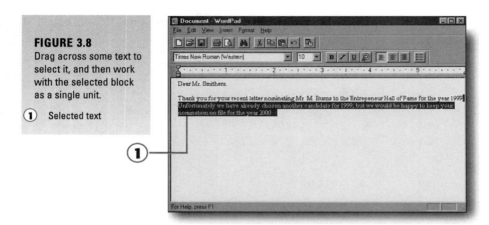

FIGURE 3.8
Drag across some text to select it, and then work with the selected block as a single unit.

① Selected text

Depending on the program, you may also be able to select text in other ways. The following are some selection shortcuts that work in many Windows-based programs:

- To select all the text in the file, press **Ctrl+A**.
- To select a word, double-click it.
- To select a paragraph, triple-click it.

Exchanging Data Between Programs

When a block of text is selected, you can copy or cut it to a special holding area called the *Clipboard*. Then, you can reposition the insertion point and paste that selection back into the document in the new location.

Copying or Moving a Selected Block of Text

1. Select the text you want to copy or move.
2. Choose **Edit**, **Cut** to move it or **Edit**, **Copy** to copy it.

3. Reposition the insertion point by clicking where you want it. You can open a different data file and/or a different program at this point if you want the selection to be placed there.

4. Choose **Edit**, **Paste**.

In most programs, you can use the following shortcut keys and toolbar buttons for the Cut, Copy, and Paste commands:

Ctrl+X for Cut

Ctrl+C for Copy

Ctrl+V for Paste

In many programs, you can also right-click a selection and choose **Cut**, **Copy**, or **Paste** from the shortcut menu.

Microsoft Office 2000 programs (Word, Excel, Access, PowerPoint, and so on) come with a more advanced Clipboard that can store multiple selections at once. If you cut or copy multiple times without having pasted, instead of the previous selection disappearing, it remains on the Clipboard, and a Clipboard toolbar appears so you can choose which of the stored selections to paste. Figure 3.9 shows the Clipboard toolbar from Microsoft Word 2000.

FIGURE 3.9
Microsoft Office 2000 programs have a Clipboard that can store multiple selections for copying and moving.

① Double-click a clip to paste it.

Saving Your Work

Unless you save your work, the data that you enter in a program (typing text, drawing a picture, and so on) is lost when you exit from that program. If you want to keep something that you have created, you must save it.

When you save your work, you can choose where to store the saved file. Some people always store all their data files in the `c:\My Documents` folder; other people like to create new folders for each project they work on. It's up to you. Just make sure you remember where you stored the file so you can open it later when you want to work with it again.

In some programs, you also have a choice of formats in which to save the file. For example, in some word processing programs, you can save the file in that program's regular format or in the format of any of several other popular word processing programs. That way, you can exchange files with someone who does not use the same word processor as you do.

Saving a File

1. Choose **File**, **Save**. The Save As dialog box appears. Figure 3.10 shows the one for WordPad; the one you see may be slightly different.

FIGURE 3.10
Save your work here.

① Choose a location.

② Type a name.

③ Select a file type to Save As.

④ Toolbar.

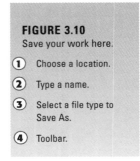
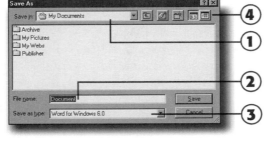

Toolbar Shortcut

🖫 Many programs have a Save button on the toolbar that opens the Save As dialog box (if the file has not yet been saved) or saves the changes made to the file (if it has already been saved before).

2. (Optional) To change the save location (the default is probably `C:\My Documents`), do the following:

   - Open the **Save in** drop-down list and choose the drive where you want to save. A list of all the folders on that drive appears.

   - Double-click the folder in which you want to save.

   - Double-click through additional levels of folders, if needed, until the name of the folder in which you want to save appears in the Save in box.

3. (Optional) To change the file format for the saved file, open the **Save as type** drop-down list and choose a different format.

4. Type the filename you want in the **File name** text box.

5. Click **Save**.

You may have noticed in Figure 3.10 that the Save As dialog box has its own mini-toolbar with several buttons. You can find out what these buttons do by pointing at them to make a ScreenTip appear. Here are two that are extremely useful:

Up One Level takes you up one level of folders. For example, if you are currently in C:\My Documents\Archive, it will take you to C:\My Documents.

New Folder creates a new folder in whatever folder is currently displayed, so you can create organizational systems on-the-fly.

SEE ALSO

➤ *To create new folders for storing a data file, see page 104.*

➤ *To find a file when you have forgotten where you saved it, see page 101.*

➤ *To save a Web page that you have been viewing on the Internet, see page 311.*

Opening Files

Saving a file enables you to open it again later when you want to edit or print it. For example, you might save a draft of your report and close it, and then open it later for more revisions.

Opening a File in WordPad

1. Choose **File**, **Open**. The Open dialog box appears. The one for WordPad appears in Figure 3.11.

2. If the saved file is in a folder other then My Documents, navigate to that folder the same way you did in the preceding steps when you saved.

3. Click the saved file on the list of files that appears.

4. Click **Open**.

File Naming Rules

Most Windows-based programs support long filenames, which means the names can be up to 256 characters and can include spaces. File names cannot include any of these symbols: forward slash (/), backslash (\), greater than sign (>), less than sign (<), asterisk (*), question mark (?), quotation mark ("), pipe symbol (|), colon (:), or semicolon (;).

Some programs (mostly older ones) require you to stick to old DOS-style filenames, which can have no more than 8 letters and cannot include spaces. Such programs will let you know if the name you have chosen is unusable.

FIGURE 3.11
Open files from here.

① Choose where the file is stored.

② Select the file.

Toolbar Shortcut

Many programs have an Open button on the Standard toolbar that opens the Open dialog box.

The Open dialog box has the same set of toolbar buttons as the Save As dialog box in Notepad, and you can use them the same way.

Some programs have fancier Save As and Open dialog boxes with more toolbar buttons and other controls. For example, Figure 3.12 shows the Open dialog box for Microsoft Word 2000. In dialog boxes such as this, you can stick to the basic controls that you just learned about, or you can explore the various buttons and options on your own.

Some programs also allow you to have more than one file open at once. In programs that do, you can switch between them by selecting the file from the **Window** menu, which lists the open files.

Printing Your Work

Most people want a *hard copy* of their work to show to others. You may have just created a fabulous advertisement for your garage sale, for example, or an important report for your business. Almost every Windows program that enables you to create something also enables you to print it.

Printing Your Work

1. Open the file containing your work.
2. Choose **File**, **Print**. At this point one of two things happens, depending on the program. Either:

- The file prints immediately on your default printer

 or

- A Print dialog box opens, in which you can set print options (which is the case with almost all other programs).

3. If a Print dialog box appears, specify the number of copies, the page range, the desired printer, and any other options the box offers. Figure 3.13 shows one for WordPad, for example.

4. Click the **Print** (or **OK**) button to close the dialog box and print your work.

Print Button

Many programs have a **Print** button on the tool-bar. Clicking it prints a single copy of the default print range (in most cases that's the entire file).

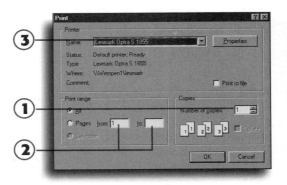

FIGURE 3.13
A typical Print dialog box.

① Set the number of copies.

② Set the page range.

③ Choose a printer, if you have more than one.

SEE ALSO

➤ *To print a Web page, see page 311.*

➤ *To control the queue for your printer, see page 225.*

➤ *To share a printer on a network, see page 226.*

➤ *To print to a network printer, see page 226.*

Switching Among Running Programs

One of Windows 98's best features is its capability to multitask—to run more than one program at a time. You can have lots of programs running at once, each in its own window. That means you can work on your report for work and then jump over to the Internet to check your stock portfolio without closing the report. Then, you can read some email, format a diskette, and come back to the business report just as you left it.

As you learned in Chapter 1, each open window has its own rectangular button on the taskbar. You can switch to any of your open windows by clicking its button there. That's the easiest way to switch among windows.

An alternate method also exists for switching: Alt+Tab. This method is great for people who prefer keyboard steps to mouse use, and it also enables you to switch to a window that does not appear on the taskbar even though it is open. (Those are rare, but they do exist. Windows 98 dialog boxes are the worst offenders here.)

Switching Among Windows with Alt+Tab

1. Hold down the **Alt** key.

2. Press and release the **Tab** key, but do not release **Alt**. A bar showing icons for all the open windows appears. See Figure 3.14.

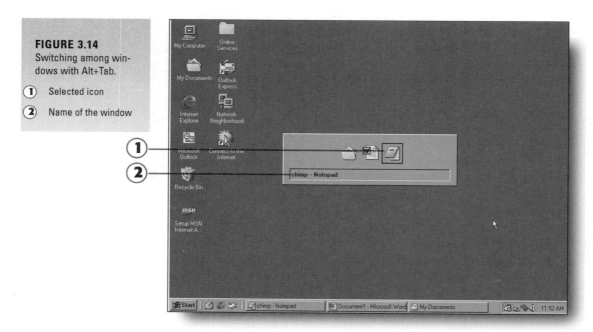

FIGURE 3.14
Switching among windows with Alt+Tab.

① Selected icon

② Name of the window

3. Press the **Tab** key to select the icon you want on the bar. Each time you press **Tab**, the selector (the outline) moves one icon to the right.

4. When the icon you want is selected, release the **Alt** key. That window appears.

Exiting a Program

Two kinds of programs run in Windows 98: programs that run automatically behind the scenes and programs that you start up yourself. You can exit either one of them.

Exiting a Running Program

To exit a program, close its window. You learned how to close Windows in Chapter 1, remember? You can exit a program by doing any of the following:

- Click the **Close** button (top right).
- Double-click the **Control menu icon** (top left).
- Choose **File**, **Exit**.
- Right-click the window's bar on the taskbar and choose **Close** from the shortcut menu.
- Shut down or restart Windows.

The only quirk when exiting a program (as opposed to closing a window that contains something else) is that in some programs it is possible to close the open data file without exiting the program entirely. In cases like that, you will see two separate commands on the **File** menu: **Close** and **Exit**. Close refers to the data file; Exit refers to the program itself.

In such programs you may also see two Close buttons in the top-right corner, one above the other. The higher one is for the program itself and the lower one is for the open data file. See Figure 3.15, which shows Microsoft Excel (a prime example).

Why Exit?

Exiting a program when you are finished with it keeps the onscreen clutter to a minimum. It also can make your other running programs run faster and better. That's because each running program consumes system resources (that is, memory), and the more programs that are running, the fewer spare system resources are available to go around.

The average computer can easily run five or six average programs at once without any noticeable slowdown, but you will probably want to exit a program when you are finished working with it, just to keep your taskbar and desktop tidy.

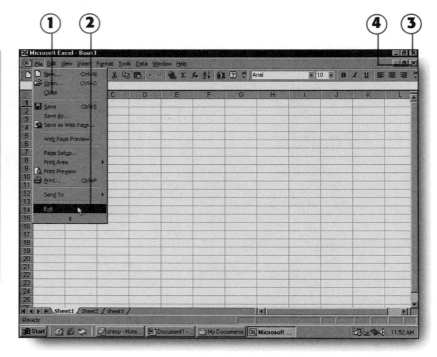

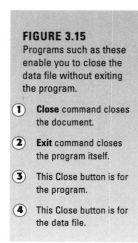

FIGURE 3.15
Programs such as these enable you to close the data file without exiting the program.

(1) **Close** command closes the document.

(2) **Exit** command closes the program itself.

(3) This Close button is for the program.

(4) This Close button is for the data file.

SEE ALSO

➤ *To exit from a program that is malfunctioning and won't exit normally, see page 460.*

Exiting a Program in the System Tray

As you learned in Chapter 1, the icons in the System tray area (the area by the clock in the bottom-right corner) represent programs that stay running all the time to perform some behind-the-scenes function such as virus protection. You usually will not need to exit these programs. They start by themselves, and they stay running the entire time that Windows 98 is running.

However, you may occasionally need to exit or disable one of them for some special reason. For example, some installation programs will not run unless you disable virus protection temporarily.

Exit a Program in the System Tray

1. Right-click the program's icon. A shortcut menu appears. The commands on the menu vary depending on the program.

2. Do one of the following:

- If an **Exit** or **Close** command is on the menu, click it.
- If no **Exit** or **Close** command exists, look for (and click) a command that pauses or disables the program.

SEE ALSO

➤ *To control which programs load at startup (and appear in the System tray), see page 123.*

➤ *To work with the programs in the System tray, see page 136.*

chapter

4

Exploring the Windows Accessories

Introducing the Windows Accessories

You will probably want to buy some software programs to run on your computer—perhaps a word processor, an accounting package, or a few games. But before you go out and spend that money, take a look at the free programs that come with Windows 98. In some cases they are just as good as those that you would pay extra for in stores.

This chapter showcases some of the free Windows accessories so you can get an idea of what they can do for you and why you might (or might not!) want to use them.

Something Missing?

If you try to run any of the programs described in this chapter and find that the program isn't there, perhaps it needs to be installed. See "Adding and Removing Windows Components" in Chapter 8, "Installing New Programs," to learn how to install any accessories that are missing.

Word Processing with WordPad

You got a sneak peek at WordPad in Chapter 3 Running Programs, when you were learning about running programs. WordPad is a simple but effective word processor that you can use to write letters, reports, and other documents. It doesn't have the fancy capabilities of a full-featured word processor such as Microsoft Word or WordPerfect, but for a person who needs a word processor only occasionally, it can serve well. To run WordPad, open the **Start** menu, point to **Programs**, point to **Accessories**, and click **WordPad**.

After WordPad is running, just start typing. You don't have to press **Enter** at the end of a line; just press it when you want to start a new paragraph. You can open, save, and print files in WordPad just as you learned in Chapter 3. Figure 4.1 shows a WordPad document.

With WordPad, you can not only create and edit text, but you can format it, too. The Formatting toolbar offers buttons you can use as shortcuts to quickly format text. Select the text and then choose from the following:

`Times New Roman (Western)` Open the Font drop-down list and choose a different font.

`10` Open the Font Size drop-down list and choose a font size.

`B` Click Bold to make text bold.

`I` Click Italic to make text italic.

`U` Click Underline to make text underlined.

Click Color to change the text color.

Click Align Left button to align the paragraph on the left.

Click Center to center the paragraph.

Click Align Right to align the paragraph on the right.

Click Bullets to make the paragraph into a bulleted one (or to remove the bullet if it already has one).

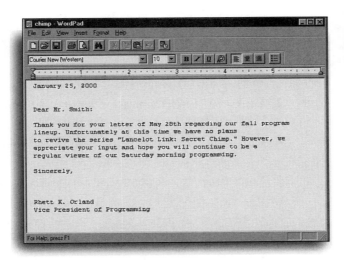

FIGURE 4.1
WordPad can create, format, save, and print simple documents.

You can do more formatting with WordPad; check out its menu system. For example, from the **Format** menu you can choose to set up tab stops. You probably have some other word processor available (because most new PCs come with a variety of software these days), so you likely won't spend much time in WordPad.

Creating Artwork with Paint

Paint is a graphics program that you can use to create simple illustrations with lines and shapes. It doesn't have the capabilities that you'll find in professional programs, but it's adequate for simple drawings. To run Paint, open the **Start** menu, point to **Programs**, point to **Accessories**, and click **Paint**.

In Paint, the screen is your blank canvas on which to create your artwork. You select a color, a tool, and any special attributes for the tool (such as the thickness of your "brush"), and then you drag on the canvas to create your art. See Figure 4.2. For more information about opening, saving, and printing files, refer to Chapter 3.

You can choose two colors for each drawing action: a foreground color and a background color. To choose your foreground color, left-click a color; to choose your background color, right-click a color.

Give it a try. The following steps show how you would draw a rectangle in Paint.

Drawing a Rectangle with Paint

1. In Paint, click the **Rectangle** tool.
2. In the options area, click the second option (the shaded rectangle with the border).
3. Click with the left mouse button on the color that you want the border to be.
4. Click with the right mouse button on the color that you want the center to be.
5. Position the mouse pointer on the canvas where you want the rectangle to start.
6. Hold down the left mouse button and drag to create the rectangle. (If you want a perfect square, hold down the **Shift** key as you drag.)
7. Release the mouse button. The rectangle appears.

FIGURE 4.2
Create simple artwork like this with Paint.

(1) Foreground color

(2) Background color

(3) (4) Choose a foreground/background color

(5) The Line tool

(6) Optional widths for the Line tool

(7) Drag the tool on the canvas.

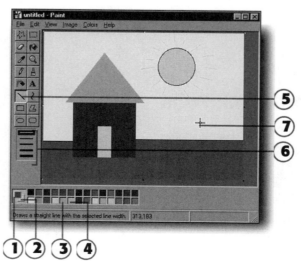

The rectangle is only one of Paint's tools. Table 4.1 shows the other tools in Paint and explains what they do. You will want to experiment with them on your own.

Table 4.1 Paint tools

Tool	Name	Purpose	Tips
	Free-form Select	Selects an irregularly shaped area.	Use to mark an area for removal or copying.
	Select	Selects a rectangular area.	
	Eraser/Color Eraser	Changes the area you drag across to the background color.	Use the right mouse button when dragging to replace the selected foreground color with the selected background one (Color Eraser).
	Fill with Color	Fills an enclosed area.	Make sure the area is fully enclosed; otherwise, the fill will "leak" and "pour out" into the background. To undo if this happens, press **Ctrl+Z**.
	Pick Color	Picks up the color of whatever you click.	Click with the left mouse button for foreground or the right mouse button for background. This is useful for matching colors.
	Magnifier	Zooms in.	
	Pencil	Draws a free-form line with the foreground color.	Use this instead of the brush for a plain, precise line.
	Brush	Draws a free-form line.	Unlike with the pencil, the Brush lets you choose from a variety of brush "tips" that make different strokes.

continues...

Table 4.1   Continued

Tool	Name	Purpose	Tips
	Airbrush	Spray-paints	Hold the mouse pointer in one spot longer for heavier coverage, just like with a real spray paint canister.
	Text	Places text in the drawing.	Aren't there some peculiarities about this tool? Click where you want the text and then type.
	Line	Draws a straight line.	Hold down the **Shift** key to draw it straight, vertical, or horizontal.
	Curve	Draws a curve.	Draw a straight line, and then drag the middle of the line to adjust the curve
	Rectangle	Draws a rectangle.	Choose between a border only (no fill), a fill only (no border), or both. Hold down the **Shift** key to draw a perfect square.
	Polygon	Draws a free-form shape consisting of multiple straight lines.	Double-click to connect the beginning to the end to complete the shape.
	Ellipse	Draws an ellipse.	Hold down the **Shift** key to draw a perfect circle.
	Rounded Rectangle	Draws a rounded rectangle.	Like a rectangle, but with rounded corners. Hold down **Shift** to make a rounded square.

Alternatives to Paint

Paint Shop Pro is an excellent mid-level graphics program, and you can download a trial version for free from http://www.jasc.com. Unless you are a professional artist, you may not need more features than it provides. PhotoDraw 2000, which comes with Office 2000, is also very good.

Moving up a level, Adobe Photoshop is widely recognized as one of the best professional graphics programs. It's also rather expensive, however (several hundred dollars), and is probably not worth the expense for casual users.

Doing Math with the Calculator

If you are always fumbling for your desktop calculator, you will appreciate that Windows 98 has one built-in. It works just like a regular calculator, too. You can either click its buttons onscreen or use your keyboard's numeric keypad. See Figure 4.3.

The Calculator is really two calculators in one: standard and scientific. To change to the scientific calculator and take advantage of its extra functions, open the **View** menu and click **Scientific**.

FIGURE 4.3
The standard calculator (on the left) and the scientific calculator (on the right).

Scanning and Annotating with Imaging

Imaging is a special-purpose graphics tool that comes with Windows 98. (Windows 95 didn't include it.) It has two rather specialized functions that you might be interested in:

- You can use it to run a scanner to acquire and then save images.
- You can use it to annotate image files in .tif, .awd (fax), and .bmp formats.

Annotation means making marks or notes on an image to comment on it. Suppose, for example, that you have some scanned photos of people that you would like to label. You can use the annotation feature to type each person's name on top of a picture, and the lettering becomes part of the picture.

To use Imaging to run your scanner, open the **File** menu and choose **Scan New**. (The controls that appear after that depend on your individual scanner.) If that command is not available, set up the scanner first by opening the **File** menu and clicking **Select Scanner**.

To annotate an image (provided it is the correct image type), use the following procedure:

File Formats

Imaging can open a variety of image formats, including .bmp, .pcx, .tif, .awd, and .jpg. However, you can annotate only .tif, .awd, or .bmp format files. In addition, when you save .awd and .bmp files, the annotations become a permanent part of the file, and you cannot remove them later.

To get around this limitation, if you have a file you want to annotate that is in the "wrong" format for it, you can save it as a .tif file with the **File**, **Save As** command.

Annotating an Image

1. Open the image. If it is not in TIF, AWD, or BMP format, save it as a TIF file (with the **File**, **Save As** command).

2. Open the **Annotation** menu and choose an annotation tool.

   If you don't see the list of tools shown in Figure 4.4, the image is the wrong type to be annotated.

FIGURE 4.4
Select an annotation tool.

3. Click the image or drag across it to create the annotation. Table 4.1 describes the available annotation tools.

   The exact procedure depends on the animation chosen. For example, if you choose the Typed Text animation, you click the image and then type the text.

Table 4.2 Annotation tools in Imaging

Tool	Purpose
Freehand Line	Draws a freehand line.
Highlighter	Draws a see-through wash of color on the image, like a transparent highlighter.

Tool	Purpose
Straight Line	Draws a straight line.
Hollow Rectangle	Draws a transparent-center rectangle.
Filled Rectangle	Draws an opaque rectangle.
Typed Text	Places the insertion point so you can type text.
Attach-a-Note	Places a rectangle into which you can type text.
Text From File	Lets you select a text file from which to import text.
Rubber Stamps	Lets you insert a saved block of text (a "stamp"), such as Received, Rejected, and so on.

The Imaging program does the job of annotation very well, but it doesn't do a very good job of editing an image's colors or shapes. For simple image editing, try Paint, covered earlier in this lesson, or download a trial version of Paint Shop Pro (http://www.jasc.com), a very good and inexpensive graphics-editing program. You may also want to experiment with PhotoDraw 2000, which comes free with some versions of Microsoft Office 2000.

Going Online with HyperTerminal

HyperTerminal is a communications program that lets you connect your PC directly to another PC through your modem, so the two can communicate.

HyperTerminal is *not* the program you will use to connect to the Internet. It does not manage a TCP/IP connection, which is probably what you need to communicate with your Internet service provider. Instead, it connects to the PC at the other end in a more primitive, direct manner, appropriate for communicating with Bulletin Board Systems (BBSes) and individual PCs (such as connecting to a friend's PC to exchange files).

The most common use these days for HyperTerminal is to connect to a company's BBS to download drivers and get technical help. Even in this golden age of the Internet, many companies still maintain such systems for the free use of their customers.

When you set up a connection for a particular BBS or other connection, it appears as an icon in the HyperTerminal folder (see Figure 4.5), and you can dial it automatically by double-clicking that icon. If you have not set up a saved connection for a particular phone number to dial, you must set it up as described in the following steps.

FIGURE 4.5
The HyperTerminal folder.

① The HyperTerminal program

② Connections to specific services already set up

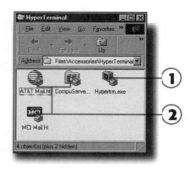

Not There?

Depending on your setup, HyperTerminal may be directly on the **Accessories** menu (**Start, Programs, Accessories**) rather than on the **Communications** menu. If it is not either place, it probably has not been installed. See Chapter 8, "Installing New Programs," to install it.

Setting Up a New HyperTerminal Connection

1. Open the **Start** menu, point to **Programs**, point to **Accessories**, point to **Communications**, and click **HyperTerminal**. A folder opens with the HyperTerminal program in it. See Figure 4.5.

2. Double-click **Hypertrm.exe**.

   You may not see the .exe part.

3. A Connection Description dialog box appears. Type a description for the new connection you want to set up.

   For example, if you are going to connect to the 3-Com Technical Support BBS, you might type **3-Com Tech**.

4. Select an icon that you want to be associated with this connection.

   This icon will be used for the saved connection file that will appear in the Hyperterminal folder later.

5. Click **OK**. The Connect To dialog box appears. See Figure 4.6.

6. Type the area code and phone number in the text boxes provided.

7. If you have more than one modem, choose the one to use from the **Connect using** drop-down list.

FIGURE 4.6
Enter the phone number to dial and choose the modem to use.

8. Click **OK**. The Connect dialog box opens.

9. Click **Dial**. Your modem dials the number and connects.

From this point, follow the prompts that appear on the screen. (It will be different for each BBS.) You will probably be prompted to enter your username (login) and password, as shown in Figure 4.7.

FIGURE 4.7
Most BBSes and other systems you dial will ask you to log in.

10. When you are finished with the call, request that the other computer terminate the call using the instructions onscreen for the BBS.

11. Open the **File** menu and choose **Exit** to exit HyperTerminal. You are asked whether you want to save the session.

12. To save the information so you can call the same BBS again in the future without going through setup again, choose **Yes**. Otherwise choose **No**.

New in Town?

If you are calling a BBS or system that accepts new users, instructions will appear at the logon screen for setting up a new account. Look carefully for such instructions to find out how to proceed.

Hanging Up

To terminate a call from your end, open the **Call** menu and click **Disconnect**. It is better to let the BBS terminate the call if you can, however, because that ensures that you log off its system properly.

If you choose Yes in Step 12, you will see a new icon in your HyperTerminal folder. You can double-click that icon later to redial the same connection.

SEE ALSO

➤ *To set up an Internet connection with your local service provider, see page 288.*

➤ *To show or hide file extensions in a file listing, see page 116.*

Playing Audio CDs

Do you like to listen to audio CDs while you work at your computer? So do I. And Windows 98 will play them, right on your CD-ROM drive. All you need is a CD-ROM drive, a sound card, and some speakers or headphones.

When you pop a CD into your CD-ROM drive, Windows scans it to see whether it contains computer data or audio files. If the latter, the CD Player utility starts automatically, and it starts playing the disc.

If the disc is already in the drive, you can start the CD player manually by opening the **Start** menu, pointing to **Programs**, **Accessories**, and **Entertainment**, and clicking **CD Player**. Or, you can eject and reinsert the CD in the drive.

The CD Player has buttons just like a regular audio CD player has:

▶ Play

II Pause

■ Stop

◄◄ Previous track

◄◄ Skip backward

►► Skip forward

►►| Next track

⏏ Eject

You can also jump to a particular track by choosing it from the **Track** drop-down list. See Figure 4.8.

FIGURE 4.8
Use the CD Player the same as you would one on your stereo system.

SEE ALSO
➤ *To troubleshoot multimedia device issues, see page 189.*

Recording Sounds

With Sound Recorder and a microphone, you can create your own sound effect files to use in Windows. Lots of ways exist to use sound files: You can add them to PowerPoint presentations, for example, or assign them to events in Windows (such as a window or menu opening or an error message appearing). I know someone, for example, who recorded Dr. McCoy on Star Trek saying, "Dammit, Jim!" and used that as the sound that played every time Windows displayed a warning box.

Recording a Sound

1. Open the **Start** menu. Point to **Programs**, **Accessories**, and **Entertainment**, and click **Sound Recorder**.

2. If you want to record from a microphone, make sure it is connected and ready.

   or

   If you want to record from an audio CD, start the CD Player and advance the CD to the spot where you want to begin recording; then click **Pause**.

3. In Sound Recorder, click the **Record** button [●]. (See Figure 4.9.) Then, quickly switch to the CD player and click **Play**, or start speaking (or singing, or whatever) into the microphone.

   As the sound records, you can watch the line in the dialog box spike and change, reflecting the sounds being recorded.

Track Sampling
You can use Sound Recorder (described in the next section) to record excerpts from CD audio discs. However, the resulting files consume a huge amount of hard disk space, so don't attempt this unless you have plenty of space to spare. A one-minute selection can take up tens of megabytes.

No Sound?
If you don't hear any sound while the CD is playing, check to make sure your speakers are plugged in and turned on. Also, check your multimedia settings (see Chapter 10, "Customizing System Settings") to make sure your sound card is set up correctly.

One more thing: To play CD audio through your sound card, a special cable must be connected from your sound card to your CD drive (inside the PC). If you can hear other sounds from your speakers but not CD audio, check inside to make sure this cable is present and connected.

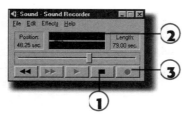

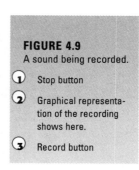

FIGURE 4.9
A sound being recorded.

① Stop button

② Graphical representation of the recording shows here.

③ Record button

4. When you have recorded the sound you want, click **Stop** [■] in Sound Recorder.

5. Open the **File** menu, choose **Save**, and save the sound file the same as you would save any other file. (Refer to Chapter 3 for more information on Save, if needed.)

Files that you create with Sound Recorder are saved in a format called Wave (with the .wav extension). You can play the recorded sounds in Sound Recorder to see if you got them right; you can also play them with Media Player (covered in the next section) or insert them in documents, presentations, spreadsheets, or other files.

SEE ALSO

➤ *To assign sound effects to system events in Windows, see page 194.*

➤ *To run the CD Player, see page 78.*

➤ *To save files in a Windows-based program, see page 57.*

➤ *To configure multimedia settings, see page 189.*

Windows Media Player

Media Player is a multipurpose player that can play a variety of files. It can play WAVE files that you record with Sound Recorder, audio CD files (CD Player does a better job of it, but Media Player will play them, too), and sounds in many other formats, too, such as the very popular MP3 and MIDI. Media player also plays a variety of video clip formats, such as QuickTime and Microsoft Streaming Video.

The best and quickest way to play a clip is to double-click it from a file listing. This opens Media Player and plays the file all in one step. But you can also start Media Player and then open a media clip by opening the **File** menu and clicking **Open**, just as you would open a file in any other program.

Media Player has the same kinds of controls as the CD Player (Start, Pause, and so on), but it has a video window where the video portion of a clip plays (if the clip has video). See Figure 4.10.

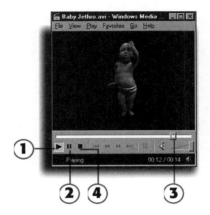

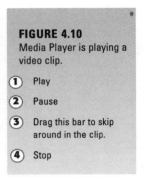

FIGURE 4.10
Media Player is playing a video clip.

(1) Play

(2) Pause

(3) Drag this bar to skip around in the clip.

(4) Stop

chapter

5

Managing Files and Folders

Choosing a File Management Method

A *file* is a collected mass of computer data stored under a single name. Many types of files are on your computer system, each serving a unique purpose, such as storing a document, running a program, or displaying a graphic.

A *folder* is a way of organizing files, much like paper folders or dividers in a filing cabinet. You create and use folders to store files of a common type or for a common purpose. For example, you might store all the files that run a game called Crazee in a folder called Crazee.

One of the easiest ways to work with files and folders is through My Computer on the upper left of your desktop. From My Computer, you can select any of your local drives (that is, any drive directly connected to your own PC, excluding network drives) and view or manage its contents. Figure 5.1 shows a My Computer window for a typical hard disk (C:).

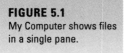

FIGURE 5.1
My Computer shows files in a single pane.

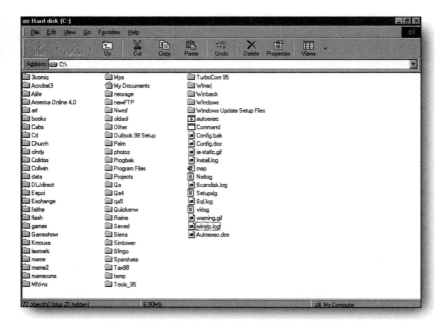

One of the most popular folders to work with is My Documents because that's where, by default, most programs store your saved data files. Therefore, My Documents has its own separate icon on the desktop. You can double-click the **My Documents** icon to display the same type of window as shown in Figure 5.1, but the window is specific to that particular folder. See Figure 5.2.

Browsing through My Computer or My Documents does not give you access to your local area network (LAN) and its files. To browse the network, use the **Network Neighborhood** icon on the desktop. (If you do not have a network connection, you may not have this icon.) From the Network Neighborhood, you can view and work with shared files on the network, as shown in Figure 5.3.

Want to manage everything in one place? And switch quickly from folder to folder and drive to drive? Then the Windows Explorer tool is for you.

Drive Shortcuts

If you browse the content of a particular drive or folder frequently, consider creating a shortcut for that drive or folder on your desktop. To do so, right-drag the drive or folder from the My Computer window to your desktop, and choose **Create Shortcut Here** from the shortcut menu that appears when you release the mouse button. See Chapter 7, "Organizing Your Programs," for more information about creating shortcuts.

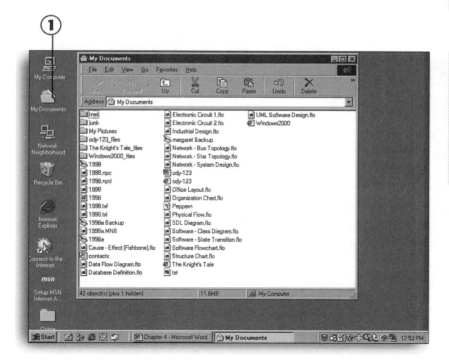

FIGURE 5.2
You can browse the My Documents folder directly from the desktop by double-clicking its icon.

① My Documents icon

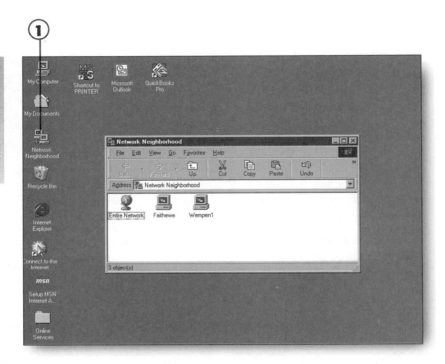

FIGURE 5.3
Network Neighborhood provides access to files on other PCs on the network.

① Network Neighborhood icon

My Documents Subfolders

You can create other folders within the My Documents folder to better organize the documents you create. Of course, you can store documents in any folder, not just this one. However, because most programs use My Documents as the default storage location, creating folders within it can save you time because you won't have to be continually changing the save location. You will learn to create folders later in this chapter.

Windows Explorer is just like My Computer and the other file management windows (Figures 5.1 through 5.3), except it has an extra pane. The navigation pane on the left shows a list of folders and drives, and you can view the contents of any of them by clicking it on that list. See Figure 5.4.

Opening Windows Explorer

Do either of the following:

- Click **Start**, point to **Programs**, and click **Windows Explorer**.
  or
- Hold down the **Shift** key and double-click **My Computer** on the desktop.

SEE ALSO

➤ *To create shortcuts on your desktop for drives or folders, see page 129.*

➤ *To create new folders, see page 104.*

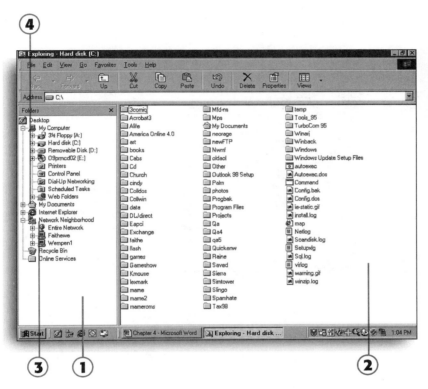

FIGURE 5.4
Windows Explorer shows the files in a certain location and provides quick access to other locations.

(1) Navigation pane

(2) File list

(3) You can see the Network from here.

(4) You can access My Documents from here.

Navigating Drives and Folders

Before you can start working with files, you need to display the drive and folder that contain those files. Therefore, we'll start out with some navigation basics.

Finding a File

If you don't know where a particular file is stored, you can use the Windows Find feature, covered later in this chapter.

Displaying a Drive or Folder in My Computer

When you open the My Computer window, you see icons for each of the drives on your PC. See Figure 5.5. You can double-click a drive's icon to open a list of folders on that drive. From there, you double-click a folder to see its contents.

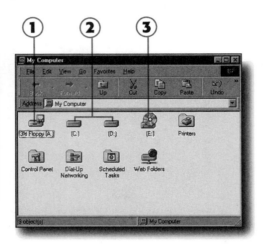

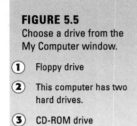

FIGURE 5.5
Choose a drive from the My Computer window.

(1) Floppy drive

(2) This computer has two hard drives.

(3) CD-ROM drive

Displaying a Drive or Folder in Windows Explorer

In Windows Explorer, you rely on the navigation pane to move around. Its "tree" of computers, drives, and folders can be collapsed or expanded. A plus sign (+) next to an item means that subordinate items exist for it that don't currently display. Click the plus sign (+) to see them (or the minus sign (–) to hide them).

When you see the name of the drive or folder you want to look at in the navigation pane, double-click it. Its content appears in the file list pane. See Figure 5.6.

SEE ALSO

➤ *To change the viewing options for a file listing, see page 112.*

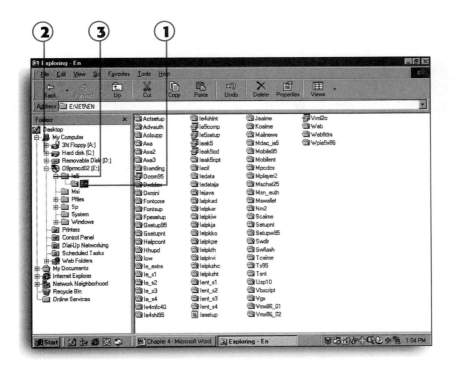

FIGURE 5.6
Use the navigation pane
on the left to select the
drive or folder you want
to see and work with.

1 This folder's content
   appears on the right.

2 Plus sign means more
   folders are hidden.

3 Minus sign means sub-
   folders are all dis-
   played.

Selecting Files and Folders

You must select a file or folder before you can do something to it.
That "something" can include moving, copying, deleting, renaming,
and so on, all of which you will learn later in this chapter.

To select a file or folder, click it. To deselect it, click somewhere else
(away from it).

You can select multiple files and folders at once and act on the group
of them as if they were a single unit. For example, you can select a
range of items to delete, and then delete them with one command.
Or, you can select a range and then copy the group to a floppy disk.
Figure 5.7 shows multiple files selected.

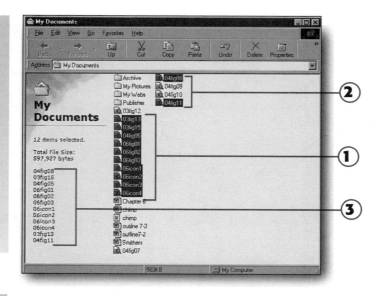

FIGURE 5.7
Multiple files are selected and are ready for a command to act on them.

① This group of files is contiguous (together).

② These files are not contiguous to the others but are still part of the selection.

③ List of selected files and their collective size.

Folders, Too

Folders can be selected, moved, copied, deleted, and renamed the same way as files. I won't say "files or folders" every time in this chapter when talking about these activities, but keep in mind that you can do the same thing to folders that you are learning to do with files.

The way you select multiple items depends on whether they are all together on the list (*contiguous*).

Selecting a Contiguous Group Of Files

1. Click the first file that you want to select.
2. Hold down the **Shift** key and click the last file. That file, and all the files between the two, are selected.
3. Release the **Shift** key.

Selecting Noncontiguous Files

1. Click the first file that you want to select.
2. Hold down the **Ctrl** key and click individually on each other file you also want to select.
3. Release the **Ctrl** key when you are finished.

Moving and Copying Files and Folders

Moving and copying files and folders are such important tasks that Windows provides many ways to accomplish them. You get to pick the method that works best for you (and for the situation at hand).

Broadly speaking, two major methods can be used:

- **Drag and drop.** You select the item(s) you want and then use the mouse to drag them to some other location.
- **Cut (or copy) and paste.** You select the item(s) you want and then Cut or Copy them to the Windows Clipboard. Then, you display the folder where you want them and paste them with the Paste command.

Each of those methods has some variations and alternatives; we'll look at all that in the following sections.

Moving or Copying with Drag-and-Drop

Drag-and-drop is a very easy way to get files and folders from Point A to Point B. You just drag them there; what could be simpler?

Well, actually it's not quite as simple as you might think. When you drag and drop, you are either moving or copying, according to the following rules:

- When you drag from one drive to another, the default is to copy the item to the new drive. If you drag without pressing any keys, it will copy.
- When you drag between folders on the same drive, the default is to move the item to a new location. If you drag without pressing any keys, it will move.
- You can force any drag-and-drop action to be a Move by holding down the **Shift** key as you drag.
- You can force any drag-and-drop action to be a Copy by holding down the **Ctrl** key as you drag.
- You can drag with the right mouse button (right-drag), and when you drop, a shortcut menu appears, letting you choose between moving, copying, and creating a shortcut.

In addition to these rules, you should be aware of one more thing: You must be able to see both the starting location and the destination location onscreen at the same time. With Windows Explorer, that is not a problem because of that handy navigation pane.

Moving or Copying in Windows Explorer with Drag-and-Drop

1. In Windows Explorer, select the files you want to move or copy.

2. Expand the tree in the navigation pane as needed so that you can see the name of the destination drive or folder.

3. Hold down the **Shift** key to move or the **Ctrl** key to copy.

4. Drag the files to the destination on the navigation tree. See Figure 5.8.

Moving or Copying?

You can tell whether Windows is moving or copying by looking at the mouse pointer. When copying, it has a small plus sign next to it.

FIGURE 5.8

Drag the files to the drive or folder where you want them.

(**1**) File being dragged

(**2**) Mouse pointer while dragging

(**3**) Plus sign indicates it is copying.

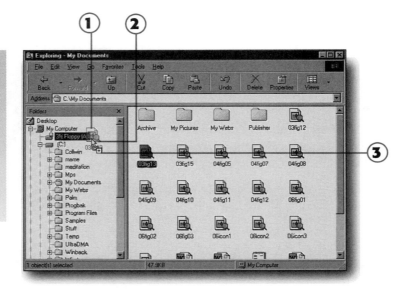

But what about with My Computer, My Documents, and Network Neighborhood? Each of these panes stands alone with no navigation tree. This makes it harder to see both the current location and the destination at once. (I didn't say impossible—just harder.) To move or copy from these, you must open a separate window in which you display the destination drive or folder.

By default, My Computer has only one open window. When you double-click a folder to see its contents, those contents appear in the same window, replacing the previously viewed contents. You can change how Windows operates, however, so that each folder you double-click in My Computer (and My Documents and Network Neighborhood) opens in its own window.

Going Up?

You can press **Backspace** or click the **Up** button to move up a level in the folder structure.

Set Up My Computer for Multiple Windows

1. In My Computer, open the **View** menu and click **Folder Options**.

2. Click the **Custom, based on settings you choose** option button.

3. Click the **Settings** button. The Custom Settings dialog box opens.

4. Click **Open each folder in its own window**.

5. Click **OK**.

After completing the preceding steps, you will be able to open multiple windows with My Computer, each one containing a different drive or folder's contents. You can then drag and drop among them.

SEE ALSO

➤ *To further customize the way files and folder windows are displayed, see page 112.*

Moving or Copying with the Clipboard

As you learned earlier in this book, the Clipboard is a temporary holding area that Windows uses to move and copy things. "Things" can be files, folders, bits of text, graphics, or anything else that can be selected.

I often use the Clipboard method of copying or moving files when I am working in My Computer and it isn't convenient to open a separate window to display the destination folder. The Clipboard method is also great for times when you need to do some other action between copying (or cutting) and pasting.

For example, suppose you want to copy some files onto a floppy disk from your My Documents folder. You aren't sure if the disk in the A: drive is empty, but it needs to be. So you copy the files first from My Documents onto the Clipboard and then display the A: drive's contents, delete any other files from it, and finally paste the files from the Clipboard onto that disk.

Drag and Drop to Shortcuts

Create shortcuts on your desktop for the drives and folders you move or copy to frequently, and then drag the files from the file listing onto that shortcut.

Moving or Copying with the Clipboard

1. Select the file(s) you want to move or copy.

2. Do one of the following:

- To copy the files, open the **Edit** menu and click **Copy**, or click the **Copy** button ▣.

- To move the files, open the **Edit** menu and click **Cut**, or click the **Cut** button ▣.

3. Display the drive or folder where you want to place the files. Not sure how? Here are some ideas:

- If the destination is a folder within the current folder or drive, double-click the folder to display its contents.

- If the destination is on the network, open Network Neighborhood and navigate to the computer, drive, and folder you want.

- If the destination is a folder on the same drive as the current one, click the **Up** button ▣ until you see the list of folders for the drive. Then, double-click the folder you want.

- Open the drop-down list for the Address line and choose a drive or folder.

4. When the destination folder's content is displayed, open the **Edit** menu and click **Paste**, or click the **Paste** button[05-04].

SEE ALSO
➤ *To move or copy text with the Clipboard, see page 56.*

Deleting Files and Folders

Deleting files (and folders, too) is very easy. Many ways exist to do it. But do you know *why* you are deleting a particular file or folder? If not, you shouldn't be doing it. Deleting files, especially ones that run programs, is serious business. Delete the wrong files in your C:\Windows folder, and Windows won't work at all. Delete the wrong word processing file, and you've just lost that 12 hours of work you did on your big report. Don't delete a file unless you are absolutely sure you don't need it anymore.

Unavailable Command?

If the **Cut** or **Copy** command is grayed out (unavailable) on the **Edit** menu, perhaps you do not have a file or folder selected. Make sure you do.

However, for some odd reason, sometimes the **Cut** and **Copy** commands will appear grayed out (unavailable) on the **Edit** menu, even when a file is selected and ready to be cut or copied. If that happens, just use one of the other Cut or Copy methods (the toolbar or the key combination).

Deleting Files

1. Select the file(s) to delete.

2. Do one of the following:

   * Press the **Delete** key.

   * Open the **File** menu and click **Delete**.

   * Right-click the files and choose **Delete** from the shortcut menu.

   * Click the **Delete** button on the window's toolbar. ☒

3. If a confirmation box appears asking whether you want to send the files to the Recycle Bin, click **Yes**.

So what should you do if you delete a file and then realize you shouldn't have? Don't worry; the file probably hasn't been destroyed yet. You go to the Recycle Bin and see whether you can fish it back out again.

Working with the Recycle Bin

Deleted files don't get destroyed right away. Instead, they are banished to the Recycle Bin, a special folder that holds files and folders you have discarded. (Kind of like *The Island of Misfit Files*.) You can empty the Recycle Bin to destroy the contents whenever you like, or you can keep them there in case you need to recover any of them.

Retrieving a File from the Recycle Bin

Open the Recycle Bin by double-clicking it on the desktop. It looks much like any other folder's window, but don't let that fool you; all the files and folders in the Recycle Bin are on Death Row. You can spare their lives with the following procedure:

Restoring a Deleted File

1. Double-click the Recycle Bin icon on the desktop to open it.

2. Select the file(s) you want to restore.

3. Open the **File** menu and click **Restore** (see Figure 5.9).

   The files vanish from the Recycle Bin. Where did they go? They went to their original locations from which you deleted them.

Deleting a File for Good

If you want to destroy a file right away, without letting it stop off in the Recycle Bin, hold down the **Shift** key as you delete it.

Other Utilities

Some add-on programs you can buy for Windows, such as Norton Utilities, add features to the Recycle Bin or replace it with their own file deletion and recovery utility. If you have such a program installed, your Recycle Bin may not work exactly as described here.

FIGURE 5.9
Restore selected files,
sparing them from
destruction.

① Select the file(s) to
restore.

② Choose Restore.

Another way to undelete a file is to drag it out of the Recycle Bin and into another folder (or onto the desktop). You can also right-click a file in the Recycle Bin and choose Restore from its shortcut menu.

Emptying the Recycle Bin

Emptying the Recycle Bin destroys all the files in it so that you can't restore them anymore.

Why in the world would anyone voluntarily limit options like that? Two words: *disk space*. When you delete a file and it goes to the Recycle Bin, you haven't really freed up any space on your hard disk. That file is still taking up as much space as ever—just in a different location. If you are trying to tidy up your hard disk so you will have more space to install more programs, deleting unneeded files is a good way to do that. But sending them to the Recycle Bin is not enough. You must then empty the Recycle Bin to free up that space.

You can do either of the following to empty the Recycle Bin:

- From the Windows desktop, right-click the **Recycle Bin** and choose **Empty Recycle Bin**. Then, click **Yes**.
- From the Recycle Bin window, open the **File** menu and click **Empty Recycle Bin**. Then, click **Yes**.

SEE ALSO
➤ *To learn other ways of freeing up disk space, see page 411.*

Setting Recycle Bin Properties

Files in the Recycle Bin are eventually destroyed if you don't do it sooner yourself by emptying it. The Recycle Bin destroys deleted files, starting with the ones that have been there the longest, after a certain amount of time or when the total size of the Recycle Bin's files exceeds the specified limit.

You can set up rules governing how long the Recycle Bin saves files and what its total capacity is. You can also choose to have separate rules for each hard drive on your system.

Configuring the Recycle Bin

1. Right-click the **Recycle Bin** on the desktop and choose **Properties**. The Recycle Bin Properties box appears. See Figure 5.10.

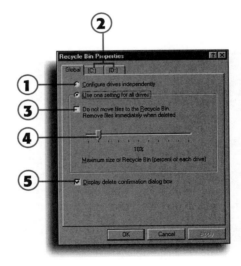

FIGURE 5.10
Set Recycle Bin properties here.

① You can configure each drive separately if you want.

② Use these tabs instead of Global if you are configuring drives separately.

③ This turns the Recycle Bin off.

④ Select how much space the Recycle Bin can use.

⑤ Disable the deletion confirmation box here.

2. (Optional) If you have more than one hard disk, and you want to configure each drive separately, click **Configure drives independently**. Then, perform the rest of these steps separately on the tab for each drive.

3. To disable the Recycle Bin so that files are destroyed immediately when you delete them, select the **Do not move files to the _R_ecycle Bin** check box.

4. To adjust the amount of space on the hard disk that the Recycle Bin can occupy, drag the slider bar to a different setting.

   For example, if you choose 10% and you have a 10-gigabyte hard disk, the Recycle Bin will be allowed to use up to 1 gigabyte on that drive. If the total size of the files in the Recycle Bin ever exceeds that amount, it will start deleting files (oldest ones first) until it comes in under the limit.

5. To turn off the confirmation box that appears when you delete files, deselect the **_D_isplay delete confirmation dialog box** check box.

6. Click **OK**.

Renaming Files and Folders

Sometimes a file or folder's name is important, and you shouldn't change it—other times not.

Generally speaking, files that run programs need to keep the same names, or the programs might not work. That's because a program usually requires many files to work, all closely related to one another. If you change the name of one of them, the others might not recognize it, and it might not work correctly. Folders that contain Windows programs should not be renamed because you won't be able to start the program from your Start menu anymore if you rename it.

On the other hand, data files and folders that you create yourself can usually be renamed without causing problems. For example, suppose you created a memo called Memo. Later, you realize that wasn't a very good name because it's not descriptive. So you decide to rename it Smith Promotion 8-1-99 instead. Good thinking. Or perhaps you have created a folder called Projects, and you want to rename it to Home Projects (and possibly create another folder for business ones). That's no problem, either.

Renaming a File or a Folder

1. Click the file or folder you want to rename.

2. Open the **File** and click **Rename**, or right-click the file or folder and choose **Rename** from the shortcut menu, or press **F2**.

    An outline appears around the current name with an insertion point in it. The name is highlighted.

3. Type a new name. It replaces the old name.

4. Press **Enter** or click away from the file or folder.

Instead of completely retyping the name in Step 3, you can edit it if you prefer. Notice that at Step 3, the old name is highlighted and an insertion point blinks at the end of it. You can click anywhere in the name to move that insertion point to the spot you want to edit, and then use the usual text editing methods (see Chapter 3) to edit the name.

SEE ALSO

➤ *To create new folders, see page 104.*

➤ *To edit text, see page 55.*

> **File Renaming Caution**
>
> Two cautions about renaming a file: First, make sure you keep the same extension for it so Windows will continue to recognize it as the same type of file. (If file extensions are not displayed, you don't have to worry about typing them when you type the new name.)
>
> Second, if you choose a name with more than eight characters and/or spaces, make sure that the program in which you will use that file can accept long filenames like that.

Working with File Properties

Each file and folder has its own properties. *Properties*, in Windows lingo, are attributes or settings. Some of these you can change, depending on the file or folder type.

First, we'll talk about some of the properties that you can't change, at least not from the Properties dialog box. A file's properties include its name, its type, its location, and its size. The Properties dialog box reports all these facts in a read-only way. See Figure 5.11.

FIGURE 5.11
The Properties dialog box for a typical data file. This one happens to be a graphic.

① File attributes

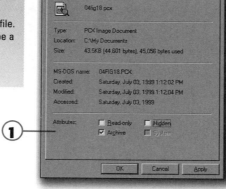

04fig18.pcx Properties	? X
General	Image	

	04fig18.pcx
Type:	PCX Image Document
Location:	C:\My Documents
Size:	43.5KB (44,601 bytes), 45,056 bytes used

MS-DOS name:	04FIG18.PCX
Created:	Saturday, July 03, 1999 1:12:02 PM
Modified:	Saturday, July 03, 1999 1:12:04 PM
Accessed:	Saturday, July 03, 1999

Attributes:	☐ Read-only	☐ Hidden
	☑ Archive	☐ System

OK   Cancel   Apply

Hidden Files Not There?

By default, Windows 98 does not show hidden or system files in most file listings. You will learn how to set them to be displayed in Chapter 6, "Setting File Management Options."

Changing Attributes: A Real Example

Suppose you have a writable CD drive and have created a disk containing backups of some of your important documents. You copy one of the files back to your hard disk later and try to edit it, but you can't. Why? Because it is read-only. All files on a CD are read-only, and when you copy one of them, the copy retains that attribute. To modify the copy, you will need to turn off the read-only attribute for it.

You can, however, change a file's attributes from its Properties box. The following is a complete description of the four attributes that each file can have (or not have):

- **Read-only.** This prevents any program or person from changing or deleting the file. Important system files often have this attribute.

- **Hidden.** This prevents the file from appearing in file listings (unless you have turned on the display of hidden files, as you learned earlier in this chapter).

- **System.** This denotes that the file is especially important to the startup or operation of the computer.

- **Archive.** This means that the file has changed since your last backup.

The first three properties you should not change without some serious thought; if a file has one of these attributes, there is probably a very good reason. For example, dire consequences may occur to your Windows operation if you modify or delete a read-only file, because some files must be read-only to ensure the proper operation of Windows. Generally speaking, you should not set or remove these properties for any files except those you have created yourself.

The last property, Archive, is less critical. If you use the Backup program described in Chapter 24, "Safeguarding Your System," to safeguard your files, you might change a file's Archive attribute to include or exclude it in the next backup operation.

Viewing or Changing File Properties

1. Do any of the following to display the selected file's properties:
   - Right-click the file and choose **Properties** from the shortcut menu.
   - Click **Properties** on the window's toolbar.
   - Open the **File** menu and click **Properties**.

   The Properties dialog box appears for that file. See Figure 5.11.

2. Select or deselect any of the Attributes check boxes as needed. (Heed my earlier warning about not changing these except for a good reason, however.)

3. Click **OK**.

SEE ALSO

➤ *To control whether hidden files are displayed in file listings, see page 118.*

➤ *To back up important files, see page 427.*

➤ *To set properties to control MS-DOS programs running from within Windows, see page 461.*

Other Properties

Some files have additional properties. For example, program files may have a Version tab that lists version information. You will seldom have to worry about any of the file's other properties, however. The exception is DOS programs. If you have an MS-DOS–based program (a game, perhaps) that you want to run in Windows, you can set various properties for it that control how the program runs. You'll find out more about these in Chapter 25, "Troubleshooting Problems."

Finding Files and Folders

Even people who are conscientious about file storage can misplace a file occasionally. Perhaps you have forgotten which project you created that really great tracking spreadsheet for, or what you named the file containing the Martinez report.

Windows has a very versatile Find feature that enables you to find files and folders, computers on a network, data or people on the Internet, and more. In this chapter, you'll learn about finding files and folders; the networking and Internet info comes later, in Chapters 14 and 18, respectively.

You can search for a file or folder using whatever shred of information you know about it. For example, you can search based on filename, file type, size, date created, or even content.

Make It Quick

Don't get too carried away with search criteria. It is often faster to specify only minimal criteria for a search and then wade through the results than it is to painstakingly create criteria that will find *only* the file you want.

If you don't know the file's full name, you can search using *wildcards*. Wildcards are symbols that can stand for any character. An asterisk (*) can stand for any number of characters; a question mark (?) can stand for any single character. So, for example, if you know the file starts with S and has a .doc extension, you would search for S*.doc. Or, if you knew the file started with S and had exactly five letters in its name, but you weren't sure of the extension, you could search for S????.*.

Finding a File or Folder

1. Click the **Start** button, point to **Find** and click **Files or Folders**. The Find window appears.

2. Enter any information that you have about the missing file or folder. See Figure 5.12. Do one or more of the following:

   • Enter the filename (or a wildcard specification that includes it) in the **Named** box.

   • Enter text that you know is in the file's content in the **Containing text** box.

   • Select the drive where you know the file is stored from the **Look in** drop-down list.

   • Choose a particular folder to search in by clicking the **Browse** button and locating the folder.

   • Include all subfolders under the chosen drive or folder by making sure the **Include subfolders** check box is marked.

FIGURE 5.12
Enter whatever you know about the file in the fields provided.

① Name criteria

② Content criteria

③ Location criteria

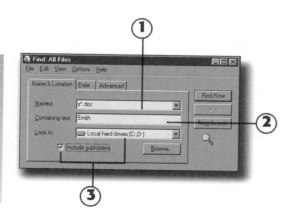

3. (Optional) To search by the date on which the file was created, modified, or accessed, click the **Date** tab and specify what you know. See Figure 5.13.

For example, if you know the file was created last week, you would set the **Find all files** drop-down list to **Created** and then look for all files in the previous seven days, as shown in Figure 5.13.

FIGURE 5.13
Narrow the search by specifying date criteria if you know it.

4. (Optional) To look only for files of a certain type, select the type from the **Of type** drop-down list on the **Advanced** tab.

5. (Optional) To look only for files of a certain size, select the size limitation (**At least** or **At most**) on the **Advanced** tab.

6. Click the **Find Now** button. A list of files appears matching your criteria. It tells where each is stored.

7. Wait for Windows to find the file(s). A list of found files appears below in a new pane, as shown in Figure 5.14.

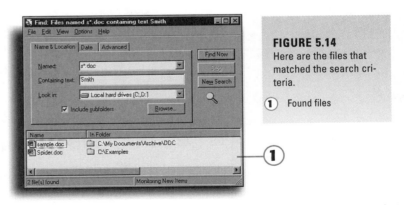

FIGURE 5.14
Here are the files that matched the search criteria.

① Found files

8. Choose from any of the following actions (or options):

- Double-click it to open it in its native application if it is a data file or to run it if it is a program file.
- Select the file and press **Delete** to delete it.
- Right-click the file and choose **Rename** to rename it.
- Right-click the file and choose **Create Shortcut** (and then click **Yes**) to create a shortcut for it on the desktop.

Drag it from the Find window to any other window to move it there.

9. Close the Find window when you are finished with it.

SEE ALSO

➤ *To find computers on a network, see page 249.*

➤ *To find people and information on the Internet, see page 317.*

Creating Folders

When you install a new program (see Chapter 8, "Installing New Programs"), the setup program usually creates a new folder to hold the program's files. You can create your own folders, too, to organize your work. For example, I have a folder called Books on my hard disk, and within that folder I have a separate folder for every book that I write or edit. You may want a separate folder for each client you work with, separate folders for each family member, or some other folder organization.

Creating a New Folder

1. Display the folder or drive that the new folder should be placed in.

2. Open the **File** menu, point to **New,** and click **Folder**. A new folder appears. Its name is highlighted so you can change it. See Figure 5.15.

FIGURE 5.15
This new folder is ready
to be named.

3. Type the name for the new folder.

4. Press **Enter** or click away from the folder to accept the name.

SEE ALSO
➤ *To install a new program, see page 142.*
➤*To delete a folder, see page 94.*

Formatting Disks

In the "olden days"—a few years ago—when you bought floppy disks you had to format them before you could use them. Formatting prepared the disks for use with your system. These days, however, most floppy disks come preformatted.

If you manage to buy unformatted floppies by mistake, or if you have a Macintosh disk, you will need to format the disk to work in your system. Formatting a disk wipes out all its content, so you should not format a disk unless it is empty, unreadable, or contains nothing that you want to keep.

It doesn't hurt a disk to format it again, even if it has been formatted before. Formatting it simply wipes out all the previous information, starting with a clean surface again on which to store your files. However, if a disk is functioning properly, there is really no reason to reformat it, either. Reformatting does not accomplish anything that deleting its contents doesn't do.

Formatting a Floppy Disk

1. Double-click **My Computer** on the desktop.

2. Place the disk to be formatted into your floppy drive.

3. Right-click **3 1/2 Floppy (A:)** in the My Computer window and choose **Format**. The Format dialog box opens. See Figure 5.16.

You Say Diskette...

The terms diskette and floppy disk are, for all practical purposes, interchangeable. In this book I'll be referring to them as *floppy disks* or simply *disks*.

Disk Problems?

If a disk is not functioning properly (for example, if it gives you errors such as `Data error reading A:"`), reformatting it may fix the disk, at least for awhile. (*Caution:* reformatting erases all the data on the disk, so it *doesn't* help retrieve whatever was stored there. To fix problems on a disk that contains important data you want to preserve, see Chapter 23.)

However, floppy disks are cheap, and after a disk has started having problems, it will probably never be totally trustworthy again. Personally, when I have problems with a floppy disk, it goes into the trash after I have retrieved any important files from it.

FIGURE 5.16
Set formatting options here, and then click **Start**.

More on Capacity

Almost all floppy disks sold today are high-density disks, which have a capacity of 1.44MB. Some older disks are double-density, however, which have a capacity of 720KB. Here's an easy way to tell which capacity to choose for a disk: Look at it from the back. Two holes (one in the top-left corner, with a sliding tab, and one in the top-right corner, with nothing) means high density. One hole (just the one with the tab, on the left) means double density.

4. Choose the formatting capacity you want from the Capacity drop-down list. The default 1.44MB should work in most cases.

5. Set the format type you want:

   • **Quick.** This reformats a disk that has already been formatted. Basically, it just erases the files on the disk. It's very fast.

   • **Full.** You must use this for unformatted disks or Macintosh disks that you want to reformat for Windows use. It checks and formats each area of the disk.

   • **Copy system files only.** This copies the files to the disk to make it bootable (that is, able to start up the PC). It works only on already formatted disks, and it does not hurt any data that may already be on the disk.

6. (Optional) If you want a label for the disk, enter it (up to 10 characters) in the **Label** box.

7. Choose any of the following check boxes to set formatting options:

   • **No label.** Formats the disk without using a label.

   • **Display summary when finished.** Displays a summary box when the disk has been formatted, reporting its capacity and any bad areas detected.

   • **Copy system files.** Copies the files to the disk to make it bootable immediately after it has been formatted.

8. Click **Start**.

9. Wait for the disk to be formatted. If you chose to display a summary, a Format Results box appears when it is finished.

10. If you see a Format Results box, click **Close** to close it.

11. Click **Close** to close the Format dialog box.

SEE ALSO

➤ *To install new hardware such as hard disks, see page 202.*

➤ *To salvage files from a malfunctioning disk, run Scandisk, described on page 406.*

Making a Boot Disk

A boot disk (a.k.a a bootable disk) is a disk that contains the necessary files to start your computer should something ever be wrong with your hard disk that prevents it from starting up. It's a smart idea to always have a bootable disk available in case of problems.

In the previous section, you saw how you can format a disk and make it bootable at the same time. A boot disk created this way does not contain any utility programs that you would need in the event of a real problem, however. To create an emergency disk that contains the helpful utilities that you need, you should go through the following process.

Creating a Windows Startup Disk

1. Click the **Start** button, point to **Settings**, and click **Control Panel**.

2. Double-click **Add/Remove Programs**.

3. Click the **Startup Disk** tab.

4. Click **Create Disk**.

5. Place a blank disk (or one that contains nothing you want to keep) in your floppy drive.

6. Click **OK**.

Label?

The label you enter for a disk when formatting it doesn't have any relationship to the paper label on the outside of the disk that you write on. The label you specify when formatting appears under the drive icon in the My Computer window when the disk is in the drive. You can use labels to help yourself remember what you plan to store on a disk.

You can change a disk's label at any time by right-clicking its icon in My Computer and choosing **Properties**, then typing a new label in the **Label** box on the **General** tab.

Formatting Hard Disks

You can format a hard disk too, but remember, formatting a disk wipes out its content. That is almost certainly *not* what you want to do to your hard disk! Only in unusual situations, such as if you have just bought a new, additional hard disk and installed it in your PC, you might want to format a hard disk. To do so, right-click the drive icon in My Computer and choose **Format** from the shortcut menu. You can do the same thing to format other removable media such as ZIP and Jaz disks.

No Miracle Cure

A boot disk will start your system, but it won't necessarily help you repair whatever problem is preventing your computer from starting normally. To troubleshoot startup problems with your PC, see Chapter 25.

7. Wait for the needed files to be copied to the disk.

    If prompted, insert the Windows 98 CD in your CD-ROM drive and click **OK** to continue.

8. When the disk is finished, choose **OK** to close the Add/Remove Programs Properties dialog box.

SEE ALSO

➤ *To use your startup disk to troubleshoot Windows problems, see page 442.*

part

II

MODIFYING YOUR SYSTEM

chapter

6

Setting File Management Options

Changing the View

Files in a window can be displayed in any of four views. See Figure 6.1. To change the view for a window, open the **View** menu and choose one of the following:

- **Large Icons.** Shows each file and folder as a large icon, much like the ones on your Windows desktop, with the name underneath. The files are arranged in rows. When only a few items are in a window, large icons are great. You can see each item very clearly. However, because fewer items will fit onscreen at once than in other views, you may have to do quite a bit of scrolling if many items are in the displayed location.

- **Small Icons.** Shows each file and folder as a small icon with the name to the right. They are arranged in rows. This display is much more compact, so you can see lots of files at once in the window without too much scrolling.

- **List.** The same as Small Icons except the icons are arranged in columns. Some people find this column arrangement easier to use than the rows of the Small Icons view.

- **Details.** Shows the files in one long column with the size, type, and date last modified for each one. This display helps you look for files with certain attributes (for example, the file that has been most recently modified or the largest file).

If you prefer, you can use the **Views** button ▦ on the window's toolbar to change the view. Just click the **Views** button to toggle between views. Or, click the **down arrow** next to the Views button to open a list of views to choose from. See Figure 6.2.

Viewing a Folder as a Web Page

You can also choose whether to view a particular folder or drive as a Web page. This may seem like an odd terminology—how can a folder window be a Web page? What it really means in practical terms is that the folder appears with a separate pane that shows the current folder's name and details about the selected file (if any are selected). Figure 6.3 shows a folder viewed as a Web page. To turn on this feature for a folder, open the **View**, **as Web Page**.

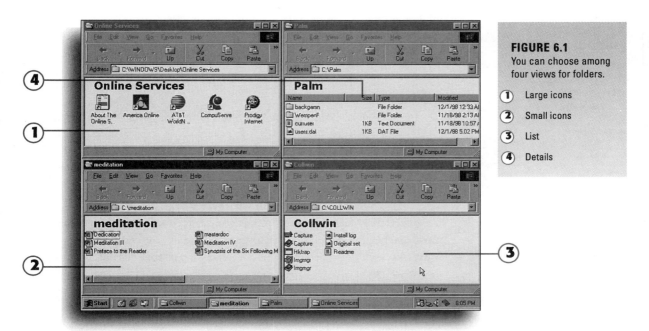

FIGURE 6.1
You can choose among four views for folders.

(1) Large icons

(2) Small icons

(3) List

(4) Details

FIGURE 6.02
Select a view from the window's toolbar.

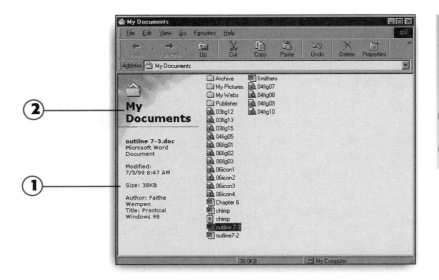

FIGURE 6.3
This folder, with View as Web Page turned on, provides more content information.

(1) Information about selected file

(2) Folder name

This Web page setting affects the individual folder in which you set it by default, so you can choose some folders to view this way and others to view normally.

SEE ALSO

➤ *To learn more about file properties, see page 99.*

➤ *For more information about viewing Windows content in Web format, see page 332.*

Sorting the File List

Web Settings

Later in this chapter, you'll learn how to control desktop update settings. If you choose Web style (or Custom style with certain options) for the desktop update setting, every folder will appear as a Web page automatically.

You can arrange a list of files by Name, Type, Size, or Date. This way, you can organize the files in whatever way makes the most sense for a particular task. For example, if you want to select and copy the most recently modified files, you might sort a list by Date. If you want to select and delete all files created in a certain program, you might sort by Type.

Sorting a File List

1. Open the **View** menu and point to **Arrange Icons**. A submenu of the four available arrangements appears.

2. Click the arrangement you want to use: **by Name, by Type, by Size,** or **by Date**.

Why Sort?

In the next section, you will learn about selecting multiple files. It is much easier to select multiple files when they are all together on the list, or contiguous. If you arrange the files so that all the files you want are together on the list, you can save yourself some time.

Showing or Hiding Toolbars and Other Window Elements

By default, folder windows have several bars that give you easy access to tools and information. If you find that you do not use them, you might want to turn them off to save space (so you can see more files at once in the window without scrolling). Figure 6.4 points them out.

- **Standard buttons.** This is the toolbar of buttons across the top that offers Back, Forward, Delete, and other helpful buttons. Turn it off or on with **View, Toolbars, Standard Buttons**.

- **Address bar.** This is the bar containing the Address text box, in which you can type the path to a folder or an Internet address to make that folder or Web page appear in the window. Turn it off or on with **View, Toolbars, Address Bar**.

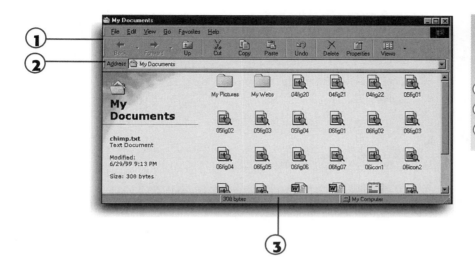

FIGURE 6.4
Default features of a folder window.

① Standard toolbar

② Address bar

③ Status bar

- **Status bar.** This is the bar across the bottom of the window that reports statistics about the window's content, such as the size of the selected file. Turn it off or on with **View**, **Status Bar**.

SEE ALSO

➤ *To browse the Internet, see page 304.*

➤ *For information about Internet radio, see page 338.*

Copying a Folder's View Settings

If you take the time to set up a folder with exactly the view that you like, you may want to copy those settings to other folders. Otherwise, every time you open a folder, you will have to set the viewing options for it individually.

When you copy a folder's view settings, the settings copied include:

- View (large icons, small icons, and so on)
- Arrangement (by name, by type, and so on)
- Web (as Web Page or not)
- Window controls (toolbars and other controls displayed or not displayed)

Other Toolbars

Two other toolbars are available from the View menu: **Links** and **Radio**—and several Explorer Bar components. You will not want to turn these on for normal file and folder management, but you may find them useful when working on the Internet. See Chapter 18.

Setting All Folders to the Same View as the Current One

1. Set up the folder with the viewing options you want.

2. Open the <u>V</u>iew menu and click **Folder <u>O</u>ptions**.

3. Click the **View** tab.

4. Click the **<u>L</u>ike Current Folder** button.

5. Click **OK**.

Advanced View Settings

So far, all the settings you have learned about affect individual folders. But you can also control a set of so-called Advanced folder settings that pertain to all folders. To access them, open the <u>V</u>iew menu and click **Folder <u>O</u>ptions** and see the list on the **View** tab. See Figure 6.5. Most of these you will probably never need to use, but the following sections tell you about two of the more commonly changed settings: hidden files and file extensions.

FIGURE 6.5
Set viewing options for all folders here.

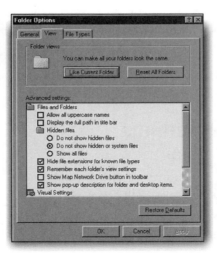

Showing or Hiding File Extensions

File extensions are codes (usually three letters) that follow a file's name that tell Windows what kind of file it is. For example, Smith.exe's extension is .exe, which means it is a program (that is, an executable file). Smith.doc's extension is .doc, which means it is a document.

By default, Windows hides the extensions for every file type that it recognizes, so you don't have to bother with seeing them. So, for example, the file Spider.doc and Spider.exe will both show up in a file listing as Spider. You can tell them apart by their icons; the icon for a program looks different from the icon for a document. See Figure 6.6.

FIGURE 6.6
These two files have the same names but different extensions. The extensions are hidden, however.

Beginners don't mind not seeing extensions because they don't know what those letters mean anyway, so the extensions don't help them. But as you become more experienced with Windows, you may want to see the extensions for the files you work with. For one thing, it helps you make more intelligent decisions about which files to move or delete. If you know that a file has an .exe extension, you would be much less likely to delete it because you can guess that it probably runs a program that you might need.

Showing File Extensions

1. In any folder or drive window, open the **View** menu and click **Folder Options**.

2. Click the **View** tab.

3. Deselect the **Hide file extensions for known file types** check box to turn on extensions.

4. Click **OK**.

With file extensions turned on, you can see that the two files in our earlier example clearly have different extensions and therefore different purposes. See Figure 6.7.

FIGURE 6.7
The file extensions are
now visible.

If you are interested in the various file extensions and what they indicate about their files, Table 6.1 explains some of the more common ones.

Table 6.1 Common file extensions

Extensions	Used For
.exe, .com, .bat	Programs
.dll, .bin, .dat, .ini, .ocx	Helper files for programs
.doc, .wpd, .wri	Word processing documents
.txt	Text files
.123, .xls	Spreadsheets
.pcx, .jpg, .bmp, .gif	Graphics
.zip	A compressed archive

Showing Hidden and System Files

In an attempt to keep beginners out of trouble, Windows excludes files of three types from normal file listings:

- **Hidden files.** These have their attributes set to Hidden, usually for a good reason. They are files that start up your computer or keep it running, and you should not disturb them. (It can be helpful to know they are there, however.)

- **System files (by attribute).** These are files that have their attributes set to System. They can have any extension.

- **System files (by extension).** These files have an extension that makes Windows consider them a "System" file. Such extensions include .dll and .ocx. They can have any file attributes set.

Intermediate and advanced Windows users may find it helpful to turn on the display of hidden and system files. For example, if you are trying to remove everything from a floppy disk, it is helpful to see what hidden and system files are on that disk so you can decide whether to include them in your deletion. Another example: If a program you are running gives you an error message saying that it cannot find a particular .dll file, you might want to view the contents of that folder and see whether it is actually there.

Displaying Hidden and System Files

1. In any folder or drive window, open the **View** menu and click **Folder Options**.

2. Click the **View** tab.

3. Click **Show all files**.

4. Click **OK**.

Hidden files appear ghosted in file listings when they are displayed at all, so that helps you remember that they are special and should not be disturbed. Figure 6.8 shows an example.

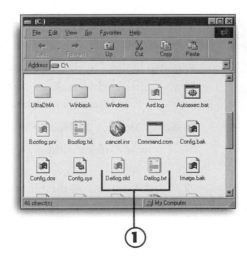

FIGURE 6.8
Hidden files appear ghosted—dimmer than the others.

① Hidden files

Changing the Windows Desktop Update Settings

Windows Desktop Update settings control to what extent you use some of the more modern features in Windows 98, such as viewing the desktop as a Web page. These features are new in Windows 98 (all versions), and some people really like them. Others don't, so you have a choice. Most of these new features are disabled by default when you first install Windows 98 so that your copy of Windows 98 seems more like Windows 95 (and therefore, more comforting and familiar.) You can enable any of the new features that interest you, however.

By the way, these settings affect all folder windows you work with and the entire desktop, not just an individual folder.

- **Web style.** Makes everything act as much like a Web page as possible. All the names of icons and folders are underlined, and you single-click instead of double-click them to activate them. And when you click a folder to display its contents, it appears in the same window rather than opening a new one. Figure 6.9 shows this in action.

- **Classic style.** The normal style of operation for Windows. You click to select and double-click to activate, and each folder that you open appears in a separate window.

- **Custom.** This style allows you to choose your own settings.

You may want to experiment with Web style and Classic style to see how you like each, but the most fun comes when you customize the settings with Custom, as shown in the following steps.

Choosing Windows Desktop Update Settings

1. From any folder window, open the **View** menu and click **Folder Options**.
2. Click **Custom** on the **General** tab.
3. Click **Settings**. The Custom Settings dialog box opens. See Figure 6.10.

Active Desktop

Web style replaces your regular desktop colors and patterns with the Active Desktop. This is a desktop mode in which you can place controls for Web content directly on the desktop, such as a stock ticker that continually updates the prices of your favorite stocks from the Internet. You will learn more about it in Chapter 19, "Bringing the Web to Your Desktop."

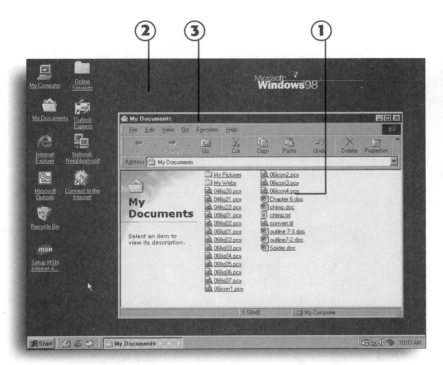

FIGURE 6.9
Windows operating in
Web style.

(1) Click anything under-
lined to activate it.

(2) Active desktop

(3) Single file-
management window

FIGURE 6.10
These are the folder set-
tings you can customize.

4. Change any of the following settings, as desired:

- **Active Desktop.** Enable Web-related content or stick with the Windows Classic desktop. I recommend you stick with the Classic version until you are ready to tackle Chapter 19.

- **Browse Folders as Follows.** As discussed in Chapter 4, you can open each folder in the same or its own window. Your choice. Personally, I prefer to have each folder in its own so that I can drag-and-drop between folders.

- **View Web Content in Folders.** This determines whether the default value for the **View, as Web Page** setting is on or off. Don't let that "with HTML content" throw you; for this purpose, regular lists of files and folders are considered HTML content.

- **Click Items as Follows.** Here you choose whether you want to single-click or double-click to open an item. The default in Windows is double-click, but in Web browsers it is single-click.

5. Click **OK** to close the dialog box.

6. Click **Close** to close the Folder Options dialog box.

SEE ALSO

➤ *To work with Active Desktop content and controls, see page 332.*

➤ *To move or copy by dragging between folders, see page 90.*

You're on Your Own...

The instructions in this book assume that you are using the double-click method of opening files; therefore, you won't be able to follow along exactly with the steps in this book if you change the Click Items as Follows setting.

chapter 7

Organizing Your Programs

Customizing the Start Menu

As you install more and more programs, your Start menu can begin to get very crowded. There may even come a point where the program names won't all fit onscreen at once. (To scroll to see the rest of them when that happens, click the arrow at the bottom, as shown in Figure 7.1.) Luckily, you can rearrange and reorganize the programs on the Start menu to make things more orderly.

FIGURE 7.1
This Programs menu has so many programs installed that it can be confusing to use it.

① Click here to scroll down and see the rest of the Programs menu.

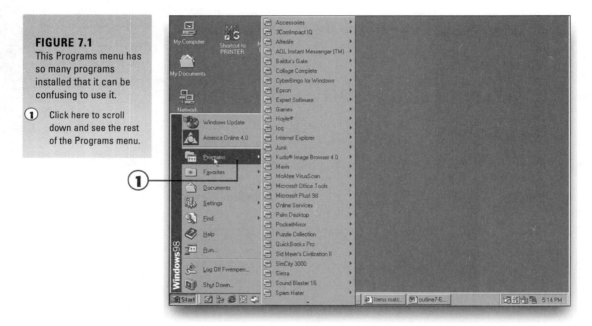

The Start menu is actually a folder on your hard disk (C:\Windows\Start Menu), and its contents are determined by the folders and shortcuts stored there. For example, the Start menu contains a folder called Programs (C:\Windows\Start Menu\Programs); that's the Programs menu you see when you click Start and point to Programs. Within that Programs folder is a folder called Accessories, and within Accessories is a folder called System Tools, and so on. So, when you create, delete, and rearrange submenus, you are actually working with folders.

The programs on the Start menu's various submenus are actually shortcuts to those programs, just like the shortcuts on your desktop. (You'll learn to create desktop shortcuts later in this chapter.) Removing a shortcut from the Start menu does nothing to the original file that runs the program; you can still run it in any of the other ways you learned in Chapter 3.

SEE ALSO

➤ *To create desktop shortcuts, see page 129.*

➤ *To learn about the various ways to start programs, see page 48.*

Rearranging Items on the Start Menu

If you just want to reposition a folder or shortcut on the existing menu system, you can drag it around, as described in the following steps. This is definitely the simpler of the two ways I'll show you.

Move an Item on the Start Menu

1. Open the **Start** menu and point to **Programs** to open the Programs menu.

2. Point to the item you want to move.

3. Press and hold down the left mouse button. (Do not click.)

4. Drag the item to the desired spot on the Start menu (or any submenu; point to a submenu to open it.) A horizontal line shows where it is going. See Figure 7.2.

5. Release the mouse button.

Restructuring the Start Menu

You might decide that your entire Start menu system needs an overhaul. (I do this every six months or so, just for general good housekeeping.) For example, perhaps you have a lot of programs installed (as in Figure 7.1) and need a way of organizing them. Or, perhaps you want to consolidate some of the folders, placing the shortcuts for similar programs together in a folder.

As I mentioned earlier, the Start menu takes its content from the `C:\Windows\Start Menu` folder. This is a regular folder that you can work with using My Computer or Windows Explorer, as you learned in Chapter 5, "Managing Files and Folders."

Shortcuts for Browsing the Start Menu

A shortcut for opening the `C:\Windows\Start Menu` folder in My Computer is to right-click the **Start** button and choose **Open**. To open it in Windows Explorer, right-click the **Start** button and choose **Explore**.

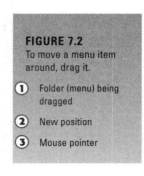

FIGURE 7.2
To move a menu item around, drag it.

① Folder (menu) being dragged

② New position

③ Mouse pointer

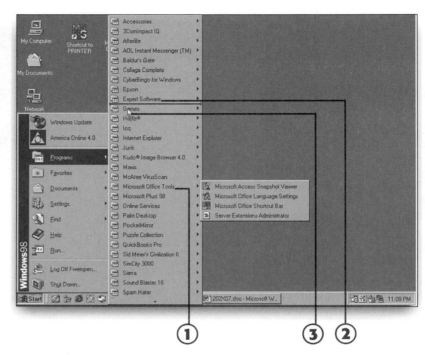

After you have opened the Start menu as a folder, you can do all the normal file operations to "prune" the tree. You can create new folders, delete folders, move shortcuts between folders, delete duplicate shortcuts, and more.

Restructuring the Start Menu

1. Right-click the **Start** button and choose **Explore**. The items on the Start button appear in Windows Explorer.

2. Double-click the **Programs** folder. All the shortcuts and folders on the Programs menu appear. See Figure 7.3.

3. Change the structure of the Programs menu system by doing any of the following:

   • Create new folders. These will become new submenus on the Programs menu.

   • Move folders into the new folders you create (or any other folders) to make them into submenus.

   • Delete any unwanted folders or shortcuts.

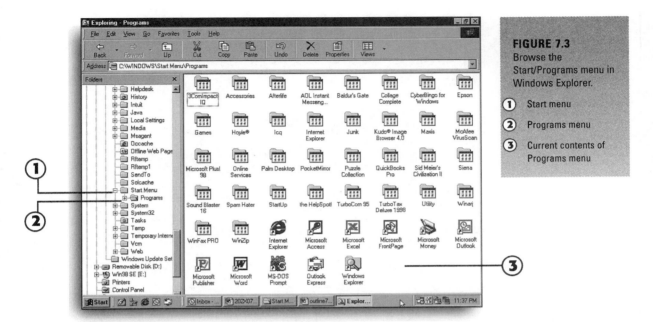

FIGURE 7.3
Browse the
Start/Programs menu in
Windows Explorer.

① Start menu

② Programs menu

③ Current contents of
Programs menu

4. Check your work by opening the Start menu. Close it again by clicking away from it without selecting a command.

5. When you are finished editing, close the Windows Explorer window.

Not sure how to reorganize things? The following are some of my favorite strategies:

- Create a few new folders with generic names such as Games, Utilities, and Business. Then, drag the shortcuts for various programs into the appropriate folders and delete all those specific folders for each application.

- Sometimes, you might not want to delete the specific folder for an application. For example, if the folder contains the program shortcut and shortcuts to several related utilities, you might want to keep the folder to keep those shortcuts grouped together.

- If you want to tidy things up without getting rid of the specific folder, drag the whole folder into one of your generic-named new folders. It becomes a submenu of it. Figure 7.4 shows the menu system from Figure 7.1 all tidied up with categories.

StartUp Folder

It's best not to rename or move the StartUp folder. This folder is special—it holds shortcuts for the programs that should load automatically at startup. If you move or rename it, Windows may not be able to find it.

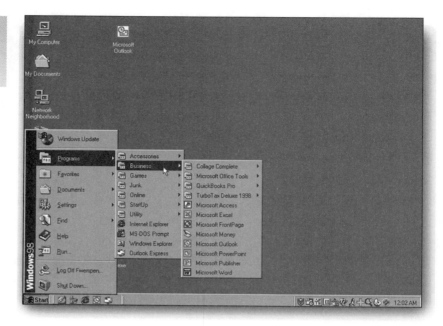

FIGURE 7.4
The reorganized, stream-lined Start menu.

- If you have a lot of programs that have installed themselves directly on the Programs menu, you can create a folder for them and place their shortcuts there instead. For example, Microsoft Office places shortcuts for all its applications on the Programs menu; you might create a folder called Office and move those shortcuts into it.

SEE ALSO

➤ *To create folders, see page 104.*

➤ *To delete files and folders, see page 94.*

➤ *To move files or folders, see page 93.*

Working with Desktop Shortcuts

As you know, your desktop contains shortcut icons to some of the most common programs and file management windows, such as My Computer, Network Neighborhood, Internet Explorer, and the Recycle Bin. Depending on what programs are installed, you may have other shortcuts, too, such as a game, an online service, or a utility program.

Repositioning a Shortcut

You can drag shortcuts around on the desktop, placing them anywhere you like. For example, you might want to move the ones that you don't use very often to an out-of-the-way corner. (For that matter, you could just delete the ones you don't use often, unless they are shortcuts that can't be deleted, such as My Computer.)

Creating New Shortcuts

You can create shortcuts on your desktop for any other programs too. *Shortcuts* allow you to bypass the Start menu and start the program more quickly. I keep about a dozen shortcuts on my desktop most of the time, for the programs I use most frequently. Figure 7.5 shows them. Note that each one has a little arrow in the bottom-left corner indicating that the icon represents a shortcut, not the original file.

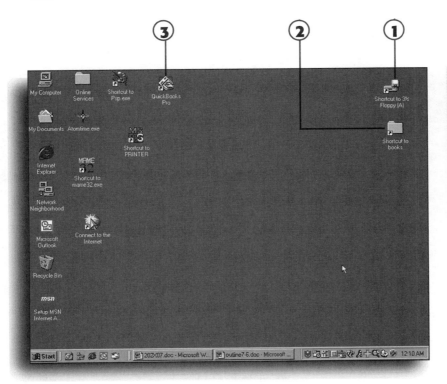

FIGURE 7.5
The desktop for my home PC, with many shortcuts I have created on it.

① Shortcut to a drive

② Shortcut to a folder

③ Shortcut to a program

Creating a Desktop Shortcut for a Folder or File

1. Locate the file or folder in a file listing.

2. Right-click the file or folder and choose **Create Shortcut**. A shortcut for that item appears in the displayed location.

3. Drag that shortcut onto the desktop, placing it there.

Creating a Shortcut for a Drive

1. Double-click the **My Computer** icon on the desktop.

2. Right-click the drive and choose **Create Shortcut**. A message appears, stating that you cannot create a shortcut in this location, asking whether you want to create the shortcut on the desktop.

3. Click **Yes**.

Alternate Method

Another (possibly quicker) way to create a shortcut is to right-drag the item (file, folder, or drive) onto the desktop. When you drop it, a menu appears. Choose **Create Shortcut(s) Here** from that menu.

You can create shortcuts anywhere, not just on the desktop. For example, suppose you have a folder called Projects in which you keep important files for the projects you are working on. One of the projects is a team effort with a friend in another office, so you have agreed to store all the files for it on the network. You could create a shortcut to that folder on the network and store the shortcut in your Projects folder. That way, you can quickly access that folder when you need it without physically placing the folder on your hard disk.

Deleting Shortcuts

Delete a shortcut the same as you would delete any file: Select it and press **Delete**, or right-click it and choose **Delete** from the shortcut menu.

SEE ALSO

➤ For more information on deleting files, see page 94.

Renaming Shortcuts

Some shortcuts will have the words "Shortcut to" in their names, which can be cumbersome. You might want to rename the shortcut to remove that. You might want to rename a shortcut for some other reason, too. For example, if you are setting up a shortcut to an installation program for a friend who is not very computer savvy, a file called Shortcut to Setup32 might confuse him. You could rename that shortcut `Double-click Here to Begin`, a much friendlier name for a novice.

Renaming a shortcut is the same as renaming any other file or folder. Select it and press **F2**, and then type the new name. (Or right-click it and choose **Rename** from the shortcut menu.)

SEE ALSO

➤ *To rename a file, see page 98.*

Changing Shortcut Properties

Each shortcut has its own properties, the same as each normal file does. You display them the same way you do for any file: Right-click and choose **Properties**.

The properties for a shortcut have some extra settings that you don't see for most other files. Figure 7.6 shows an example. For a shortcut, you can set the following:

- **Target.** This is the path to the file that runs the program. It is what the shortcut points to. If you aren't sure of the path, use the **Find Target** button to locate it.

- **Start in.** This specifies the default folder for data created in that program if the program doesn't have its own default separate from its own folder.

- **Shortcut key.** This assigns a shortcut key combination that you can use to activate that shortcut.

- **Run.** This lets you choose between Normal Window, Minimized, or Maximized.

You can also change the shortcut's icon, as described in Chapter 9, "Customizing the Screen Appearance."

SEE ALSO

➤ *To change an icon, see page 174.*

General Tab

The General tab for a shortcut shows the same information as for any other file, including the size, the date, and the attributes.

FIGURE 7.6
Properties for a shortcut.

Customizing Toolbars

As you learned in Chapter 3, the Quick Launch toolbar appears on the taskbar, providing easy access to Internet Explorer, Outlook Express, and more. You can control which buttons appear on that Quick Launch toolbar. You can also display one of the other toolbars that comes with Windows 98 or create your own toolbars.

Customizing the Quick Launch Toolbar

Too Many Buttons

Remember that the Quick Launch toolbar shares space onscreen with the rest of your taskbar. Don't go overboard adding buttons to the Quick Launch toolbar, or there won't be much room left to display the buttons for your running programs.

You can add buttons to and remove them from the Quick Launch toolbar as desired. For example, I have added a button to mine that starts my Internet connection. If you use a certain few programs a lot, you might want to add shortcuts to them to the Quick Launch toolbar. The advantage of having a shortcut on the Quick Launch toolbar rather than (or in addition to) on the desktop is that the toolbar is always visible, whereas the desktop may not be without minimizing some windows.

Adding a Button to the Quick Launch Toolbar

1. Select the file, folder, drive, or existing shortcut that you want to place on the Quick Launch toolbar.

2. Drag the item and drop it on the Quick Launch toolbar in the spot where you want it.

Deleting a Button from the Quick Launch Toolbar

1. Right-click a button on the Quick Launch toolbar.

2. Choose **D**elete from the shortcut menu.

The above procedures showed you how to create and delete shortcuts for the Quick Launch toolbar, but keep in mind in the next sections that you can add buttons the same way to any other toolbar, including one that you create yourself.

Displaying Other Toolbars in the Taskbar

Three other toolbars come with Windows 98; you can display them in addition to the Quick Launch toolbar if you like. However, they take up a lot of space on the taskbar, so you will probably not want to have them displayed all the time.

- **Address.** Provides an Address box into which you can type URLs and other addresses that you want to browse, either on the Web, on your local network, or on your own PC.

- **Links.** Provides buttons that link to various Web pages.

- **Desktop.** Provides buttons for the shortcut icons on your desktop so that you don't have to minimize all the windows for access to them.

Figure 7.7 shows all the toolbars displayed at once. Notice that you can't see all the tools on any of them. When a toolbar has hidden tools, a >> button appears at its right. You can click that button to see the remaining tools in menu form.

Choosing Which Toolbars to Display

1. Right-click the Quick Launch toolbar or any visible toolbar.

2. Point to **T**oolbars. A submenu appears.

3. Click the name of the toolbar you want to toggle on or off.

After you have displayed a toolbar, you can turn off its name label if you want. (By default, its name appears to the left of its buttons, but that name takes up valuable space onscreen.) To turn off the name, right-click the toolbar and choose **Show Title** to remove the check mark next to that command.

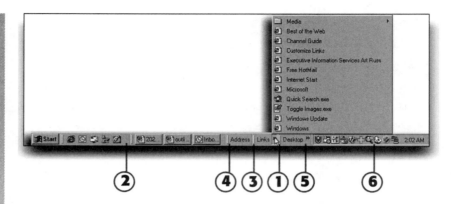

FIGURE 7.7
With all the toolbars turned on, they must all share the limited space available.

① Click here to see the rest of the buttons for the toolbar in menu form.

② Quick Launch toolbar

③ Links toolbar

④ Address toolbar

⑤ Desktop toolbar

⑥ System tray

SEE ALSO
➤ *To increase the size of the taskbar vertically so that each toolbar can have its own row, see page 181.*

Creating Your Own Toolbars

Not interested in any of the toolbars that Windows 98 provides? You may want to create your own toolbar to hold just the shortcuts that you specify.

Why would this be better than adding your shortcuts to the Quick Launch toolbar? Well, it isn't necessarily better. If you want to create shortcuts for programs that you use all the time, the Quick Launch toolbar is the better location for them because you will probably leave it displayed all the time.

However, if you use a group of programs or folders only under certain circumstances (such as when working for a particular client), you might create a special toolbar for them. Then, you could display that toolbar only when you are working on things for that client.

Toolbars are created based on existing folders; you can't just create one out of thin air. So, you must create a folder first, with the name you want to give your toolbar. If you plan to create multiple toolbars, you may even want to create a special folder (perhaps C:\Windows\Toolbars) in which you store the folders that should each become toolbars.

Creating a New Toolbar

1. Using Windows Explorer or My Computer, create the new folder to be used as a toolbar.

2. (Optional) Create shortcuts in that folder for the items you want to appear on the new toolbar. (You can also add the shortcuts later, as you'll see.)

3. Right-click a toolbar and point to **Toolbars**, then click **New Toolbar**. The New Toolbar dialog box opens.

4. Locate and select the folder that you want to make into a toolbar.

5. Click **OK**. That folder appears as a new toolbar on the taskbar.

6. Add shortcuts to the new toolbar. Those shortcuts are placed in the folder you created.

SEE ALSO

➤ *To change the size and appearance of the taskbar, see page 194.*

Controlling Programs Running in the System Tray

When you start your PC, Windows loads, of course, but so do some other programs (which ones depend on what you have installed). For example, your virus protection program loads if you have one. Other programs that might load at startup include the Windows task scheduler, your fax software, and system utilities such as Norton Utilities or CrashGuard.

It's not a hard-and-fast rule, but most of these startup programs show their icons in the system tray to help you remember they are running and to help you manage them. (You'll learn how to do just that in the next section.) Figure 7.8 shows the system tray for my PC, with some of the background programs identified. Yours will probably be different.

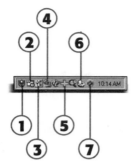

FIGURE 7.8
Each of the icons in the System tray represents a program that is running in the background.

1. Virus protection
2. Task scheduler
3. Volume control
4. Internet Connection Sharing
5. Crash protection
6. Fax manager
7. HotSync for PalmPilot

Managing Background Programs in the System Tray

When you point at a System tray icon, a ScreenTip appears. Depending on the program, it may tell you the program's name, or it may report the status of the program. For example, when I point at the icon for my fax manager, its ScreenTip tells me `Automatic Receive is Disabled`.

To control a System tray program, right-click it. A menu of things you can control for it appears.

The exact commands you see depend on the program, of course, but most programs give you a way to exit the program (or at least disable it temporarily). You may also see a command that lets you configure the program options (perhaps Properties, Configure, or Options) and one that opens the program window (such as Restore, Open, or Run). See Figure 7.9 for some examples.

FIGURE 7.9
Menu examples for System tray icons.

Specifying Which Programs Load at Startup

Why does a particular program load at startup? Good question.

One reason might be that the shortcut for the program is in the StartUp folder. Open the **Start** menu, point to **Programs**, and point to **StartUp**, and you'll see a list of shortcuts. All these programs load automatically each time you start or restart your PC. (This menu is in every other way like a normal menu; you can use the shortcuts on it to restart one of the programs if you have exited it.)

To prevent one of these programs from loading at startup, remove it from the StartUp submenu.

If you want to make a certain program load at startup that currently doesn't, add a shortcut for it to the StartUp submenu.

Some programs give you options for turning a program's startup status on or off from within the program itself. Figure 7.10 shows such a program.

Double-Click

When you right-click a System tray icon, the menu that appears may have one command on it that is bold. That's the command that will execute if you were to double-click the icon. If no bold commands are present, double-clicking the icon does nothing, or it opens the same menu as right-clicking does.

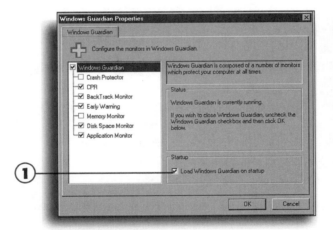

FIGURE 7.10
From within the program's options, you can configure some programs to start automatically.

① Deselect the check box and the program will no longer start up automatically.

Other programs have lines in a configuration file called *Win.ini* that load them. `Win.ini` is a text file in `C:\Windows` that contains configuration information. Each time Windows starts, the instructions in it execute. I do not recommend that you add programs to Win.ini, but if a program always loads automatically and you can't turn it off in other ways, you may be able to edit Win.ini to stop it.

Removing Startup Programs from Win.ini

1. Browse the contents of C:\Windows and locate the file Win.ini.

2. Double-click Win.ini to open it for editing in Notepad.

3. Look at the top of the file for LOAD= and RUN= lines. Programs listed after the equals sign on either line are set to run at startup.

   For example, Figure 7.11 shows one program set to load at startup.

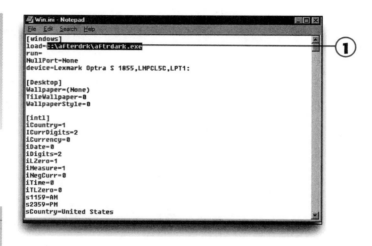

FIGURE 7.11
The contents of Win.ini.

1 To prevent this program from loading, delete this text.

4. Delete the reference to any program that you don't want to load or run at startup. Leave the LOAD= and RUN= text there.

5. Close Notepad, saving your changes.

6. Restart Windows.

SEE ALSO

➤ *To add or remove shortcuts from the Start menu, see page 124.*

➤ *To edit text, see page 55.*

Load Minimized

Remember earlier in the chapter, when we looked at the Properties for a shortcut? You could choose between Normal, Minimized, and Maximized for the program's startup. If you are placing a shortcut in the StartUp folder, you will probably want to set it to run minimized so that you don't see a window onscreen for it at startup.

Load Versus Run

LOAD starts up a program minimized; RUN starts it up in an open window.

Installing New Programs

Adding and Removing Windows Components

As you learned in Chapter 4, Windows 98 comes with several accessory programs, such as WordPad, Paint, and HyperTerminal. If you upgraded from Windows 95, Windows 98, during setup, automatically installed the same accessory programs as were previously installed. For example, if you had Paint, HyperTerminal, or the Phone Dialer in Windows 95, you also have them in Windows 98. If you installed Windows 98 from scratch, however, you had the opportunity to choose which accessories you wanted during setup. (See Appendix A, "Installing Windows 98," for more information about Windows Setup.)

You can change the accessories installed at any time, adding or removing them as desired. (Why might you want to remove one? One of the best reasons is to save disk space on a full hard disk. But you might also want to clean up the Accessories menu, removing programs that you never use.)

When you add or remove Windows components, you choose a category (see Figure 8.1) and then choose programs within that category. For example, if you want to add or remove Calculator, you would find it in the Accessories category. (You can browse the categories freely to find the program you want.)

FIGURE 8.1
Select a category of program.

(1) Information about the category appears here.

(2) Click Details to see a list of components in the category.

On the category list, each category has one of three check box states next to it:

- A cleared check box means none of the components in that category are installed.

- A marked check box with a gray background means that some, but not all, of the category's components are installed.

- A marked check box with a white background means that all the category's components are installed.

Adding or Removing a Windows Component

1. Click **Start**, point to **Settings**, and click **Control Panel**.

2. Double-click **Add/Remove Programs**.

3. Click the **Windows Setup** tab.

4. To add or remove an entire category, click its check box to place or remove a check mark there. Then, skip to Step 8.

   or

   To add or remove a specific component, click the name of the category that contains the program you want to install or remove. See Figure 8.1.

5. Click the **Details** button, or double-click the category. A list of programs in that category appears. Figure 8.2 shows the ones for the Accessories category, for example.

FIGURE 8.2
Programs in the Accessories category.

When Is a Category Not a Category?

Two of the categories are not actually categories: Address Book and Outlook Express. They are individual components that just happen to be right there on the Categories list. (No, I don't know why Microsoft chose to put them there.) When you select these, the Details button is unavailable because there are no choices to make.

6. Place check marks next to the ones to install, and remove check marks next to the ones to remove.

7. Click **OK** to return to the category list.

8. Repeat Steps 4–7 for other categories, if desired.

9. Click **OK**.

10. If prompted, insert the Windows 98 CD-ROM and click **OK**. (You may not see this.)

Depending on which components you are adding or removing, you may be prompted to restart Windows. Choose **Yes** if prompted; Windows might not work correctly if you don't restart.

SEE ALSO

➤ *To install Windows 98, see page 470.*

➤ *To use some of the popular Windows accessory programs, see page 68.*

Installing a New Program

In the olden days of PCs, programs were so small that the entire program could fit on a single floppy disk. You could run the program directly from the floppy, without having to install it anywhere. (That was a good thing because most PCs didn't have hard disks back then, either!)

Nowadays, however, almost every program requires you to run a setup utility. The setup utility does two important things: It decompresses and copies the needed files to your hard drive so that you don't need to have the setup disk in the PC at all times, and it sets itself up in Windows to know that the program is installed and available for use.

The following sections explain how to install programs from different sources. You can read it all, or you can skip to the section that pertains to your situation at the moment.

Installing a New Program from a Setup Disk

The software that you buy in stores comes on a setup disk (usually CD-ROM, these days). Depending on the program, when you put the CD-ROM in your drive, the installation program may start automatically. (Nice feature!) Just follow the prompts onscreen to install it.

If you pop the CD in the drive and nothing happens, or if the program comes on floppy disk instead, use the following procedure to start the ball rolling.

Install a New Program from CD or Disk

1. Make sure the setup disk for the program is in one of your drives.

2. Click **Start**, point to **Settings**, and click **Control Panel**.

3. Double-click **Add/Remove Programs**.

4. On the Install/Uninstall tab, click the **Install** button. The Install Program from Floppy Disk or CD-ROM Wizard appears.

5. Click **Next**. Windows scans your drives, looking for the setup program.

6. A box appears showing the path and file it found. See Figure 8.3.

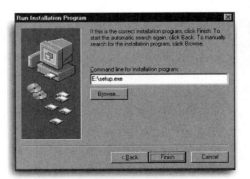

Auto Startup

If your installation program doesn't automatically start, Windows 98 may not have Auto Insert Notification turned on. To turn Auto Insert Notification on, double-click the **System** icon in the Control Panel. Then, on the **Device Manager** tab, click the plus sign (**+**) next to CD-ROM. Then, right-click the device under CD-ROM and click **Properties**.

Click the **Settings** tab and select the **Auto insert notification** check box. Click **OK** and then exit Control Panel.

Your installation programs will now start automatically—unless the particular disc you are using doesn't support the feature.

FIGURE 8.3
Windows finds and suggests a setup program to run.

If it did not find the right setup program, click the **Browse** button and locate the setup program yourself.

7. Click **Finish**. The setup program runs, and the program installs itself on your PC.

Start It Up Yourself

If you are very comfortable with Windows file management, you may choose to bypass the previous procedure by manually searching for the file that starts the installation. You can browse the disk in Windows Explorer to look for a file with a likely name (a name such as `Setup.exe` or `Install.exe` is usually a dead giveaway), and then double-click it.

Freeware Versus Shareware

Have you ever seen one of those honor-system snack bars, where you are supposed to take what you want and drop your money into the slot? That's what *shareware* is. The developers allow you to download the program without paying, but they ask that you pay for it if you like the program. Most of the software distributed on the Internet today is shareware.

You may also find programs designated as *freeware*. That means it's free to anyone who wants it, but you cannot make modifications to it. (Most of us don't have the programming skills anyway!) *Public Domain*, a third kind, is not only free, but modifications are allowed.

Of course, the setup program requires some interaction from you, but each program is different, so just follow the onscreen prompts.

SEE ALSO

➤ *To remove an installed program, see page 149.*

➤ *To browse a disk's file listing, see page 87.*

Installing a New Program from a Download

The Internet is a very attractive source of new software. Thousands of programs are waiting out there for free (or at least free trial) or for a modest fee, usually payable by credit card. More and more people are acquiring new programs by downloading them.

When you download software, it usually comes in one of two formats:

- An executable setup program (with an .exe extension) that you can download and run. It decompresses and installs all the needed files.

- A compressed archive, such as a zip file (with a .zip extension). This file contains all the files needed to run the program (or to run its setup program), but you need a special utility program to decompress them.

If you need to extract the contents of a zip file, you can download a variety of freeware or shareware utilities that will do the job. My personal favorite for Windows 98 is WinZip, a shareware program that performs just as well as a commercial program you might pay big bucks for. You can download it from the Web site `http://www.winzip.com`. The file you will download will be an executable (.exe); when you run it, you will install WinZip. From then on, you can double-click a zip file (.zip) to see and extract its contents.

Downloading a Program

As you surf the Web (see Chapter 18, "Exploring the Web"), you will probably find files you want to download. (If you haven't found any yet, surf on over to `http://www.shareware.com` to find some.) The following steps take you through the process:

Downloading a Program from a Web Site

1. Click a link on a Web page to a downloadable file. A dialog box appears, asking what you want to do with it. See Figure 8.4.

FIGURE 8.4
Your choices when downloading a file.

2. Choose **Save this program to disk** and then choose **OK**. A Save As dialog box opens.

3. Select the drive and folder in which you want to save the file, and then choose **OK**.

4. Wait for the download to take place. A box onscreen shows a progress bar and an estimate of the remaining time.

5. Depending on your setup, you may see a Download Complete box when it's finished; if so, click **OK** to close it.

Installing a Downloaded Program

After you have downloaded the file, navigate to the folder where you stored it and double-click it. If a setup program starts, you're home free. Just follow the onscreen prompts.

If you see a box asking what program Windows should use to open the file, it's probably a zip file and you don't have a zip utility installed. Visit `http://www.winzip.com` and download and install the latest version of WinZip. Then, try again to double-click the original file. It should open in WinZip.

Where Should I Save It?

When you run the setup program, it will create the new folders needed to hold the installed program. Therefore, the location where you store the download is not all that important because it's just a temporary holding area.

I have created a folder called Temp on my hard drive where I always store the files I download. That way, I don't have to remember where I have saved a particular file; they are all there. Occasionally, I clean out this folder by deleting the setup programs for programs I have already installed.

Keep On Surfing

As the file is downloading, you can view other Web pages or even close Internet Explorer; the download will continue. Do not disconnect your Internet connection until the download is finished, however.

When you open a compressed archive in WinZip, WinZip displays a list of the files in the archive. It may look something like Figure 8.5. You will need to extract all these files (it's best if you extract them into a new folder created for that purpose) and then run the installation program.

Extracting Setup Files from a Zip File with WinZip

1. Download and install WinZip. (You will need to reboot your computer after installing.) If asked which mode you want to operate in, choose WinZip Classic.

2. Double-click the zip file to open. WinZip opens the file, displaying the compressed files within it. See Figure 8.5 for an example.

FIGURE 8.5
A sample compressed archive's contents.

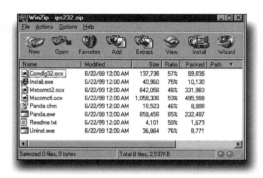

3. Click **Extract**. The Extract dialog box opens. See Figure 8.6.

FIGURE 8.6
Select a location for the extracted files.

4. Enter the folder into which you want to place the setup files in the **Extract to** text box, or select it from the **Folders/drives** list.

   If you want to create a new folder to hold the files, click the **New Folder** button, enter the folder name, and click **OK**.

5. Make sure the **All Files** button is selected and then click
   Extract. The files are extracted into the folder you specified.

6. Close WinZip and open Windows Explorer.

7. Navigate to the folder where you placed the files and examine
   the extracted files. Then, do one of the following:

   • If one of the files looks like an installation program (usually
     a file called either **Setup** or **Install**), double-click it to
     install.

   • If you don't see any installation program, the program may
     need to be manually installed. Look for a Readme file
     (`Readme.txt`, `Readme.doc`, and so on) and double-click it to
     read what to do. See the following section for help.

SEE ALSO

➤ *To work with files and folders in Windows Explorer, see page 87.*

Setting Up a Program with No Installation Utility

A setup program takes care of the following important tasks:

- It makes changes in the Windows Registry as needed to allow
  the program to run.

- It copies the right files to the right locations.

- It creates a shortcut on the Start menu with which to run the
  program.

Some programs, particularly shareware or freeware programs, don't
come with any kind of setup utility. When you unzip their zip file,
you will find all the files needed to run the program, but nothing
about "Setup" or "Install." With such programs, you don't need to
make any changes to the Windows Registry, but you do need to take
care of the latter two steps (copying the files and creating the shortcut).

In the following steps, I show you a way to place new programs on
your Start menu. You have already seen (in Chapter 7) how to modify the Start menu in other ways; this is simply an alternate method.

Setting Up a Program Manually

1. Create a new folder on your hard disk and extract all the files
   from the zip file into it.

Which File Starts the Program?

The file that starts the program usually has an .exe extension and has a name similar to the name of the program itself. If you can't see the file extensions in your file listing, turn on their display, as you learned in "Showing or Hiding File Extensions" in Chapter 6.

2. In Windows Explorer, navigate to the new folder and double-click the program's executable (.exe) file, making sure that it will run. Then, exit the program.

3. Right-click the taskbar and choose **Properties**.

4. Click the **Start Menu Programs** tab.

5. Click the **Add** button. The Create Shortcut dialog box appears.

6. Type the path to the new program (including the file name that runs the program), or browse for it with Browse. Then, click **Next**.

7. Select which existing folder on the Start menu you want to put the new program into. (Or create a new folder with the **New Folder** button.) See Figure 8.7. Then, click **Next**.

FIGURE 8.7
Choose a location for the new program on the Start menu.

8. Type a name for the shortcut. The default is the name of the chosen file. Then, click **Finish**.

9. Click **OK** to close the Taskbar Properties dialog box.

SEE ALSO

➤ *To modify the Start menu in other ways, see page 124.*

➤ *To show or hide file extensions in a file listing, see page 116.*

Removing an Installed Program

The time may come when that exciting new program isn't exciting anymore—in fact, it's not even useful. Perhaps you solved the puzzle; perhaps you decided you had no use for a cross-stitch pattern creation program; perhaps the *Swimsuit Babes on Ice* screen saver was prompting complaints from your co-workers. Whatever the reason, you may want to remove a program from your system.

Uninstalling a Program

Some programs have an uninstall feature built into them. For such programs, an Uninstall command is usually located in their folder on the Start menu. For example, in Figure 8.8, you can see that TurboTax provides an Uninstall utility. If a program offers this, by all means, take advantage of it! Just choose the **Uninstall** command from the program's folder on the **Start** menu and follow the prompts.

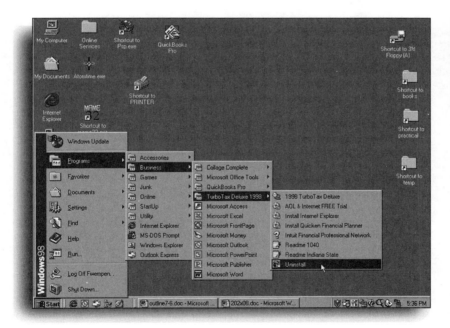

FIGURE 8.8
Some programs include a utility that lets you uninstall.

No such luck as to find an Uninstall program? Then, fall back on the next-best thing. If you installed the program using a Windows-based setup program, you may be able to uninstall it using the Uninstall feature built into Windows itself. The following steps show how to use it.

Uninstalling a Program

1. If the program you want to uninstall is running, exit from it.
2. Click **Start**, point to **Settings**, and click **Control Panel**.
3. Double-click the **Add/Remove Programs** icon.
4. On the **Install/Uninstall** tab, scroll through the list of installed programs and click the one you want to remove. See Figure 8.9.

FIGURE 8.9
Choose a program to uninstall.

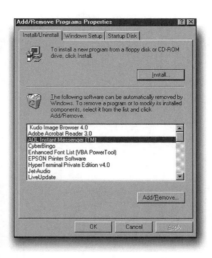

5. Click the **Add/Remove** button.
6. Follow the prompts to remove the program. Depending on the program, it may uninstall automatically at this point with no further prompts, or you may be prompted to choose between adding options, removing options, and removing the entire program.
7. If prompted to keep or remove a shared file, choose to keep it.
8. If prompted, restart the PC when the removal is finished.

Removing Leftover Program Elements

Sometimes, an uninstall does not remove all the files associated with a program. For example, if you have created data files in a program, Uninstall usually leaves them intact, in case you want to use them later with a different program. If all the files in the program's folder are not removed, the folder itself won't be removed either.

Keep or Remove?

One or more dialog boxes may ask whether you want to keep or remove specific shared files. If you have any doubts at all, choose **Keep**. Removing a shared file that another program still needs can make that other program malfunction (or not function at all), and it's difficult to tell which other programs may be using it.

My general rule is this: If the file it is asking about is located in the folder for the program being removed (for example, in `C:\Quickbooks` if I'm removing Quickbooks), I choose to remove it. However, if the file in question is in a common folder such as `C:\Windows`, I choose to keep it.

You can clean up after an Uninstall by deleting the folder(s) left behind by the program, along with any files in them. Transfer any data files that you want to keep to another location first (such as `C:\My Documents`).

Some programs may also leave behind their shortcuts on the desktop, on the Start menu, or in both places. You can delete those easily enough, or you can run the Disk Cleanup utility that comes with Windows, which identifies and deletes any shortcuts that point to nonexistent programs.

SEE ALSO

➤ *To run Disk Cleanup, see page 411.*

➤ *To delete shortcuts from the desktop, see page 130.*

➤ *To delete programs from the Start menu, see page 125.*

TweakUI

If you end up with programs on the list in Figure 8.9 that shouldn't be there (perhaps the program has already been removed), you can clean up the list with a utility called TweakUI. You can download it from Microsoft's Web site or you can install it from the Windows 98 Resource Kit on your Windows 98 CD-ROM (in Tools\ResKit).

Not a Clean Sweep

The program may have left behind a few files in a shared location such as `C:\Windows`, but don't worry about removing those. It is risky to remove files from `C:\Windows` or its subfolders because some other program may need those files, too.

chapter 9

Customizing the Screen Appearance

Adjusting Video Settings

Why Would the Current Video Settings Be Wrong?

When you install Windows (or when it is installed at the factory if your PC came with it preinstalled), Windows is supposed to detect your hardware and install the appropriate drivers. (That's called Plug and Play.) Sometimes it works; sometimes not. For this reason it's known in techie circles as Plug and *Pray*.

Sometimes, Windows thinks it has detected a piece of hardware, but it is mistaken. Usually, the settings for the device it thinks you have are very similar to the settings for your actual stuff, so the device will probably function, more or less. Some features may not work just right, however, because Windows is using a driver for it other than its own.

The display you see onscreen is controlled by (and limited by the capabilities of) your video card and your monitor as a team. In other words, your display will look only as good as the weaker of those two components can manage.

The following sections take you through the following steps:

- Making sure that Windows 98 has correctly identified your video card and monitor
- Choosing a color depth and display resolution appropriate for your needs (and your monitor size)
- Setting the refresh rate for optimal viewing

These are not the "fun" settings (those come later in the chapter), but they are important settings to make sure are correct before going further.

Describing Your Video Card and Monitor to Windows

For the best display, Windows needs to have accurate information about the video card and monitor you are using. That way, Windows can take advantage of the full capabilities of the devices. These are the settings in Windows that describe your video card and monitor:

- **Adapter.** This is the make and model of video card you have.
- **Monitor.** This is the make and model of monitor you have.

Depending on what you choose for the preceding items, different driver files are installed in Windows. These drivers are extremely important for two reasons. First, they control the interaction between Windows and the devices. Second, they specify which display resolutions, color depths, and refresh rates you will be allowed to choose. (All those things are covered later in this chapter.)

SEE ALSO

➤ *To change the color depth or display resolution for your display, see page 161.*
➤ *To change the refresh rate for your monitor, see page 164.*

Are You Really Interested?

Techies may find this stuff about video drivers fascinating, but the average person probably won't. Unless you are having a problem with your video drivers, feel free to skip the following sections. Pick up reading again at "Changing the Display Mode" later in this chapter.

Checking to See What Is Already Set Up

If you are not sure whether your PC is set up for the correct video card and monitor, you should check. The following steps show how to check:

Checking the Video Driver and Monitor

1. Right-click the desktop and choose **Properties**.

2. Click the **Settings** tab.

3. Click the **Advanced** button. The properties for your video card appear.

4. Click the **Adapter** tab and check to see what video card is listed at the top. See Figure 9.1.

    If the correct video card name does not appear, see "Changing the Video Driver" later in this chapter.

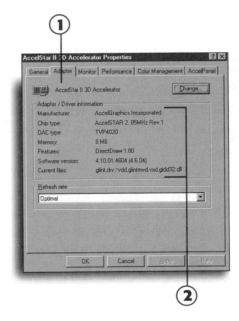

FIGURE 9.1
Check to see which video card Windows 98 thinks you have.

① Name of the video card

② Information about the video card

5. Click the **Monitor** tab and check to see which monitor is listed at the top. See Figure 9.2.

    If the correct monitor name does not appear, see "Changing the Monitor" later in this chapter.

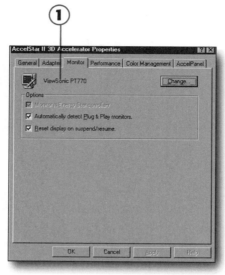

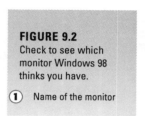

FIGURE 9.2
Check to see which
monitor Windows 98
thinks you have.

(1) Name of the monitor

6. Click **OK**.

7. Click **OK**, which closes the Display Properties box.

Following are two procedures. Use the first one, "Updating the Video Driver," if your video card is correctly identified but you want to see if a better driver is available for it. Use the second, "Changing the Video Driver," if Windows has not correctly identified your video card.

Updating the Video Driver

You may want to update the video driver if the correct video card name appears, but the video display doesn't seem right for some reason. For example, one of my clients was having a problem with his video display. Every time he would change it to a higher resolution and number of colors (as you will learn to do later in this chapter), it would default back to 16 colors and 640×480 resolution every time he restarted his PC. We were able to fix the problem by reinstalling the video driver from the disk that came with his PC. If that hadn't worked, I would have checked the video card manufacturer's Web site next to see whether an updated driver was available.

Updating the Video Driver

1. Right-click the desktop and choose **Properties**.

2. Click the **Settings** tab.

3. Click the **Advanced** button.

4. Click the **Adapter** tab.

5. Click the **Change** button. The Update Device Driver Wizard runs.

6. Click **Next**.

7. Choose **Search for a better driver** and then choose **Next**. A list of locations to search appears. See Figure 9.3.

FIGURE 9.3
Choose where you want
Windows to search for
an updated driver.

8. Place a check mark next to each place you want to search for a new driver:

- **Floppy disk drives.** Mark this if you have a driver on a floppy disk that you think may be better than the current one. Choose this if you have a floppy disk from the manufacturer.

- **CD-ROM drive.** Choose this if you have a driver on a CD-ROM that you think may be better. Choose this if you have a CD-ROM from the manufacturer.

- **Microsoft Windows Update.** Choose this if you want to check for a better driver on Microsoft's Web site. I always mark this; it doesn't hurt to check. (You can do this only if your copy of Windows 98 is registered—see Chapter 1.)

Connection Prompt

If you chose Microsoft Windows Update, and your Internet connection is not running, you may be prompted to connect so that the Microsoft Web site can be checked.

- **Specify a location.** Choose this, and then type (or browse for) a folder on your hard disk where a driver is stored. (If you downloaded new drivers from the manufacturer's Web site and placed them in a folder, for example, you would specify that folder here.)

9. Insert any needed disks into your floppy or CD-ROM drive, depending on what you specified in Step 8.

10. Click **Next** and wait for Windows to look for better drivers.

11. A message appears telling you whether a better driver was found. (The message may say that the best driver is already installed.) Click **Next** to install the new driver or to leave the old one in place, as recommended.

12. Click **Finish**.

13. Click **Close** to close the Properties box for your video card.

14. Click **Close** to close the Display Properties box.

15. If prompted to restart your computer, click **Yes**.

SEE ALSO

➤ *To install a program after downloading it, see page 144.*

Changing the Video Driver

If the video driver shown in the Display Properties box does not match the make or model that you think you have, you can try using a different driver. For example, if Windows 98 thinks that your video card is VGA, but you know that it's really an AccelStar II 3-D model, you will want to change to the correct driver.

Changing the Video Driver

1. Right-click the desktop and choose **Properties**.

2. Click the **Settings** tab.

3. Click the **Advanced** button.

4. Click the **Adapter** tab.

5. Click the **Change** button. The Update Device Driver Wizard runs.

6. Click **Next**.

Setup Program?

Some video cards come with their own setup program on disk. Browse the disk that came with yours; if a `Setup.exe` file is on it, go ahead and run that program instead of using the following steps (see Chapter 8 for details on installation and running setup programs). The setup program will automatically set up the video card and install any utility programs that came with it.

Other video cards come with a disk that simply contains the drivers, with no setup utility. In that case, you must install the drivers as explained in the following steps.

7. Choose **Display a list of all the drivers** and then choose **Next**.

A list of drivers appears for the card that Windows thinks you have.

8. Choose the **Show all hardware** button. A list of video card manufacturers appears in the left pane.

9. Do one of the following:

- If you have a disk that came with your PC or your video card that contains Windows 95/98 drivers for it, insert that disk and then click the **Have Disk** button. Then, click **Browse** and navigate to the drive and folder that contains the drivers and click **OK**.

- If you do not have a disk, choose the video card manufacturer and model from the list that Windows provides. See Figure 9.4. Then, choose **Next**.

10. When prompted that Windows is ready to install the new driver, click **Next**.

You may be prompted to insert the Windows 98 CD or the disk that came with your video card; if you see this prompt, insert whatever disk is requested and click **OK**.

If you see a message telling you that a file being installed is older than the file already on your system and asking whether you want to skip that file, click **Yes**.

I Don't Have a Disk!

If you are prompted to insert a disk that you don't have, you may be able to work around it. Perhaps the needed file is already on your hard disk from a previous installation, and the setup program simply doesn't know where to look.

Click **OK**, as if you had inserted the disk. A box will appear informing you that the file is not in that location and allowing you to browse for it. It also gives you the file's name that it is looking for. Jot down that file's name, and then use the Find feature in Windows (**Start, Find, Files or Folders**) to see whether a copy of that file is already on your hard disk somewhere. If it is, use **Browse** to point the installation program to it.

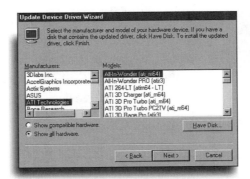

FIGURE 9.4
Find the correct video card manufacturer and model.

11. When you see a message that the installation of the new driver is complete, click **Finish**.

12. Click **Close** to close the Properties box for the video card.

13. Click **Close** to close the Display Properties box.

14. If prompted to restart your computer, click **Yes**.

SEE ALSO

➤ *To use the Find feature in Windows to find a file, see page 101.*

Changing the Monitor

As I mentioned earlier, the overall display quality is limited by the combined capabilities of your monitor and your video card. In the preceding sections, you set up the video card just right; now, it's time to take a look at the monitor.

Windows has probably detected your monitor as a Plug-and-Play Monitor. That's fine, unless your system is capable of higher refresh rates than what is specified by the plug-and-play monitor driver. (See "Changing the Display Refresh Rate" later in this chapter for details about that.) For the best quality image onscreen, you should set up Windows for the specific monitor you have, if possible.

Changing the Monitor Setup

1. Right-click the desktop and choose **Properties**.

2. Click the **Settings** tab.

3. Click **Advanced**.

4. Click the **Monitor** tab.

   If the correct monitor name is shown, you're done; click **OK** and then click **OK** again. Otherwise, go on to Step 5 to change the monitor name listed.

5. Click the **Change** button.

6. Click **Next**.

7. Click **Display a list of all the drivers**.

8. Click **Next**.

9. Click **Show all hardware**.

10. Select your monitor's manufacturer and model, and then click **Next**. (Or if your monitor came with a disk, click **Have Disk** and browse to that disk.)

11. Click **Next**.

    If prompted, insert the Windows 98 CD-ROM and click **OK**.

12. Click **Finish**.

13. Click **Close**.

14. Click **OK** to close the Display Properties box.

15. If prompted to restart your PC, click **Yes**.

You're done! Windows now knows the correct video card and monitor for your system, and the correct drivers are installed for them. Now, you can move on to setting the display mode you want to use.

Changing the Display Mode

Based on the video card and monitor, Windows will let you choose among several display modes. The display mode is made up of two factors: resolution and color depth.

Resolution is the number of individual pixels (dots) that make up the display mode. The higher the numbers, the smaller the dots and the sharper the image (and also the smaller the image). Figures 9.5 and 9.6 show the same screen in 640×480 and 800×600 resolution.

Common resolutions are 640×480, 800×600, and 1024×768. Which resolution is best? It all depends on what you plan to do with your PC and on the size of your monitor. As you can see in Figures 9.5 and 9.6, a higher resolution makes everything onscreen look smaller. If you have a large monitor, you can use a very high resolution without straining your eyes to see things. On a small monitor, you may want to stick with a lower resolution. Think, too, about how you use your PC. Someone who works with large spreadsheets may appreciate a higher resolution because it allows him or her to see more spreadsheet cells on the screen at once. But someone who spends a long time sitting at the computer reading email each day may find that a lower resolution prevents eyestrain because things are easier to see.

Old Monitor Blues?

If you have a really old monitor that doesn't have controls to adjust the image's vertical and horizontal sizes, you may see a big black ring around the outside of the image onscreen. You can sometimes minimize it by changing to a different monitor driver from the same manufacturer.

FIGURE 9.5
A Windows screen in 800×600 resolution.

Color depth is the number of colors that can be displayed simultaneously onscreen. Standard VGA is 16 colors; most people run Windows in at least 256-color mode. High color (16-bit) and True Color (24-bit) are higher modes that show more colors.

Why is color depth important? Well, if you are displaying photographs or video clips onscreen, they will look much better at higher color depths because the colors shown onscreen will be closer to reality. When you use a lower color depth, such as 16 colors, Windows attempts to simulate the other colors by blending two or more colors in a cross-hatch pattern. This is called *dithering*. From a distance it looks okay, but when you examine it closely it looks fuzzy. When you use a higher color depth, Windows has more "real" colors to work with, so it doesn't have to dither as much.

In general, more color depth is better. However, if you want to use a program (usually a game) that works best at a particular color depth (such as 256 colors), you may want to temporarily set the color depth for a lower setting than the maximum your system is capable of. Such programs usually state in the documentation, onscreen, or in both places that they prefer a certain color depth.

Changing the Display Mode

1. Right-click the desktop and choose **Properties**.

2. Click the **Settings** tab.

3. Open the **Colors** drop-down list and choose the color depth you want.

4. Drag the **Screen area** slider to the setting you want. For example, in Figure 9.6 it is set for 800×600.

5. Click **OK**.

6. Do one of the following:

    - If you are changing only the resolution (not the color depth), a box appears telling you that Windows will now change the display. Click **OK** to accept that. Then, a box appears asking whether you want to keep the new settings; click **Yes**.

    - If you are changing the color depth, a box appears suggesting that you restart Windows. Click **Yes**.

      If you do not restart your PC after changing the color depth, the colors may not look quite right, depending on which color depth you are changing from and to and the capabilities of your video card.

SEE ALSO
➤ *To use a different font size for onscreen text (such as in title bars), see page 166.*

Video Memory

Video cards have their own built-in video memory (usually between 1 and 16 megabytes). It is much like the regular memory in your PC, but it is used only for video processing. The higher the resolution and the greater the color depth, the more video memory is required for the mode.

For the techies, here is how the maximum resolution/color depth is calculated. If you have a 16-color display, you need 4 bits to control each dot because 16 combinations are possible with a 4-digit binary number (2 to the 4th power, or 16). If you multiply the number of dots in the resolution by the number of bits required for each dot, you have the amount of memory required to display that resolution. For example, 640×480 and 16 colors would be 640×480×4, or 1,228,800 bits. There are 8 bits in a byte, so that would be 153,600 bytes (approximately 154KB). Therefore, if your video card had 1MB of video memory, you could have the following:

- 640×480 in 24-bit color (922KB required)

- 800×600 in 16-bit color (960KB required)

- 1024×768 in 8-bit color (786KB required)

- 1280×1024 in 4-bit color (655KB required)

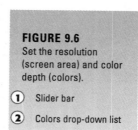

FIGURE 9.6
Set the resolution
(screen area) and color
depth (colors).

① Slider bar

② Colors drop-down list

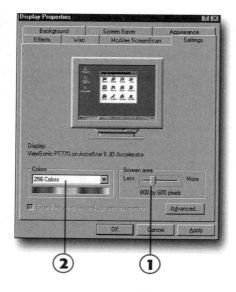

Changing the Display Refresh Rate

The *refresh rate* is the rate at which the image onscreen is
"refreshed," or repainted, by the light beams inside the monitor. The
higher the refresh rate, the less flicker in the display.

If you have ever seen video footage of a computer system in which
the monitor appeared to be scrolling or blinking, that was because of
a refresh rate on the monitor that is out of sync with the video-
recording speed. The human eye doesn't notice it as much, but it is
obvious on video. The flicker of a low refresh rate (under 72Hz) can
make your eyes tired if you look at such a display for a long time.

The following are several choices of refresh rate:

- **Adapter default.** This is the default setting for your video card.
  It is not always the highest setting possible, but it works with
  every monitor, so it is a safe setting.

- **Optimal.** This is the highest setting possible, given the monitor
  and video card that you have told Windows you have. Windows
  examines the capabilities of both devices and calculates the best
  setting.

- **Specific settings.** You can choose a specific setting, in Hertz (Hz). Larger numbers are better.

If the refresh rate you choose exceeds the capabilities of either your monitor or your video card, the screen can become distorted or even scrambled.

Setting the Refresh Rate

1. Right-click the desktop and choose **Properties**.
2. Click the **Settings** tab.
3. Click the **Advanced** button.
4. Click the **Adapter** tab.
5. Open the **Refresh rate** drop-down list and choose the setting you want. See Figure 9.7. If you do not know what to pick, choose **Optimal**.

FIGURE 9.7
Set the refresh rate on the Adapter tab.

6. Click **OK**. A message appears that Windows is going to adjust your refresh rate.
7. Click **OK**. The refresh rate changes and a message appears asking whether you want to keep the setting.
8. Click **Yes**.
9. Click **OK** to close the Display Properties box.

Not Just Colors

Some color schemes include not only colors but also font choices. If you have a hard time seeing the tiny type onscreen in your chosen video resolution, you might want to choose a scheme that includes larger fonts, such as Pumpkin (Large) or Windows Standard (Extra Large).

After adjusting the refresh rate and video mode (resolution/color depth), the image you see onscreen may be slightly off-center, slightly too large (edges cut off), or too small (black ring around the outside) for the monitor. On most monitors, you can adjust the image size and positioning somewhat with its built-in controls. See the manual that came with your monitor for details. If that's not an option, try a different refresh rate or monitor driver.

Changing Color Schemes

Now comes the fun part—changing the colors on your display. These color changes don't have any direct bearing on image quality; they're just fun little tweaks that you can use to express your personality on your Windows desktop.

You can change the colors of nearly all onscreen elements: the desktop, the window title bars, the menus, and so on. You can select one of the dozens of preset schemes, or you can customize any of the color schemes to fit your exact wants.

Choosing a Different Color Scheme

1. Right-click the desktop and choose **Properties**.

2. Click the **Appearance** tab.

3. Open the **Scheme** drop-down list and choose a different color scheme. A sample of it appears above the list. See Figure 9.8.

FIGURE 9.8
Select the color scheme you want.

① Sample area

② Scheme drop-down list

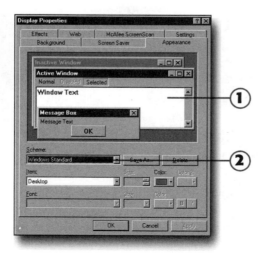

4. When you are happy with the chosen scheme, click **OK** to accept it.

You can customize any color scheme, so if a scheme is not exactly as you want it, you don't have to settle. For example, perhaps a certain scheme is perfect except for the background color or the font size. First select the scheme, and then customize it. Then, you can save your customized scheme as a new scheme to reuse whenever you want.

Customizing a Color Scheme

1. Right-click the desktop and choose **Properties**.

2. Click the **Appearance** tab.

3. Open the **Scheme** drop-down list and choose the scheme on which you want to base your new settings.

4. Select the element you want to change in that scheme. To do so, you can either click the element in the sample area or open the **Item** drop-down list and choose its name.

5. Set the **Size** and **Color** for the chosen element using the controls to the right of the **Item** drop-down list. See Figure 9.9.

No Background Change?

If you change the color of the desktop but you don't see the change onscreen, your desktop may be covered by wallpaper. See "Dressing Up the Desktop" later in this chapter to learn how to remove the wallpaper so that you can see the chosen desktop color.

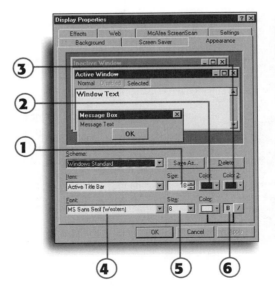

FIGURE 9.9
Customize the chosen item.

(**1**) Choose a different size.

(**2**) Choose a different color.

(**3**) Some items can have two colors in certain display modes.

(**4**) Choose a font.

(**5**) Set a font size.

(**6**) Set font color and other properties.

Two Colors?

If you have your color depth set for 16-bit or 24-bit color, you can have two colors for some elements. If you choose two colors, they will appear as a gradient—a fade from one color to the other. Title bars look especially nice with a two-color gradient. If you do not want a gradient, set both color settings to the same color.

6. To change the font, open the **Font** drop-down list and choose a different one.

7. To change the font size, color, and/or attributes (bold and italic), use the controls to the right of the **Font** drop-down list. See Figure 9.10.

8. (Optional) To save your customized color scheme as a new scheme, type a new name in the **Scheme** box.

9. Click **OK** to apply the new settings.

SEE ALSO

➤ *To change the color depth (that is, the number of colors used in your display mode), see page 161.*

Apply Versus OK

The Apply button applies the new color scheme without closing the Display Properties dialog box. That way, you can find out whether you like the new scheme before you close the Display Properties box.

Dressing Up the Desktop with Patterns and Wallpaper

The desktop can be any color, as you just learned, but a plain, solid-color desktop can be boring. You can dress up a plain desktop in two ways. One is to apply a pattern to it; the other is to apply wallpaper. A *pattern* is a small design that repeats on the desktop, with the chosen desktop color showing through behind it. See Figure 9.10. *Wallpaper* is a picture that appears on top of the desktop, obscuring the chosen color and pattern partly or completely. See Figure 9.11.

FIGURE 9.10
The desktop with a pattern applied.

① This pattern is a small plaid.

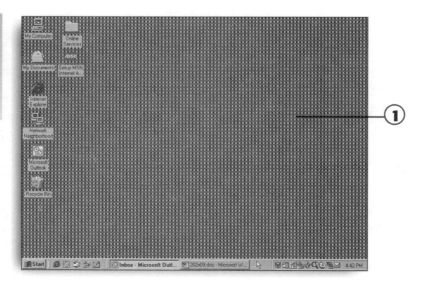

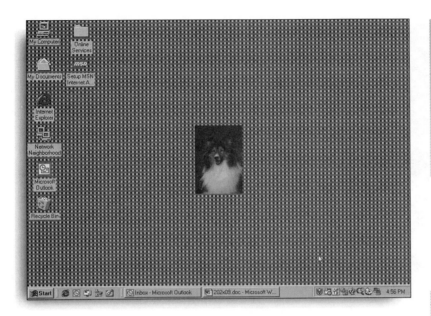

FIGURE 9.11
The desktop with both a pattern and wallpaper applied.

(**1**) This image is the wallpaper.

(**2**) Behind the image you can see the desktop with its pattern.

Choosing a Desktop Pattern

1. Right-click the desktop and choose **Properties**.

2. Click the **Background** tab.

3. Click the **Pattern** button.

4. Select a pattern from the **Pattern** list. See Figure 9.12.

Create Your Own Pattern

You can click the Edit Pattern button shown in Figure 9.13 to open a window where you can edit the chosen pattern, creating any pattern you want.

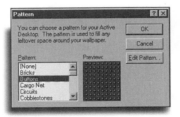

FIGURE 9.12
Select a pattern to use.

5. Choose **OK**.

6. Choose **OK** again, closing the Display Properties dialog box.

Wallpaper appears on top of the desktop, so it does not affect any color or pattern you have chosen. It merely covers them up. You can choose to center the image on the desktop (as in Figure 9.11) so that the desktop peeks out from the edges, or you can tile the image so that it repeats, covering the desktop entirely, as in Figure 9.13. You can also set it to **Stretch**, which enlarges (and distorts) the image so that a single copy of it exactly fills the screen.

FIGURE 9.13
The wallpaper image is tiled, filling the entire screen.

① This is the wallpaper image; see how it is repeated.

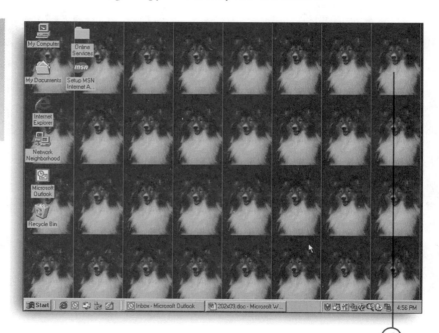

Make Your Own Wallpaper

You can use any picture for wallpaper; the one in Figure 9.14 is a picture of my dog. To make an image appear on the list of wallpapers, simply save it in .bmp format using a paint program and place it in the C:\Windows folder.

Choosing Wallpaper

1. Right-click the desktop and choose **Properties**.

2. Click the **Background** tab.

3. Select the picture you want to use. Or, to remove the wallpaper, choose **None**.

4. Open the **Display** drop-down list and choose **Center**, **Tile**, or **Stretch**. (Skip this if you chose **None** in Step 3.)

5. Click **OK**.

Using a Screen Saver

The *screen saver* is a moving image or pattern that kicks in when your computer has been idle for a specified amount of time. The original job of a screensaver was to display a continuously changing image to prevent *burn-in* on your monitor.

A side benefit of using a screen saver is that you can assign a password to it so that the screen saver will not turn off until you type the password. That way, if you step away from your computer for awhile, no unauthorized "visitors" can snoop.

Setting Up Your Screen Saver

Set Up a Screen Saver

1. Right-click the desktop and choose **Properties**.

2. Click the **Screen Saver** tab.

3. Open the **Screen Saver** drop-down list and select the screen saver you want to use. (Choose **None** to turn the screen saver off.) See Figure 9.14.

   If you are not sure which one you want, choose one and click **Preview**. The screen saver appears onscreen until you move the mouse or press a key to stop it.

Wallpaper from the Web

On a Web page, if you see an image that you would like to use as your Windows wallpaper, right-click it and choose **Set as Wallpaper** from the short-cut menu. This copies it to your C:\Windows folder under the name Internet Explorer Wallpaper.bmp.

Burn-In

You have probably seen burn-in on old ATM displays or video games, where you can see a ghosted image of the text or picture that appears there most of the time (such as "Please Insert Card" on an ATM display). With today's advanced monitors, burn-in is no longer a problem, but screen savers are so much fun that people continue to employ them anyway.

FIGURE 9.14
Choose the screen saver, and then set its Settings, Password, and so on.

4. To change the settings for the chosen screen saver, click the **Se_ttings** button. Make changes in the dialog box that appears, and then click **OK**.

5. (Optional) To assign a password to the screen saver, do the following:

Select the **_Password protected** checkbox.

Click the **_Change** button to change the password.

Type the password you want to use in the **New Password** box.

Type it again in the **Con_firm new password** box. See Figure 9.15.

FIGURE 9.15
Type and then retype the password to use.

Click **OK**. A message appears that the password has been changed.

Click **OK** again to close the confirmation box.

6. Enter the number of minutes to wait before activating the screen saver in the **_Wait** box.

7. Click **OK**.

Waking Up a Screen Saver

To wake up your computer when it is running the screen saver, press a key or move the mouse.

If you have assigned a password, a box appears prompting you to type it. Type the password and press **Enter** to wake up the computer.

If you forget the screen saver password, you can't wake up the computer. To get back in, you must shut off the computer (which is not a good idea to do routinely, as I explained in Chapter 1). When it restarts, go back to **Display Properties**, go to the **Screen Saver** tab, and change the screen saver password or disable it completely.

SEE ALSO

➤ *To recall why you should not shut off your computer's power while Windows is running, see page 28.*

Setting Energy-Saving Settings for Your Monitor

Many of the newer monitors have energy-saving features that allow them to shut themselves off after a certain period of inactivity. This can save your electric bill because the monitor takes quite a bit of electricity to stay powered up. This feature may already be enabled, depending on how Windows 98 detected your monitor.

On a laptop computer running on batteries, saving energy is especially critical. By setting your monitor to shut off after, say, 3 minutes of inactivity, you save your battery life during those times when you are called away from the computer unexpectedly and it is left running.

Use the following steps to check and change the settings.

Changing Your Monitor's Energy Settings

1. Right-click the desktop and choose **Properties**.

2. Click the **Screen Saver** tab.

3. Click the **Settings** button. (If the Settings button is unavailable, you do not have a monitor that supports this feature.) The Power Management Properties dialog box opens. See Figure 9.16.

FIGURE 9.16
Set the power management properties for your monitor here.

Where Do Icons Come From?

You can use icons from .ico, .exe, and .dll files. The .ico files are icon files; they are simply a single image for use as an icon. The .exe files are program files, most of which store multiple icons in them. (You don't have to use the program in any way to borrow an icon from it.) The .dll files are helper files for programs. They too often contain multiple icons.

You can search for icons by trial and error, opening each .exe and .dll file on your system to see if any interesting icons are present. But that takes forever. Many interesting icons can be found in `C:\Windows\System\Pifmgr.dll`, `C:\Windows\Progman.exe`, and `C:\Windows\Moricons.dll`; try some of these first.

4. Open the **Turn off monitor** drop-down list and choose an amount of idle time it should wait before turning off.

   I typically set this to **After 1 hour** for a desktop on AC power or **After 5 minutes** for a laptop on batteries, but it's up to you.

5. Click **OK**.

SEE ALSO

➤ *To learn more about power management settings for laptops, see page 270.*

Changing Icon Appearance

The icons associated with each data file and each program help you determine what they are for. The Recycle Bin looks like a trash can; the My Computer icon looks like a computer, a word processing document looks like a piece of paper, and so on. Beginners find this extremely helpful, as you can imagine.

But in time you may grow tired of the same old icons. In the following sections you will learn how to choose different icons, both for items on your desktop and for individual files.

Changing the Desktop Icons

The icons on your desktop (for the Recycle Bin, My Computer, Network Neighborhood, and so on) can be customized. For example, you might want to use a different icon for the Recycle Bin or the My Documents folder.

Changing Desktop Icons

1. Right-click the desktop and choose **Properties**.

2. Click the **Effects** tab.

3. Click the icon you want to change in the Desktop icons pane. See Figure 9.17.

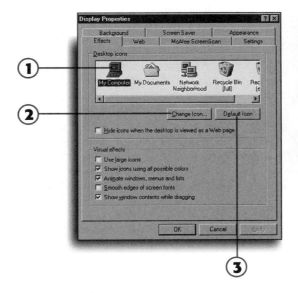

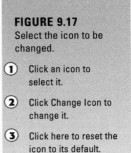

FIGURE 9.17
Select the icon to be changed.

① Click an icon to select it.

② Click Change Icon to change it.

③ Click here to reset the icon to its default.

4. Click the **Change Icon** button. A box showing some alternate icons appears. See Figure 9.18.

FIGURE 9.18
Select a different icon to use.

5. Do one of the following.

- Choose one of the alternate icons.

  or

- Click the **Browse** button and locate the file containing the icon you want to use.

6. Click **OK** to accept the chosen icon.

7. Click **OK**, closing the Display Properties dialog box.

SEE ALSO

➤ *To change all the desktop icons at once, as well as other appearance settings, check out Desktop Themes, described on page 178.*

Changing an Individual File's Icon

Each file has a default icon. Most program files have icons that uniquely describe the program. For example, the icon for Microsoft Word 2000 has a big W on it. Most data files have icons evocative of the program used to create them. For example, the icon for Microsoft Word documents looks like a piece of paper with a little W on it (for Word).

But you can choose any icon for any file. For example, if you have shortcuts to several files of the same type on your desktop (perhaps several word processing files), you can change the icon for each one to make it unique at a glance.

Changing an Icon for Any File

1. Right-click the file and choose **Properties**.

2. Click the **Change Icon** button. A list of the icons associated with that file appears, as in Figure 9.18.

3. Do one of the following:

    • Choose one of the alternate icons.

        or

    • Click the **Browse** button and locate the file containing the icon you want to use.

4. After selecting the icon you want, click **OK**. The Properties box for the shortcut reappears.

5. Click **OK** to close the Properties box.

SEE ALSO

➤ *To set other file properties, see page 99.*

Setting Visual Effects

You may have noticed on the Effects tab that there are a few other miscellaneous appearance settings you can control. See Figure 9.19. Here's a brief description of them, along with my biased comments. To set any of these, right-click the desktop and choose **Properties**, and then make your selections on the **Effects** tab.

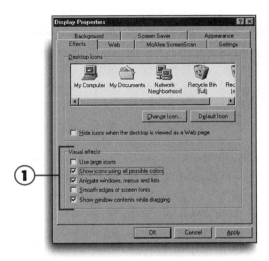

FIGURE 9.19
Change any of these visual effect settings as desired.

① Visual effects

- **Use large icons.** This makes the icons for all items and short-cuts on your desktop very large so that they are easier to see. Good for someone with a visual impairment; not useful for most people.

- **Show icons using all possible colors.** This enhances the look of your icons when you are using a large color depth setting (16-bit or 24-bit). A nice little extra that doesn't hurt anything; I leave this enabled.

- **Animate windows, menus, and lists.** This makes windows, menus, and lists open and close with a kind of "flourish". A big waste of computing power if you ask me, but some people like it.

- **Smooth edges of screen fonts.** Makes text onscreen look smoother by dithering any ragged edges. (Not necessary, in my opinion, but try it for yourself and see if you notice a difference.)

- **Show <u>w</u>indow contents while dragging.** Makes the mouse pointer look like it is dragging a shadowy version of the icon for a file you are moving or copying with drag-and-drop. It also shows the window contents when you drag an open file across the desktop.

Using Desktop Themes

Desktop themes were introduced in the Microsoft Windows 95 Plus Pack. They were so popular that Microsoft included them for free with Windows 98.

A desktop theme is a combination of wallpaper, mouse pointers, icons, color schemes, fonts, sounds, and screen savers based on a particular topic or theme. For example, the one for the '60s has tie-dye wallpaper, a peace sign for a mouse pointer, and so on. A theme takes over many of the settings that you learned to control individually in this chapter, but you can always change a setting back if you don't like the one the theme has provided.

Applying a Desktop Theme

1. Click **Start**, point to **<u>S</u>ettings**, and click **<u>C</u>ontrol Panel**.
2. Double-click the **Desktop Themes** icon. The Desktop Themes dialog box opens. See Figure 9.20.

Installing Themes

The Desktop Themes feature may not be installed by default on your PC. Use **Add/Remove programs** to add the Desktop Themes component, as you learned to do in Chapter 8.

FIGURE 9.20

Choose a desktop theme to use.

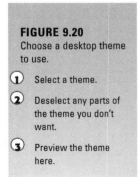

① Select a theme.

② Deselect any parts of the theme you don't want.

③ Preview the theme here.

3. Open the **Theme** drop-down list and choose a theme. A preview of it appears in the window beneath the list.

4. Deselect any check marks along the right side for parts of the theme that you would prefer not to apply.

For example, if you want to keep your current wallpaper rather than using the wallpaper associated with the theme, deselect the **Desktop wallpaper** checkbox.

5. (Optional) To see a preview of the screen saver associated with the scheme, click the **Screen saver** button. Move the mouse or press a key to return.

6. (Optional) To see a preview of the mouse pointers associated with the scheme, click the **Pointers, Sounds, etc.** button. Check out the various pointers, sounds, and icons, and then click **Close** to return.

7. Click **OK**. The scheme is applied.

If you ever decide you don't want to use a theme anymore, return to these steps and choose the **Windows Standard** theme. This resets everything back to normal.

SEE ALSO

➤ *To add Windows components such as Desktop Themes, see page 140.*

➤ *To choose different sounds for system events (without using a desktop theme), see page 194.*

➤ *To use different mouse pointers (without using a desktop theme), see page 188.*

> **Delete a Scheme**
> Schemes take up a great deal of space on your hard disk. If you don't like one of the schemes and know you will never use it, you can remove it by selecting it from the **Theme** list and clicking the **Delete** button. You can also choose certain themes to uninstall from **Add/Remove Programs**. See Chapter 8.

Changing How the Taskbar Operates

The taskbar in Windows is a great little tool for controlling both running programs and programs that you would like to run. You have seen in earlier chapters how to use it; now, you'll learn how to change its appearance and functionality.

Changing the Taskbar Size

You will quickly find that when you turn on the display of several toolbars, as you learned to do in Chapter 7, your taskbar fills up and there is no room to see the buttons for the running programs and open windows. One solution for a crowded taskbar is to enlarge it vertically.

Just position the mouse pointer over its top edge and drag upward, creating extra rows for it. That way each toolbar can have its own row. Figure 9.21 shows an expanded taskbar with several of the extra toolbars turned on.

FIGURE 9.21
The taskbar takes up a lot more space now, but everything is more readable.

SEE ALSO
➤ *To display or hide toolbars in the taskbar, see page 133.*

Auto Hiding the Taskbar

Missing Taskbar

Here's a problem that clients bring to me more often than you would think. Their taskbar is simply gone. There is a thin line at the bottom of the screen where it is supposed to be. Can you guess what has happened?

That's right, they have accidentally resized their taskbar right out of existence. The solution: Point at that thin bar and drag upward, enlarging the taskbar to its normal size again.

You probably don't use the taskbar every moment you're on the computer, so why have it displayed all the time, especially when it's monster-sized as shown in Figure 9.21? You can set it to **Auto hide**, which makes it go away entirely when you aren't using it. Whenever you want to see the taskbar, move the mouse pointer to the bottom of the screen and it pops up automatically.

Auto Hiding the Taskbar

1. Right-click the taskbar and choose **Properties**. The Taskbar Properties dialog box appears. See Figure 9.22.
2. Select the **Auto hide** check box.
3. Click **OK**.

FIGURE 9.22
Choose whether to Auto hide the taskbar.

You can repeat this procedure and deselect the check box to stop auto hiding at any time.

Setting Taskbar Properties

You may have noticed the other settings in the Taskbar Properties dialog box in Figure 9.23. These are less common to change, but you can experiment with them if you like:

- **Always on top.** If the taskbar is not set to Auto Hide, this controls whether it always appears on top of whatever else is onscreen. I don't recommend that you turn this off; it makes the taskbar hard to access.

- **Show small icons in Start menu.** This switches the icons that appear on the first level of the Start menu to a smaller size. No big deal either way.

- **Show clock.** This shows or hides the clock in the system tray. You could turn this off, but why? It's so handy.

SEE ALSO
➤ To work with other items in the system tray, see page 136.

Docking the Taskbar in a Different Location

The Windows taskbar appears at the bottom of the screen by default, but it's not locked there. You can move it to the top, right, or left side of the screen if you prefer. (However, if you move it to one of the sides, some of the buttons may be harder to read and/or use.) Figure 9.23 shows it docked at the right.

FIGURE 9.23
The taskbar docked on the right.

To move the taskbar, simply drag it. Position the mouse pointer over a blank area on the taskbar and drag to another side of the screen. You won't see the bar moving as you drag, but when you release the mouse button, the taskbar will appear in the new spot.

SEE ALSO
➤ To control which toolbars appear on the taskbar, see page 132.
➤ To control the height of the taskbar, see page 180.

chapter 10

Customizing System Settings

Controlling Keyboard Properties

The keyboard may seem like a straightforward device—you press keys and characters appear onscreen. Nevertheless, you can control several settings for it.

For example, when you hold down certain keys, such as the period (.) key, the character types continuously onscreen. This is called *character repeat*, and you can use it to create long lines of a particular character quickly without pressing the key over and over. The rate at which it repeats the character onscreen is the *repeat rate*. The delay between when you press and hold the key and when the character starts repeating onscreen is the *repeat delay*.

You can also set the cursor blink rate. This is the speed at which the insertion point blinks when it is in a text box. (This is a really minor setting, and most people don't bother with it.)

Setting Keyboard Properties

1. From the **Control Panel**, double-click the **Keyboard** icon. The Keyboard Properties dialog box opens. See Figure 10.1.

FIGURE 10.1
Set keyboard properties here.

2. On the **Speed** tab, drag the **Repeat delay** slider bar to the setting you want.

3. Drag the **Repeat rate** slider bar to the setting you want.

4. Test the settings by clicking in the text box below the sliders and holding down a key. Adjust the settings as needed.

5. Drag the **Cursor blink rate** slider to the setting you want. A sample cursor blinks to the left of the bar, showing how it will look.

6. Click **OK**.

The Keyboard Properties dialog box also has a Language tab. See Figure 10.2. It enables you to use keyboards for other languages with Windows 98, and to specify which keyboard you want to use. On the **Language** tab, use the **Add** button to add a keyboard layout and set properties for the chosen language with the **Properties** button. Choose a key combination in the Switch Languages section to choose how you will switch among the keyboards.

FIGURE 10.2
Users of foreign language keyboards can control them here.

Controlling Mouse Settings

Few things are more annoying than a mouse that doesn't behave the way you want. Fortunately, Windows provides many adjustments that can fine-tune your mouse's operation to your exact specifications.

Jumping Mouse?

If your mouse pointer jumps erratically onscreen or "sticks" sometimes (that is, you move the mouse, nothing happens, and then it jerks into motion), the mouse settings described here won't help you. Your mouse is probably dirty; you can take it apart and clean it with alcohol and a cotton swab. If that doesn't work, you may need a new mouse; they do wear out eventually. I wear out a mouse every 6–9 months (but then I use my computer a lot—at least 8 hours a day).

Some mice come with their own software that replaces the default Mouse Properties controls with their own. So, if the controls you see onscreen don't match what's described in the following sections, don't worry. Consult the manual that came with your mouse to find out how to set its controls.

Depending on your setup, you may have an actual mouse, or you may have a trackball or a touchpad. (The latter are very common on laptop PCs.) The Mouse controls in Windows adjust them all the same way, however, unless they have their own special software.

Switching the Mouse Buttons

The idea of clicking with the left mouse button was developed by right-handed people because the strongest finger on the right hand, the index finger, is on the left side of the hand. Left-handed people may prefer to work the mouse with their left hand, on which the strong index finger is toward the right.

Lefties can switch the functioning of the mouse buttons so that the right mouse button "clicks" and the left mouse button "right-clicks."

Switching Mouse Button Operation

1. From the **Control Panel**, double-click the **Mouse** icon. The Mouse Properties dialog box appears. See Figure 10.3.

FIGURE 10.3
Set the mouse button operation here.

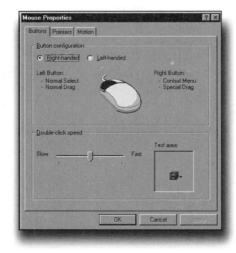

2. On the **Buttons** tab, click <u>**Right-handed**</u> or <u>**Left-handed**</u>.

3. Click **OK**.

Changing the Double-Click Speed

The double-click speed is the speed at which you must press and release the mouse button for it to be considered a double-click rather than two single clicks in succession. If the double-click speed is set too high, it is difficult to click fast enough for your actions to be interpreted as a double-click. If it is set too low, you may find Windows interpreting two clicks in a row as a double-click when that wasn't what you intended. A medium setting (halfway between Fast and Slow) works well for most people.

Changing the Double-Click Speed

1. From the **Control Panel**, double-click the **Mouse** icon. The Mouse Properties dialog box appears. See Figure 10.3.

2. On the **Buttons** tab, drag the <u>**Double-click speed**</u> slider to the desired setting.

3. Click **OK**.

Changing the Pointer Speed

The *pointer speed* is the distance that the pointer moves onscreen when you move the mouse a certain amount. With a faster pointer speed, the mouse is more sensitive, so you can move the pointer a greater distance onscreen with a smaller movement of the mouse. If the pointer speed is too slow, you may find yourself "rowing" (that is, picking up the mouse and repositioning it on the mouse pad because you have run out of room to move in a direction). If the speed is too fast, you may have trouble positioning the pointer.

You can set the pointer speed on the **Motion** tab of the Mouse Properties dialog box.

Adjusting the Pointer Speed

1. From the **Control Panel**, double-click the **Mouse** icon. The Mouse Properties dialog box opens.

2. Click the **Motion** tab. See Figure 10.4.

Pointer Trails

Another setting is available on the Motion tab: Pointer trails. Turning on pointer trails makes a "trail" when you move the mouse pointer, so you can see easily where it has come from and where it is going. This can help some people with visual impairment locate the pointer, but for most people it is merely irritating. Go ahead and turn the feature on temporarily, just so you can see what it is like; you will quickly want to turn it off again.

FIGURE 10.4
Adjust the pointer movement here.

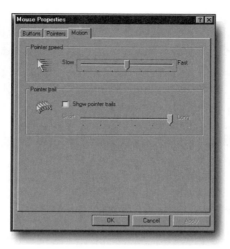

3. Drag the **Pointer speed** slider bar to the desired setting.

4. Click **OK**.

Choosing a Different Pointer Scheme

The default mouse pointer is a small white arrow. It can also take on a variety of other forms depending on the task you are performing, as you saw in Chapter 1. This set of default pointers for various tasks and situations is a *pointer scheme*. You can choose from among several pointer schemes that come with Windows 98.

Pointer schemes are not just for fun—you can choose a scheme that uses larger pointers, such as Windows Standard (Extra Large), if you have trouble seeing the regular-sized mouse pointers onscreen.

You can also choose a specific pointer image for a specific position in the scheme. For example, perhaps you want to use the Windows Standard scheme except for the Busy hourglass; you would prefer the hourglass from the Window Standard (Extra Large) scheme. The following steps include directions for setting that up, too.

Changing the Pointer Scheme

1. From the **Control Panel**, double-click the **Mouse** icon. The Mouse Properties dialog box opens.

2. Click the **Pointers** tab.

Install Pointer Schemes

Two pointer schemes are always available: Animated Hourglass and Windows Standard. Three other schemes are available, too: 3D, Windows Standard (Large), and Windows Standard (Extra Large). However, these latter three are not installed by default with a standard Windows installation. If you want to install these extra pointer schemes, see "Adding and Removing Windows Components" in Chapter 8.

3. Open the **Scheme** drop-down list and select the scheme you want. See Figure 10.5.

FIGURE 10.5
Choose a pointer scheme.

4. (Optional) To use a specific pointer for a specific position, do the following:
   - Select the pointer you want to change.
   - Click the **Browse** button.
   - Select the file for the pointer you want to use. The pointers that come with Windows are in the `C:\Windows\Cursors` folder.
   - Click the **Open** button.

5. Click **OK**.

SEE ALSO

➢ *To add Windows components such as pointer schemes, see page 140.*

Controlling Multimedia Settings

Multimedia settings control how your audio, video, MIDI, and audio CDs will play. In most cases the default settings will do nicely, so you don't have to tackle this section if you're not up for it. But intermediate and advanced Windows users may find it interesting to explore these settings.

Use the Default Pointer

To use the default pointer (the Windows Standard pointer) for a particular position, select it from the list and click the **Use Default** button.

More MIDI

You can do much more with MIDI device configuration than I will cover in this chapter. MIDI devices, such as keyboards, can be set up to do an amazing number of interesting things, but that's the subject of an entire other book.

Audio Multimedia Settings

Audio settings are settings that affect your audio input and output devices. Most people's systems have one audio output device, a sound card, and one audio input device, a microphone.

One of the most common multimedia settings to change is to display or hide the Volume Control icon in the System tray. When you install a sound card, Windows may automatically enable the volume control, but it may not, especially if your sound card comes with its own setup software that might install its own version of the volume control.

Check and Change Audio Settings

1. From the **Control** Panel, double-click the **Multimedia** icon.
2. On the **Audio** tab (see Figure 10.6), do any of the following:
   - To change the default audio playback device (for example, if you have more than one sound card), choose it from the **Playback** drop-down list.
   - To change the default audio input device (for example, if you have several microphones or other inputs devices), choose from the **Recording** drop-down list.
   - To use only the selected preferred devices, mark the **U̲se only preferred devices** check box. (I normally leave this unmarked for greater flexibility.)
   - To turn the volume control on the System tray on or off, select or deselect the **S̲how volume control on the taskbar** check box.
3. Click **OK**.

Video Multimedia Settings

Video multimedia settings is somewhat misleading in the preceding heading. Only one setting exists: You can choose at what size video clips will appear by default. You can choose to have the clip play in a window at a variety of sizes, or you can choose to have clips play full screen.

FIGURE 10.6
Set multimedia proper-
ties for audio devices.

On the surface, it would seem that "bigger is better" and that you
would want the largest size you can get. But a video clip's quality
degrades as you expand it past its original size, so a larger clip may
actually be harder to watch. That's why I leave this setting at
Original—for maximum clip quality at whatever the default size happens to be for that clip.

Setting Video Clip Playback Size

1. From the **Control Panel**, double-click the **Multimedia** icon.

2. Click the **Video** tab. See Figure 10.7.

FIGURE 10.7
Choose how video
clips will play back on
your PC.

3. Choose one of the following:

  • **Window.** Play clips in a window.

  • **Full screen.** Play clips in full-screen mode.

4. If you chose Window, open the drop-down list and choose a size for the clip, or choose **Original size**.

5. Click **OK**.

MIDI Multimedia Settings

Unless you are a musician who has multiple MIDI devices, these settings will not mean much to you; most people can skip this part.

MIDI (Musical Instrument Digital Interface) is a type of computer-created music in which the computer simulates the sound of one or more real-life instruments. MIDI can be either an input format (for example, you might plug a keyboard into your sound card and record a song that you play on the keyboard) or an output format (for example, a game you are playing might have recorded MIDI files that play through your sound card). The settings we are talking about in this section are the MIDI *output* settings.

You can choose a specific MIDI instrument to play MIDI output, or you can set up a custom scheme that uses different MIDI devices for different channels. Sixteen channels are available, and each one can be set for a different instrument, so you can get really fancy! But as I said earlier, these settings are really for people who use their PCs for music, not just for ordinary users who play the occasional game.

Choosing MIDI Output Devices

1. From the **Control Panel**, double-click the **Multimedia** icon.

2. Click the **MIDI** tab. See Figure 10.8.

3. Choose one of the following:

  • **Single instrument.** Choose this, and then choose the output instrument you want to use from the list.

  • **Custom configuration.** Choose this, and then choose the MIDI scheme you want from the list. Click the **Configure** button to set up MIDI schemes. (I won't go into this in this chapter, but it's relatively self-explanatory if you read the instructions onscreen.)

Adding an Instrument

(Optional) To add a new MIDI instrument, you can click the **Add New Instrument** button and then work through the MIDI Instrument Installation Wizard that appears. You can also use the procedure you will learn in Chapter 11 in "Installing a New Driver for an Existing Device."

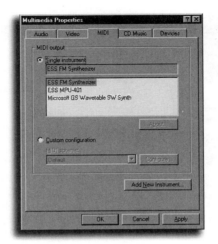

4. Click **OK**.

SEE ALSO

➤ *To install new hardware, see page 211.*

CD Music Multimedia Settings

If you have more than one CD-ROM drive, you may want to choose the one that you will use to play audio CDs. You can play audio CDs with any drive, but the one you pick in the multimedia settings will be the one that works automatically with your CD Player utility.

You can also set the CD audio volume through the multimedia properties, but this is not a big deal because you can also set it through your volume control in the system tray (and in fact it's much easier to access it that way).

And finally, you can choose digital playback from the CD-ROM drive. This doesn't work with all CD-ROM drives that play audio, but it can result in better-sounding output.

Setting Audio CD-ROM Playback Settings

1. From the **Control Panel**, double-click the **Multimedia Settings** icon.

2. Click the **CD Music** tab. See Figure 10.9.

FIGURE 10.9
Control CD audio device
settings here.

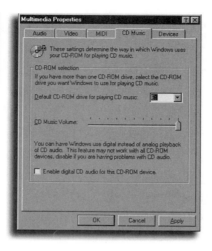

FIGURE 10.9
Control CD audio device
settings here.

3. To choose a different default drive for CD audio, open the **Default CD-ROM drive for playing CD music** drop-down list and choose a drive letter.

4. Drag the **CD Music Volume** slider bar to change the CD audio volume setting.

5. To enable digital CD playback, select the **Enable digital CD audio for this CD-ROM device** check box.

   If you aren't sure whether your drive supports this setting, try it; you can always deselect it later if you experience problems.

   Click **OK**.

SEE ALSO
➤ *To use the CD Player utility, see page 78.*
➤ *To use the Windows volume control, see page 196.*

Setting System Sound Effects

I remember back in the late '80s, I had a friend who had a Macintosh computer. He had it set up to make all kinds of interesting noises when certain system events occurred. Whereas my DOS-based PC had only one generic beep, his had Captain Kirk saying, "Ahead, Warp Factor One" each morning when he turned it on. And his onscreen error messages were accompanied by rude noises that

System Event?

A *system event* is any activity that Windows controls. System events include (but are not limited to) windows opening, windows closing, error messages appearing, system startup, system shutdown, and emptying the Recycle Bin. You do not have to assign sounds to every system event; you can pick and choose so that you hear noises only occasionally.

approximated various bodily functions depending on the error type. I was quite envious!

Nowadays Windows can do the same thing. You can associate any sound with any system event—and never have a moment's silence in your office again.

You can choose sounds for each event individually, or you can apply one of Windows 98's sound schemes. Several schemes are available, each centered around a theme, such as music or nature. Another way to apply a set of sounds is to choose a desktop theme, as you learned in Chapter 9. Each of the desktop themes comes with a full complement of system event sounds.

Choosing System Event Sounds

1. From the **Control Panel**, double-click the **Sounds** icon.

2. To choose a sound scheme, open the **S̲chemes** drop-down list and click a scheme.

4. To preview a sound for a particular event (to see if you like it), do the following:

   • Click the system event on the **Events** list.

   • Click the **Play** button in the Preview area. The sound plays. See Figure 10.10.

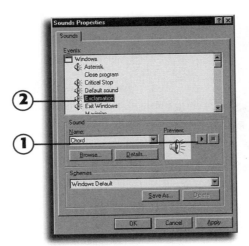

> **No Schemes?**
>
> If you do not see any schemes other than No Sounds and Windows Default on the list in Step 3, the sound schemes are not installed. Use **Add/Remove Programs** to add the schemes. See Chapter 8, "Installing New Programs," for help.

FIGURE 10.10
Check out an event's sound by previewing it.

① Play button

② Speaker symbol means a sound is associated with this event.

Use Your Own Sounds

To use a sound that you have recorded yourself or downloaded from the Internet, click the **Browse** button next to the Name drop-down list and locate/select the sound file.

Use Your Own Sounds

To use a sound that you have recorded yourself or downloaded from the Internet, click the **Browse** button next to the Name drop-down list and locate/select the sound file.

No Speaker Icon?

If you don't see a speaker icon in the System tray, perhaps you are using software that replaces the default speaker icon with some other symbol. For example, Enqoniq, a popular sound card brand, provides a volume control that uses this icon: ▣. If you are sure that none of the icons in your system tray are for the volume control, perhaps you need to enable its display there; see "Audio Multimedia Settings" earlier in this chapter.

5. To change the sound associated with an event, do the following:
   - Select the event from the **E̲vents** list.
   - Open the **N̲ame** drop-down list and choose a different sound. (Preview it if you are not sure what it sounds like.)

6. To save a changed sound scheme, click the **Save As** button, enter a new scheme name, and click **Save**.

7. Click **OK**.

SEE ALSO

➤ *To choose a desktop theme, see page 178.*

➤ *To install Windows components (such as sound schemes), see page 140.*

Controlling the Volume

You can easily access the volume control for your PC by double-clicking the speaker icon in the System tray. (Or, if it's not there, you can open the Start menu and choose **Programs, Accessories, Entertainment, Volume Control.**)

The Volume control panel has a master volume control on the left, followed by controls for each device type. Depending on your setup, you might see ones for CD, Wave, MIDI, Synthesizer, Microphone, Line, Auxiliary, Video, and/or Modem. Each device can be adjusted separately by dragging its slider bar up or down. See Figure 10.11.

You can control which devices have volume controls in this panel. The ones in Figure 10.11 are the devices I have chosen to display there because they are the devices I work with frequently. You can use the **Options** menu and select or deselect the available controls. The menu shown in Figure 10.12 may be a little different from the one you see on your system, depending on the sound card you have and its drivers.

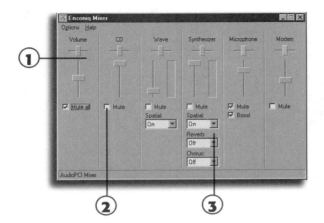

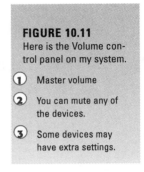

FIGURE 10.11
Here is the Volume control panel on my system.

① Master volume

② You can mute any of the devices.

③ Some devices may have extra settings.

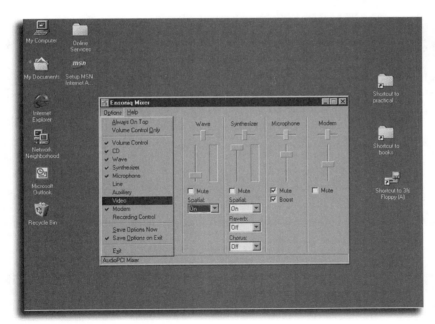

FIGURE 10.12
Control which devices appear.

Setting the Date and Time

When you install Windows 98, you confirm (and change if needed) the date and time. You can update the date and time settings whenever you like (for example, if you move to a different time zone or if your computer's built-in clock loses or gains time).

Losing Time
If your PC's clock loses time consistently (more than a minute or so), your computer's battery may be low.

To display the Date/Time Properties dialog box, double-click the clock in the System tray or double-click the **Date/Time** icon in the **Control Panel**. See Figure 10.13.

FIGURE 10.13
Check and change the date and time here.

Auto Adjust

The Automatically Adjust check box is unavailable in Figure 10.13 because Indiana is chosen for the time zone, and Indiana does not change for Daylight Savings Time. Incidentally, Indiana and Hawaii are the only time zones in the world that do not change.

Then, set the date and time as needed. Click **OK** when finished.

- To change the date, choose a month and year from the **Date** drop-down lists, and then click a day on the calendar to choose a day.

- To set the time, type a new time in the **Time** box under the clock face.

- To choose your time zone, make your selection from the **Time zone** drop-down list.

- To automatically adjust for Daylight Savings Time (or not), select or deselect the **Automatically adjust clock for daylight saving changes** check box.

Adjusting Regional Settings

The term "region" loosely refers to country. In different countries, the unit of measurement, the currency, and/or the way dates are written can be different. By choosing a region, you choose all the appropriate settings for it.

To access the Regional Settings properties, double-click **Regional Settings** in the **Control Panel**. Then you can do one of the following:

- Select a country or region from the **Regional Settings** tab, as shown in Figure 10.14, and let Windows choose the appropriate formats for you.

  or

- Select a country or region as a starting point, but then customize the date format, currency, and other items on the corresponding tabs in the dialog box. For example, the settings for Currency appear in Figure 10.15.

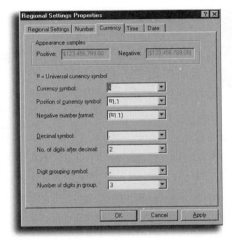

FIGURE 10.14
By simply choosing a country, you set all the settings on all the other tabs automatically.

chapter
11

Installing Hardware

Devices You Can Install

New hardware: Nearly everyone wants some, right? If your PC is more than a few months old, chances are that you wish you had a new *something*. Perhaps it's a bigger monitor, a DVD drive, a scanner, or a printer.

Entire books are written about the physical installation of new devices. (I have even written one myself, called *Upgrade Your PC in a Weekend*.) But I'll save you the money and tell you the secret of successful upgrading: *Read the instructions*. Each new piece of hardware comes with a manual—or at least an instruction sheet. Read it and follow the directions to the letter.

You can add lots of devices to your system, but they all boil down to a few categories:

- **Cards.** These are circuit cards you plug into expansion slots on the motherboard (inside the case). The card has a connector on it (usually) into which you can plug either an internal device (such as a drive) or an external device (such as a scanner).

- **Drives.** These are metal boxes that you install in drive bays inside the case. (Examples: CD-ROM, DVD, hard disks, floppies, zip drives). You connect cables to them that run to your motherboard or a card (see above) and to the PC's power supply.

- **External devices.** These plug into ports at the back of your PC. The port may be one that came with the PC or one that you added yourself with a card (see above). Printers, scanners, and some digital cameras fall into this category. External devices require their own power supply, so you must plug them into an AC outlet in addition to hooking them up to your PC. (Keyboards and mice are the exception; they don't require separate power.)

- **Memory.** Mini-cards or individual chips that plug into the motherboard or a card. They increase the memory of an existing component (either the system as a whole or a particular device, such as the video card).

BIOS Setup

Most of these devices are fairly straightforward to install. You just hook them up as described in their directions. (Make sure your PC's power is off before installing or removing a device, of course.) The only wrinkle is that some devices (notably drives) may require you to set them up in the BIOS setup program.

When you start your PC, you probably see a message onscreen briefly that reads Press F1 for Setup—or Delete, F2, or some other key. If you follow that instruction (quickly, before the message goes away), you enter the BIOS setup.

When you are in the BIOS Setup program, look for a place to set the drive type.

For floppy or CD-ROM drives, set the drive type to the appropriate setting if it is not already correct. (Instructions onscreen should tell you how to change a type.) Most BIOS programs have specific drive types for CD-ROM and floppy. Some have a specific drive type for SuperDisks and zip drives, too.

If you are setting up a hard disk, set the drive type to **Auto,** or use the **AutoConfigure Drive Type** feature if one is available. (Sorry I can't be more specific, because every BIOS program is different.)

Then, exit the BIOS program (try the **Esc** or **F10** keys) and save your changes.

Setting Up Device Drivers in Windows

After you have installed a new piece of hardware in your PC (following the instructions that came with it to the letter, of course), you're ready to see how it will interact with Windows 98.

Most new devices that you buy these days are plug-and-play compatible. That means that, in theory anyway, you just plug them in (that is, install them), and they play (that is, operate) without any special setup. It's a nice idea, but it doesn't always work.

Automatic BIOS Setup

Some of the most modern computers detect new devices automatically and set up the BIOS for you so that you do not have to enter the BIOS setup program and manually configure a new drive.

BIOS? CMOS?

The BIOS is an automatically executed startup routine that runs certain tests and checks for installed hardware. The BIOS program is stored on a Read-Only Memory (ROM) chip mounted on the motherboard. Most systems have a setup program built into the BIOS that displays the BIOS settings and enables you to customize them. The customizations are stored on a special microchip called a CMOS chip (Complementary Metal-Oxide Semiconductor).

As the PC starts up, it first reads the "house rules" from the BIOS chip. Then, it reads the exceptions to the rules that you have set up on the CMOS chip. The exceptions override any of the house rules that they contradict. For example, if the BIOS says "you have one floppy drive" but the CMOS says "you have two floppy drives," then the "two drives" setting will reign.

203

Turn on your PC, and let Windows start up. Depending on the device, one of several things might happen:

- Windows automatically detects the new device and installs one of its own built-in drivers for it. Windows comes with drivers for hundreds of popular devices, so if you buy a name-brand device, this is more likely to happen to you. (Lucky dog.)

- Windows automatically detects the new device and prompts you to insert the disk that came with it. Just do as you're told onscreen.

- Windows acts as though it detected the device and installed a driver, but the device doesn't work. This usually means you need to run a special setup program on the disk that came with the new device. (It also can mean a resource conflict exists; see Chapter 25, "Troubleshooting Problems.")

- Windows doesn't detect the device automatically at all, and you must use the Add New Hardware Wizard to ask Windows to look for it.

All the above scenarios except the last one are easy to handle, so we'll take a look at the Add New Hardware Wizard in the following section.

SEE ALSO

➤ *To run a setup program for a device, see page 143.*

➤ *To troubleshoot device problems, see page 453.*

Using the Add New Hardware Wizard

First, some bad news. If Windows did not detect the new device automatically, and it's a device that's supposed to be Plug and Play, there is probably a problem with it, such as a resource conflict or a mechanical failure. (Or maybe you just don't have it installed correctly.)

However, the next proper step, before you start troubleshooting (see Chapter 25), is to run the Add New Hardware Wizard, in the hopes that something will shake loose and Windows will suddenly recognize the device. You can also use the Add New Hardware Wizard to configure an older, non-Plug-and-Play device in your system.

Turn It On

Windows cannot automatically detect an external device, such as a printer or scanner, unless the device is turned on and online.

Running the Add New Hardware Wizard

1. Close all running programs.

2. From the Control Panel, double-click **Add New Hardware**.

3. Click **Next**, and then click **Next** again. The Wizard searches for new Plug-and-Play devices.

4. It then asks whether you want to search for non-Plug-and-Play devices. Click **Yes**, and then click **Next**, and then **Next** again.

5. Wait for the detection results to appear.

   • If you see a message that it did not find any new hardware, click **Cancel**. It didn't work. See Chapter 25 for troubleshooting help.

   • If you see a message that it found new hardware, click the **Details** button to see what it found. A list of the detected devices appears, as shown in Figure 11.1.

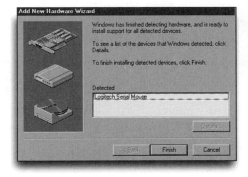

FIGURE 11.1
The new device(s) detected.

6. To install the device(s) listed, click **Finish**. Or, if the device(s) found is not the device you thought you were installing, click **Cancel** and see Chapter 25.

You can also use the Add New Hardware Wizard to manually set up a new device. This might be useful if you want to set up a device that is not currently connected to your PC. Perhaps you share the device with some other user and that person currently has "custody" of it. You can still set it up in Windows so that the device will work when it does become available.

Setting Up a Device Manually with the Add New Hardware Wizard

1. Close all running programs.

2. From the Control Panel, double-click **Add New Hardware**.

3. Click **Next**, and then **Next** again to search for Plug-and-Play devices.

4. When asked whether you want to search for non-Plug-and-Play devices, click **No, I want to select the hardware from a list**, and then click **Next**.

5. A list of device types appears, as shown in Figure 11.2. Click the type you want, and then click **Next**.

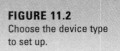

FIGURE 11.2
Choose the device type to set up.

6. Depending on the device type you chose:

   • A wizard may start for the device type chosen. (Printers, infrared devices, and modems fall into this category). Work through the wizard by following the prompts.

   • A list of device manufacturers and models may appear, as shown in Figure 11.3. Choose the model you want to set up, and then choose **Next**.

Got Disk?

If you have a disk that came with the device, insert it in Step 6 at the list of manufacturers screen, and then click the **Have Disk** button.

7. Follow the prompts that appear to install the drivers for the device. You may be asked to insert the Windows 98 CD-ROM, to reboot, or to answer some other questions, depending on the device type.

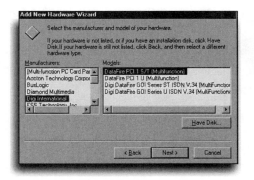

FIGURE 11.3
Some device types let you choose from a list of makes and models.

8. Shut down the PC and install the new device if it is not already installed and available.

9. Check the device to see if it is working. If not, see Chapter 25 for troubleshooting help.

Setting Up a Printer

Many times, Windows will detect a new printer automatically or at least detect it when you run the Add New Hardware Wizard. But if it doesn't, you can use the Add Printer Wizard to set it up.

The procedure for setting up a local printer is different from that of a network printer, so we'll look at local printers first.

Adding a Local Printer

1. Open the **Start** menu, point to **Settings**, and click **Printers**.

2. Double-click the **Add Printer** icon.

3. Click **Next** to start the Add Printer Wizard.

4. Choose **Local printer** and then click **Next**.

5. Do one of the following:

   Choose the printer's manufacturer and model from the list provided, and then click **Next**.

   or

   Insert the disk provided by the manufacturer, then click **Have Disk,** and follow the prompts to select the model.

Its Own Setup Program?

Don't use the Add Printer Wizard if the printer comes with its own setup program on disk; use its own setup program instead. The setup program will accomplish everything that the Add Printer Wizard will, and it will install any extra software that came with the printer.

6. Select the port that the printer is connected to from the list of ports that appears. Then click **Next**.

   The ones for my system appear in Figure 11.4; your list may be different. (Hint: Most local printers are connected to LPT1.)

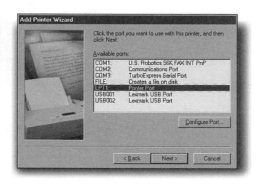

FIGURE 11.4
Choose the port to which the printer is connected.

7. Type a descriptive name for the printer in the **Printer name** text box.

   This description will appear in the Print dialog box in applications from which you print.

8. Choose **Yes** or **No** to choose whether this printer is your default printer. Then, click **Next**.

9. Choose **Yes** to print a test page or **No** to skip it.

   If you chose to print a test page, a box appears asking whether it printed okay. Click **Yes** (assuming it did) or click **No** to open a print troubleshooting box, and then follow along with it to fix the problem.

10. Click **Finish**. The printer's drivers are installed.

    If prompted, insert the Windows 98 CD-ROM into your drive and click **OK** to continue.

After you have installed the printer's drivers, that printer appears in the Printers folder (**Start, Settings, Printers**) and also in all printer listings (such as in the Print dialog box in an application).

If you are setting up to print from a network printer (that is, a printer that is not physically attached to your own PC, but to some other PC on your network), the Add Printer Wizard is the best way to accomplish that, as shown in the following steps. After you set up a network printer, it appears in all printer listings, the same as a local printer, and works the same way.

Adding a Network Printer

1. Open the **Start** menu, point to **Settings**, and click **Printers**.

2. Double-click the **Add Printer** icon.

3. Click **Next** to start the Add Printer Wizard.

4. Choose **Network printer** and then click **Next**.

5. Click the **Browse** button and locate the printer you want to use. Figure 11.5 shows a printer being found on another PC. Then, click **OK**.

FIGURE 11.5
Browse the network to find the printer you want to share.

6. Click **Next**.

7. Type a descriptive name for the printer in the **Printer name** text box.

   This description will appear in the Print dialog box in applications from which you print.

8. Choose **Yes** or **No** to choose whether this printer is your default printer. Then, click **Next**.

9. Choose **Yes** to print a test page or **No** to skip it.

If you chose to print a test page, a box appears asking whether it printed okay. Click **Yes** (assuming it did) or click **No** to open a print troubleshooting box, and then follow along with it to fix the problem.

SEE ALSO

➤ *To make your local printer available to others on a network, see page 226.*

➤ *To browse a network, see page 245.*

➤ *To control a print queue, see page 225.*

Setting Up a Scanner

When working with a scanner, it is extremely important that you follow the instructions that came with the device. That's because so many brands and types of scanners are available, and each one works a little differently.

First, the physical installation of a scanner varies depending on what interface it uses. Some scanners plug into your PC's USB (Universal Serial Bus) port; others share your parallel port with the printer; still others require a SCSI connection (a special add-on circuit card) or come with their own interface cards that you install.

After you perform the physical installation and turn on the PC, Windows may automatically detect the scanner. However, you should always run the setup software that comes with a scanner because it will install a program that you can use to scan and edit pictures. (Many scanners come with a program called PhotoDeluxe for this purpose; others come with their own proprietary software.)

TWAIN Compatible

Most scanners these days conform to a standard called TWAIN. Such scanners can be used in a variety of programs to scan directly into that program. (Most of the Microsoft Office 2000 programs allow you to do this, for example.) That means you don't have to use the software that comes with the scanner if you don't like it.

Setting Up a Digital Camera

As with scanners, you must be very careful to read the instructions that come with your digital camera because every one is different.

The camera is basically a standalone device; you connect it to your PC only to transfer pictures from it. Some cameras save the pictures on floppy disks (notably the Sony Mavica cameras), so you don't have to do any setup at all in Windows. Simply copy the .jpg files from the camera disk to your hard drive.

Other cameras require you to connect them to one of the PC's ports temporarily to transfer the images. Some cameras connect to a USB port, others to a serial port, a SCSI port, a PC Card port (for laptops only), or an infrared port. The setup program that comes with the camera will install the appropriate software to enable you to make the connection. Windows does not normally auto-detect a digital camera.

Still another kind of camera attaches more-or-less full-time to one of your PC's ports and is used to capture and broadcast video images for videoconferencing. These are cameras, but in a different sense than is popular today. To use one of these, follow the instructions that come with it.

Installing a New Driver for an Existing Device

If you upgraded to Windows 98 from an earlier version of Windows, the drivers for some of your devices may not be as good as they could be. Drivers written for a device for Windows 95 will usually work with Windows 98, but they may not always work very well. If you started having problems with a device (such as a scanner, a printer, a video card, a modem) after upgrading to Windows 98, a driver update might provide the fix you need.

Several ways exist to acquire an updated driver. The device's manufacturer may have a Web site where you can download one, for example. (Such downloads often come with their own setup programs; if so, you do not have to go through the procedure in the following steps. You run the provided setup program instead.) You can also get a new driver using Windows Update, a free service provided by Microsoft. (You'll see it at work in the following steps.) Or you can use a driver from a disk that you have ordered from the manufacturer. (Check the device's manual to see whether there is a phone number to call to order device driver updates.)

Updating a Device Driver

1. From the Control Panel, double-click the **System** icon.

   (Or right-click **My Computer** on the desktop and choose **Properties**.)

2. Click the **Device Manager** tab.

3. Select the device whose driver you want to update.

4. Click **Properties**.

5. Click the **Driver** tab.

6. Click the **Update Driver** button. The Update Device Driver Wizard opens.

7. Click **Next** to begin.

8. When asked what you want to do, choose **Search for a better driver than the one your device is using now.** Then, click **Next**.

9. If you have a disk containing the new driver, insert it into your floppy or CD-ROM drive.

10. Mark the check boxes for all the locations where you want Windows to search. See Figure 11.6. Then, click **Next**.

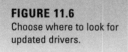

FIGURE 11.6
Choose where to look for updated drivers.

11. Follow the recommendation that appears, depending on what Windows finds.

    It may find, for example, that you are already using the best driver. Or it may recommend an update. Continue working through the wizard to its completion.

Removing Drivers for a Removed Device

Sometimes, when you remove a device from your system, Windows detects that fact and removes the drivers for it. But more often, it doesn't, and you must remove the drivers yourself.

The Control Panel contains several icons for specific device types, such as Modems and Network, and you can remove devices from these Properties dialog boxes. Just select the component to remove and click the **Remove** button. Figure 11.7 shows the Modems Properties dialog box, for example.

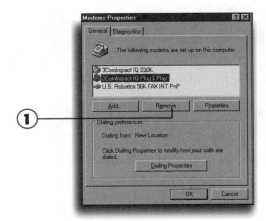

FIGURE 11.7
To remove a specific type of device from Windows, choose Remove from the Properties for that device type.

① Remove button

It's even easier to remove a printer. Just display the Printers window (**Start, Settings, Printers**), click the icon for the printer, and press the **Delete** key.

You can also remove components from the Device Manager. The Device Manager presents a list of all the devices on your system, much like the tree in Windows Explorer. The following steps show how:

Deleting a Device Driver from Device Manager

1. From the Control Panel, double-click the **System** icon.
2. Click the **Device Manager** tab.
3. Click the plus sign (**+**) next to the type of device you want. A list of installed devices of that type appears, as shown in Figure 11.8.

Do I Have To?

If you don't remove the drivers for the removed device, probably nothing bad will happen. However, that device will continue to appear on lists of available devices, which might be confusing, especially to someone else using your PC. In addition, if the device driver is still loaded, Windows is still allocating system resources to the device, which is wasteful.

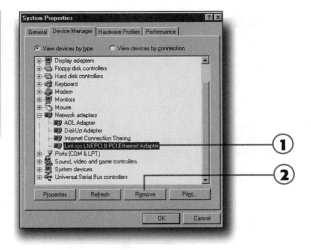

FIGURE 11.8
Devices can also be removed through Device Manager.

① Selected device

② Remove button

Remove to Reinstall

If a plug-and-play compatible device isn't working correctly, it can sometimes be coaxed into working by removing its driver from Device Manager and then clicking **Refresh** to force Windows to re-detect it.

4. Click the device for which you want to remove the driver.

5. Click the **Remove** button.

6. Click **Close** to close the System Properties dialog box.

SEE ALSO

➤ *For more information about Device Manager, see page 453.*

chapter 12

Managing Fonts and Printers

Working with Fonts

Font Versus Typeface

Some people maintain that a font is a particular typeface at a particular size with certain attributes, such as Courier 12-point Bold, but I tend to use the terms font and typeface interchangeably to mean a named family of characters, such as Arial, Times New Roman, or Courier.

Fonts are typefaces that you can use onscreen and in printed documents. The more fonts you have, the more flexibility you have in creating documents with exactly the look you want. For example, you might create a newsletter that uses Arial for the headings, Times New Roman for the body text, Arial Black for the page numbers, and so on.

Windows 98 comes with several fonts, including Courier, Times New Roman, Arial, and Symbol. You may also have other fonts installed, depending on what other software you have. (For example, Microsoft Office comes with many fonts.) Figure 12.1 shows samples of some of the fonts on my PC. You can install more fonts yourself, as you'll learn in "Installing New Fonts" later in this chapter.

FIGURE 12.1
Sample fonts.

One way to see a list of the installed fonts is to open the Font drop-down list or the Font dialog box in one of your word processing programs. For example, Figure 12.2 shows the Font drop-down list in Microsoft Word 2000. From that list you can choose the font you want to apply to the selected text (or to text that you are about to type).

Font Previews

Office 2000 allows you to see a real sample of each font on the Font drop-down list in its programs, as shown in Figure 12.2. Not all word processing programs do that; in most of them, you see only the font names on the Font drop-down list in plain lettering.

Another way is to open the Font listing from the Control Panel, as shown in the following steps. From here, you can not only view the installed fonts but also do the activities described in the following sections (sorting, filtering, adding/removing, and so on).

Displaying the List of Installed Fonts

From the Control Panel, double-click the **Fonts** icon. A window containing the fonts appears, as shown in Figure 12.3.

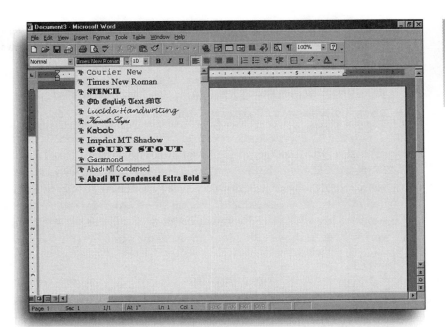

FIGURE 12.2
Most word processing programs let you browse the list of available fonts.

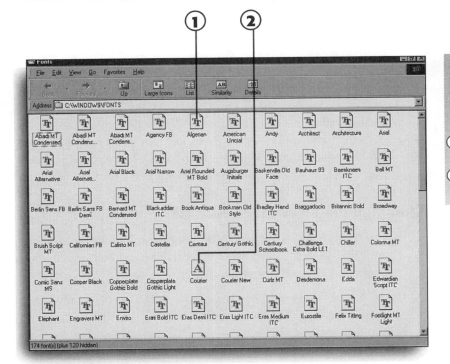

FIGURE 12.3
The Fonts window shows all installed fonts for your PC.

① TrueType fonts (TT icons)

② Non-TrueType font (A icon)

Most of the fonts on your system are probably TrueType fonts, designated by a TT icon. These are fonts designed for use in Windows (or on a Macintosh). You may also have a few other types of fonts available (for example, fonts that are built into your printer). In Figure 12.3, notice that the icon for Courier is different—it has an A on it, indicating a non-TrueType font.

Try to use TrueType fonts whenever you can in your work. They offer several advantages over other fonts. For starters, TrueType fonts are scalable—that is, you can use them in any size you want. (Other fonts may or may not be.) TrueType fonts can also be embedded in word processing documents (in some programs) so that a person working with your document on another PC can see and print it correctly even if he or she does not have the same fonts installed as you do.

If you have a PostScript printer, you probably have access to 35 or more built-in, scalable PostScript typefaces. If you will be exchanging files with a professional printing service, the service may want you to use those PostScript fonts to create your work because they will be printing your final copy on a PostScript printer, too.

Fonts are not just for printouts; you can also use different fonts in your Web pages and other documents designed for onscreen viewing. Keep in mind, however, that whoever views the page or document will need to have that same font installed on his or her own screens, or the document won't look the same. You can provide the needed fonts for download on your Web page (subject to any copyright restrictions placed on a particular font by its creator, of course), but it is easier to stick with common fonts when designing Web pages, such as Arial, Times New Roman, and Courier.

Using Unusual Fonts on Web Pages

If you want to use a font on your Web page that most of your viewers won't have, consider creating a graphic of the text to use instead. To create a graphic from typed text, use the **Paint**, and use the **Text** tool to type the text in whatever font you want. Then save the file as a graphic and place the graphic on the Web page.

Changing the View of the Font List

The Fonts window appears to be a regular folder, but it is special in several ways. First, it has its own special toolbar with which you can display the fonts in any of four ways:

Large Icons. Displays the fonts as large icons, as shown in Figure 12.3. This is the default.

List. Displays the fonts in a list, with small icons.

Similarity. Displays a special view in which you can determine how similar one font is to another. (More on this shortly.)

 Details. Displays details about each font, such as file size and date last modified.

Of these four views, three will seem familiar. The odd one here, Similarity, can be used to sort fonts according to their similarity to a font that you choose.

You might want to sort by similarity for several reasons. One of the most common is to weed out fonts that are virtually identical to another font so that you do not have to scroll through lots of similar fonts to find the font you need.

If you have two fonts that look almost the same, you probably won't want to have both installed and taking up space; you will want to keep one and discard the other. By choosing a font and then deleting any fonts that are marked Very Similar, you can trim your font list to a more manageable and useful size.

Viewing Fonts by Similarity

1. In the Fonts window, click the **Similarity** button .

2. Open the **List fonts by similarity to** drop-down list and choose the font that you want to compare all others to. See Figure 12.4.

3. Examine the list of fonts. They are sorted from most similar to the chosen font to least similar.

SEE ALSO
➤ *To delete an unwanted font (from any view), see page 222.*

One other viewing option: You can display or hide the variations for each font. For example, suppose separate font files exist for Arial, Arial Bold, Arial Italic, and Arial Bold Italic. If you choose to hide the variations, you would see only one file on the list: Arial. To display or hide variations, open the **View** menu and choose **Hide Variations**.

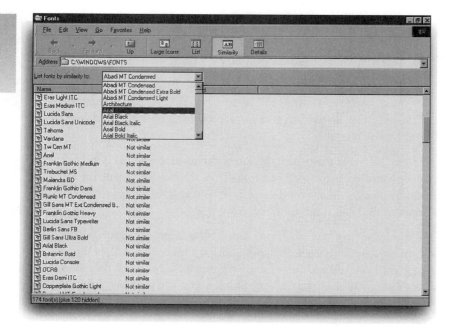

FIGURE 12.4
Choose a font to compare to others.

Printing a Font Sample Page

It's hard to tell what a font looks like just from the name, although some of the names are rather descriptive (such as Comic or Stencil). But you can easily see and print a sample page for a font to remind yourself what it looks like.

Printing a Sample Page for a Font

1. From the Font window, double-click a font. A window opens showing the sample for it. The one for Arial Black is shown in Figure 12.5.

2. To print the sample page, click the **Print** button.

3. In the Print dialog box that appears, click **OK**.

4. Click **Done** to close the sample window.

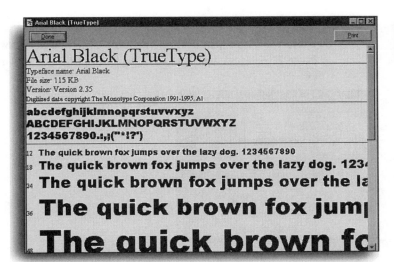

Installing New Fonts

Most of the ways of getting new fonts come with their own installation utility, so you will seldom need to manually install fonts. For example, if you buy a CD full of fonts, it probably contains a font browser and installation utility. Or, if you buy a new word processing program that comes with fonts, the same setup program that installs the word processor probably installs the fonts, too.

However, you may occasionally need to install fonts through Windows. For example, if a colleague provides a font to you on disk (or emails it to you), you may need to install it. Or, if you bought an inexpensive disk full of fonts, no installation utility may be provided.

When you install a font, you can choose whether to copy the font to the Fonts folder. (The default is to copy it there.) If you choose not to copy the font, the font will not take up any space on your hard disk. (For a single font this is not a big issue, but if you're dealing with dozens or hundreds of fonts, it can add up.) However, the font will not be available unless the disk from which it came is available. For example, if you leave the fonts on the network, and the network is down, you won't be able to use the font.

Alternative Method

Instead of steps 1 and 2, you can select the font and then open the **File** menu and choose **Print**, or you can right-click the font and choose **Print** from the shortcut menu. Then, pick up the procedure at Step 3.

Fonts Online

You can find a variety of freeware and shareware fonts available for download on the Internet. Some sites will try to sell them to you, but many free fonts are available that are just as good as the commercial ones. See "Downloading a Program" in Chapter 8, "Installing New Programs," for information about locating and downloading files online.

Installing Fonts

1. From the Fonts window, open the **File** menu and choose **Install New Font**. The Add Fonts dialog box opens. See Figure 12.6.

FIGURE 12.6
Add new fonts here.

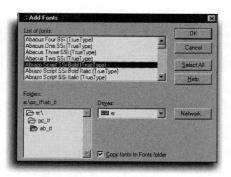

2. Navigate to the folder/drive containing the new font(s).

   To do so, first choose the drive from the **Drives** list and then choose the folder from the **Folders** list. Or to browse the network, choose the **Network** button.

3. Click the font you want from the **List of fonts**.

   To select more than one font, hold down the **Ctrl** key as you click the ones you want. Or click the **Select All** button to select all the fonts in the chosen folder.

4. To copy the fonts to your hard disk (recommended), make sure the **Copy fonts to Fonts folder** check box is marked.

5. Click **OK**. The fonts are installed.

Removing Fonts

To remove a font from your system, simply delete it from the Fonts folder as you would delete any file. (That is, select it and then press the **Delete** key.)

Deleted fonts go to the Recycle Bin, so you can restore them from there as you learned in Chapter 5.

SEE ALSO
➤ *To restore a deleted font from the Recycle Bin, see page 95.*

Controlling a Printer

Most of the time, you will control your printer through the Print dialog box of whatever program you are using. For example, in Word 2000, you would work with the Print dialog box shown in Figure 12.7. The Print dialog box enables you to choose how many copies and what portion of the current document you would like to print. (This was covered in Chapter 3.)

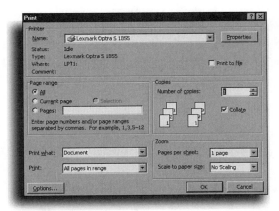

FIGURE 12.7
A typical Print dialog box for an application.

In addition to setting how a particular print job will print, you can also set up the printer itself. You can set properties that control how it operates, you can control its queue (that is, the list of documents waiting to be printed), and you can choose to share your local printer on a network. You will learn about each of those things in the following sections.

Setting Printer Properties

Each printer has an array of properties you can set for it. The exact properties available depend on the type and model of printer; each one is slightly different. For example, some printers allow you to manage color settings; others don't have color capability, so it's not an issue.

Working with Printer Properties

1. Open the **Start** menu, point to **Settings**, and click **Printers**. This displays the Printers folder.

Different Versions of the Printer Properties

You can access a printer's Properties dialog box from an application's Print dialog box in many cases. For example, in Figure 12.7 notice the Properties button, which will take you to the Properties dialog box. However, the Properties box that appears may not contain a complete set of options for the printer. For full access to its properties, use the following steps instead.

2. Right-click a printer and choose **Properties** from the shortcut menu.

   (Or select the printer and then open the **File** menu and click **Properties**.)

3. Make any changes desired to the printer settings. (See Table 12.1 for guidance.)

4. Click **OK**.

Because the properties for each printer are slightly different, I can't give you a full list of the properties and what they do. However, Figure 12.8 shows the Properties box for one of my printers so that you can see the various tabbed sections, and Table 12.1 lists some of the more common properties that you may find for a printer and explains something about them.

FIGURE 12.8
A Properties box for a typical laser printer.

Table 12.1 Common printer properties

Setting	Description
Port	The port that the printer is attached to.
Copies	The number of copies the printer will print unless otherwise specified in an application.

Setting	Description
Orientation	Page direction, portrait or landscape, unless otherwise specified in an application.
Form Size	The dimensions of the paper being used unless otherwise specified.
Tray	The default paper tray to use, if the printer has more than one.
Resolution	The image quality. Higher quality may equal slower printing speed.
Dithering	The fineness (or coarseness) of the dots that make up a shaded image.
Font Substitutions	Which of the printer's built-in fonts (if any) should be used instead of certain TrueType fonts.
Sharing	Whether the printer should be available to other users on your network. (More on this shortly.)

SEE ALSO
➤ *To print from a program, see page 60.*

➤ *To set up a new printer in Windows, see page 207.*

Managing the Print Queue

Each printer has its own queue in which documents wait to be printed. Most home users print only one document at a time and have only one PC and printer, so the queue will not be a big issue. However, if several people share a printer on a network, there may sometimes be a list of several documents waiting for their turns at being printed. You can view this list and (if you have the appropriate network permissions) rearrange and even delete print jobs on it.

Managing the Print Queue for a Printer

1. From the Printers folder (**Start, Settings, Printers**), double-click the printer you want. The print queue for the printer appears. Figure 12.9 shows an example.

Print Icon in System Tray

When your default printer has print jobs to be printed, a Printer icon appears in your System tray. You can double-click it to open the print queue for that printer instead of performing Step 1, if you prefer.

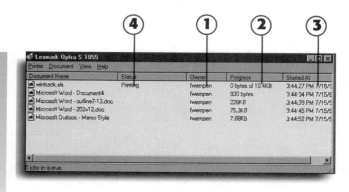

FIGURE 12.9
A print queue with several documents waiting.

① Owner of the print job

② Size

③ When started

④ Job status

2. Do any of the following:

- To pause a particular print job, select it and then choose **Pause Printing** from the **Document** menu. To resume it, repeat.

- To pause the entire printer, choose **Pause Printing** from the **Printer** menu. To restart it, repeat.

- To delete a particular print job, select it and choose **Cancel Printing** from the **Document** menu, or press the **Delete** key.

- To delete all print jobs, choose **Purge Print Documents** from the **Printer** menu.

- To move a certain document higher or lower in the queue, drag it with drag-and-drop, just as you would drag any object on the desktop or in a file listing.

3. When you are finished with the printer's queue, close the window.

SEE ALSO

➤ *To learn more about the System tray, see page 135.*

➤ *For more information on drag-and-drop, see page 91.*

After You, Please!

Another way to move an item to the bottom of the queue is to pause it and let all the other jobs continue around it; then, release it when the others have finished.

Sharing a Printer on the Network

If you are on a network, you may want to share your printer with others. For example, I have three computers in my home, networked, and two printers. Each computer can print to any printer, thanks to network sharing.

Networking is not necessarily a two-way street. Just because you can access files or printers on the network does not mean that others can automatically access yours. You must specifically set up permissions to do so. The following steps assume that you have a network already set up; if you don't, see Chapter 14, "Using Network Resources."

Sharing a Local Printer on the Network

1. From the Printers folder, right-click the printer and choose **Properties**.

2. Click the **Sharing** tab.

3. Click **Shared As**.

4. Type a name for the printer in the **Share Name** box. This name will appear when others on the network are browsing your resources.

5. (Optional) Enter a comment that others will see when browsing your resources.

6. (Optional) Enter a password to use the printer, if you want to require it. That way, you can restrict the printer use to those to whom you give the password.

   Figure 12.10 shows a completed Sharing tab.

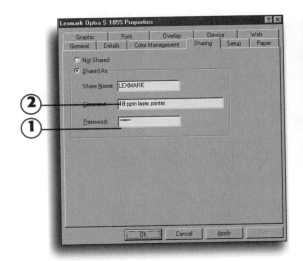

FIGURE 12.10
Fill out the Sharing tab to specify how others will be able to use your printer.

① Password is optional.

② Comments are optional.

7. Click **OK**. Now others can view your printer on the network and set it up to be used from their own PCs, as explained in "Setting Up a Printer" in Chapter 11, "Installing Hardware."

SEE ALSO

➤ *For more information about file and printer sharing on a network, see page 251.*

➤ *To set up a network printer to be used on your PC, see page 207.*

SHARING RESOURCES

chapter

13

Sharing a PC with Multiple Users

Setting Up Multiuser Operation

In an ideal world, each worker in your office (and each family member at home) would have his or her own computer, and nobody would have to share. But, of course, in reality budgets are tight, and often several people end up sharing one machine.

Sharing isn't so bad, except that people may have different ideas about what constitutes attractive screen colors or a useful arrangement of commands on the Start menu. Especially if you have kids that use your home computer, you may find that their screen appearance choices are not your own!

Luckily, Windows allows each person to customize his or her own settings. When you log on with the multiple users feature enabled, Windows identifies you and loads your settings. Windows is not set up for multiple users by default, however, so some initial configuration is involved. You will learn how to set it up in this chapter.

First things first: You need to turn on multiuser operation and create your first user. (That's probably you!) Then, you'll add more users and perhaps change the settings for particular users or delete them. The following sections show how.

Enabling Multiuser Operation

One User, Multiple Purposes

Even if you don't share your PC with others, you may want to set up separate "users" for various tasks. For example, you might have a "business user" set up with shortcuts on the desktop to all your business applications. Then, you might create another "user" for when you are playing games with the PC, with shortcuts to your favorite games.

To enable Windows to keep track of separate settings for each user, you must turn the User Profiles feature on. Doing so sets up Windows to keep track of a separate desktop and Start menu for each user. That desktop and menu can be customized freely without affecting those of any other user.

Enabling User Profiles

1. Click **Start**, point to **Settings**, and click **Control Panel**.
2. Double-click the **Users** icon. The Enable Multiuser Settings Wizard appears (see Figure 13.1).

   If it does not appear, user profiles may already be turned on for this PC. See the following section to add, delete, or configure user settings.

FIGURE 13.1
You'll see this if multiple users are not already set up.

3. Click **Next**. The Add User dialog box appears.

4. Type the name of the first user you want to set up, and then click **Next**.

5. If you want to use a password for this user, type it in the **Password** box, and then again in the **Confirm Password** box. Leave both boxes blank if you don't want to use passwords. Then, click **Next**.

6. On the list that appears (see Figure 13.2), place a check mark next to each item that you want to personalize for this user.

Password Protection?

Using a password for a user profile will not keep others from using your PC because anyone can create a new username at logon. To password-protect your PC, see "Setting and Changing Passwords" later in this chapter.

FIGURE 13.2
Specify which settings should be customizable for this user.

7. Choose how you want the user settings to be managed:

- Choose **Create copies of the current items and their content** to duplicate all the chosen items on the list (Step 6) for each user you create. I recommend you choose this if you are not sure.

- Choose **Create new items to save disk space** to reduce the amount of hard disk space consumed by the feature. This creates new folders only for user content that differs from the default.

8. Click **Next** to continue.

9. Click **Finish**.

10. When prompted to restart Windows, click **Yes**.

11. At the Welcome to Windows logon box, type your username and password and click **OK**. You are now logged on as yourself, and you are ready to set up other users.

Adding Users

After the initial multiuser setup that you went through in the preceding section, you will probably want to add other users. To do so, revisit the Users properties from the Control Panel. This time, instead of the wizard running, a User Settings dialog box appears, as shown in Figure 13.3.

FIGURE 13.3
Add users and manage the settings for existing ones here.

① Click here to add a new user.

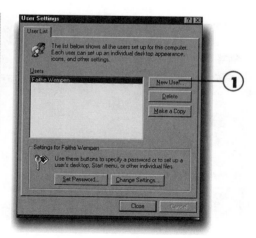

Add a User

1. From the **Control Panel**, double-click the **Users** icon.

2. Click **New User**. The Add User dialog box appears. (This will seem familiar; you saw it in the preceding steps.)

3. Click **Next** to begin.

4. Type the name of the user, and then click **Next**.

5. If you want to use a password for this user, type it into the **Password** box, and then again in the **Confirm Password** box. Leave both boxes blank if you don't want to use passwords. Then, click **Next**.

6. Place a check mark next to each item that you want to personalize for this user.

7. Choose how you want the user settings to be managed, just as you did in the preceding steps. If in doubt, choose **Create copies of the current items and their content**.

8. Click **Next** to continue.

9. Click **Finish**.

10. Click **Close** to close the User Settings dialog box.

You can also create a new user by copying the settings from an existing one. To do so, from the **Users** list select the user to copy and then click **Make a Copy**. The Add User Wizard starts, the same as in the preceding steps, except that the default settings are the ones from the user you are copying.

New users can also set themselves up. When Windows starts and the Welcome to Windows box appears, if you type a new name in the **User** box, Windows Networking will detect that this is a new person and will ask the following:

You have not logged on at this computer before. Would you like this computer to retain your individual settings for use when you log on here in the future?

Click **Yes** to set up that person as a new user on-the-fly. Choosing **No** allows the person to log in to Windows but does not retain any of their settings.

SEE ALSO

➤ *To switch between users, see page 236.*

➤ *To delete a user, see page 236.*

➤ *To change a user's properties, see page 237.*

➤ *To change a user's password, see page 239.*

Working on a Multiuser System

Now that you have some user profiles set up, you can customize your Windows environment freely, confident that nobody else will have to put up with your choice in color schemes or your menu arrangement. The following sections explain how to use and configure a multiuser Windows PC.

Switching Between Users

Each time Windows starts, you are prompted to log in to Windows by providing your username and password. That's how Windows determines whose settings to load.

To change users without restarting the PC, follow these steps:

Switching Users

1. Click **Start** and then click **Log Off** *name*, where *name* is the user currently logged on. The Log Off Windows box appears.

2. Click **Yes**. The Welcome to Windows box appears.

3. Type the username and password (if any), and click **OK**.

Deleting a User

When you delete a user, Windows deletes all the customized settings for that user. Because the settings for each user take up disk space, it is good housekeeping to delete any users who will no longer be using your PC.

Deleting a User

1. From the **Control Panel**, double-click the **Users** icon.

2. Click the user that you want to delete.

3. Click the **Delete** button. A confirmation box appears.

4. Click **Yes**.

5. Click **Close** to close the User Settings dialog box.

Changing a User's Settings

The settings that you specify when you create a user are merely a starting point; you can change them at any time. For example, you may decide that users should not have separate Favorites folders and want to disable personalized settings for that item for each user. Or, you may decide that you don't want separate copies of everything for each user taking up space on your hard disk.

Changing User Settings

1. From the **Control Panel**, double-click the **Users** icon.

2. Click the user whose settings you want to change.

3. Click the **Change Settings** button. The Personalized Items Settings dialog box opens. (This is the same box that you saw in Figure 13.2.)

4. Select or deselect items to be personalized.

5. Choose how you want them personalized (**Create copies of the current items and their contents** or **Create new items to save disk space**).

6. Click **OK**.

7. Click **Close**.

Changing Global Options for User Profiles

The settings you learned about in the preceding section must be set individually for each user. But you can also control a couple of important settings for all users as a whole. You can

- Include desktop icons and Network Neighborhood contents in user settings.

- Include Start menu and Program groups in user settings.

(Those are the actual names of the check boxes, as you can see in Figure 13.4.) If you disable either of these, no user profiles will allow individual versions of those features, even if the individual profile has them turned on.

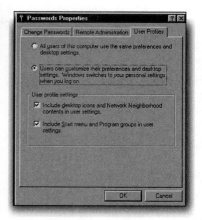

FIGURE 13.4
You can control which settings are available for each user's customization.

Setting Global User Profile Options

1. In the **Control Panel**, double-click the **Passwords** icon.

2. Click the **User Profiles** tab.

3. Select or deselect either of the check boxes in the User-profile settings area. See Figure 13.4.

4. Click **OK**.

Turning Off Multiuser Operation

If you stop sharing your PC with others, you may want to disable the multiuser capability. This can save time because you won't be faced with a logon box every time you start Windows (provided you have not set a Windows logon password).

Turning off multiuser operation does not delete the user profiles that you may have set up, or any settings from those profiles. It simply stops using them and reverts to the original settings that were in place before you turned on multiuser operation. If you later re-enable multiuser operation, all the former users will reappear in the User Settings dialog box's user list.

Turning Off Multiuser Operation

1. In the **Control Panel**, double-click the **Passwords** icon.

2. Click the **User Profiles** tab.

3. Click **All users of this computer use the same preferences and desktop settings**.

4. Click **OK**.

5. When prompted to restart your computer, click **Yes**.

Setting and Changing Passwords

Passwords exist to prevent unauthorized individuals from using a particular PC or other resource, or to prove that someone is who he or she claims to be. If you need that kind of security, they're great. But don't assume that everyone must use passwords simply because Windows prompts for them.

Personally, I don't use passwords at all on my home PCs because there is simply no need. I don't have anything to protect or keep secret from others in my household. If prompted for a password, I leave the box blank. However, your situation may differ. For example, if you work on a network in an office, you probably have a network password that you use to log on to the network. You may also have other passwords that you need to enter each time you start your PC, depending on what kind of equipment your employer has provided and how its security is set up.

Changing a User's Windows Password

When you have user profiles enabled, as you learned earlier in this chapter, Windows always prompts for a username and password at startup. This enables you to specify which user is logging on. You don't have to use a password for this if you don't want to; you can just ignore the Password box. As I stated earlier, the protection offered by a Windows logon password is very minimal because anyone can log on to the computer by creating a new username on-the-fly. So, you may want to save time in your logon by changing your password to be nothing (that is, no characters at all).

You can change your Windows password in either of two places. You can change it from the User Settings dialog box or from the Passwords dialog box. (Both are accessible from the Control Panel.) The following steps show how to do it from the User Settings, which is the slightly more versatile method because it allows you to change the password for any user, not only the one currently logged on.

Change a Windows Logon Password

1. From the **Control Panel**, double-click **Users**.

2. Click the user for whom you want to change the password.

3. Click **Set Password**. The Change Windows Password dialog box opens, as shown in Figure 13.5.

4. Type the old password in the **Old password** box. (You must know the old password or you can't change it.)

5. Type the new password in the **New password** box and then retype it in the **Confirm new password** box.

6. Click **OK**. A message appears that the password has been successfully changed.

7. Click **OK** to close the message.

8. Click **Close**.

Other Passwords

Depending on your network setup, you may also be able to change your network password. Double-click the **Passwords** icon in the **Control Panel**, and look on the **Change Passwords** tab. If the **Change Other Passwords** button is available, click it and change your network or other passwords from there.

You can also set screen saver passwords so that when you step away from your desk for awhile, nobody can use your PC while you are away. See "Using a Screen Saver" in Chapter 9, "Customizing the Screen Appearance," for details.

Alternative Method

If you do not have multi-user operation enabled, you can still change your Windows password. Instead of steps 1–3, double-click **Passwords** in the Control Panel, and then click the **Change Windows Password** button on the **Change Passwords** tab.

SEE ALSO

➤ *To set a screen saver password, see page 171.*

➤ *To use network resources, see page 244.*

Choosing Which Logon to Present at Startup

By default, the logon that appears when you start or restart Windows
is the Windows logon. But you can change that. For example, you
might want your network logon prompt to appear when you start
Windows.

To choose which logon you use, double-click the **Network** icon in
the **Control Panel** and choose a logon from the **Primary Network
Logon** drop-down list on the **Configuration** tab. See Figure 13.6.
You'll be prompted to restart your computer; click defaultYes.

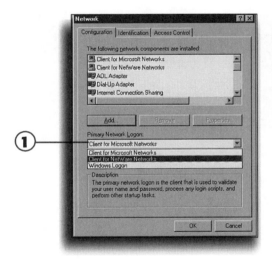

FIGURE 13.6
Choose which logon
should be your
defaultdefault.

① Select a logon.

SEE ALSO

➤ *To work with networks, see page 244.*

chapter 14

Using Network Resources

Accessing Network Files ●

Printing to a Network Printer ●

Finding a Computer on the Network ●

Sharing Your Own Files and Printers ●

Installing Network Components ●

Connecting Computers with Direct ●
Cable Connection

Working with Network Resources

Is your PC connected to a network? If it isn't, it probably will be someday. Networking has exploded in popularity in the last few years, and nowadays, even homes have networks that link their PCs to share files and devices.

The term *network* can refer generically to any situation in which two or more computers are linked. The Internet qualifies as a network, as do local area networks (LANs), wide area networks (WANs), and so on. But in this chapter, I will be focusing mostly on LANs. (You'll learn more about the Internet in later chapters.)

Some LANs are *server-driven*. That is, one computer on the network exists for the sole purpose of keeping the network running and "serving up" files from its hard disk to other computers as requested. The server's hard disk functions as a repository for shared files. In such networks, if you want to share a particular file with your colleagues, the best way is to copy it to a shared network drive or folder. Having a server is desirable because it takes the network processing load off of the other computers. But homes and small businesses may not be able to afford to dedicate one PC to LAN administration.

Permission Needed

You may not always have permission to access every drive, folder, or printer on your network. For example, the network administrator may have set up certain drives or folders for read-only access. That means you can open and examine files there, but you can't make changes to them.

If you are trying to use a network resource but receive messages that you don't have permission, or if you receive a prompt for a password that you don't know, contact your network administrator.

Other networks are serverless, or *peer-to-peer*. In a peer-to-peer network, all the computers are connected to one another without the help of a server, and all equally share the administration duties. Such networks are popular in homes and small businesses where no extra computer can be spared for a server.

Network resources are any files or devices that are directly connected to one PC but that can be used by another through the network. Examples could include a file or folder, a printer, or a modem (with Windows 98 Second Edition; see Chapter 15, "Sharing an Internet Connection"). These devices can be connected either to the server or to any of the individual PCs in the network.

SEE ALSO

➤ *To share a modem, see page 260.*

Accessing Network Files

You can browse shared files on the network through Network Neighborhood. It works just like My Computer, except that it shows you network files instead of local ones.

Browsing the Network with Network Neighborhood

1. Double-click **Network Neighborhood** on the desktop. A window showing the computers on your network appears (see Figure 14.1).

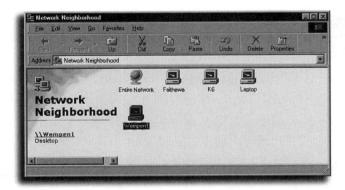

FIGURE 14.1
This network has four computers.

2. Double-click the computer whose files you want to browse. Icons for each of its shared drives appear. Figure 14.2 shows an example.

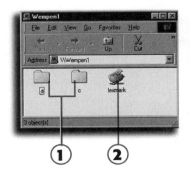

FIGURE 14.2
The shared drives and printers on the selected networked PC.

① Shared drives

② Shared printer

Enabling Sharing

Each shared resource must be set up to be shared. See "Sharing Your Files and Printers" later in this chapter if you need to enable sharing for a device.

3. Double-click the drive you want. Then, work with its files normally, as you would local files on your hard disk (provided you have the needed permissions). See Chapter 5, "Managing Files and Folders."

or

Double-click the printer you want. Then, work with its print queue normally, as you would the queue for your local printer. See Chapter 12, "Managing Fonts and Printers."

In many programs, you can also open files from (and/or save files to) network locations. (For example, all the programs in Microsoft Office allow this.) To do so, open the **Look in** (or **Save in**) drop-down list and choose **Network Neighborhood**. Then, navigate to the drive and folder you want, as you did in the preceding steps. Figure 14.3 shows the Open dialog box from Microsoft Word with the Network Neighborhood selected.

FIGURE 14.3
In some programs, you can browse the network from the Open and Save As dialog boxes.

(1) Network

(2) Computers on the network

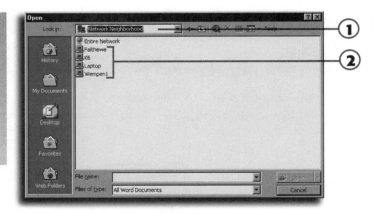

SEE ALSO
➤ *To select which of your own files and printers should be shared, see page 251.*
➤ *To work with files and folders, see page 84.*
➤ *To manage a printer's queue, see page 225.*

Mapping a Network Drive

Not all programs allow you to browse the network freely, as shown in Figure 14.3. Some programs can recognize only local drives. For the benefit of such programs, you can trick Windows into thinking that a particular drive or folder on the network is actually a local drive on your system. This is called *mapping a network drive*. You create a connection that leads all programs from an imaginary new drive letter on your system to the network location you desire. For example, you could assign the drive letter J: to a folder on the server called D:\Arts, so that whenever you display the contents of your J: drive, you are actually displaying the contents of that folder.

Mapping a Network Drive

1. In Network Neighborhood, locate the drive or folder that you want to map.

2. Right-click it and choose **Map network Drive** from the shortcut menu. The Map Network Drive dialog box appears. See Figure 14.4.

3. Open the **Drive** drop-down list and choose the drive letter to use.

4. To reestablish this connection each time you log on to the network, mark the **Reconnect at logon** check box.

5. Click **OK**. The chosen drive or folder opens for browsing.

   As you can see in Figure 14.5, the title bar shows the new drive letter designation, and the Address line shows it, too.

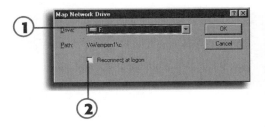

FIGURE 14.4
Select the drive letter that should refer to this location.

① The first free drive letter appears by default.

② Click here to automatically reestablish this connection at startup.

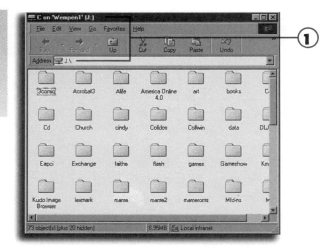

FIGURE 14.5
The C: drive on the computer Wempen1 has been mapped as drive J:.

① Drive designation

After mapping a drive, the new letter appears in all drive listings. For example, Figure 14.6 shows the My Computer window with the networked drive, and Figure 14.7 shows the Open dialog box in a program called Collage (which does not support network browsing), with the J: drive listed on the Drives list.

FIGURE 14.6
You can access the mapped drive from your My Computer window.

① Mapped network drive

SEE ALSO
➤ *To work with the My Computer window, see page 84.*
➤ *To print from a program, see page 60.*

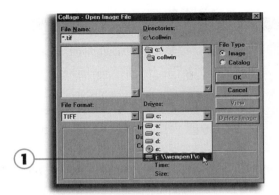

FIGURE 14.7
This program can access the network through the mapped drive.

(1) The mapped drive is a choice on the Drives list.

Printing to a Network Printer

After you set up a network printer (see Chapter 12), it works the same as a local printer in all your applications. Simply select the printer from the Print dialog box in whatever program you are printing from. For example, Figure 14.8 shows the Print dialog box from Word.

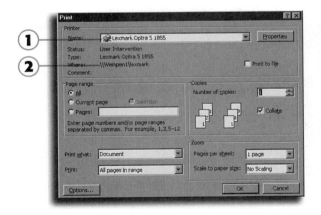

FIGURE 14.8
Select the network printer from the Name drop-down list, the same as you would any printer.

(1) Name drop-down list

(2) Network path to the printer

SEE ALSO
➤ *To set up a network printer, see page 226.*

Finding a Computer on the Network

If you are working on a large LAN with many servers, more computers may be connected than you can easily browse. For example, suppose each department in your company has its own server, and all the servers are linked. You are looking for John Smith's computer, but you don't know what department John Smith is in, so you don't know which server to browse.

Each computer has a name on the network. No fixed naming convention exists, but many companies set up a consistent naming scheme for convenience, such as JSMITH for John Smith's computer.

If you know the name of the computer you want to locate, you can search for it with the Windows Find feature.

Locating a Computer on the Network

1. Click **Start**, point to **Find** and click **Computer**. The Find: Computer dialog box opens.

2. Type the name of the computer into the **Named** box.

   You can enter a partial name if you don't know the whole name. For example, entering SMITH will find SMITH, JSMITH, and SMITH1.

3. Click **Find Now**. A list of computers with names that include the text you typed appears. Figure 14.9 shows the result of searching for the computer named Wempen1 on my network.

FIGURE 14.9
Use **Find** to locate a particular computer.

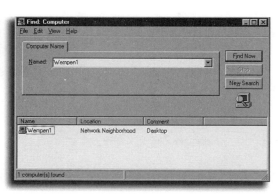

4. (Optional) To browse that computer's contents, double-click it.

Sharing Your Files and Printers

Just being connected to a network does not automatically make any part of your PC accessible to others. By default, nothing of your local PC is shared. You must specify which drives, folders, and/or printers you want to share.

Enabling Sharing

First, you must make sure that your PC is set up to share files and printers in general. This may already be set up, depending on how your network is configured. Follow these steps to check out the status and enable the sharing, if needed.

Enabling Sharing on Your PC

1. From the **Control Panel**, double-click **Network**.

2. Make sure that the list of networking components on the **Configuration** tab includes this item:

   File and printer sharing for Microsoft Networks

   If it does not, see "Installing Network Components" later in this chapter.

3. Click **File and Print Sharing**. The File and Print Sharing dialog box opens. See Figure 14.10.

FIGURE 14.10
Make sure the check boxes are marked for what you want to share.

4. Make sure that both check boxes are marked to share both files and printers.

5. Click **OK**.

6. Click **OK** to close the Network dialog box.

7. If prompted to restart your computer, click **Yes**.

Sharing Specific Devices or Folders

To set up a specific printer, drive, or folder to be shared, right-click it and choose **Sharing**. Then, set up the sharing specifications on the **Sharing** tab.

You have several choices to make when it comes to sharing, as you can see in Figure 14.11:

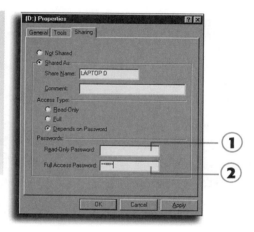

FIGURE 14.11
Set the sharing options for the chosen printer, drive, or folder.

(1) Everyone will have read-only access.

(2) Only those who know this password will have full access.

- **Share Name.** This will be the name that the device is known by on other computers.

- **Access Type: Read-only.** This gives others the right to examine but not change files (or print jobs). **Full** grants full read/write permission. If you choose **Depends on Password**, you must specify two separate passwords: one for read-only access and one for full access.

- **Read-Only Password.** This box is enabled only if you chose Depends on Password for the access type. To give free read-only access to everyone, leave this box empty.

- **Full Access Password.** You can assign a password for full access here. To give everyone free access, leave it empty.

Sharing a Specific Device

1. Right-click the drive, folder, or printer that you want to share, and choose **Sharing**.

2. Make sure that the **Shared As** option button is selected.

3. Type a name for the device in the **Share Name** box. (Type a description in the **Comment** box, if desired.)

4. Choose an access type: **Read-Only**, **Full**, or **Depends on Password**.

5. Enter any passwords you want to use in the **Passwords** section.

6. Click **OK**.

SEE ALSO

➤ *To share an Internet connection, see page 260.*

Installing Network Components

In most businesses, the end user is not responsible for setting up the network components. Your company probably has a computer expert who installs and maintains the network. However, if you have a home network or a small office, you may have to take care of network setup yourself.

Each PC must have a Network Interface Card, or NIC, installed. This can be a circuit card you install (on a desktop PC) or a PCM-CIA card (on a laptop). Most cards come with their own setup software that installs the correct drivers. However, because networks vary, that setup software may not install all the needed network protocols in Windows.

Installing Network Components

1. From the **Control Panel**, double-click **Network**.

2. Check the list of components on the **Configuration** tab. (See Figure 14.12.)

3. If you do not see your NIC listed, run the software that came with it to install it. Then, reboot and return to this dialog box.

4. If you do not see the client you need for your network (Client for Microsoft Networks or Client for Netware Network), do the following:

   a. Click **Add**.

   b. Click **Client**.

   c. Click **Add**.

   d. Click **Microsoft**. A list of Microsoft-provided clients appears, as shown in Figure 14.13.

Sharing Individual Folders

You can specify different sharing rights for various folders on your hard disk. You might, for example, set up the entire drive to be shared Read-Only, but then grant Full rights to a specific folder that contains files that several people will need to work on a project with you.

Protocol? Client?

A *protocol* is a language that computers speak to one another. A network requires that each machine have a common protocol installed so that all the PCs in the network can communicate using a common language. The most common networking protocol is IPS/SPX, but others include NetBEUI and TCP/IP.

You must also have the appropriate driver for your network *client*. This is either the Client for Microsoft Networks or the Client for NetWare Networks, whichever is appropriate for your server software. (If you are running a peer-to-peer network with no server, use Client for Microsoft Networks.)

253

 e. Click the client you need to install.

 f. Click **OK**.

 g. If prompted to insert the Windows 98 disk, do so and click **OK**. You are turned to the Configuration tab when you're finished.

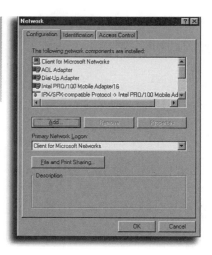

FIGURE 14.12
These are the network components currently installed.

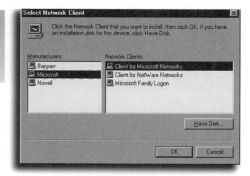

FIGURE 14.13
Select a network client to install.

 5. If you do not see IPX/SPX-compatible protocol on the list, do the following:

  a. Click **Add**.

  b. Click **Protocol**.

  c. Click **Add**.

  d. Click **Microsoft**.

    e. Click **IPX/SPX-compatible protocol**.

    f. Click **OK**.

    g. If prompted to insert the Windows 98 disk, do so and click **OK**. You are turned to the Configuration tab when you're finished.

  6. If you do not see NetBEUI on the list, repeat Step 4, except choose NetBEUI at Step e.

  7. Open the **Primary Network Logon** drop-down list and choose the client for your network (for example, **Client for Microsoft Networks**).

  8. Click **OK**.

  9. If prompted to restart your computer, click **Yes**.

SEE ALSO
➤ *To install new hardware, see page 202.*

➤ *To run a setup program for your new hardware, see page 143.*

Linking to Another PC with Direct Cable Connection

Direct cable connection is a substitute for networking. If you need to transfer files from one PC to another, but you do not have any networking equipment, you can accomplish the transfer by temporarily hooking the two computers together with a null modem cable.

Before you begin, choose which machine should be the *host* and which should be the *guest*. The host computer is the one containing the resources to be accessed; the guest computer is the one that will be accessing those resources. Then, follow these steps.

Connecting Two Computers with Direct Cable Connection

  1. Make sure the Direct Cable Connection feature is installed on each PC.

  2. Shut off both PCs and connect a null modem cable from one PC's serial port to the other. Then, restart both PCs.

    You can also use the parallel port, which provides faster transfer speeds, but a null cable for the parallel port is more expensive. These steps will assume you are using the serial ports.

> **Modem Cable?**
>
> The term *null modem cable* does not have anything to do with modems per se. It simply refers to a cable that provides a direct pass-through of information.
>
> When you hook up most devices via cable, you use a cable with one male end (pins) and one female end (holes). A null modem cable is the same on both ends (female) because it connects from one PC's serial port to the other, and both of the serial ports are male.

255

Is It There?

The Direct Cable Connection feature is not installed by default when you install Windows 98; to install it, refer to "Adding and Removing Windows Components" in Chapter 8, "Installing New Programs."

If you are not sure whether it is installed, click **Start**, point to **Programs**, point to **Accessories**, point to **Communications**, and survey the programs available there; if installed, Direct Cable Connection should appear on that menu.

3. On the host machine, click **Start**, point to **Programs**, point to **Accessories**, point to **Communications**, and click **Direct Cable Connection**. The Direct Cable Connection Wizard starts.

4. Click **H**ost and then click **N**ext. A list of available ports appears, as shown in Figure 14.14.

5. Click the port you want to use, and then click **N**ext.

6. Click **Finish**.

7. On the guest computer, click **Start**, point to **Programs**, point to **Accessories**, point to **Communications**, and click **Direct Cable Connection**. The Direct Cable Connection Wizard starts.

8. Choose **G**uest and then click **N**ext.

9. Choose the port to use and then click **N**ext.

10. Click **Finish**.

11. Wait for the connection to be established. When it is, the contents of the host computer appear in a window, the same as if you had connected via Network Neighborhood. See Figure 14.15. You can work with the files normally from there.

12. When you are finished working on the guest PC with the host's files, click **Close** to close the connection.

13. Back on the host machine, display the Direct Cable Connection box and click **Close** to close the connection on that end.

14. Shut down both PCs and disconnect the cable.

FIGURE 14.14
These ports are available for use.

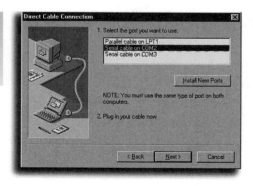

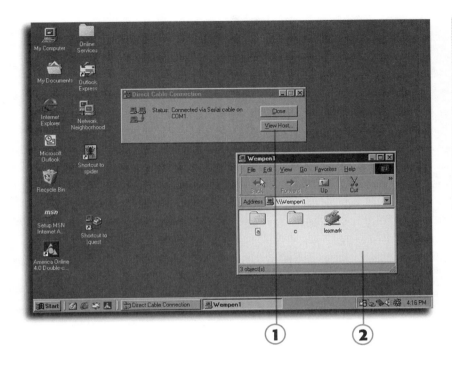

FIGURE 14.15
This window looks like a
Network connection, but
it is actually established
via Direct Cable
Connection.

① Click here at any time
to reopen the window
containing the host's
files.

② Window containing the
host PC's shared files.

SEE ALSO
➤ *To shut down a PC, see page 28.*
➤ *To work with files and folders, see page 84.*

chapter
15

Sharing an Internet Connection

Introducing Internet Connection Sharing

If you have Windows 98 Second Edition, you can take advantage of its capability to share an Internet connection over your home (or office) network. This is one of those "dream come true" features that folks have been asking Microsoft to provide for years; now, it's a reality. Multiple PCs can use the same Internet connection (through a single phone line) and all be online at the same time.

The only drawback is speed. If several computers try to send or receive information from the Internet at once, nobody's request will be processed as quickly as a single request would be. It's not a big issue if the shared Internet connection is a very fast and powerful one (ADSL, cable modem, satellite), but with a shared 56K modem, be prepared for some delays. The speed is also limited by the network connection itself.

To use Internet Connection Sharing (ICS), your PCs must be networked. That means they must have network cards installed and networking must be set up in Windows 98. (You learned about that in Chapter 14, "Using Network Resources.")

When you set up ICS, it uses those network connections to relay Internet data. For example, suppose Tom's PC has a very fast Internet connection (suppose it's a cable modem—lucky Tom). Gloria's computer, which is also on the network, connects to the Internet through Tom's computer. It's kind of like sharing a network printer; one computer "owns" the device but all the others can use it.

How It Works: The Techie Version

For those of you who care about this sort of thing: The PC with the Internet connection provides private IP addresses and name resolution services for the other computers on the network, the same as if it were a service provider. In a sense, it is a service provider for its Internet connection.

When a PC on the network sends data to the Internet, its private IP address is transmitted to the computer controlling the connection, which translates it to its own Internet IP address and sends it on to the Internet. When the results come back, the controlling computer translates the IP address back again and routes it back to the PC to which it belongs.

Installing Internet Connection Sharing

The Internet Connection Sharing (ICS) feature is not installed with a default installation of Windows 98 Second Edition; therefore, you will probably need to install it. You install ICS on the *gateway* PC—that is, the one that has the modem or other connection. The machines that will use the connection through the network do not have to be running Windows 98 Second Edition; they can have Windows 95, Windows 98, or Windows NT.

Installing the ICS Component

Internet Connection Sharing is a Windows accessory, so you install it the same as you would install any other accessory program—from Add/Remove Programs. Then, you must set it up on the gateway PC and create a disk that sets up the other PCs. The following steps show how.

Installing Internet Connection Sharing

1. Click **Start**, point to **Settings**, and click **Control Panel**.

2. Double-click **Add/Remove Programs**.

3. Click the **Windows Setup** tab.

4. Click **Internet Tools** on the list.

5. Click **Details**.

6. Place a check mark next to **Internet Connection Sharing**. See Figure 15.1. (If a check mark is already there, click **Cancel** and go on to the next section.)

FIGURE 15.1
Select the Internet Connection Sharing feature to install.

7. Click **OK**.

8. Click **OK** again.

9. If prompted, insert the Windows 98 Second Edition CD into your drive and click **OK**.

10. Wait for the Internet Connection Sharing Wizard to start. When it does, click **Next** to begin.

11. If you see a list of adapters, select the adapter you want to use for the shared connection. See Figure 15.2. (You might not see this screen at all, depending on your setup.) Then, click **Next**.

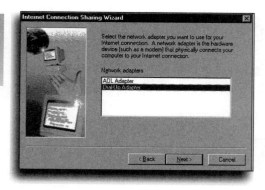

FIGURE 15.2
Select the adapter to share.

Choosing an Adapter

For most people the right choice will be the Dial-Up Adapter, but if you have some special kind of Internet connection, it might be something else (such as AOL adapter if you use America Online).

12. If asked what type of connection you have (dial-up or network, click the appropriate button and click **Next**. (You might not be asked.)

13. When you see a message that the wizard will now create a client configuration disk, click **Next**.

14. When prompted, place a blank disk (or one that contains nothing you want to keep) in your floppy drive and click **OK**.

15. When prompted, remove the disk from the drive and click **OK**.

16. Click **Finish**.

17. When prompted to restart your computer, click **Yes**.

SEE ALSO

➤ *To add/remove other Windows components, see page 140.*

➤ *To set up a network, see page 253.*

If you ever want to remove Internet Connection Sharing, return to the Add/Remove Programs dialog box (Steps 1–4) and remove the check mark from the Internet Connection Sharing check box.

Configuring Internet Connection Sharing

The next step is to set up the gateway PC. The default settings may work fine, so this procedure may not be necessary, but it never hurts to check out the settings and confirm that they are as you want them to be.

Configuring ICS Settings on the Gateway PC

1. Click **Start,** point to **Settings,** and click **Control Panel**.

2. Double-click the **Internet Options** icon.

3. Click the **Connections** tab.

4. Click the **Sharing** button under LAN Settings. The Internet Connection Sharing dialog box opens. See Figure 15.3.

FIGURE 15.3
Configure Internet connection sharing here.

5. If the **Enable Internet Connection Sharing** check box is not marked, click to select it.

6. To show an icon for it in the System tray area, select the **Show Icon in Taskbar** check box.

I recommend doing this, and I'll show you how to use that icon later in this chapter to control the connection.

7. To change the adapter you use to connect to the Internet, choose a different one from the **Connect to the Internet Using** drop-down list. This should not normally be necessary because you chose it when you installed the feature.

No Sharing Button?

If you don't see a sharing button even after you have installed ICS, see the section "No Sharing Button" later in this chapter for troubleshooting help.

8. To change the adapter you use to connect to your local network, choose a different network adapter from the **Connect to My Home Network Using** drop-down list. This should not be necessary because you probably have only one network adapter in your PC.

9. Click **OK**.

Configuring Other Computers in Your Home Network

Use the disk that you created when you installed the Internet Connection Sharing earlier in this chapter to set up each of the other PCs. You can set up any Windows 95 or Windows 98 PC with this disk.

Before you go through this procedure, make sure that the gateway PC is turned on, logged on to the network, and connected to the Internet.

Setting Up Another PC to Use the ICS Connection

1. Put the ICS Setup disk that you created into the drive and display its file list.

2. Double-click the **icsclet** icon (looks like a globe). The Browse Connection Setup Wizard starts.

3. Click **Next** to begin.

4. Click **Next** again to allow the Wizard to check and change your browser settings.

5. To try out the connection right now, mark the **To Immediately Connect** check box.

6. Click **Finish**.

Sharing the Connection

To share the Internet connection from one of the other PCs, first establish the connection on the gateway PC. Then, on the other PC, start Internet Explorer, your email program, or whatever Internet

---

Windows NT or Windows 2000

The setup disk won't work with Windows NT PCs, but Windows NT machines should work automatically with the connection without special setup because NT is a more network-aware operating system. If the Internet connection does not work automatically on the NT machine, run the Internet Connection Wizard in Windows NT and set Internet Explorer to connect through the LAN that way.

program you want to use. The connection establishes itself automatically through the network.

Managing the ICS Connection from the Gateway PC

When you right-click the ICS icon in your System tray (see Figure 15.4), the shortcut menu gives you four options. Use any of these as needed:

- **Status.** Tells you how many computers are using the Internet connection.
- **Options.** Reopens the same Internet Connection Sharing dialog box you learned about earlier in this chapter (see Figure 15.3).
- **Disable Internet Connection Sharing.** Temporarily prevents other computers from sharing your Internet connection. Right-click and choose Enable Internet Connection Sharing to allow it again later.
- **Hide Taskbar Icon.** Just what the names says—it hides the icon in the system tray.

FIGURE 15.4
Manage your ICS connection from the System tray icon.

Troubleshooting ICS Problems

If not everything goes smoothly for you, see whether one of the following sections has the answer.

No Sharing Button

Installing ICS should place a Sharing button in your Internet Properties dialog box (on the Connections tab). If you don't see one, you need to update two files on your PC: `Inetcpl.cpl` and

Inetcplc.dll. This is a confirmed bug in Windows 98 Second Edition. Follow these steps to take care of it:

Installing a Sharing Button

1. Click **Start** and then click **Run**.

2. Type `sfc.exe` and click **OK**.

3. Click **Extract One File from Installation Disk**.

4. Type `inetcpl.cpl` in the **Specify the System File You Would Like to Restore** box.

5. Click **Start**.

6. In the **Restore From** box, type the drive letter and path to the Windows 98 Second Edition files. (For example, if your CD-ROM drive is E, it might be `E:\Win98`.)

7. In the **Save File In** box, type `c:\Windows\System`.

8. Click **OK** when prompted for a backup folder.

9. Click **OK**.

10. Repeat Steps 6 through 9 to restore the `Inetcplc.dll` file, too.

Other Computers Can't Access the Internet Connection

If your network seems to be running fine but your other computers can't use the gateway's Internet connection, the problem is probably a lack of a TCP/IP pathway between them.

Networks exchange information between PCs using protocols. Protocols are like languages—the two computers must speak the same language if they are to communicate. Normally, they can communicate using any of several languages (TCP/IP, IPX/SPX, NetBEUI). But when sharing the Internet, both computers must use a specific language: TCP/IP. Even if your network works perfectly without TCP/IP in other ways, you must make sure that TCP/IP is installed on both machines and bound to your network adapter.

On some networks, ICS won't work unless Internet Explorer on the gateway PC is set up to automatically dial the connection whenever Internet Explorer is opened. To set this up, in Internet Explorer open the **Tools** menu and click **Internet Options**. On the **Connections** tab, choose **Always Dial My Default Connection**.

SEE ALSO

➤ *To add protocols such as TCP/IP and bind them to specific adapters, see page xx (Installing network components, ch 14)*

Need More Help?

If you are stumped as to why you can't get ICS running, check out the Microsoft Knowledge Base at `http://support.microsoft.com/support`. Search for help with Windows 98 using the keyword **ICS**.

You can also call Microsoft technical support at (425) 635-7222 for help. (You get 90 days of free technical support with Windows 98 Second Edition.)

SEE ALSO

➤ *To search for help articles online, see page 43.*

chapter

16

Traveling with a Laptop

Conserving Battery Power   •

Controlling PCMCIA cards   •

Synchronizing Files with My Briefcase   •

Hardware Profiles   •

Laptops and Windows 98

More and more people these days are opting for the convenience and portability of a laptop computer. Even people who don't travel can take advantage of the small size and go-anywhere flexibility.

Laptops present a few special challenges in Windows 98, and you'll learn about them in this chapter. Unlike regular computers, for example, a laptop has a battery that can be used to power the PC when no electrical outlet is available. And almost all laptops have a special slot called a PCMCIA into which you can insert credit-card–sized devices such as modems and network cards. In this chapter, we'll take a look at the laptop's special hardware and you'll learn how to control it.

Some people who have a laptop also have a desktop PC, and they sometimes need to transfer files between the two. This chapter also explains a feature called My Briefcase that can help synchronize files between PCs simply and effectively.

Other Portable PCs

Laptop computers are just like regular computers except for their portability. However, a variety of other, smaller devices are available that run on different operating systems, such as Windows CE. These hand-held devices are often called PDAs, or Personal Digital Assistants. Their primary function is to store contact information and scheduling data, but some of them also have games, email readers, and even mini-versions of popular Microsoft applications such as Word, Excel, and PowerPoint.

To transfer data between a PC (laptop or desktop) and one of these handheld computing devices, consult the documentation that came with the device. I have a Palm III, for example, and to sync it with Outlook, I place it in its cradle and push a button on the cradle. Each device works a little differently, however.

Controlling Power Management Settings

The biggest issue for most laptop users is battery life. The computer's battery never seems to last long enough before it needs recharging. Some people carry extra batteries when they travel, but laptop batteries can be expensive ($200 or more for some models) and heavy (up to several pounds).

The intelligent use of power-management features in Windows can help you stretch your battery life as much as possible. These power-management features shut off the computer's screen and hard disk after a certain number of idle minutes so that the battery is not being used up when you aren't actively working. The screen and hard disk spring wake up immediately when you press a key or move the mouse.

Different power-management strategies may be appropriate in different situations. It can be rather annoying to have the screen black out if you pause to think for a moment, so you probably will not *always* want the most conservative settings. For example, if you are on an airplane and you need to make your only battery last for a 5-hour flight, you want to be extremely conservative with power. On the other hand, if you have an extra battery with you on that flight, you could afford to be more liberal and let the monitor and hard disk stay active longer. Windows lets you create multiple power-management schemes and choose which scheme is most appropriate for a given situation.

You can also set alarms and indicators that warn you when your battery is getting low so that you can change it or switch to AC power (or simply shut down to avoid losing data).

SEE ALSO

➤ *To set a screen saver password, see page 171.*

➤ *To set and change your Windows password, see page 239.*

Creating and Editing Power Schemes

Windows comes with three power schemes. The one you pick depends on what kind of computer you have and how you use it:

- **Home/Office Desk.** Use this for a desktop PC or a laptop that is docked in a docking station.

- **Portable/Laptop.** Use this for a laptop that is not docked.

- **Always On.** Use this for a desktop PC that you leave turned on all the time.

You can customize any of these schemes, or you can create your own schemes.

When you work with power schemes on a laptop, you see two sets of drop-down lists for each setting, as shown in Figure 16.1. On a desktop PC, you see only a single drop-down list for each one because the desktop PC does not have a battery. On a desktop PC, you also will not have all the tabs shown in Figure 16.1; you will see only the Power Schemes and the Advanced tab.

What's a Docking Station?

A docking station is a desktop PC case that the laptop slides into. It has an external monitor, keyboard, and mouse, so it looks and feels almost like a regular desktop PC. Having a docking station is the next-best thing to having two computers. It gives you the flexibility of having both a desktop unit at your desk and a laptop that you can disconnect and take with you when you travel.

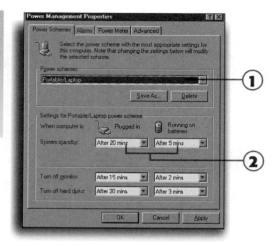

Setting a Power Scheme

1. From the Control Panel, double-click **Power Management**.

2. Open the **Power schemes** drop-down list and choose the
   appropriate scheme. For most laptops, it would be
   Portable/Laptop.

3. In the **System standby** section, set the amount of idle time
   before the system goes on standby, both when plugged in and
   when using batteries.

   In Figure 16.1, for example, it is set to 20 minutes when plugged
   in and 5 minutes for batteries.

4. From their drop-down lists, set the amount of idle time for turning off the monitor and turning off the hard disks (see Figure
   16.1).

5. (Optional) To save your settings as a new scheme, click the **Save
   As** button. Enter a scheme name and click **OK**.

6. Click **OK** to close the Power Management Properties box.

Setting Power Alarms and Indicators

Your power scheme will do its best to preserve battery power, but
eventually your battery will run low and require recharging. The
Alarms tab in the Power Management Properties dialog box enables
you to set alarms that warn you when the battery is getting low.

As you can see in Figure 16.2, you can set two alarms: Low Battery and Critical Battery. You can define when these will go off and what will happen.

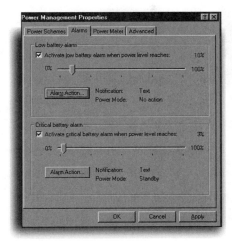

When setting the action for an alarm, you can choose either **Standby** or **Shutdown**. *Standby* suspends the computer's operation but allows it to wake up again with a keypress or mouse movement. *Shutdown* shuts the computer off completely so that you will need to restart when you return to it. If you shut down, your PC stops using the battery altogether; if you stand by, it uses only a tiny amount of battery power.

Suspend to Disk
Some laptops have a "suspend to disk" feature that copies the contents of memory to disk. This allows the computer to stand by instead of shutting down, even when the battery is almost completely drained. Consult your laptop's manual to see whether you have this feature, and if so, how to activate it.

Setting Battery Alarms

1. From the Control Panel, double-click **Power Management**.

2. Click the **Alarms** tab.

3. To use the low battery alarm, make sure its check box is marked.

4. Drag the slider bar beneath it to a percentage of battery life that should trigger the alarm. (The default is 10%.)

5. Click the low battery alarm's **Alarm Action** button. The Low Battery Alarm Actions dialog box opens, as shown in Figure 16.3.

FIGURE 16.3
Specify what should happen when the alarm goes off.

What to Pick?

I recommend that you set the Low Battery Alarm to **no action** (in other words, leave the check box in Step 7 deselected). For the Critical Battery Alarm, you may wish to shut down or stand by.

6. Select or deselect the Notification check boxes as desired:

   - **Sound alarm.** Emits an audible beep.

   - **Display message.** Presents a warning box onscreen.

7. If you want an action to be taken, select the **When the alarm goes off, the computer will** check box, and then choose either **Standby** or **Shutdown** from the drop-down list.

8. (Optional) To shut down or stand by even if a program is not responding, mark the check box to that effect.

9. Click **OK** to return to the Alarm tab.

10. To use the Critical Battery Alarm, make sure its check box is marked.

11. Drag its slider bar to a percentage that should trigger its alarm. (The default is 3 percent.)

12. Click the critical alarm's **Alarm Action** button and configure the alarm action the same as you did in steps 6–9.

13. Click **OK** to close the Power Management Properties box.

Viewing the Power Meter

By default on a laptop, a power icon appears in the System tray. When the laptop is connected to electrical current, the symbol is a plug; when it's running on battery power, the symbol is a battery. To turn off this icon, on the **Advanced** tab of the Power Management Properties box, deselect the **Always show icon on the taskbar** check box.

You can get information about the battery's power status on the Power Meter tab of that dialog box, as shown in Figure 16.4.

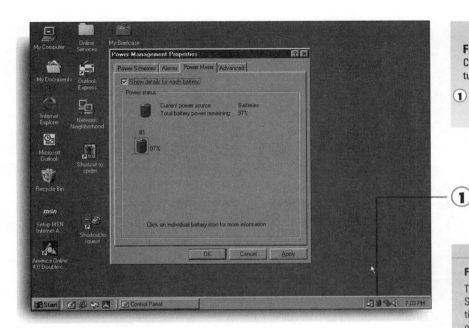

FIGURE 16.4
Check the battery's status here.

1 Battery icon in the System tray

Setting Wakeup Options

You can set Windows to prompt for a password whenever the computer is waking up from Standby mode. This acts somewhat like the password on a screen saver, which was discussed in Chapter 9, "Customizing the Screen Appearance," except that the password it wants is your Windows password. To do so, on the **Advanced** tab of the Power Management Properties dialog box, select the **Prompt for password when computer goes off standby** check box.

Controlling PCMCIA Devices

Windows 98 manages PCMCIA devices (PC cards) for you, so you don't have to run any special management program for them. And unlike other devices, you don't have to wait until the PC is off to plug in a PC card; it can be inserted at any time.

Force It?

The setting described in Step 8 has some ramifications that may not be obvious. If a program is waiting for you to answer a dialog box question (such as `Save changes to your document?`), the program is considered unresponsive to shutting down. Marking the check box in Step 8 will allow Windows to shut down anyway, even if a program is waiting for an answer.

This can be good because if your system is going to shut down shortly anyway because it is out of power, a controlled shutdown is better than an uncontrolled one. (During a controlled shutdown, Windows closes all open files so that you don't have file corruption potential.) But it also doesn't give you the opportunity to respond to a prompt that might save your work.

When you insert a PC card, Windows detects it and you may hear an audible beep. If you are inserting it for the first time, Windows detects it and walks you through its setup. (See Chapter 11, "Installing Hardware," for hardware installation info.)

SEE ALSO

➤ *To set up new hardware, see page 203.*

To manage your PC cards, double-click the **PC Card (PCMCIA)** icon in the Control Panel. Or, if you have a PC Card icon in your System tray, double-click that instead. (See Figure 16.5.)

FIGURE 16.5
Work with PC cards here.

① PC Card icon in System tray

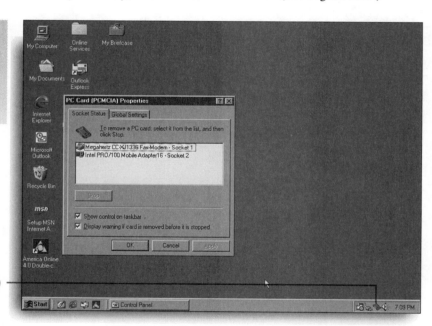

Although you can insert a PC card at any time, you should not remove one as freely. The device might be in use, and you could corrupt files or harm the device by removing it before it has stopped its current action. To ensure that a device has stopped, use the following procedure prior to removing it.

No Icon?

If you don't have an icon in the system tray, select the **Show control on taskbar** check box in the PC Card (PCMCIA) Properties box to place one there in the future.

Stopping a PC Card

1. From the Control Panel, double-click the **PC Card (PCMCIA)** icon.

2. Click the device you want to stop.

3. Click the **S**top button.

4. Wait for a message to appear telling you it is safe to remove the card.

5. Remove the card.

6. Click **OK** to close the dialog box.

The exact procedure for physically removing a PC card varies depending on the laptop model, but most laptops have separate eject buttons for each PC card slot.

Synchronizing Files with My Briefcase

If you use both a desktop and a laptop—or different computers of any type—you will appreciate the My Briefcase feature in Windows. It enables you to synchronize the copies of files between PCs.

For example, suppose you are working on a report at work, and you want to take the latest draft home with you over the weekend. You copy the report from your desktop computer to the Briefcase on your laptop (using either a disk or your LAN). Then, you work on the report at home, and when you return to the office, you synchronize your Briefcase, copying the latest version back to the desktop to overwrite the older version.

Copying Files to My Briefcase

The first step in using My Briefcase is to copy the files from the PC containing the files (the *main PC*) to the My Briefcase folder on the computer that you will be working with (the *remote PC*). You can either use a disk or your local area network.

Copying Files to My Briefcase with a Disk

1. Double-click the My Briefcase icon on the main PC's desktop. The My Briefcase folder opens.

   If you see an introductory box, as shown in Figure 16.6, click **F**inish.

Install It

The Briefcase feature is not installed by default in Windows 98. It needs to be installed on both PCs. To install the Briefcase feature, use Add/Remove Programs, as you learned in Chapter 8, "Installing New Programs."

FIGURE 16.6
You'll see this box the first time you open My Briefcase on the PC.

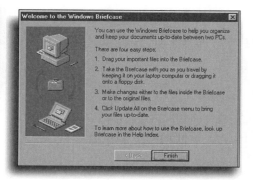

2. Copy the files you want to work with into the My Briefcase folder.

   Copy files to it the same as you would copy any other files from one folder to another. Figure 16.7 shows the My Briefcase window with four files copied into it.

FIGURE 16.7
The My Briefcase folder is like any other folder except for a few different toolbar buttons.

① Buttons unique to the My Briefcase window

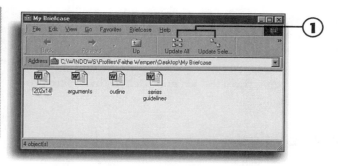

3. Close the My Briefcase window.
4. Insert a blank disk into your floppy drive.
5. Drag the **My Briefcase** icon from the desktop onto the **A: drive** icon in the My Computer window. The entire briefcase is moved there.
6. Insert the disk into the remote PC and display its contents. You'll see a My Briefcase folder there.
7. Double-click the My Briefcase folder on the A: drive. The My Briefcase window appears, listing the copied files. Use these files for your editing work.

If you use the disk method above, you must edit the files from the floppy disk and then transfer that same floppy disk back to your main PC later for synchronization.

If you are lucky enough to have a network connection between the PCs, use the following procedure instead, which is simpler and does not require a floppy disk.

Copying Files to My Briefcase on a Network

1. Make sure both PCs are logged on to the network and that file sharing is enabled on the main PC (the one containing the files).

2. Double-click the **My Briefcase** icon on the *remote* PC's desktop. The My Briefcase folder opens.

   If you see an introductory box, click **Finish**.

3. Still on the remote PC, open **Network Neighborhood** and navigate to the files you want to copy.

4. Drag the files from the Network Neighborhood window to the My Briefcase window.

Now, you can disconnect from the network and take the remote PC with you. Edit the files in My Briefcase while you are on the road. Then, use the procedure in the following section to synchronize them when you get back.

> **Yes, the Remote One**
> In the preceding procedure, you began at the main PC's briefcase, but here you must begin at the remote PC's.

SEE ALSO

➤ *To copy files between folders, see page 90.*

➤ *To work with Network Neighborhood, see page 245.*

➤ *To enable file sharing, see page 251.*

Synchronizing Briefcase Files

When you synchronize files, you overwrite the originals with the updated versions from My Briefcase. You can update all the files from the briefcase or only selected ones.

To see which files in the briefcase need updating, view the My Briefcase window in Details view. The Status column gives you the answer, as shown in Figure 16.8.

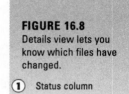

FIGURE 16.8
Details view lets you know which files have changed.

① Status column

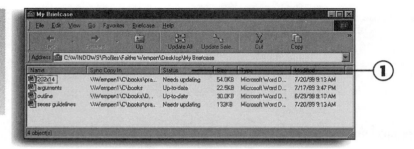

When you are ready to synchronize, use one of the following procedures, depending on whether you are using the disk or the network method.

Synchronizing Briefcase Files from Disk

1. Insert the floppy disk containing the briefcase files into the main PC.

2. Display the content of the A: drive and drag the **My Briefcase** icon onto the desktop, moving it back there.

3. Double-click **My Briefcase**, opening it.

4. Do one of the following:

   • To update all files, click **Update All** or open the **Briefcase** menu and choose **Update All**.

   • To update only certain files, select them and then click **Update Selection,** or open the **Briefcase** menu and choose **Update Selection**.

5. Examine the report in the Update My Briefcase window (see Figure 16.9), to make sure it lists the actions you want to perform.

FIGURE 16.9
Modified files will replace the originals; unmodified ones will be deleted.

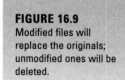
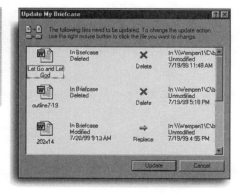

6. Click **Update**.

The following steps show the network method:

Synchronizing Briefcase Files from the Network

1. Make sure both PCs are connected to the network.

2. Double-click **My Briefcase** on the remote PC, opening its window.

3. Do one of the following:
   - To update all files, click **Update All,** or open the **Briefcase** menu and choose **Update All**.
   - To update only certain files, select them and then click **Update Selection,** or choose **Briefcase, Update Selection**.

4. Examine the report in the Update My Briefcase window (see Figure 16.9), to make sure it lists the actions you want to perform.

5. Click **Update**.

If you decide that you want to discard a particular revision in the briefcase, simply delete it as you would delete a file from any folder.

If you want to keep a revision but save it separately from the original, select it and then open the **Briefcase** menu and choose **Split from Original**.

Read Only

If a message appears that some of the files are read-only and were not updated, that may indicate that the files that needed to be updated were in use on the main PC.

part

IV

USING THE INTERNET

chapter
17

Setting Up Online Connectivity

Checking Your Modem

Unless you are connecting to the Internet through a network, you will need a modem. A modem uses your telephone line to connect to an online service or an Internet provider.

Most modems these days are Plug and Play; Windows detects and configures them automatically when you install them. (Look back at Chapter 11, "Installing Hardware," if needed, for hardware installation help.)

To make sure your modem is installed and is working correctly, go through the following procedure.

Checking Modem Operation

1. From the Control Panel, double-click **System**.
2. On the **Device Manager** tab, click the plus sign (+) next to **Modem**. A list of installed modems appears.

FIGURE 17.1
Browse the list of installed modems on your system.

(1) The modem should be listed here.

(2) No warning symbols should be next to it.

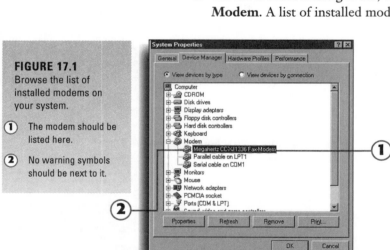

3. Locate and click the modem you want to check.

   If you see a red X or a yellow exclamation point next to the modem, a problem exists with its installation; see Chapter 25, "Troubleshooting Problems," for help.
4. Click **Properties**. The properties for the modem appear.
5. Look on the **General** tab in the **Device status** area. It should read: This device is working properly.

6. Click **OK**, closing the modem properties, and then click **OK** again, closing the system properties.

7. From the **Control Panel**, double-click **Modems**. The Modems Properties box appears.

8. Click the **Diagnostics** tab. Click the entry in the Port column for your modem, as shown in Figure 17.2.

FIGURE 17.2
Choose the port for the modem that you want to check out.

① Port for the modem

9. Click **More Info**.

Windows checks the modem by sending it certain commands and noting the responses. If the modem is working correctly, results appear in a More Info box, as shown in Figure 17.3. If an error message appears instead, a problem exists with the modem.

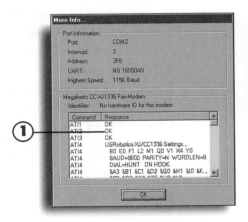

FIGURE 17.3
This modem is functioning properly.

① OK on at least some lines indicates that the modem is working.

10. Click **OK**, and then click **OK** again.

If you ran into any problems or error messages in the above procedure, something is wrong with the modem. Perhaps it is not installed correctly, or perhaps it has a resource conflict with another device. See Chapter 25 for troubleshooting help.

If your modem passes all the preceding tests, but you still can't connect to the Internet or your online service, check out the section "Troubleshooting Connection Problems" later in this chapter.

SEE ALSO

➤ *To troubleshoot problems with modems and other devices, see page 453.*

Running the Internet Connection Wizard

The Internet Connection Wizard (ICW) automates the process of setting up your PC for Internet connectivity. If you don't have an Internet account yet, it can suggest a service provider in your area. If you already have an account, it can help you set up your PC to use it.

The first time you run Internet Explorer on the PC, the ICW runs automatically. You may also have an icon for it on your desktop. If not, you can access it from the Start menu. (Click **Start**, point to **Programs**, then to **Accessories, Internet Tools**, and then click **Internet Connection Wizard**.)

The first screen of the ICW (see Figure 17.4) invites you to choose one of three options:

America Online

If you want to use America Online, run the setup program on your America Online disk. Do not go through the Internet Connection Wizard. America Online's software is separate and different.

- **I want to sign up for a new Internet account. (My telephone line is connected to my modem.)** Choose this if you do not have an Internet account and do not know which Internet Service Provider (ISP) you want to use. The wizard will provide several offers from which you can choose.

- **I want to transfer my existing Internet account to this computer. (My telephone line is connected to my modem.)** Choose this if you already have an Internet account with a national provider such as MSN or Concentric Network, and you want to use the same account on this computer.

- **I want to set up my Internet connection <u>m</u>anually, or I want to connect through a local area network (LAN).** Choose this if you want to share an Internet connection on your LAN (see Chapter 15, "Sharing an Internet Connection") or if you use a local ISP that isn't likely to be on Microsoft's list of providers.

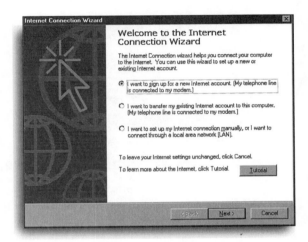

FIGURE 17.4
Select the option that most closely matches your situation.

Depending on which option you choose, skip to the appropriate section that follows.

SEE ALSO

➤ *To learn more about TCP/IP, IPX/SPX, and other network protocols, see page 253.*

➤ *To share an Internet connection through a LAN, see page 260.*

Setting Up a New Internet Account

If you choose to sign up for a new account from the Internet Connection Wizard (see Figure 17.4), it dials a toll-free number that retrieves a current listing of available ISPs in your area.

Review the offers for the various providers (see Figure 17.5), select one, and then work through the wizard to sign up for the service.

Disabling File and Printer Sharing

At some point during the Internet setup process, you may see a warning that file and printer sharing is running on the same TCP/IP connection you will use to access the Internet. It lets you know that the file and printer sharing will be disabled. Click **OK** to continue, and then click **OK** to restart your computer if prompted. When you restart, the Internet Connection Wizard picks up where you left off automatically.

File and printer sharing should still work even after you have disabled its association with TCP/IP; it will simply work with one of the other network protocols instead, such as IPX/SPX. See Chapter 14, "Using Network Resources," for more information about networking.

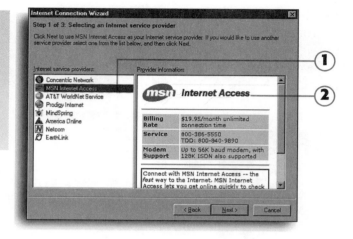

FIGURE 17.5
Compare the offers presented, and then click **Next** to continue through the wizard to sign up.

(1) Selected provider

(2) Current offering

Not a Comprehensive List

The list of providers you see includes only providers who have made arrangements with Microsoft to appear on the list. Most of these are national providers, such as MSN (Microsoft Network), Netcom, and EarthLink. Most local providers will not appear.

I personally use a local service provider in the Indianapolis area: Iquest. (I chose it because it offers really good prices.) You won't find out about local ISPs from the wizard, however. Check your local newspaper or ask at a local computer store to find out what providers offer service in your area. Then, call a local provider and ask for a startup kit. The kit will come with directions for setting up your connection.

Setting Up an Existing Internet Account

Choosing the second option from the Internet Connection Wizard (see Figure 17.4) dials the same toll-free number as in the preceding section and retrieves a similar list of providers. Figure 17.6 shows the list that came up on my PC. If your provider is listed—great. Click it. If not, choose **My Internet service provider is not listed**.

If your provider is one of the ones listed, select it and click **Next**, and the Wizard will dial your provider and help you configure the connection. The rest of the steps in the Wizard depend on the provider; Figure 17.7 shows what information is requested by Concentric Network, for example.

If your provider is not listed, a message appears letting you know that you will need to configure the connection manually. (See the following section to learn how to do that.)

Setting Up the Internet Connection Manually

Most people will end up going through the connection setup manually because at this time, the Internet Connection Wizard supports relatively few service providers directly. But don't worry—manual setup is not difficult.

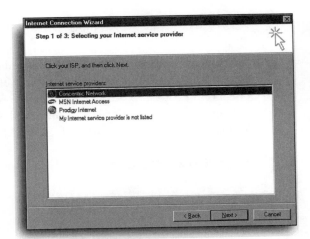

FIGURE 17.6
The wizard presents a list of providers in your area. (As before, however, this list is not comprehensive.)

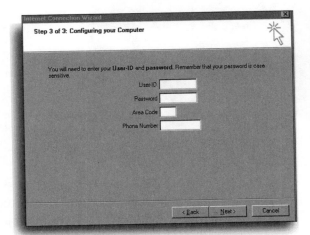

FIGURE 17.7
If your provider is listed, the wizard walks you through transferring your settings to this computer.

To set up a new or existing account on this PC, you will need the following information from your service provider:

- The telephone number for your modem to dial.

- Your username (such as jdoe199).

- Your password (which may be case-sensitive).

- The incoming and outgoing mail servers to use. These will probably be something like `pop.mysite.net` for the incoming and `smtp.mysite.net` for the outgoing.

- The IP address and/or DNS server address to use, if your provider requires that you use specific ones. These will be four sets of numbers separated by periods, such as 198.70.36.70.

Then, plug that information into the blanks provided as you work through the wizard.

If you need to enter a specific IP address and/or DNS server address, click the **Advanced** button on the Step 1 of 3 screen. An Advanced Connection Properties box opens. Click the **Addresses** tab and then enter the IP address and/or the Primary and Secondary DNS server addresses on that tab, as shown in Figure 17.8.

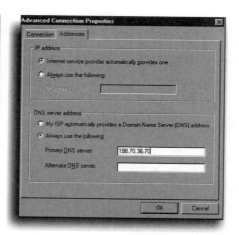

FIGURE 17.8
If your ISP requires specific IP or DNS addresses, enter them here.

Establishing Your Internet Connection

You can establish your Internet connection either manually or automatically. The manual method lets you choose when to connect; the automatic method connects whenever you open a program that requires Internet access. Both methods are explained in the following sections.

Connecting Manually

Working through any of the options in the ICW results in a dial-up networking connection being created. You can view it in the Dial-Up Networking folder from My Computer. (Mine is shown in Figure 17.9.) To establish your Internet connection, double-click its icon.

FIGURE 17.9
Use the Dial-Up Networking connection to connect to the Internet.

Connecting to the Internet with Dial-Up Networking

1. From the Dial-Up Networking window, double-click the icon for your connection. A Connect To dialog box appears.

2. Confirm that your username is correct, and enter your password if it does not already appear. As shown in Figure 17.10, the password appears as asterisks for security reasons.

   To save your password for future use, click the **Save password** check box.

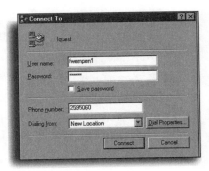

FIGURE 17.10
Change any settings as needed, and then click **Connect**.

3. Check the phone number. If it is incorrect, correct it.

4. (Optional) If you have multiple dialing locations set up (see "Configuring Telephony Settings" later in this chapter) and want to choose a different one, open the **Dialing from** drop-down list and make your selection.

5. Click **Connect**. Your Internet connection is established, and you are ready to surf! See Chapter 18, "Exploring the Web."

> **Connection Shortcuts**
>
> I find it inconvenient to open the Dial-Up Networking folder every time I want to connect, so I usually create a shortcut to the icon on my desktop or on my Quick Launch toolbar.

> **Unneeded Area Code?**
>
> If a 1 and the area code appear in the Phone Number box and you don't want it to, you need to change your telephony settings, as you will learn later in this chapter. Click the **Dial Properties** button and make sure that the correct area code appears in the Area Code box and the Dial as a Long Distance Call check box is not marked.

If your modem connects to your ISP, but the speed reported is less than your modem's maximum speed, don't worry too much about that. A 33.6K modem might connect at 31K, for example, or a 56K modem at 52K. The connection speed is negotiated between the two modems involved (yours and the one that answered the phone); therefore, it may vary from call to call.

SEE ALSO

➤ *To create shortcuts on the desktop, see page 129.*

➤ *To add an icon for your Internet connection to the Quick Launch toolbar, see page 132.*

Connecting Automatically

Depending on how your Web browser and email programs are set up, your Internet connection may dial itself automatically whenever either of those programs needs to go online.

To set up Internet Explorer and Outlook Express to connect automatically to the Internet, if they aren't set up that way already, use the following procedure. (Outlook Express shares Internet Explorer's connection settings, so making the change in Internet Explorer affects both programs.)

Configure Internet Explorer to Dial Automatically

1. Make sure that you are *not* connected to the Internet.
2. Start Internet Explorer (click the **e** icon on the Quick Launch toolbar).

   If your modem dials and a Web page loads, Internet Explorer is already set up to dial automatically.
3. Open the **Tools** menu and click **Internet Options**.
4. Click the **Connections** tab. (It's shown in Figure 17.11.)
5. Click **Dial whenever a network connection is not present**.
6. Click **OK**.

SEE ALSO

➤ *To use Internet Explorer to surf the Internet, see page 304.*

➤ *To use Outlook Express for email, see page 348.*

Password Saved?

If you have not saved your password (see Figure 17.10), the Connect To box will reappear when Internet Explorer needs to connect to the Internet rather than the connection being made automatically. That way, you can enter your password each time.

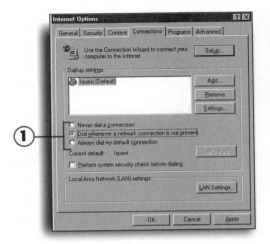

FIGURE 17.11
Configure Internet Explorer to dial your connection as needed.

(1) Automatic dialing controls

Configuring Telephony Settings

Telephony settings control such mundane but important options as whether to dial an area code and whether to dial using tone or pulse service. You can also set telephony to use a calling card, to disable call waiting, and more.

Telephony settings are based on locations. A *location* is a profile based on a particular dialing situation. For example, you might have a location called Home in which you specified that you are in area code 217, you do not need to dial 9 for an outside line, and you must disable call waiting. Another location might be 765 Hotel, in which you are in area code 765, in a hotel that requires you to dial 9 for an outside line, and in which there is no call waiting.

When you install Windows, you are prompted to create a dialing location. Those settings you specified appear in the Dialing Properties box by default. You can change them, or you can create a different location. The following procedure shows you how to examine and change telephony settings and create a new dialing location if needed.

Call Waiting

You should disable call waiting before placing a call with your modem because the short beeps or pulses that signal another call can disrupt the modem communications.

Working with Dialing Location Settings

1. From the Control Panel, double-click the **Telephony** icon. The Dialing Properties dialog box opens (see Figure 17.12).

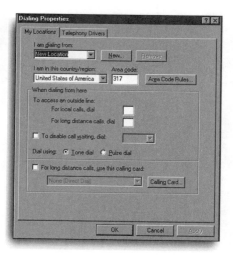

FIGURE 17.12
Set the dialing options here.

More Locations

To add a new location, click the **New** button and then click **OK**. To remove the selected location, click **Remove**.

2. (Optional) Change the name of the location in the **I am dialing from** box. (The default name is New Location, but you will probably want something more specific.)

3. Choose a country or region and specify your area code.

4. (Optional) To set specific rules for the area code, click the **Area Code Rules** button and then set any of the following in the Area Code Rules dialog box (see Figure 17.13):

   - To always dial the area code even when the number being dialed has the same area code as your own, mark the **Always dial the area code (10-digit dialing)** check box.

   - To specify certain prefixes that require a 1 to be dialed but not an area code, click the **New** button in the top area. Enter the prefix, and click **OK**. Repeat for each prefix to add to that list.

   - To specify certain area codes for which dialing 1 is not needed, click the **New** button in the bottom area. Enter the area code, and click **OK**. Repeat for each area code desired.

5. To dial a number to reach an outside line for local calls, enter it in the **For local calls, dial** box.

6. To dial a number to reach an outside line for long distance calls, enter it in the **For long distance calls, dial** box.

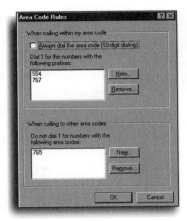

FIGURE 17.13
Set up rules here for
when to dial 1 and when
to dial area codes.

7. To disable call waiting, click the **To disable call <u>w</u>aiting, dial** check box and then choose the needed code from the drop-down list. The most commonly used code is *70, but check with your local phone company.

8. Choose <u>**T**</u>**one dial** or <u>**P**</u>**ulse dial**, whichever matches your phone service.

9. To set up a calling card, click the **For long distance calls, <u>u</u>se this calling card** check box, and then set up your calling card by clicking the **Calling Card** button and filling in the dialog box that appears.

   After you have set up a calling card, it appears on the drop-down list next to the Calling Card button, and you can choose among several calling cards for different situations.

10. When you have finished with the dialing properties, click **OK**.

Tone or Pulse

If you hear musical tones when you dial your telephone, you have tone dialing. If you hear a series of clicks when you dial, you have pulse dialing. Tone phone systems will still work if you set them to Pulse dialing in this dialog box, but not vice versa.

Troubleshooting Connection Problems

Problem: *I hear the modem dialing, but then it keeps making those connection noises endlessly, until I finally have to abort it. Once in a great while, it does connect okay.*

This is often indicative of a poor-quality phone line. The phone line is probably so full of static that a connection can't be established. It may be good enough to talk on, but your modem isn't liking it. Ask the phone company to come out and check your line; there may be a loose connection somewhere.

Problem: *I hear the modem dialing and it sounds like it's connecting, but the service provider's computer always hangs up on me without making a successful connection.*

Several possible causes exist. One may be that your service provider is simply busy at some times and unable to accept more connections. If you are sometimes able to connect, this is probably the case.

If you are never able to connect, perhaps you do not have your connection configured properly for your service provider. In the Dial-Up Networking window, right-click the icon and choose **Properties**. Then

- Check the phone number on the **General** tab.
- Check the modem settings by clicking the **Configure** button on the **General** tab.
- On the **Server Types** tab, click **TCP/IP Settings** and make sure that if your provider requires a specific IP address or DNS server address, they are configured correctly here, as shown in Figure 17.14.

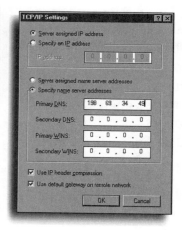

FIGURE 17.14
If your provider requires specific IP or DNS settings, check to make sure they are entered.

- On the **Server Types** tab, make sure that the **TCP/IP** check box is marked. You can deselect the **NetBEUI** and **IPX/SPX Compatible** check boxes.

If none of these help, make sure that TCP/IP is installed in your Networking properties. From the Control Panel, double-click **Network**. If TCP/IP is not on the list, add it with the following procedure.

Adding the TCP/IP Protocol

1. In the Network dialog box (from the Control Panel), click the **A̲dd** button.

2. Click **Protocol** and then click **A̲dd**.

3. Click **Microsoft** and then click **TCP/IP**.

4. Click **OK**. If prompted to insert the Windows 98 CD-ROM, do so.

5. If prompted to restart your PC, do so.

After rebooting, return to the Network window and confirm that TCP/IP now appears on the list. It should look like this: **TCP/IP -> Dial-Up Adapter,** as shown in Figure 17.15.

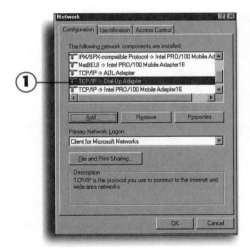

FIGURE 17.15
Check to see which devices TCP/IP is bound to.

① TCP/IP bound to Dial-Up Adapter

If you don't see the Dial-Up Adapter part, display the properties for the Dial-Up Adapter item on the list (click the **P̲roperties** button), and on the **Bindings** tab, make sure a check mark is next to **TCP/IP -> Dial-Up Adapter**. See Figure 17.16.

Problem: *When I try to dial, I see a message,* No dial tone. *The modem checks out okay, though.*

Plug a phone into that same line that is currently going into the modem. Do you hear a dial tone on the phone? If not, the cord (or its connection to the wall outlet) is faulty.

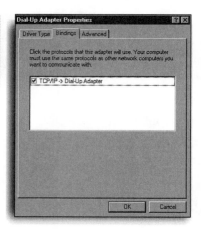

FIGURE 17.16
Check the bindings for
the Dial-Up adapter.

If you do hear a dial tone from the phone, reconnect the modem and
try it again.

Some modems have a pass-through that enables you to connect a
phone to the modem so that the modem and phone can share the
line. The two jacks on your modem should be labeled Phone and
Line, or Out and In. Make sure that you don't have them switched.
Some modems will not work if you have the incoming line attached
to the Phone or Out jack.

Problem: *When I try to use the modem, the computer sometimes (or
always) freezes up.*

This sounds like a device conflict to me. See the section
"Troubleshooting Problems with a Device" in Chapter 25.

Exploring the Web

Choosing Your Browser

When most people talk about the Internet, they mean the *World Wide Web*, or Web for short. The Web is a vast network of documents, or *pages*, that are available for online viewing. You can visit a specific page if you know its *URL* (which stands for Uniform Resource Locator—in other words, its address), or you can hop from page to page by following *hyperlinks*. Millions of Web pages are available for your free, anonymous viewing pleasure, with information about every subject from Aardvarks to Zulus.

Before you can use the Web, however, you must decide which Web browser software you want to use. Windows 98 comes with Internet Explorer, which is a very good, feature-rich Web browser. It's the only browser I use anymore; not only is it free, but it's already installed, and it does everything I want to do (and then some).

However, you may prefer instead to use Netscape Navigator, a competing browser that is just as good (some say better) and that is also free (although you may have to download it from http://www.netscape.com). Figures 18.1 and 18.2 show the same page in Internet Explorer and Netscape Navigator, respectively, so you can see the difference. (There really isn't much difference.) The examples in this chapter will all be based on Internet Explorer, but you are free to use either browser.

SEE ALSO

➤ *To download and install new software (such as Netscape Navigator), see page 144.*

User Profiles in Navigator

Netscape Navigator uses a system called User Profiles to allow multiple users to share a copy of the software, each with their own saved favorite links. The first time you start Netscape after downloading and installing it, you will be prompted to create a user profile. Just work through the wizard, answering the questions in the boxes provided.

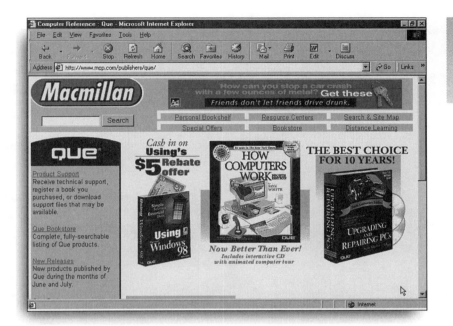

FIGURE 18.1
Microsoft Internet Explorer, which comes with Windows 98.

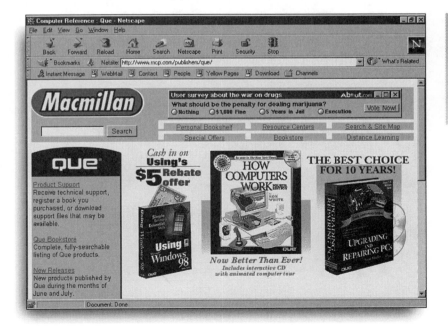

FIGURE 18.2
Netscape Navigator, the browser component in the free, downloadable Netscape Communicator package.

Working with Web Pages

Change Your Home Page

You can easily choose a different page as your home page. In Internet Explorer, open the **Tools** menu, choose **Internet Options**, and on the **General** tab, specify a new address in the **Address** line.

When you start your browser, your Home page loads. (The default Home page for Internet Explorer is shown in Figure 18.3.) This is the page that your browser is configured to begin with each time. From there, you can click any of the links provided or type an address on the Address line.

You can return to the Home page at any time by clicking the **Home** button 🏠.

FIGURE 18.3
The Home page loads each time you open the browser.

① Graphical hyperlink

② Text-based hyperlink

③ Mouse pointer

④ ScreenTip describing the hyperlink being pointed at

⑤ Home button

⑥ Back button

⑦ Forward button

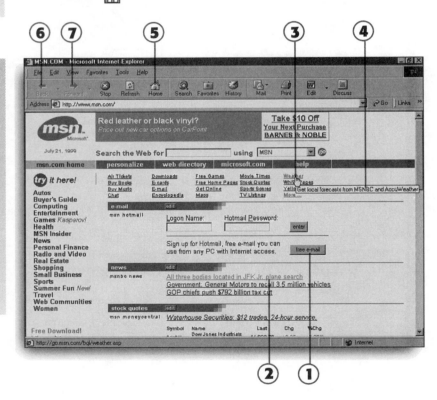

SEE ALSO
➤ *To set program options for Internet Explorer, see page 322.*

Understanding Hyperlinks

Hyperlinks are pointers to other Web pages. When you click a hyperlink, its associated Web page displays, replacing whatever page was showing before.

You will encounter two types of hyperlinks on Web pages. Text-based hyperlinks look like regular text, except that they are a different color, underlined, or both. Graphical hyperlinks, as the name implies, are graphics with hyperlinks associated with them. Figure 18.3 shows both types.

Regardless of the type of hyperlink, when you position your mouse pointer over a hyperlink, it turns into a pointing hand, indicating that clicking in that spot will display a different page. Sometimes a ScreenTip appears too, indicating where that hyperlink will take you.

Non-Web Hyperlinks
Some hyperlinks point you to something other than another Web page. Mail-to hyperlinks, for example, open a window where you can compose an email message to a certain recipient.

Browsing the Web

Click any hyperlink to view the page associated with it. You can surf the Web by jumping from link to link all day and probably never run out of links!

Use these buttons on the Internet Explorer toolbar to help you explore:

The Back button returns to the previously viewed page.

The Forward button takes you forward again after using the Back button; if you have not gone Back, Forward is not available.

The Refresh button reloads the current page. This is useful when an error occurs in loading or when the page contains information that you want to update (such as stock quotes).

The Stop button stops a page loading in progress. It is not available if a page is not currently loading. It is useful when a page is taking too long and you don't want to wait.

The Home button returns you to your Home page.

Back, Back, Back
The Back button has a down arrow to its right. Click it to open a list of previously viewed pages, and then click one of those pages to jump directly to it. The Forward button works the same way.

Viewing a Specific Page

How many times have you been watching TV and seen a Web site address flash across the screen? Whether it's Pepsi or Pepcid AC, it seems as though every product and movie has its own Web site these days.

Displaying a Specific Web Page

1. Type the address of the page into the **A̲ddress** box, replacing whatever is there.

2. Press **Enter** or click the **Go** button 　.

For example, Figure 18.4 shows the result of entering www.microsoft.com/windows98.

FIGURE 18.4

Type an address in the Address box and press Enter to visit that page.

① To get here, I typed http://www.microsoft. com/windows98.

Just Guess It

If you don't know the address for a specific movie, company, or product, sometimes you can guess it by taking the name and adding www. to the beginning and .com to the end. For example, www.reebok.com takes you to the Reebok Web site. This trick works for hundreds of brands and products.

As a typing shortcut, you can leave out the http:// part, and Internet Explorer will assume it as long as the address starts with www. Or you can leave out the www part and Internet Explorer will assume it as long as you type the http:// part.

Visiting Favorite Places

Internet Explorer comes with several lists on its Favorites menu of suggested Web sites to visit. Yes, all of them appear on the list because of some commercial arrangement with Microsoft, so it's not really an unbiased list of the best spots. But most of the links are to interesting, professionally done Web pages, so you may want to check them out.

Loading a Page from the Favorites List

1. Click **Favorites**. The Favorites menu opens.
2. Click the link to the page you want to visit. (You may have to go through one or more layers of submenus, as you do with the Start menu. See Figure 18.5 for an example.)

> **Favorite**
>
> A *favorite* is a stored hyperlink to a page. Internet Explorer comes with many favorites, and you can add your own favorite places to the list, too. You will learn to do so in the next section.

FIGURE 18.5
The favorites on the Media list provide a good starting place if you are looking for something to browse.

Managing the Favorites List

The Favorites list is a great help; you can use it to store all those interesting links that you want to visit regularly. (You saw it in action in Figure 18.5.) Whether you're checking the weather in your area every morning or checking your stocks every night, it pays to have your favorites set up on the Favorites menu and at your fingertips.

In the following sections, you will learn how to add and remove items from the Favorites menu (you can even remove the ones that come preinstalled) and how to rearrange items on the Favorites menu to meet your needs.

Adding a Favorite

Alternate Method

An alternative to step 2 is to right-click the page and choose **Add to Favorites** from the shortcut menu.

As you saw in the preceding section, the Favorites list comes pre-loaded with some interesting pages to visit. But you will surely want to add your own favorites to it as well. Even if you've been using the Web only for the last 15 minutes, you have probably already found a Web page that you want to refer to again later. By adding it to your Favorites list, you create an easy-to-access shortcut to it.

Adding a Page to the Favorites List

Make Available Offline?

You will learn about the Make Available Offline feature later in this chapter, in the "Making Favorites Available for Offline Browsing" section.

1. Display the page.

2. Open the **Favorites** menu and click **Add to Favorites**. The Add Favorite dialog box opens (Figure 18.6).

3. The page title appears in the **Name** box. To use different wording for the menu item, change it there.

4. (Optional) To place the item in a submenu of the Favorites menu, click **Create in**. The dialog box expands, as shown in Figure 18.7. Click the folder in which you want it stored.

New Folder

To create a new folder, click the **New Folder** button, type a name, and click **OK**.

5. Click **OK**. The page is added to your Favorites list.

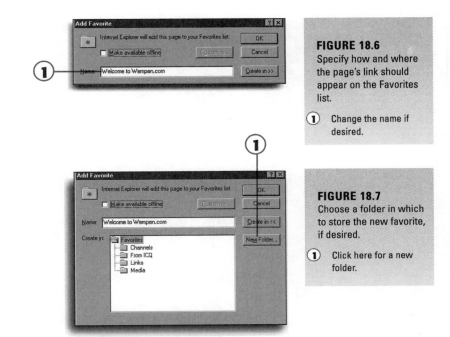

Removing a Favorite

In time you may tire of a particular Web page, or it may become
unavailable. For example, if you have added a page for an online auction to your Favorites list, that auction will end in a few days, and
then the link will be outdated. Fortunately, you can remove any link
from the Favorites menu.

Removing a Link from the Favorites Menu

1. Open the **Favorites** menu and click **Organize Favorites**. The
   Organize Favorites dialog box opens, as shown in Figure 18.8.

2. Click the item you want to delete.

   If it is in a folder, double-click that folder and then click the
   item.

3. Click the **Delete** button.

4. Click **Close** to close the Organize Favorites dialog box.

You can also use the above procedure to delete entire folders; simply
select the folder instead of a file before clicking **Delete**.

FIGURE 18.8
Manage your favorites list from here, including deleting items.

Organizing Your Favorites

As you might guess from the Organize Favorites dialog box (Figure 18.8), you can do a lot with the Favorites list besides adding and removing. Here are some ideas:

Another Way to Rearrange

Another way to move an item or folder is to drag it in the listing, the same as you move items around on the Start menu. You can use this method to reorder items within a menu as well as to move items from one menu to another.

- To rename a favorite, select it in the Organize Favorites dialog box and click the **Rename** button. Then type a new name and click **OK**.

- To create a new folder, click the **Create Folder** button. A new folder appears. Type a name for it and press **Enter**.

- To move that new folder, or any other folder or item, to a new location in the list, select it and then click **Move to Folder**. A Browse for Folder box appears, as shown in Figure 18.9. Click the folder to move it, and then click **OK**.

FIGURE 18.9
Choose where you want to move the selected item or folder within the Favorites menu structure.

Saving Web Content for Offline Use

Web browsing can be addictive—so much great information is out there! I rarely surf the Web without finding some unexpected treasure that I want to save for later rereading and enjoyment. Saving an item to the Favorites list is one way to mark it, but the item will be available only while you are online.

Lots of ways exist to capture the information from a Web page and make it available offline. You can print a hard copy of it or save the page itself to your hard disk, for example. You can also subscribe to the page, so that it is available through Internet Explorer even when you are not online. You'll learn all those techniques in the following sections.

Printing Content from the Web

You can print any Web page easily. For a printout of the entire page (a single copy, on the default printer), simply click the **Print** button 🖨. To print with more options available, use the following procedure instead.

Printing a Web Page

1. Display the page you want to print.
2. If the page has multiple frames (that is, multiple panes separated by divider bars), click in the frame that you want.
3. Open the **File** menu and click **Print**. The Print dialog box opens (see Figure 18.10).
4. Select the printer, the page range, and the number of copies.
5. If the page contains multiple frames, the Print frames area of the dialog box is enabled, as shown in Figure 18.10. Select how you want the frames to be handled:
   - **As laid out on screen.** Prints the page as it appears, with all frames together on the printout.
   - **Only the selected frame.** Prints only the content of the frame you clicked in step 2.
   - **All frames individually.** Prints each frame's content on a separate page.
6. Click **OK**. The page prints.

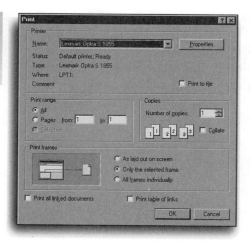

You may have noticed in Figure 18.10 that a couple of special-purpose check boxes are available in the Print dialog box. They are:

- **Print all linked documents.** Beware—this generates a lot of paper! It prints not only the current Web page, but all the pages that are hyperlinked to it.

- **Print table of links.** This prints a listing of all the hyperlinks on the page.

SEE ALSO

➤ *For general information about printing and Print dialog boxes, see page 60.*

➤ *To control a printer's settings or queue, see page 223.*

Saving Web Pages on Your Hard Disk

When you view a Web page, your browser does not save that whole page to your hard disk; it merely displays it onscreen. When you log off the Internet, that page will no longer be available for viewing until you log back on again.

You can save a Web page to your hard disk, however, so that it is available any time. You can also open and edit saved Web pages using Microsoft Word or some other program that supports that format.

You can save a Web page in four formats:

- **Web Page, complete.** Saves the entire page, including any graphics, frames, and style sheets.

- **Web Archive for email.** Saves all the information needed to display the page in a single MIME-encoded file (for mailing in Outlook Express). If you don't have Outlook Express 5 installed, this choice is not available.

- **Web Page, HTML only.** Saves only the current Web page, but not the graphics or other files.

- **Text File.** Saves only the text from the current Web page.

The default is Web Page, complete. I use this to retrieve the contents of public-domain books online (such as at www.greatliterature.com) and then save the book files to disk. Then I use Word to open the saved HTML files, and I can read them in Word whenever I want.

If a page contains lots of graphics and you aren't interested in saving them, Web Page, HTML only may be a better choice. This saves hard disk space by not saving anything except the text and the HTML formatting codes.

Save a Web Page

1. Display the page.
2. Open the **File** menu and click **Save As**. The Save Web Page dialog box opens (shown in Figure 18.11).

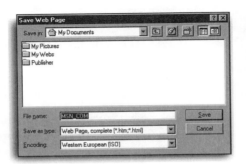

3. Change the save location if desired.
4. To change the file name (the default is the page title), type a different name in the **File name** box.

Web Cache

Some Web browsers include a caching feature that saves each page you view into a temporary file so that if you want to view the same page again later, it will load more quickly. However, this is not the same as really saving the page to disk yourself because those saved temporary files are for the browser's use only; you can't work with them directly. You will learn to empty the cache later in this chapter.

FIGURE 18.11
Save a Web page to your hard disk.

5. Open the **Save as type** drop-down list and choose the format you want.

6. Click **Save**.

SEE ALSO

➤ *To open Web pages for editing, see page 393.*

Opening a Saved Web Page

To open a saved page later, open the **File** menu, click **Open**, and then select the Web page to open, the same as you would open a file in any program. You can be either online or offline; because the page is saved on your hard disk, your connection status doesn't matter.

The exception is if you have chosen the format Web Page, HTML Only, and the page has graphics or other elements that were not saved. In that case, when you load the page in Internet Explorer, you will need to be online or those unsaved elements will not display.

Saving an Individual Graphic from a Web Page

To save a particular graphic that you find online, right-click it and choose **Save Picture As**. Then use the Save Picture dialog box to save it in either JPEG or bitmap format.

Making Favorites Available for Offline Browsing

You learned earlier in the chapter how to add pages to your Favorites list so that you can revisit them later. But the Favorites items are accessible only while you are online.

You can set certain favorites to also be available when you are offline, however. In addition, you can set them so that all the pages linked to them are also available. (You can go several levels deep with this!) That way, you can peruse an entire Web site at your leisure offline.

Here's how it works: when you turn on the Make Available Offline option for a page, Internet Explorer immediately transfers that entire page (and other related pages, if specified) to your hard disk, in a temporary folder. It waits there for you to choose it from the Favorites menu. Then periodically (according to the schedule you specify), it updates the stored version of the page to synchronize it with the latest version on the Web.

Making a Favorite Available Offline

1. Open the **Fa̲vorites** menu and click **O̲rganize Favorites**.

2. Click the item you want to make available.

3. Click the **Make available o̲ffline** check box. A **Properties** button appears, as shown in Figure 18.12.

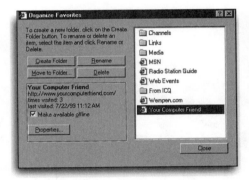

FIGURE 18.12
Select a page from the list and then mark the **Make available offline** check box.

4. Click the **P̲roperties** button. The Properties box for that link appears.

5. Click the **Schedule** tab.

6. Choose a scheduling option for updating this page:

    • **O̲nly when I choose Synchronize from the Tools menu (the default)**

    • **U̲sing the following schedule(s)**

    If you choose the latter, you must create at least one schedule. Click the **A̲dd** button and specify a schedule, as shown in Figure 18.13. You can have different schedules for different links; some pages you may want to update daily, whereas others need updating less often.

7. Click the **Download** tab (shown in Figure 18.14).

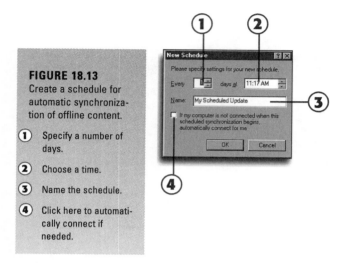

FIGURE 18.13
Create a schedule for automatic synchronization of offline content.

1 Specify a number of days.

2 Choose a time.

3 Name the schedule.

4 Click here to automatically connect if needed.

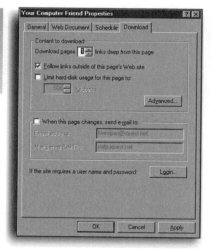

FIGURE 18.14
Specify how much information will be downloaded to your hard disk.

    8. Set options for the associated pages:

        • Specify a number of levels of links you want to download in the **Content to download** area. For example, to download all the pages that are linked from this page, choose **1**. To download all that and all the pages linked to all those pages, too, choose **2**.

- To download only pages from this same Web site (that is, with the same domain address), deselect the **Follow links outside of this page's Web site** check box.

- To limit the total amount of hard disk space that these downloads can consume, select **Limit hard-disk usage for this page to** and then enter a number of kilobytes.

- To omit images, sounds and video, or ActiveX controls and Java applets, click the **Advanced** button and deselect the undesired objects from the box that appears. (Then click **OK** to return.)

9. Set any other options for the page as needed:

   - If you want an email sent to you when the page changes, click the **When this page changes, send e-mail to** check box and enter your email address and mail server.

   - If the page requires you to log in, click the **Login** button and specify your username and password for that site.

10. Click **OK**, closing the Properties box for the page.

11. Click **Close**, closing the Organize Favorites box.

    The chosen pages are immediately downloaded to your hard disk. You can now view them any time from the Favorites menu, even when offline.

Finding People and Information

One of the first questions people ask when they start using the Internet is "How do I find X?" X can be anything: a person, a bit of information, a Web site for a particular company, and so on. The answer, unfortunately, is "Well, it depends." No single directory exists that lets you find everything. However, many very good partial directories are available, and by visiting several of them, you are likely to find your answer.

Using Web Search Engines

Search engines are a great way to look for information online. Search engine sites are organized around giant databases of Web page links, and they are free (that is, advertiser supported). You type in certain words, and it spits back to you a list of Web pages that match. The

My Favorite Search Engine

Of these, Yahoo! is the one I choose most often because the pages it lists are actually checked and reviewed by real human beings, and only the best pages are included. Most of the other sites use computers to gather and index Web content, so they have more matches for a particular query. You may wonder why more matches wouldn't be better—and it is better to a certain extent. But suppose I'm searching for information about Shetland Sheepdogs. On Yahoo, I get a list of 74 sites that have been checked and deemed useful by a real human. On Infoseek, I get 2,040 matches, including some really good sites and lots of crummy sites. Which would *you* rather wade through?

following are the addresses of some of the more popular search engines:

http://www.yahoo.com

http://www.excite.com

http://www.lycos.com

http://www.webcrawler.com

http://www.infoseek.com

http://www.altavista.com

http://www.hotbot.com

The basic process for using a search site is simple. Type the keywords you are looking for, and then press **Enter** or click the button that activates the search (Find, Go, Seek, Search, and so on—it depends on the site). It presents you with a list of addresses, usually with some descriptive paragraph beneath each one, as shown in Figure 18.15. Each of the addresses is a hyperlink, and you can click any of them to visit that page. Use **Back** to return to the list and try another.

FIGURE 18.15
The results of a typical keyword search. This one is from Webcrawler.

① Hyperlink to the described site

② Pages are ranked by relevance to your keywords.

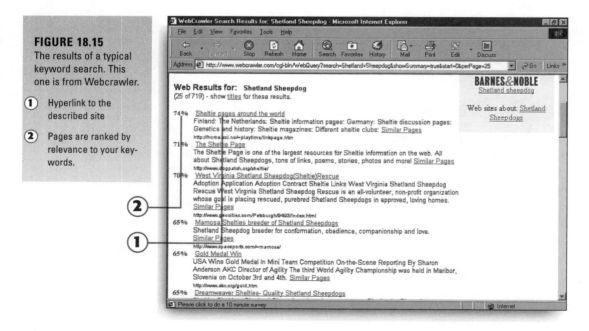

Using Internet Explorer's Search Pane

When you click the **Search** button 🔍 on Internet Explorer's toolbar, a separate Search pane opens to the left of the main browser window.

This new pane provides access to several popular search engines and reports the search results in that same pane. That way, you can run a search without leaving the current Web page that you are working with. Figure 18.16 shows a search for Shetland Sheepdog. To close the Search pane, click the **Search** button 🔍 again, or click the **X** in the top-right corner of the pane.

By default, the Search feature uses different search engines to be fair to all the major players (or at least those who have paid a promotional fee to Microsoft!). However, the Search feature can be customized to use particular search engines—or even one specific one—all the time.

Customizing Internet Explorer's Search Pane

1. With the Search pane open, click **Customi̲ze**. This opens the Customize Search Settings dialog box (see Figure 18.17).

2. In the Search pane, select which search engines you want to use by selecting or deselecting their check boxes.

3. Make your choices of search services for each of the other categories. (Scroll down in the dialog box to see the others.)

4. Click **OK**.

Finding Contact Information for People

Finding a person can be more difficult than finding a bit of information. A certain fact may be found on hundreds of pages; you need only to locate one page that happens to contain it. But a person is unique.

To find a person, you can visit one of the popular directories, such as

http://www.bigfoot.com

http://www.four11.com

http://www.worldpages.com

http://www.infospace.com

Search Syntax

Most search engines have a particular syntax you need to use for more complex searches. Unfortunately, the syntax is different for almost every site. On some sites, for example, to exclude a particular word you can type a minus sign before it. The search "bear–teddy" would find all pages that contained the word "bear" but that did not contain "teddy." But on other sites, the minus sign doesn't work at all—perhaps they use parentheses around the item to exclude, instead.

If you are interested in narrowing down your search with criteria like that, read the directions at the site to find out how to proceed.

FIGURE 18.16
The Search pane enables you to search without leaving your current page.

FIGURE 18.17
Choose which search engines should be used when you search for specific data types.

1. Scroll down for more data types.

2. Select or deselect a site.

3. Click here to reset the defaults.

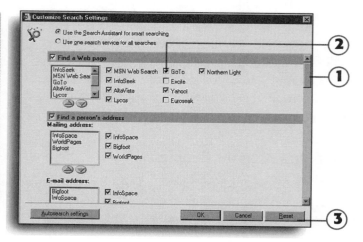

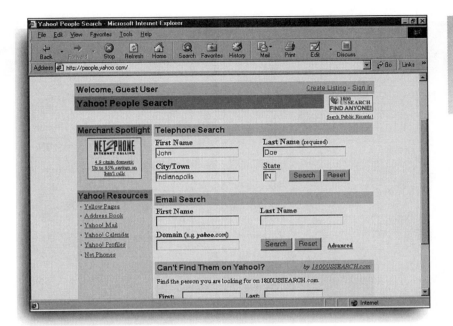

FIGURE 18.18
Search for a person at a search engine site designed for that purpose.

Then fill in the blanks provided to search for the person based on what you know. For example, Figure 18.18 shows a search in progress at Four11.com. You can use this site to search either for email addresses or real-world contact information (that is, street address and phone number).

As with the information searching, you can also use Internet Explorer's Search pane to access popular directories. To do so, open the Search pane and then click **Find a person's address**. Then fill in the details you know (see Figure 18.19) and click **Search**.

Is It Accurate?

The contact information you get from a search directory online may be out-of-date. Sites typically don't update their records very frequently, so if the person has moved within the last year or so, you may get the old info.

321

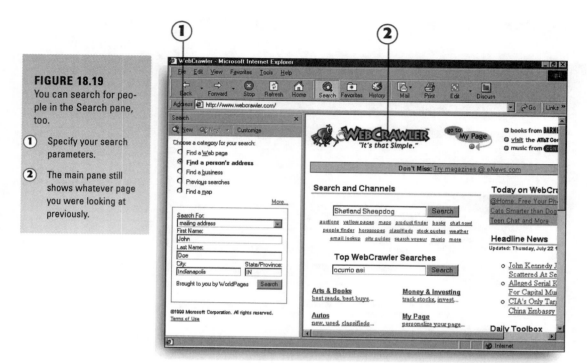

FIGURE 18.19
You can search for people in the Search pane, too.

① Specify your search parameters.

② The main pane still shows whatever page you were looking at previously.

Customizing Internet Explorer

Like most good programs, Internet Explorer is fully customizable. You can change everything from which toolbars appear to how security is handled.

Rather than going into exhaustive detail about the available settings, we'll look at them in some general categories. This will give you an idea of what you can change and where you might start looking for the setting that changes it.

Most of the settings you'll learn about in the following sections (with the exception of the first section that follows) are controlled from the Internet Options dialog box. To display it, open the **Tools** menu and click **Internet Options**.

Changing the Internet Explorer Window

On the View menu, you'll find some commands that affect how the Internet Explorer window appears and how content looks within it:

- **Toolbars**, **Status Bar**, and **Explorer Bar**. These are the same in any Windows 98 window; refer to Chapter 6 if you need a refresher.
- **Text Size**. This controls how large text appears by default on the Web pages you display. (In most cases, Web content does not specify its own font size; it relies on the browser to choose the font.) The default is Medium.
- **Encoding**. The default character set used. This is mostly an issue when viewing non-English pages. The default is Western European (Windows).

Setting General Options

On the General tab of the Internet Options dialog box (Figure 18.20), you'll find the following settings:

- **Home page.** Specify a different Home page (that is, start page) here if you like. You can use a Web address here (http://*something*) or a file on your hard disk (C:*something*).
- **Temporary Internet Files.** Internet Explorer caches the pages you visit in a temporary folder on your hard disk to make the pages load more quickly when you visit them again. Click **Settings** in this section to set up this feature, or click **Delete Files** to clear the current cache.
- **History**. Internet Explorer saves links to pages you have visited in the History folder so that you can call up the pages again later. Specify an amount of time a link should remain in History, or clear the current list with **Clear History**.
- **Colors**. Click here to open a box where you can set default colors for Web page display.
- **Fonts**. Click here to open a box to choose a default font for text. (To choose a default size, see the preceding section, "Changing the Internet Explorer Window.")

Create Your Own Home Page

Here's an idea: create an HTML document in Word or some other program that saves in that format. Include hyperlinks to the Web sites you visit most often. Then make that page (saved on your hard disk) the Home page, and it will load each time you start Internet Explorer. From there, you can click any of the hyperlinks to go to your favorite spots.

Cookies

A cookie is a file created on your hard disk when you visit a Web page that helps the company providing the Web page to identify you when you return for another visit. Generally, cookies are very useful because they can identify you without your having to log in when you visit a site. However, some people consider them a violation of privacy. You can set Internet Explorer to a higher security level to prevent it from accepting cookies or to force it to ask your permission before each cookie is accepted.

- **Languages.** Click here to open a box to select a language. (This is not necessary unless you plan to view pages in different languages.)

- **Accessibility.** Click here to open a box to set features that allow you to bypass a page's formatting to make it easier to see onscreen.

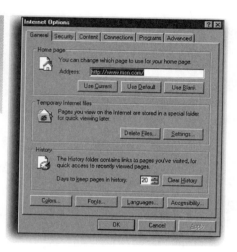

FIGURE 18.20
General options include screen appearance and saved file and link options.

Setting Security Options

Many people are worried about security when they go online. *Will a rogue program take over my PC? Will a virus destroy my hard disk? Will the government—or some evil secret agent—spy on me?*

When browsing the Web, you must decide how secure you want to be and balance that with how many of the newest whiz-bang features you want to take advantage of. The highest security levels in Internet Explorer let you explore completely anonymously, with no fear of anything. However, these very high security settings also prevent you from, for example, online ordering, viewing multimedia content, and playing Java-based games.

On the Security tab (Figure 18.21), you'll find several content zones defined: Internet, Local intranet, Trusted sites, and Restricted sites. You can set a security level for each zone individually and specify which sites are part of that zone. (Click the **Sites** button to manage the list for a particular zone.) Any sites that are not on the list for the Local intranet, Trusted sites, or Restricted sites are automatically assumed to be in the general Internet zone.

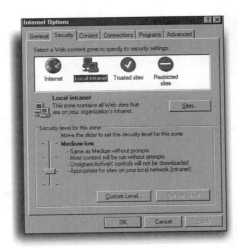

FIGURE 18.21
Manage the security settings for each zone.

Each zone has a slider bar that you can drag to control the security level. The default for the Internet zone is **Medium**, which offers a good compromise between safety and capability. It lets you do almost anything that the page offers, but it prompts you to let you know what is happening before anything happens that could potentially be a security risk.

You can also customize the security level for a zone by clicking the **Custom Level** button. This opens an exhaustive list of security settings (see Figure 18.22) that you can change for the zone, to specify how you want various types of content to be handled.

Setting Up Content Ratings

If you are a parent of minor children who use your PC, you may be concerned about your kids being exposed to adult content online. This is a valid concern! Internet Explorer provides a content rating feature that can help prevent some of the obvious smut from reaching your desktop. However, it is not perfect and can't be relied on to filter out 100% of the material that you may find objectionable.

No Cookies, Thanks

To set your security so that you receive a prompt each time a Web page wants to transfer a cookie to your PC, click the **Settings** button and click the **Prompt** option button under **Allow cookies that are stored on your computer**.

Watch Your Kids!

In my opinion, children should not be allowed to go online without an adult nearby, at least casually observing the action. Security measures and content filtering are helpful tools, but they are not a substitute for parental involvement in a child's online experience.

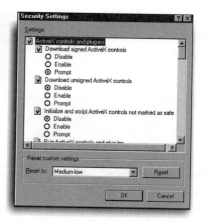

FIGURE 18.22
You can customize the
security level for a zone
here.

The Content Advisor works by comparing the settings you choose to the ratings for a particular site. Not all sites have ratings, so you can choose whether you want sites that have no rating to be viewable on your PC. (If you go to all the trouble of setting up content ratings, I strongly suggest that you block sites with no rating; many explicit sites are without ratings.) You can also specify a password that can be typed to override the block (so that adults in the household may view sites that the children, who don't know the password, cannot).

Setting Up Content Restrictions

1. Start in the Internet Options dialog box (open the **Tools** menu and click **Internet Options**) on the **Content** tab.

2. Click the **Enable** button. The Content Advisor dialog box opens.

3. On the Ratings tab, set a rating for **Language**, **Nudity**, **Sex**, and **Violence**. Drag the slider bar to choose an acceptable level. For example, in Figure 18.23, the Violence rating is set to Level 2. A description of what that entails appears below the slider bar.

4. (Optional) To block or allow certain sites, type the address on the Approved Sites tab, and then click **Always** or **Never** to set its status. For example, in Figure 18.24, the site http://www.wempen.com is set to always be viewable, regardless of its content, whereas the site http://www.hardcore.com is set to never be visible.

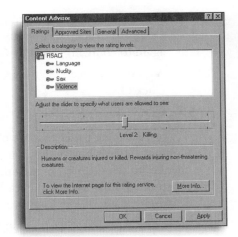

FIGURE 18.23
Set the allowable level for each of the four categories.

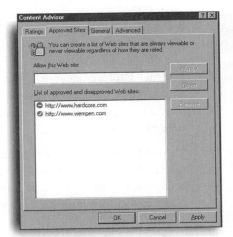

FIGURE 18.24
Specify certain sites to always be or to never be viewable.

5. On the **General** tab, do any of the following:

   - Select or deselect the **Users can see sites that have no rating** check box. If this is marked, all sites with no rating are assumed to be objectionable.

   - Select or deselect the **Supervisor can type a password to allow users to view restricted content** check box.

   - Set a password by clicking **Change Password**.

   - Find and use other rating systems by clicking **Find Rating Systems**. (Some systems require you to pay to use them.)

6. Click **OK** to accept the new settings.

Advanced Tab

I intentionally skipped the Advanced tab in this dialog box because little is here that most Web users would need. If you are using a special ratings service that requires you to set up a ratings bureau or PICS rules, the service will provide instructions for setting the required options on the Advanced tab.

7. If you chose to use a supervisor password, the Create Supervisor Password dialog box appears. Type a password (and then type it again to confirm) and click **OK**.

8. A message appears that the Content Advisor has been enabled. Click **OK**.

9. Click **OK** to close the Internet Options dialog box.

Try to visit some pages that are objectionable, to see whether the Content Advisor blocks them successfully. If you need to make changes to the settings, reopen the Internet Options dialog box (open the **Tools** menu and click **Internet Options**) and click the **Settings** button on the **Content** tab.

To stop using content ratings, click the **Disable** button on the **Content** tab. When prompted for the password, type it and click **OK**.

Setting Program Options

Internet Explorer can't do all Internet activities single-handedly; it sometimes requires helper programs. For example, when you want to send email, Internet Explorer relies on a separate email program to take care of your request.

On the **Programs** tab of the Internet Options dialog box, you can select which program should be associated with various external activities. For example, in Figure 18.25, notice that Outlook Express is the chosen program for both email and newsgroups.

FIGURE 18.25
Select which programs should start when Internet Explorer needs help.

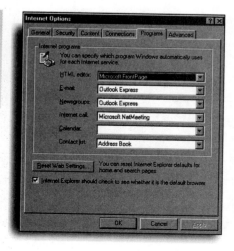

SEE ALSO

➤ *To use Outlook Express for email, see page 344.*

➤ *To use Outlook Express for newsgroups, see page 370.*

➤ *To use NetMeeting, see page 369.*

➤ *To manage addresses, see page 359.*

Advanced Options

Most people never need to bother with the Advanced options in the Internet Options dialog box. These allow you to make very specific technical changes, and most people don't understand the bulk of them—and don't need to. That's why I'm not devoting a special section to them in this chapter.

However, you may occasionally run into some Internet game or other Web activity that requires you to make a change or two here. For example, I like to play an online Bingo game that required me to enable the Java console on the Advanced tab the first time I tried to play it. So just remember that these advanced options are there, and if you never have to work with them, lucky you.

chapter 19

Bringing the Web to Your Desktop

Working with the Active Desktop ●

Adding Active Controls ●

Listening to Internet Radio ●

Push Technology in Windows 98

In the preceding chapter, you learned how to go out onto the Web and find information. The Web is a *pull technology* because you are pulling the information from the Web with your commands. Nothing comes to your PC that you haven't requested at that moment.

In this chapter, you'll learn about *push technology*. Push technology delivers content to your desktop at regularly scheduled intervals so that you don't have to manually request it each time. (Another name for push technology is *Internet broadcasting*.) Push technology can be a great time-saver if you find yourself looking up the same information frequently on the Web, such as the latest stock prices or weather forecasts.

Enabling the Active Desktop

To employ push technology through Windows 98, you must enable the *Active Desktop*.

The Active Desktop, as you may recall from Chapter 6, "Setting File Management Options," is an operating mode in which the desktop can support active controls. An *active control* is a window or a box that contains Internet content and that is automatically updated at a specified interval as long as you are connected to the Internet. For example, one very popular active control is the Microsoft Investor Ticker. It reports the latest prices for the stocks you specify. Figure 19.1 shows the Active Desktop turned on and the Microsoft Investor Ticker ticking away.

Other Push Programs

You can use a variety of other programs to receive Internet broadcasting; push technology is not limited to Windows 98's active controls. At the end of this chapter, I'll provide a list of other content providers you can explore.

FIGURE 19.1
The Microsoft Investor Ticker is a popular active control.

(1) Stock price

(2) Financial headline news—click to read the story.

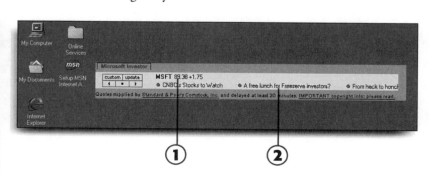

Viewing the Desktop as a Web Page

The Active Desktop is one of several Web-style features you can enable or disable through the Windows Desktop Update features, covered in Chapter 6. When you turn on the Active Desktop, you set the desktop to be viewed as a Web page.

You must set the desktop to be viewed as a Web page to use active controls. To check this and to turn the feature on if needed, use the following procedure.

Enabling the Active Desktop

1. Right-click the desktop and choose **Active Desktop**.
2. If no check mark is next to **View as Web Page**, click it to place one there.

SEE ALSO

➤ *To turn on or off other parts of the Windows Desktop Update, see page 120.*

➤ *To change the wallpaper, see page 168.*

Adding Active Controls

After the Active Desktop is enabled, you will want to add some active controls to it. You don't have to display every control at all times; you may want to add many controls upfront and then choose a few at a time to display.

Adding an Active Control

1. Establish your Internet connection if it is not already running.
2. Right-click the desktop and choose **Properties**.
3. Click the **Web** tab.
4. Make sure the **View my Active Desktop as a web page** check box is marked.
5. Click **New**.
6. If you see an explanation box telling you that you need to connect to the gallery, click **Yes**. The Active Desktop Gallery page appears in Internet Explorer.

What's with the Blue Wallpaper?

When you turn on the Active Desktop, your wallpaper may switch to one called Windows 98. It's a blue background with a Windows 98 logo in the top-right corner. You don't have to keep it to use active controls, however; you can turn it off by changing the Background to **None**, as you learned in Chapter 9, "Customizing the Screen Appearance."

Channel Bar

Internet Explorer 4.0 and Windows 98 (the original edition) come with an active control called the Channel bar. It's a bar that appears on your desktop, from which you can select any of a variety of multi-media "channels" (somewhat like Web pages). Windows 98 Second Edition doesn't come with this, but if you have upgraded from the original Windows 98, it will still be available.

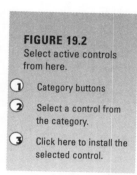

Investment Ticker

The Microsoft Investor Ticker may attempt to install itself automatically at this point. If you see a box asking whether you want to install the Microsoft Investor Ticker, click **Yes** or **No**, depending on whether you want that control.

7. On the Active Desktop Gallery page, click a button for a category (News, Sports, Entertainment, and so on). A list of the available controls in that category appears. See Figure 19.2.

8. Click the name of the active control you want to install. Information about it appears.

9. Click **Add to Active Desktop**. A prompt appears asking whether you want to add an item to your Active Desktop.

10. Click **Yes**. A box appears letting you know you have chosen to add a component to your desktop.

11. Click **OK**. The control itself downloads, along with the latest version of its content. This may take several minutes.

   When the download is finished, the control appears on your desktop.

12. Return to Internet Explorer and add more controls, or close Internet Explorer if you are finished.

FIGURE 19.2
Select active controls from here.

(1) Category buttons

(2) Select a control from the category.

(3) Click here to install the selected control.

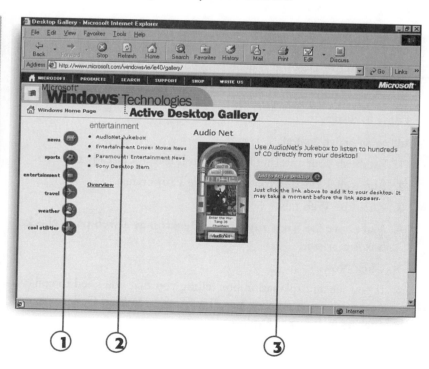

Using Active Controls

You might not be able to get much benefit from an active control simply by looking at it. On the stock ticker, for example, the stocks and headlines scroll by, but you need to click a headline or a stock price to display the full information.

The exact procedure for using a particular control may vary, but clicking them can activate most items, just as with any hyperlink on a Web page. For example, in Figure 19.3, the Audio Net Jukebox control appears; I can choose an artist or a format by clicking the corresponding buttons. Also in Figure 19.3, the Microsoft Investor ticker appears, along with a weather map. I can click any part of those windows to open an Internet Explorer window with details.

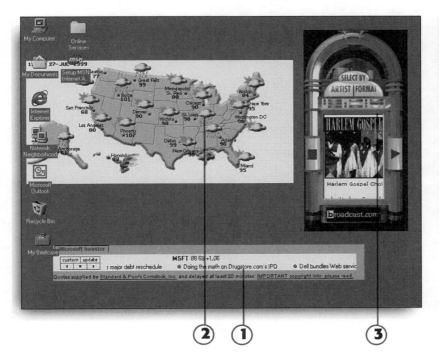

FIGURE 19.3
Each active control has its own controls, but most work by clicking them.

(1) Click an article to read it.

(2) Click an area to see its weather forecast.

(3) Click Artist to see a list of artists from which to choose.

Customizing Active Controls

Some controls can be customized as to the content they provide; others can't. For example, in Figure 19.3, the jukebox and the weather map have no customization capability, but the stock ticker does. (You can tell because the stock ticker has a Custom button in its window, whereas the others don't.)

Because the stock ticker is such a popular item to use, I'll review the procedure for customizing it in the following steps.

Customizing the Microsoft Investor Stock Ticker

1. Click the **Custom** button in the stock ticker window. A Properties box appears for it, as shown in Figure 19.4.

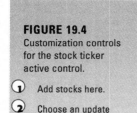

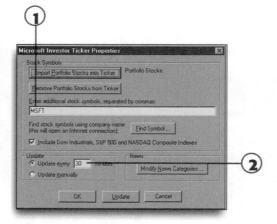

FIGURE 19.4
Customization controls for the stock ticker active control.

① Add stocks here.

② Choose an update interval.

> **Update Customization**
>
> All controls can be customized as to their update interval (that is, how often their content is updated, and in what manner). See the following section, "Setting the Update Interval," for details.

2. Type the stock symbols you want to track, separated by commas, in the **Enter additional stock symbols** box.

3. Choose an update interval in the **Update** area. You can choose automatic or manual update. (If you choose manual, you will need to click the **Update** button in the stock ticker window when you want an update.)

4. (Optional) To choose different news headlines to appear, click the **Modify News Categories** button and add or remove categories from the list, as shown in Figure 19.5. Then, click **OK** to return to the Properties box.

5. Click **OK**, closing the Properties box.

Each of the active controls (the customizable ones, that is) has its own properties that you can set; the ones in the preceding steps are just an example.

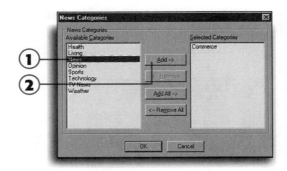

FIGURE 19.5
Select which news categories should be used for your scrolling headline ticker.

① Click a category.

② Click Add to add it to the list.

Setting the Update Interval

You can control the update settings for each active control separately. These include the update interval, how much information is downloaded with each update, and more.

Setting Update Properties for Active Controls

1. Right-click the desktop and choose **Properties**.

2. Click the **Web** tab.

3. Click the control you want to modify.

4. Click the **Properties** button. The Properties box for that control opens.

5. Click the **Schedule** tab.

6. Choose one of the following:

    * **Only when I choose Synchronize from the Tools menu.** For manual updates only.

    * **Using the following schedule(s).** For automatic updates, in addition to any manual updates you may perform.

7. If you chose to use an update schedule, do any or all of the following as needed to set the schedule:

    * Place or remove check marks next to any of the schedules on the list.

    * Edit a schedule by selecting it and clicking **Edit**.

    * Add a schedule by clicking **Add** and completing the New Schedule dialog box.

Creating Schedules

You learned about creating update schedules in Chapter 18, "Exploring the Web," in the section "Making Favorites Available for Offline Browsing."

337

8. (Optional) To specify how much information can be downloaded during an update, click the **Download** tab and make your selections there, as shown in Figure 19.6.

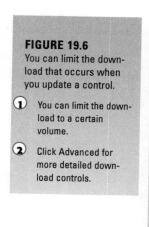

FIGURE 19.6
You can limit the download that occurs when you update a control.

(1) You can limit the download to a certain volume.

(2) Click Advanced for more detailed download controls.

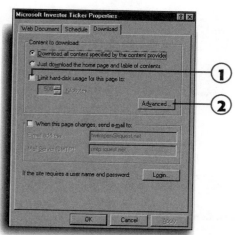

9. Click **OK** to accept the new properties for the control.

SEE ALSO

➤ *For more information about update and synchronization schedules, see page 314.*

Working with Internet Radio

Internet Radio works much like the active controls you saw in the preceding sections, except it is audio. I love Internet Radio because it enables me to listen to many of my local radio stations as I work (as long as I'm connected to the Internet)—without investing in a radio tuner for my PC and without worrying about static or antennas.

Displaying the Internet Radio Controls

You access Internet Radio through Internet Explorer. Remember back in Chapter 6 that you learned about the various toolbars available in a window? One of them was Radio. Turning on this toolbar gives you access to the radio controls.

Displaying the Internet Radio Toolbar

1. Start Internet Explorer.

2. Open the **View** menu, point to **Toolbars**, and click **Radio**. The Radio toolbar appears, as shown in Figure 19.7.

Choosing a Radio Station

You can select which radio stations you want to appear on your list and then switch freely between them, just as you would switch to a Web page from your Favorites list. But first things first—which stations do you want? The following steps explain how to add them to your Favorites list.

Adding a Station to the Favorites List

1. Click the **Radio Stations** button on the Radio toolbar. A menu opens.

2. Click **Radio Station Guide**. A Web page appears, listing the available stations, as shown in Figure 19.8.

3. Select any station from the listing by clicking its link. That station immediately begins broadcasting.

4. If you decide you want to add this station to your Favorites list, click the **Radio Stations** button again and click **Add Station to Favorites**.

5. Create a Favorites item for the station, the same as you would to add a favorite Web page. (Refer to Chapter 18 for help.) You may want to add it to the Radio folder on the Favorites list to keep all your radio station links together.

Local Stations

To locate the radio stations in your area that broadcast on the Internet, enter your ZIP code on the Radio Station Guide page and click **Go**.

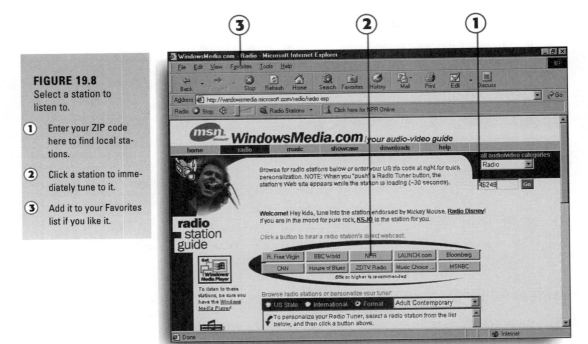

FIGURE 19.8
Select a station to listen to.

1. Enter your ZIP code here to find local stations.

2. Click a station to immediately tune to it.

3. Add it to your Favorites list if you like it.

After adding the desired stations to your Favorites list, choose them from there any time you want to listen to them.

SEE ALSO

➤ *To add items to your Favorites list, see page 308.*

Other Sources of Internet Broadcasting

Hungry for more broadcasts? Visit some of the following Web sites, each of which can help you get set up to receive more content. Some of these are full broadcasting systems, complete with their own software that you will be prompted to download and install; others are simply links to RealAudio content. If you don't have the RealAudio player, a box will prompt you to download it; go ahead and work through that for the installation if needed.

Broadcast.com

http://www.broadcast.com

ChannelSEEK

http://www.channelseek.com

DENtv

http://www.dentv.com/

The Media Channel

http://www.mediachannel.com/

Radio-on-the-Internet.com

http://www.radio-on-the-internet.com/

Yahoo! Internet Live

http://www.zdnet.com/yil/content/depts/ylive/ylive.html

chapter 20

Working with Email

Choosing Your Email Program

Dozens of perfectly good email programs are out there, and most are available for free or as a trial download on the Web. Some of the most popular include Eudora, Pegasus, and Netscape Mail. Each has its own special set of features to recommend it; serious mailing-list participants or managers like Pegasus, for example, because of its excellent sorting and filtering capabilities.

Owners of Microsoft Office also have a powerful program available called Outlook. Outlook not only handles email, but it also manages contacts, tasks, and calendars. I use Outlook for my personal email on my home PC. Figure 20.1 shows Outlook's Inbox, where incoming mail comes.

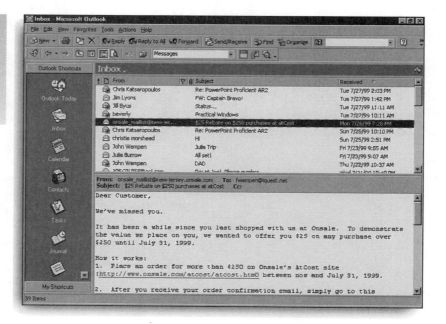

FIGURE 20.1
Outlook comes with Microsoft Office. This is Outlook 2000, the version that comes with Office 2000.

Another program, Outlook Express, comes free with Windows 98 itself. As its name implies, Outlook Express is a slimmed-down version of Outlook, focusing on email and newsgroup management only. Figure 20.2 shows Outlook Express.

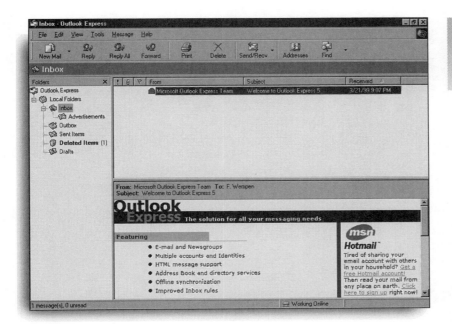

FIGURE 20.2
Outlook Express comes
free with Windows 98.

This chapter focuses on Outlook Express because that's a program
that everyone has available. No matter which email program you
choose, you will want to do the same activities: sending, receiving,
replying, and so on. However, the steps for accomplishing those
activities will vary somewhat from those presented here.

SEE ALSO

➤ *To work with newsgroups, see page 370.*

➤ *To download programs from the Internet, see page 311.*

Introducing Outlook Express

Outlook Express has a button on the Quick Launch toolbar; you
can start it by clicking there. Or you can click **Start**, point to
Programs, and click **Outlook Express**.

When you first start Outlook Express, it may open to an introductory screen such as the one shown in Figure 20.3. From there, you
can click any of the various hyperlinks to do certain tasks, such as
create a message, set up a newsgroup account, and so on.

AOL Users

If you have decided to go
with an online service such
as America Online, your
email program is built into
the service, and you won't
be able to use a separate
email program such as
Outlook Express.

Need Setup?

If the Internet Connection
Wizard runs when you start
Outlook Express, it means
that your Internet connection has not yet been set
up on this PC. See Chapter
17, "Setting Up Online
Connectivity," for help
with it.

FIGURE 20.3
Outlook Express's opening screen, unless you have set it to jump directly to the Inbox at startup.

(1) Click here to bypass this opening screen in the future.

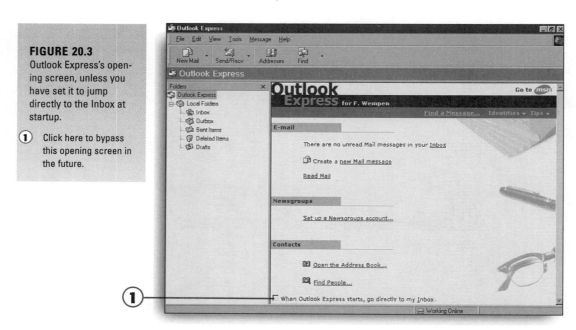

When you click the **Inbox** icon in the folder tree or click the **Read Mail** hyperlink, you see your Inbox, shown in Figure 20.4. The Inbox is divided into three panes. The left pane lists the available folders, just like in Windows Explorer (see Chapter 5, "Managing Files and Folders"). The top-right pane lists the email messages in your Inbox, and the bottom-right pane previews the selected email. As with most Windows programs, a toolbar across the top provides shortcuts to the most common activities.

In addition to the Inbox, Outlook Express uses several other special-purpose folders automatically for certain tasks:

- **Drafts.** Holds messages that you are currently composing. When you issue the command to send one, it moves to the Outbox.

- **Outbox.** Holds outgoing messages until they are sent to your ISP's outgoing mail server. After being sent, a message moves to the Sent Items folder.

- **Sent Items.** Holds a copy of each message you send so that you can refer to it later.

- **Deleted Items.** Holds messages that you delete, in case you want to retrieve them. (They are destroyed eventually, after a specified waiting period.)

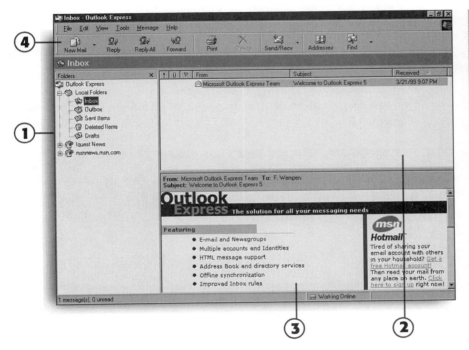

FIGURE 20.4
Familiarize yourself with the parts of the Outlook Express screen.

(1) Folder tree

(2) Incoming messages

(3) Preview pane

(4) Toolbar

Outlook Express uses each of these folders, as needed, automatically; you do not need to do anything special to them. However, you can display a folder's content at any time by clicking its name in the folder tree.

SEE ALSO

➤ *To configure your Internet connection with the Internet Connection Wizard, see page 288.*

➤ *To navigate folders in a folder tree, see page 88.*

➤ *To create your own folders in which to organize incoming messages, see page 352.*

Receiving Email

Multiple Mail Accounts

If you have more than one mail account, you can send and/or receive from a specific one by choosing it from the bottom of the Send and Receive menu instead of choosing **Send and Receive All**.

Receiving email includes not only reading your new messages, but also deciding what to do with them afterward. You can delete them, print them, file them, and more.

Outlook Express may already be set up to receive new mail when you start the program (provided your Internet connection is established). To get your new mail at any time, open the **Tools** menu, point to **Send and Receive**, and then click **Send and Receive All**. Or, you can click the **Send/Recv** button.

New messages appear in your Inbox. Unread messages are bold, so you can distinguish them from messages you have already read. See Figure 20.5.

FIGURE 20.5
The Inbox contains one new and one old message.

① Old (already read) message

② New messages appear in bold.

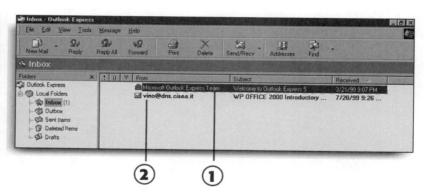

Reading New Email

Outlook Express gives you a Welcome email in your Inbox the first time you run it, so you will have some mail to work with. It's shown in Figure 20.5. Notice that the message is selected in the list of messages, and a preview of it appears in the preview pane.

You can read all your mail from the preview pane if you like, but you can also double-click the message in the list to open the message in its own window, as shown in Figure 20.6. This window features a message header area listing the sender, date, time, and subject.

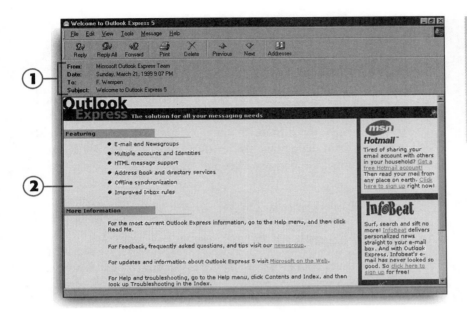

FIGURE 20.6
The "Welcome" message displayed in its own window.

① Message header

② Message

The Welcome message in Figure 20.6 is elaborately formatted with graphics, different fonts, different colors, and so on. It looks a lot like a Web page in that regard. That's because it takes advantage of Outlook Express's capability to read HTML formatting in messages. But most of the messages you receive will probably be in plain text format, such as the junk advertisement shown in Figure 20.7 (which, by the way, is a total rip-off in my opinion, so don't even think about calling the number shown and ordering the product).

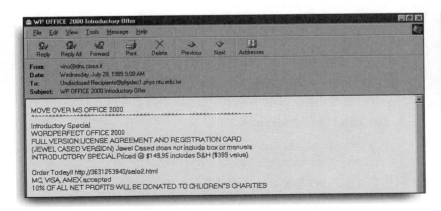

FIGURE 20.7
Most email messages from individuals come in Plain Text format like this.

SEE ALSO

➤ *To add formatting to your own outgoing messages, see page 362.*

Printing a Message

To print a message, either display it (by double-clicking it on the list) or simply select it on the list. Then, to print it, click the **Print** button ![printer icon] or open the **File** menu and click **Print**. The latter method opens the Print dialog box, from which you can select the printer, the page range, the number of copies, and so on.

SEE ALSO

➤ *For more information about printing, see page 60.*

Reading and Saving an Attachment

Some messages come with attachments. An attachment can be any kind of file: a picture, a word processing document, a compressed archive (for example, a zip file), or any other type. If a particular message has an attachment, a little paper clip appears next to it in the message list. When you open the message in its own pane, the attachment appears there, as shown in Figure 20.8.

FIGURE 20.8
This message contains an attached word processing file.

① Attachment

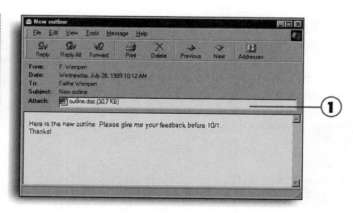

Saving an Email Attachment

1. Select the message on the message list or double-click it to display it in its own window.

2. Open the **File** menu and click **Save Attachments**. The Save Attachments dialog box opens (see Figure 20.9).

FIGURE 20.9
Save attachments to
your hard disk using this
dialog box.

3. If needed, click **Browse** and choose a different folder in which
   to save the file.

4. Click **Save**. The attached file is saved to the specified location.

You do not have to save an attachment to view it. Simply do one of
the following to open the attachment in whatever program it is associated with:

- Double-click the attachment name in the message (when the
  message is open in its own window).

- In the message preview pane, click the large paper clip in the
  top-right corner. A menu opens showing the attachments.
  Click the attachment to open from that menu, as shown in
  Figure 20.10.

Deleting a Message

To delete a message, select it from the message list and press **Delete**,
or click the **Delete** button ☒. This moves the message to the
Deleted Items folder.

Change your mind? You can undelete a message by locating the message in the Deleted Items folder and dragging it to the Inbox icon on
the folder tree.

To delete a message completely so that no record of it exists, switch
to the **Deleted Items** folder and delete it there. (Of course, you
can't undelete the message after that.)

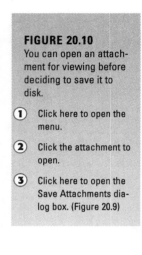

FIGURE 20.10
You can open an attachment for viewing before deciding to save it to disk.

(**1**) Click here to open the menu.

(**2**) Click the attachment to open.

(**3**) Click here to open the Save Attachments dialog box. (Figure 20.9)

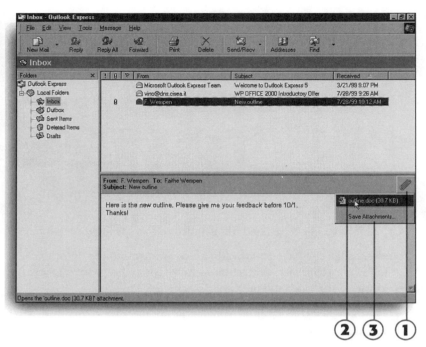

Organizing Incoming Mail

It is perfectly okay to leave received messages in your Inbox as long as you like, but in time your Inbox will become crowded.

If you get a lot of email (for example, if you participate in a mailing list, as explained in Chapter 21, "Participating in Online Discussions"), you may wish to create subfolders within your Inbox in which to organize the mail. For example, you could create a folder for each mailing list you participate in, a folder for correspondence from your family, and a folder for advertisements that you may be interested in looking at when you have time.

Creating a Mail Folder

1. Open the **File** menu, point to **Folder**, and click **New**. The Create Folder dialog box opens.

2. Click the **Inbox** to place the new folder as a subfolder of the Inbox.

3. Type a name into the **Folder Name** box.

4. Click **OK**. The new folder appears beneath the Inbox in the folder tree.

Then, to move messages into the new folder, simply drag them from the Inbox's message list onto the new folder's name on the folder tree.

If that seems like a lot of work to drag each message where you want it—you're right. It is. Fortunately, you can create message-handling rules that do the work for you based on criteria you specify. The following section explains how to set it up.

Creating Message Handling Rules

Rules let you specify what should be done to a particular message based on one or more facts about it. Those facts could include who the sender is, what the subject line contains, what size the attachment(s) are, and so on. For example, suppose you belong to a mailing list called FunStuff. You could create a rule that automatically moved any messages addressed to the list into a special folder that you have created, called FunStuff.

Creating a New Rule

1. Open the **Tools** menu, point to **Message Rules**, and click **Mail**. The Message Rules dialog box opens.

2. Click the **New** button. The New Mail Rule dialog box opens. (If you have not created any rules yet, you won't need to click New; the New Mail Rule box appears automatically.)

3. Click a check box in the **Select the Conditions for your rule** list to indicate the type of conditions you want to set.

For example, to base the rule on a particular email address (or group of addresses) in the Sender field, choose **Where the From line contains people**.

4. In the **Message Description** area, click the hyperlink to open a box in which you can specify the condition.

For example, in Figure 20.11, the hyperlink is **Contains people**, and clicking it opens a **Select People** dialog box.

> **Rules in Other Programs**
>
> This chapter focuses on Outlook Express Version 5, which is what comes with Windows 98 Second Edition. If you have a different version of Outlook Express, or if you use Outlook instead, the procedure for setting up message-handling rules will be different for you than what is shown here.

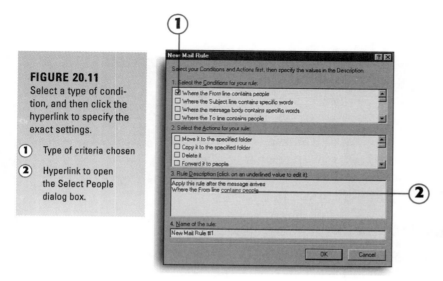

5. In the dialog box that appears (Select People, for example), set up the conditions for the rule. For example, in Figure 20.12 I have chosen two certain email addresses for the rule to apply to.

6. Click **OK** to return to the New Mail Rule dialog box. The conditions you specified now appear in the Rule Description area.

7. (Optional) Choose other criteria types from the **Select the Conditions for your rule** list, and set them up as you did the first one.

8. Choose an action from the **Select the Actions for your rule** list.

9. Click the hyperlink in the **Rule Description** area for the action you just added and specify its parameters in the dialog box that appears. Click **OK** when finished.

For example, if you chose **Move it to the specified folder** from the Actions list, you would click the word *specified* in the Rule Description to open a list of folders from which to choose.

10. Type a name for the rule in the **Name of the rule** box. Make it descriptive—something you will understand later when you see it.

11. Click **OK** to create the new rule. The new rule appears in the Message Rules box.

12. Click **OK** to close the Message Rules box. Your new rule will be applied to any new incoming messages.

To modify or delete a rule later, return to the Message Rules box and use the **Remove** or **Modify** buttons there.

Blocking Certain Senders

You can create rules (see the preceding section) that filter out some of the mail that you don't want. For example, you could create a rule that would delete all messages with the word "XXX" in the subject line without having them ever appear in your Inbox.

To block certain senders from sending you messages, you can create a rule, or you can use the Blocked Senders list. The Blocked Senders list is a bit easier to set up than a full-blown rule, and you can quickly add senders to it on-the-fly. When you block a sender, any mail received from that sender is immediately moved to the Deleted Items folder.

Blocking a Sender Who Has Sent You a Message

1. Select a message from the sender.

2. Open the **Message** menu and click **Block Sender**. A message appears stating that the sender has been blocked and asking whether you want to remove all messages from the sender now.

3. Click **Yes** or **No**.

4. If you chose Yes, a confirmation box appears; click **OK**.

You can also block mail from senders who have not sent you anything yet. When you do it this way, you can block email, newsgroup messages, or both for the sender.

Blocking Any Sender

1. Open the **Tools** menu, point to **Message Rules**, and click **Blocked Senders List**. The Message Rules dialog box opens with the Blocked Senders tab on top.

2. Click **Add**. The Add Sender dialog box opens (Figure 20.13).

FIGURE 20.13
Enter the address of the sender to be blocked.

3. Type the address in the **Address** box.

4. Choose an option button describing what you want to block: **Mail messages, News messages**, or **Mail and News messages**.

5. Click **OK**. The address appears on the list of blocked senders.

6. Click **OK** to close the Message Rules dialog box.

You can make changes to the list of blocked senders at any time. Just redisplay the dialog box (see Figure 20.14). Then, select or deselect the check boxes next to each address. To remove an address from the list completely, click it and then click **Remove**.

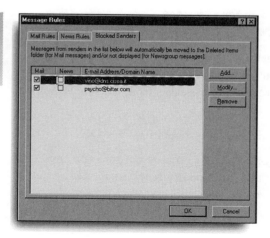

FIGURE 20.14
Manage your list of blocked senders here.

Sending Email

Now that you can handle your incoming mail with ease, it's time to tackle the other half of the equation: sending mail. You can reply to a message that you've received, or you can create a whole new message. You can rely on plain-text format (for maximum flexibility) or dress a message up with formatting (for greater impact). In the following sections you'll learn how to create, format, and send messages to others.

Replying to a Message

The easiest way to send a message is to reply to one that you've received. This is great because you don't have to look up the person's email address or the subject; when you reply, the correct address and the previous subject are inserted automatically.

When you reply to a message, the original message appears quoted below your reply. Each line of it is preceded by a symbol (such as >) that indicates the text is quoted and not original. You can type your reply above this quoted block, or you can insert the lines of your reply between the quoted lines to respond individually to certain points that the original writer made.

Replying to a Message

1. Select the message that you want to reply to, or open it in its own window.
2. Click the **Reply** button ![icon]. A new message pane opens.
3. Type your reply. See Figure 20.15.
4. Click **Send** ![icon]. The message moves to your Outbox.

    The message will be sent the next time Outlook Express is scheduled to send and receive messages.
5. To send the message immediately from the Outbox instead of waiting for the next scheduled delivery, click the **Send/Recv** button ![icon].

When you reply to a message, its icon changes in the Inbox to show a little arrow, like this: ![icon]. You can use this to tell at a glance which messages you have sent replies to and which you haven't.

> **Email Addresses**
>
> In Figure 20.15, the recipient's full name appears instead of the email address. That's because I have set this recipient up in my Address Book under her full name. When I send the message, however, Outlook Express will look up her correct email address and use it.

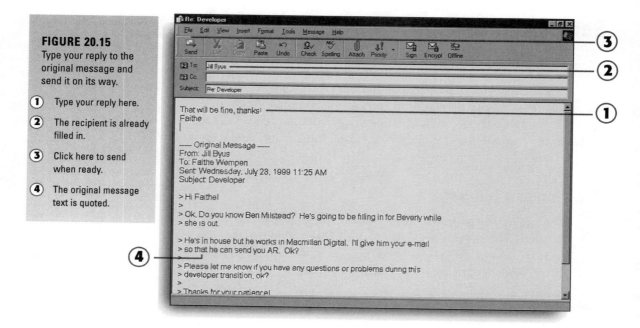

FIGURE 20.15
Type your reply to the original message and send it on its way.

① Type your reply here.

② The recipient is already filled in.

③ Click here to send when ready.

④ The original message text is quoted.

SEE ALSO
➤ *To work with the Address Book, see page 359.*
➤ *To specify when Outlook Express sends and receives automatically, see page 366.*

Composing New Messages

Bcc:

Bcc stands for blind carbon copy. It is like a Cc, except that the other recipients don't see the name on their copies, so they don't know it was sent to the person.

Outlook Express does not include the Bcc: field on new messages, but you can choose names for Bcc copies when you select from the Address Book, as you will see in the next section.

Composing a new message is almost like replying, except that you need to specify the recipient's address. You can look it up in your Address Book (see "Managing Addresses" later in this chapter), or you can type it.

Creating a New Message

1. Click the **New Mail** ▢ button on the toolbar. A new message window opens.

2. Type the recipient's email address into the **To:** box, or select it from the Address Book, as described in the next section.

3. (Optional) To send copies to other recipients, type their addresses into the **Cc:** box.

4. Type a subject into the **Subject** box. This should be a descriptive title that will help the recipient know what the email is about.

5. Type your message into the **Message** area. Figure 20.16 shows a completed message, ready to send.

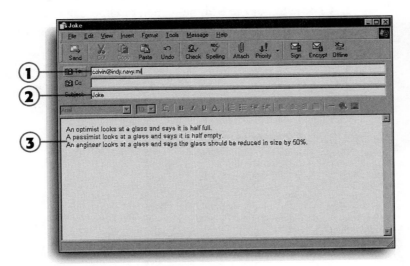

FIGURE 20.16
A ready-to-send message.

① Recipient

② Subject

③ Message

6. Click the **Send** button 🖃. The message moves to the Outbox.

7. To deliver the message immediately (before the next scheduled Send/Receive), click the **Send/Recv** button 🖃.

SEE ALSO

➤ *To control how often messages are sent and received automatically, see page 366.*

Managing Addresses

Fortunately, you do not have to remember everyone's email addresses. You can store them in Outlook Express's Address Book and use them whenever needed.

Adding Addresses to the Address Book

You can add someone to your address book in several ways. One of the easiest is to copy the address from a message that you've received. The person need not have been the sender; he can be one of the other recipients.

Full Contact

The Address Book lets you record much more information about a person than simply the email address. You may decide to go ahead and fill in complete contact information for each person, but you may prefer to include only the email addresses and keep the other contact information in some other program (or even on paper, the old-fashioned way!). If you synchronize your contact list with a portable device such as a PalmPilot, you may wish to store complete information in the Address Book so it will be handy while you are traveling.

Adding an Address Book Entry from a Received Message

1. Display the message in its own window.

2. Open the **Tools** menu and choose **Add to Address Book**. A submenu appears.

3. Choose **Sender** to add the sender, or choose one of the other addresses on the submenu to choose one of the other recipients.

A Properties box appears for the new address.

4. To file the person under her real name (not the email address), click the **Name** tab and type the correct First, Middle, and Last names into the boxes provided, as shown in Figure 20.17.

FIGURE 20.17
Type the person's full name on the **Name** tab if you want to use it for filing purposes.

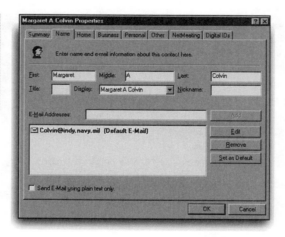

5. (Optional) Fill in any other information about the person on the other tabs (such as Home, Business, and so on).

This is not necessary to send email to the person, but you may want to keep the information for your own records.

6. Click **OK**, adding the person to your Address Book.

You can also add a new address to the Address Book from scratch (that is, without having received any mail from that person). The following steps show how.

Adding a New Address to the Address Book

1. From the Inbox (or another folder), click the **Addresses** button ▦.

You can't do Step 1 from a message composition window because no Addresses button is present on the toolbar in those windows.

2. Click the **New** button. A menu appears.

3. Click **New Contact**. A Properties box for the new contact appears.

4. Type the person's email address into the **Email addresses** box, and click **Add** to add it to the list.

   You can store multiple email addresses for a person. To choose which is the default, select it and then click **Set as Default**.

5. Fill in any fields for the new contact, as desired. I recommend that you at least fill in the First and Last names.

6. Click **OK**, adding the person to the Address Book.

7. Close the Address Book window when you are finished with it.

Selecting Addresses for an Email

When composing an email, you can click the **To:** or **Cc:** buttons to open a Select Recipients box. It lists all the addresses in your Address Book and enables you to select any of them as primary recipients (To:), secondary or "copy" recipients (Cc:), and secret recipients (Bcc:).

Addressing an Email with the Address Book

1. From the message composition screen, click the **To:** button or the **Cc:** button. The Select Recipients box appears.

2. Click a name on the list, and then click the **To:**, **Cc:**, or **Bcc:** button to move the name to the appropriate list. Figure 20.18 shows two primary recipients and one copy recipient.

3. Repeat Step 2 as needed to add more recipients.

4. Click **OK**. The names appear in the To and/or Cc fields in the message composition window.

You can also start a new email and address it to a single recipient directly from the Address Book. With the Address Book open, click a name, and then click the **Action** button on the toolbar and choose **Send Mail** from the menu that appears.

FIGURE 20.18
Choose who should receive the email in one of the three manners.

(1) Select a person.

(2) Click a button to add the person to the list.

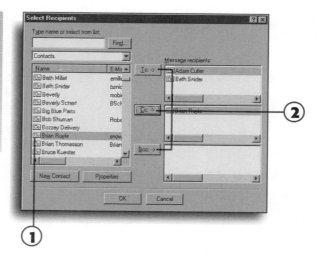

Modifying or Deleting an Address

To modify an address, return to the Address Book (click the **Address Book** button on the toolbar) and double-click a name. The Properties box reopens for it, and you can make your modifications.

To delete an address, return to the Address book and select the name. Then, click the **Delete** button or press the **Delete** key on the keyboard.

Formatting a Message

You can send messages in either Plain Text or Rich Text format. Rich Text enables you to apply formatting such as bold, italic, various fonts, various colors, bullets, and so on.

It might seem like a no-brainer: *of course* you want to use formatting if you can, right? Well, not necessarily. If you are sending email to someone whose email program cannot understand Rich Text formatting, your message will not look right on the recipient's screen. It would be better for you to send a plain-text message to such a person because at least you can be confident in how it will appear on the other end. So how do you know? You don't. You can send a test message and find out whether it was received with formatting intact, or you can simply stick with text-only format and not have to worry.

Printing the Address Book

Click the **Print** button on the Address Book's toolbar to open a Print dialog box. From there you can choose to print all or selected addresses in any of three styles (Memo, Business Card, or Phone List).

Alternate Access

You can also open the Address Book even when Outlook Express is not running. Just click Start, point to **Programs**, point to **Accessories**, and click **Address Book**.

But for now, let's assume that you do want to include formatting in your message. When you click in the message area when composing an email, the Formatting toolbar may become available. If it does, you are already in Rich Text mode. If it doesn't, open the **Format** menu and choose **Rich Text (HTML)**. (Conversely, you can switch to Plain Text mode by opening the **Format** menu and choosing **Plain Text**.)

Then, just use the Formatting toolbar's buttons to format the message text as you type. It works the same as the toolbar in Microsoft Word or most other word processing programs. Figure 20.19 shows the toolbar, along with a formatted message. Additional commands are also available on the Format menu that let you add backgrounds, use stationery, and work with Font and Paragraph dialog boxes. I won't go into the formatting in detail because you dabbled in formatting back in Chapter 4, "Exploring the Windows Accessories," when you worked with WordPad, and the controls here are similar.

> **Default Format**
>
> You can set a default format for new messages by opening the **Tools** menu, clicking **Options**, and choosing a **Mail Sending Format** from the **Send** tab.

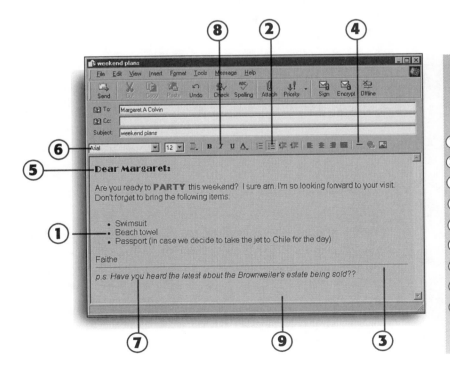

FIGURE 20.19
You can use the Formatting toolbar when composing a message.

1. Bulleted list
2. Bulleted list button
3. Horizontal line
4. Horizontal line button
5. Different font
6. Font drop-down list
7. Italic text
8. Italic button
9. Background color chosen with the Format, Background command

If you are sending a message to someone whom you are certain has a compatible email program, you may want to take advantage of Outlook Express's Stationery feature. It uses a graphic as a background to the message to make it look like you are typing on fancy paper. Figure 20.20 shows some stationery in use. To choose a stationery design, open the **Format** menu and choose **Apply Stationery**. If the recipient can't use stationery in his email program, the stationery appears as an attached graphic file, which he can simply ignore.

FIGURE 20.20
You can choose stationery to dress up the background of your message.

① Graphic from stationery

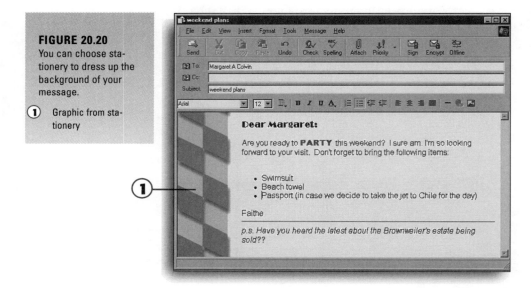

Sending Attachments

You may sometimes want to attach files to your email messages. For example, I often send my editor updated versions of my outline as email attachments. I write the outline in Word, save it as a Word file, and attach it to my message; when my editor receives it, she saves it to her hard disk and opens it for viewing in her own copy of Word.

Before sending an attachment, you need to make sure that the person receiving your message has the appropriate program to open and read the attachment. For example, if you send an Excel file to someone who doesn't have Excel, the file will be useless to the recipient.

As a workaround if you aren't sure, you can use the Clipboard (Copy and Paste) to copy text from a program such as Word, Excel, and so on, directly into an email message. That way, the pasted information becomes part of the message and not an attachment that relies on a particular program to open it.

Attaching a File to a Message

1. From the message composition window, click the **Attach** 🔘 button. The Insert Attachment box opens.

2. Select the file to attach, changing drives and folders if needed.

   To select more than one file at once, hold down **Ctrl** as you click each file (in the same folder only).

3. Click **Attach**. The file(s) become attached to the email.

4. Finish and send the email normally.

Use a bit of caution when emailing attachments to others. People with slow Internet connections will not appreciate the several minute wait required to receive a message containing a large attachment. In addition, some mail servers don't allow incoming attachments greater than a certain size and will lock up the person's mailbox if such an email is received.

Forwarding a Message

Forwarding a message is somewhat like replying to it, in that the original message's text is quoted. However, when forwarding, you specify the recipient. You might use Forward to send a joke that you have received to some other friends or to distribute a memo from your supervisor to the employees who report to you.

Forwarding a Message

1. Select the message from the list of messages.

2. Click the **Forward** button 🔘. A new message appears, containing the quoted text from the original message.

3. Enter or choose recipients as you normally would.

4. Type any comments you want to make in the Message area.

5. Send the message as you normally would.

As with replied-to messages, forwarded messages have a special icon in the Inbox: ![icon], indicating that you have forwarded them.

Setting the Delivery Schedule

The *delivery schedule* is the interval at which Outlook Express connects automatically to your mail server to send and receive mail. The default setting is 30, which means Outlook Express will send and receive mail every 30 minutes, but you can change this to any interval. You can also specify whether it should establish your Internet connection automatically as needed.

Setting the Delivery Schedule

1. From the Inbox, open the **T**ools menu and choose **Options**.
2. Click the **General** tab.
3. Set the following options in the **Send/Receive Messages** section:

   - **P**lay sound when new messages arrive. When enabled, this plays whatever sound is associated with new messages in the Sounds scheme. (Set this from the Sounds area of the Control Panel, as described in Chapter 10, "Customizing System Settings.")

   - **S**end and receive messages at startup. When enabled, this sends and receives messages each time you start Outlook Express.

   - **C**heck for new messages every ___ minutes. When enabled, this sends and receives email at the specified interval.

   - **If my computer is not connected at this time.** Choose what action to take from this drop-down list. Your choices are Do not connect, Connect only when not working offline, and Connect even when working offline.

4. Click **OK**, closing the dialog box.

If you have multiple email accounts set up in Outlook Express, you can specify whether a particular account is to be included in a general Send/Receive Mail operation. To do so, follow these steps.

Online Versus Offline

You can place Outlook Express in Offline mode, so that it will not automatically connect to the mail server at the specified interval unless the above option is set to Connect even when working offline. To do so, open the **File** menu and choose **Work Offline**.

Including or Excluding a Mail Account from Automatic Send/Receive

1. Open the **T**ools menu and click **A**ccounts.

2. Click the **Mail** tab if it is not already displayed.

3. Click the account you want, and then click **P**roperties.

4. On the **General** tab, select or deselect the **I**nclude this account when receiving mail or synchronizing check box.

5. Click **OK**.

6. Click **Close**.

SEE ALSO

➤ *To change which sound is associated with new mail, see page 194.*

chapter
21

Participating in Online Discussions

Reading Newsgroups •

Posting Messages to Newsgroups •

Chatting with Microsoft Chat •

Creating Interactive Chat Comics •

Working with Newsgroups

Newsgroups are like bulletin boards. One person leaves a message that everyone can read; someone else posts a reply (again, which everyone can read), and so on. The whole conversation is completely public, and hundreds or even thousands of people may be chiming in with their own posts on the subject. Chaotic? Yes. But *interesting*. You can post a request for help on a certain subject and receive dozens of informative replies from experts.

Outlook Express has a newsreader component that you can use to read and post to newsgroups. You learned about Outlook Express in Chapter 20, "Working with Email," so its operation should be familiar to you. Many other newsreader programs are available, too, but because Outlook Express is free and already installed, this chapter uses it as the focus.

Setting Up Your News Account

Your ISP probably provides a news server as well as a mail server, and its name is probably listed somewhere in the startup paperwork you received when you signed up. You will need that news server name to configure Outlook Express to read newsgroups.

It's possible that the news server is already set up on your PC; perhaps someone else set it up, or perhaps the Internet Connection Wizard walked you through entering the needed information. If you see your news server listed on Outlook Express's folder tree (at the bottom), it's already taken care of and you can skip the following steps.

Setting Up a News Account

1. Start Outlook Express if it is not already running.

2. Open the **Tools** menu and click **Accounts**, and then click the **News** tab.

3. Click **Add**, and then click **News**. The part of the Internet Connection Wizard that sets up newsgroup accounts runs.

4. Type the name by which you want to be known in newsgroup postings into the Display Name box, and then click **Next**.

   You may not want to use your real name here because newsgroup postings are very public.

Don't Know the Name?

Your news server name is probably *news*-dot-whatever comes after the @ sign in your email address. For example, if your email address is psycho@mysite.com, your news server is probably news.mysite.com.

5. Enter your email address into the Email address box, and then click **Next**.

6. Type the news server name in the News (NNTP) Server box.

This is probably something like *news.yourprovider.com*.

7. If the news server requires a logon, select the **My news server requires me to log on** check box.

Some providers require you to log in to the news server with your username and password to ensure that nobody except their members can access it. Other providers are more flexible and do not require this.

8. Click **Next**.

9. If you selected the check box in Step 7, prompts appear for your username and password. Enter them and click **Next**. You won't see this if you didn't mark the check box in Step 7.

10. Click **Finish**. The new news account appears on the account list.

11. Click **Close** to close the Internet Accounts dialog box. A message appears, asking whether you want to retrieve a list of newsgroups from the server.

12. Click **Yes**.

13. Wait for the list of newsgroups to appear.

14. Subscribe to the newsgroups you want, as explained in the following section.

You should have to do the above procedure only once unless you want to use a different news server. For example, as a Microsoft beta tester, I have access to a special news server set up for testers to post messages. So I might add a new news account to Outlook Express by repeating the preceding steps for that new server.

Subscribing to Newsgroups

Each provider decides which newsgroups it will carry on its server. More than 30,000 newsgroups are available, but some of them are pretty "adult" (and beyond!), so some providers choose to exclude some of the more disgusting ones. (Of course, disgusting is a matter of opinion, so if your provider doesn't carry a newsgroup you want, you can always ask for it to be made available, provided you have the guts to ask.)

Microsoft News

Set up the news server `msnews.microsoft.com` to view a list of public newsgroups maintained by Microsoft. You can often get help with Microsoft products by reading here or by posting your own messages about problems you are having.

The list of newsgroups may already be displayed if you just finished setting up your news account. If not, click the **Newsgroups** button on the toolbar to open the list. (See Figure 21.1.) Then, select and subscribe to the groups you want, as explained in the following steps.

FIGURE 21.1
The list of newsgroups provided on my ISP's news server; yours may be different.

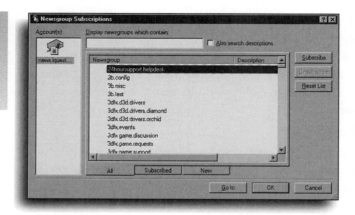

Subscribing to Newsgroups

1. Start in the list of newsgroups (Figure 21.1). If it doesn't currently appear, click the **Newsgroups** button [icon].

2. Scroll through the list of groups to locate a group that interests you.

    Type a word or phrase describing a topic that interests you to narrow the list to only groups that include that word in the name.

    For example, Figure 21.2 shows the list narrowed to groups that contain "dogs" in the title.

3. When you find a group that interests you, click it, and then click **Subscribe**.

4. Subscribe to other groups (repeat Steps 2–3). When you are finished, click **OK**.

You can subscribe to more newsgroups at any time simply by repeating the preceding steps.

To unsubscribe to a newsgroup, right-click it and choose **Unsubscribe**.

FIGURE 21.2
You can narrow the list
by typing words that you
want to find.

① I typed here.

② Each group on the list
includes the word
"dogs."

Retrieving Messages from Subscribed Groups

After subscribing to the groups you want, the newsgroups appear on
a list in Outlook Express, as shown in Figure 21.3. (If you don't see
this list, click the name of the news server in the folder tree.)

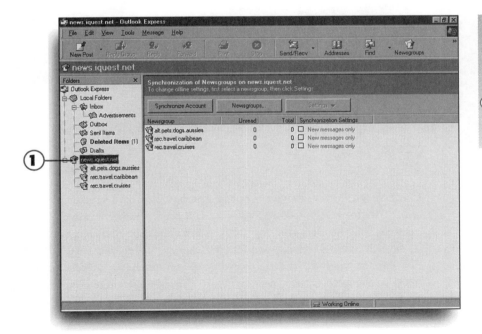

FIGURE 21.3
These are the news-
groups I have chosen to
subscribe to.

① Click the server on the
folder tree to display
this list.

To retrieve the message headers in a newsgroup, click the newsgroup name. Its message subject lines appear in the upper-right pane, and a preview of the selected message appears in the lower-right pane, the same as with email (see Chapter 20). Figure 21.4 shows the new messages in one of my newsgroups, ready to read.

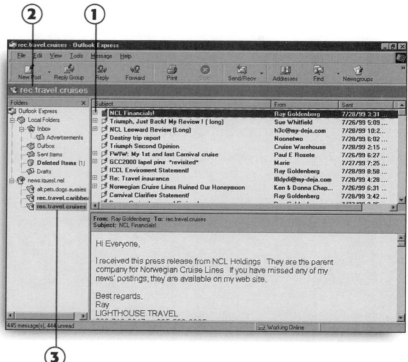

FIGURE 21.4
Here are the messages from the newsgroup rec.travel.cruises, one of my favorites for vacation daydreaming.

(1) Plus sign indicates there are replies.

(2) Name of the displayed newsgroup.

(3) Newsgroup chosen on the folder tree.

Outlook does not retrieve the entire message until you specifically choose that message to display. Instead, it retrieves the message headers. The headers contain information about the message, such as its subject line, its date, its sender, and its size. When you read a message, as you'll do in the following section, Outlook Express connects to the news server and downloads the message's actual content.

Reading a Message

Reading a newsgroup message is almost exactly like reading an email message. Click it to make it appear in the Preview pane, or double-click it to make it appear in its own window.

Replies to a message appear immediately beneath the original. (See Figure 21.4 for examples.) If you see a plus sign next to a message, click it to see the replies. Then, read any of the replies the same as you would read a normal message.

An unread message appears in bold; already-read ones appear in regular text. This is the same as the messages in your Inbox, as you learned in Chapter 20.

SEE ALSO

➤ *To read email messages, see page 348.*

Sorting Messages

You can sort the messages according to any of the columns in the display by clicking the column name. For example, to sort by subject, click **Subject**. You can sort in ascending or descending order; click the same column heading again to toggle between the two. Figure 21.5 shows a newsgroup's content sorted by subject.

You might want to sort by a particular column for several reasons. Here are some ideas to get you started:

- When you're scanning messages for information about a particular subject (for example, for information about Princess Cruises in the rec.travel.cruises group), sort by the Subject column.

- Because messages that have graphic images tend to be larger than those that are replies and comments, when you're scanning a newsgroup that contains graphics, sort by the Size column to place all the larger messages together.

- When you're looking for posts from a particular sender, sort by the From column.

300 at a Time

Outlook Express retrieves only 300 message headers at a time. If the newsgroup contains more messages than that, you won't see them. However, you can ask it to retrieve 300 more by opening the **Tools** menu and clicking **Get Next 300 Headers**. You can repeat this until all message headers for the newsgroup appear, or until enough messages appear to make you sufficiently weary of reading them!

You can also set up Outlook Express to retrieve a different number of messages at a time. Open the **Tools** menu and click **Options**; on the **Read** tab, change the **Get ___ headers at a time** setting to some other number.

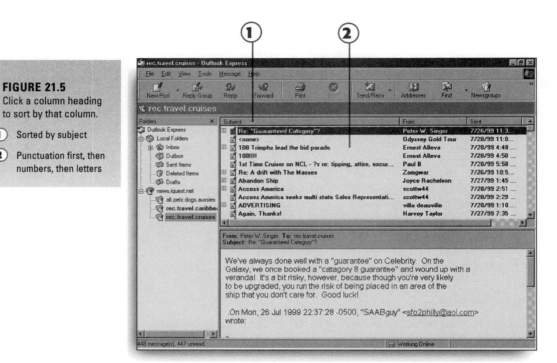

FIGURE 21.5
Click a column heading to sort by that column.

(1) Sorted by subject

(2) Punctuation first, then numbers, then letters

Marking Messages as Read

When you read a message, it becomes marked as read. It stops being bold on the message list.

You may not be interested in reading every single message, especially those on a particular subject in which you have no interest. To mark a group of messages as read, select them, and then open the **Edit** menu and click **Mark as Read**. To mark the entire contents of the message list as read, choose **Edit, Mark All Read**.

Using Mark All Read affects only the displayed message headers in the current newsgroup; if more headers have not been downloaded yet (for example, if the 300-message limit has been reached and you have not yet selected **Get Next 300 Headers** from the **Tools** menu), those are not affected.

Displaying or Hiding Already-Read Messages

One important reason to mark messages as read is to prevent them from showing up the next time you view this newsgroup. That way, only the messages you have not yet seen will appear on the list.

Sometimes, however, you may want already-read messages to appear on the list. For example, you might want to refer back to a message that you read yesterday, having thought of an appropriately witty reply to it overnight.

You can choose whether to include read messages in the listing by opening the **View** menu, choosing **Current View**, and selecting **Show All Messages** or **Hide Read Messages**.

If you have set Outlook Express to hide read messages but they still appear, switch to another newsgroup and then back again. The list should change so that only the unread ones appear.

Downloading Messages for Offline Reading

As I said earlier, by default only the message headers are down-loaded. This saves a lot of time because you probably don't want to read every single message in the newsgroup, anyway.

However, if you need to limit your time online, you may want to download the messages so that you can read them offline.

Downloading Messages

1. Display the newsgroup you want to download from.
2. Open the **Tools** menu, point to **Mark for Offline**, and click **Download All Messages Later**. This marks all the messages in the newsgroup.
3. Open the **Tools** menu and choose **Synchronize Newsgroup**. The Synchronize Newsgroup dialog box opens.
4. Mark the **Get the Following Items** check box.
5. Choose **All messages**.
6. Click **OK**. The messages are transferred to your PC.

Now you can hang up your Internet connection and, in Outlook Express, open the **File** menu and click **Work Offline**. The messages in that newsgroup will continue to be available for reading.

Posting a Reply

You can reply to a newsgroup posting either publicly or privately. Usually you will want to reply publicly, to share your information with others. (It's considered good manners to *share* in newsgroups.)

To reply to a message publicly, select the message and then click the **Reply Group** button 🖻. A message composition window appears, as shown in Figure 21.6. Notice that the complete text of the message appears, along with the name of the person who wrote the message you are replying to. Compose your reply and click **Send** 🖻.

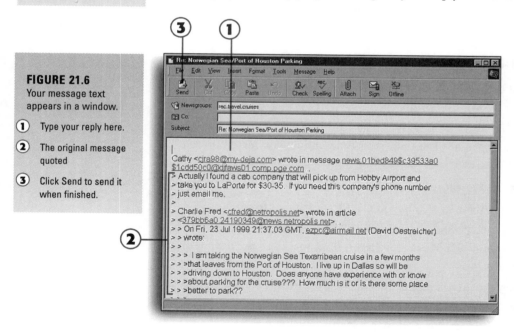

FIGURE 21.6
Your message text appears in a window.

① Type your reply here.

② The original message quoted

③ Click Send to send it when finished.

To reply privately using email, select the message and then click the **Reply** button. Compose your email in the window that appears and click **Send** 🖻.

SEE ALSO

➤ *For more information about creating reply emails, see page 357.*

Posting a New Message

To post a new message in the active newsgroup, click the **New Post** button 🖼. Then fill in the subject and your message, as shown in Figure 20.7, and click **Send** 🖼. You do not specify a recipient; that information is already filled in based on the newsgroup that was active when you clicked the New Post button.

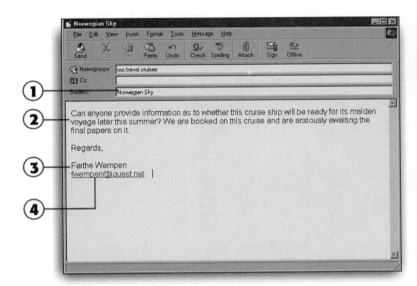

FIGURE 21.7
Compose a new message the same as you would compose an email.

① Subject

② Message

③ Include your name.

④ Include your email address if you want private replies.

Chatting with Microsoft Chat

Microsoft Chat is a program that enables you to "chat" with other people in real-time (that is, live). Chatting involves typing messages that appear immediately onscreen where everyone else who is in the same chat room can see them. Then, other people reply to your message, and their replies appear onscreen for all to see, too. It's like a newsgroup, but much more immediate.

Microsoft Chat is not installed by default; to install it, go through **Add/Remove Programs**, as you learned in Chapter 8, "Installing New Programs."

Then, to run it, click **Start**, point to **Programs**, point to **Accessories**, point to **Internet Tools**, and click **Microsoft Chat**.

Instant Messaging

A variation on chat, Instant Messaging, allows you to send personal, one-on-one messages back and forth with friends who are also online. To do this, you must download and install Microsoft's MSN Messenger program. You'll find it at `http://messenger.msn.com`.

SEE ALSO

➤ *To add Windows components such as Microsoft Chat to Windows 98, see page 140.*

Configuring the Chat Server the First Time

The first time you start Microsoft Chat, you're prompted to choose a chat server, as shown in Figure 21.8. You have two choices to make on the Connect tab: the chat server and the chat room.

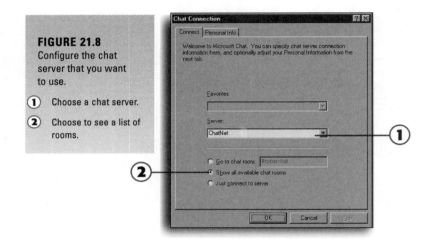

FIGURE 21.8
Configure the chat server that you want to use.

(**1**) Choose a chat server.

(**2**) Choose to see a list of rooms.

Be Cautious

Don't disclose personal information to strangers, especially your home address and phone number! If you have children who chat online unsupervised (which is a very bad idea to begin with, in my opinion), make sure you stress to the child that he or she should never reveal such information.

As the names imply, the chat server is the server that runs a particular collection of chat rooms. The room itself is where you meet and talk with other people.

If you want a particular chat server (for example, if all your friends already use a specific server), choose it from the **Server** list.

If you know of a particular chat room you want to start in, enter its name; otherwise, I recommend that you start with the list of rooms.

Before you move on, click the **Personal Info** tab and fill in whatever information you want others who are chatting to see about you. You don't necessarily have to use your real name or fill in any of the other blanks, either; they're all optional. For example, in Figure 21.9, I have created a bit of "mystery" about myself! When finished, click **OK** to start chatting.

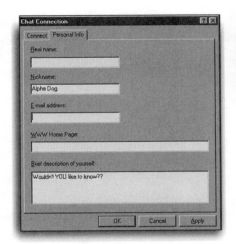

FIGURE 21.9
Enter what you want others to know about yourself.

You will need to do the above configuration only once, but you can change the configuration later by opening the **View** menu and choosing **Options**.

Finding and Entering a Chat Room

If you chose to start with the list of rooms, it appears (after a Tip of the Day box, which you can immediately close).

If you didn't choose to start with the list, you can display the list by opening the **Room** menu and choosing **Room List** or clicking the **Chat Room List** button on the toolbar.

As you will immediately see (Figure 21.10 shows an example), most of the rooms on the list are for entertainment. And many of them are sex-oriented. This is not the appropriate place to turn your kids loose! The other thing you will notice right away is that people have caught on to how room names are alphabetized and have created names that include the letter A and then some junk characters to place the name higher on the list. (How annoying!)

To narrow the list, you can type a word or phrase in the **Display chat rooms that contain** text box, the same as you did when searching for newsgroups earlier in this chapter. You can also mark the **Show only registered rooms** check box to screen out the junk, but this may screen out too much; when I tried this, I was left with only one chat room on the list.

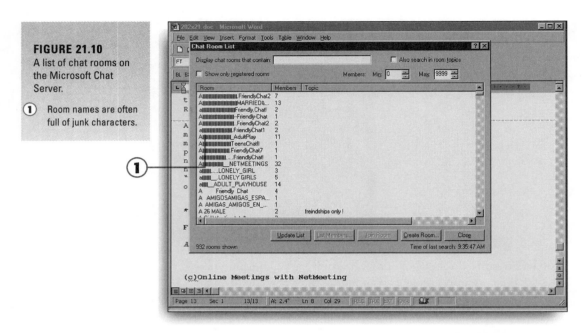

FIGURE 21.10
A list of chat rooms on the Microsoft Chat Server.

(1) Room names are often full of junk characters.

When you've located a room you want to enter, click it, and then click **Join Room**. (You can also create your own room by clicking **Create Room**.)

If you don't see any rooms that you want to enter, try a different chat server. To change servers, open the **Room** menu and choose **Disconnect**, then reopen **Room** and choose **Connect**, and then select a different server from the **Connect** tab. ChatNet is a popular chat server; you might have better luck there in finding someone with whom you can hold an intelligent, nonsexual conversation.

Chatting in a Chat Room

When you arrive in the chat room, many conversations may already be in progress. Sit back for a moment and get your bearings. As shown in Figure 21.11, the right pane lists the other people in the room. The top left shows what has been said, and you can type your own comments in the bottom left.

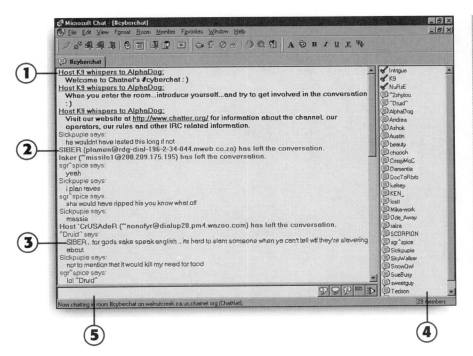

FIGURE 21.11
A typical chat room, with conversation flying every which way.

(1) Messages specifically to you are underlined.

(2) Messages in different colors are system messages.

(3) These are public statements individuals have made.

(4) List of room participants

(5) Type your own messages to the group here.

When you are ready to jump in, type something in the bottom-left pane, and then click the **Say** button 🖳 to say something to the whole group or the **Whisper** button 🖳 to say something to an individual privately.

To leave a chat room to visit another room on the same server, choose another room from the **Chat Room List** (🖳). To leave the entire server, open the **Room** menu and choose **Disconnect**.

Using Comic Chat

There are two chat modes: Text and Comic. You start out in Text. To switch to Comic, click the **Comic** button 🖳. To go back to text, click the **Text** button 🖳. Comic view shows each statement in comic-strip format, as shown in Figure 21.12.

Chat Room Etiquette

To avoid getting "flamed" (that is, bawled out for having bad manners), observe these chat room proprieties:

Don't type in ALL CAPS. It is hard to read.

Don't use too much punctuation, such as !!!GREAT NEWS!!!!!!!!. It's annoying and juvenile.

Don't use words that can't be used on the radio and TV. (That is, don't swear.)

Don't issue public invitations for sex. (Duh!)

Don't present your opinions in an aggressive or obnoxious way.

FIGURE 21.12
Comic view can liven up a boring chat.

(1) Double-click here to select your character.

(2) Choose an expression to send along with text you type.

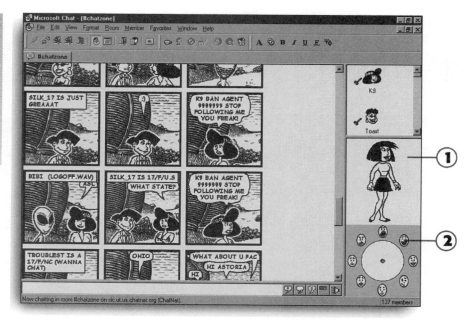

To control your own character in the comic strip, use the controls on the right (shown in Figure 21.12). Double-click the character to open a box where you can choose a new character. Then, choose an expression for your character from the palette of expressions in Figure 21.12.

Other Chatroom Activities

There's a lot to learn about the Chat software; you will pick up on things as you go along. But the following are some pointers to get you started:

- To search for a particular user on the server, use the **User List**.
- To let people know you are stepping away for a moment, click the **Away from keyboard** button.
- To find out the details about a person, double-click the name, or click the name and then click the **Get Identity** button.

To ignore a person (so that his or her messages do not appear on your screen), click the name and then click the **Ignore** button.

To have a private conversation with someone, click the name and then click the **Whisper Box** button.

- Use the formatting buttons at the right end of the toolbar to dress up the text that you type, the same as you did with email formatting in Chapter 20.

- To add a room to your Favorites list, choose **Favorites**, **Add to Favorites**. The favorites list works just like the one in Internet Explorer (Chapter 18, "Exploring the Web").

SEE ALSO

➤ *To format email, see page 362.*

➤ *To work with Favorites, see page 308.*

chapter

22

Creating and Publishing Web Content

Understanding Web Page Creation

To understand how Web pages are created, you need to know one important fact: The Web (in fact, the whole Internet) is, at its heart, a text-only medium. It transfers only numbers, letters, and symbols. It can't directly work with programs, graphics, text-formatting commands, or other nontext items.

Of course, without formatting and graphics, most Web pages would be deadly dull. And they *were*, in the early days, until some clever programmers hit upon a solution. They embedded formatting codes in plain text files and struck a deal with browser manufacturers to include translation for them in their software. Therefore, the Web designer, for example, might have a line in the text file like this:

```
<p>Abba is the <b>coolest</b> rock group of all time!</p>
```

The Web browser program recognizes everything in angle brackets (<>) as a formatting code and translates the preceding line as follows:

`<p>`	Start a new paragraph.
`<b>`	Make the following bold.
`</b>`	Stop making text bold.
`</p>`	End the paragraph.

The result in the Web browser would look like this:

`Abba is the `**`coolest`**` rock group of all time!` Because of all these codes needed to generate the page, the file itself (a.k.a. the *source code*) is hardly the attractive document you see in your browser. Instead, it's a jumble of text and symbols that the Web browser translates into the proper formatting. For example, Figure 22.1 is a page I created that shows off my vacation pictures. Figure 22.2 shows the same page's *source code* (that is, the codes that compose it).

Content-wise, you can put anything on your Web page that you want. For security reasons, it might be best to avoid publishing your address and phone number, and it's only good manners to avoid inflammatory rhetoric. But other than that, your Web page is absolutely your own.

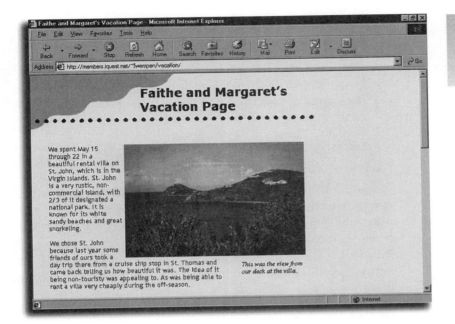

FIGURE 22.1
My vacation pictures in Internet Explorer.

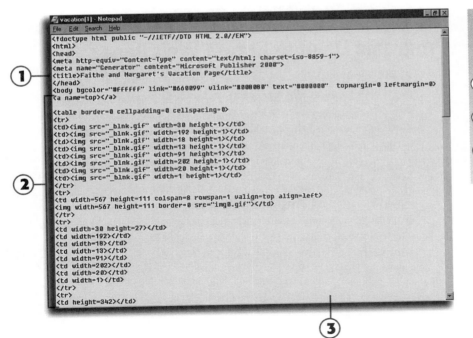

FIGURE 22.2
The source code for the vacation page.

(1) This line produces the page title.

(2) All these lines define the page layout.

(3) The rest of the text is further down in the file.

Structurally, your Web page should contain one or more of the following elements:

- Text
- Graphics
- Hyperlinks to other pages
- Tables
- Forms for readers to provide information to you
- Forms readers can use to search your site

Almost all Web page creation software can create all the preceding objects, although some do it much more easily than others. If you plan to use only text, graphics, and hyperlinks, any program will do; if you plan to create forms, you will have a much easier time of it with a high-quality program such as FrontPage or Word 2000. The next section takes a look at your Web page program options in more detail.

SEE ALSO

➤ *For an explanation of hyperlinks, see page 305.*

Programs Used to Create Web Pages

In the early days of the Web, people who wanted to create Web pages had to manually type each line of coding, as shown in Figure 22.2. People who created Web pages were rightly called Web programmers because the HTML codes needed to create the pages constituted a real programming language to be mastered.

Nowadays, however, a variety of programs are available that can create Web pages almost as easily as a word processor can create documents. These programs make it easy for people with no programming experience (like me) to create good-looking Web pages like the one you saw in Figure 22.1. It's possible to create pages "from scratch" in a text editor such as Notepad, but why would anyone want to?

You probably have several programs on your system already that can be used to create Web pages. See how many of these are available to you. I've listed them in order of preference:

- **FrontPage.** Microsoft's full-blown Web site creation software. This is a top-of-the-line tool that allows you to create multipage Web sites with links between them. And the newest version, FrontPage 2000, is very easy to use. FrontPage 2000 comes free with some versions of Office 2000, and you can also buy it separately.

- **Microsoft Word.** Word 97 and Word 2000 can both hammer out a very respectable-looking Web page with ease. Of the two, Word 2000's Web capabilities are much greater. Like FrontPage, Word 2000 can also create multipage sites that have pages that are automatically linked to one another.

- **FrontPage Express.** This program comes free with Windows 98. As the name implies, this program is a stripped-down version of FrontPage. It's useful for creating very simple pages, but I don't recommend it if you have either of the previously mentioned programs available.

Creating Web Pages with FrontPage

FrontPage really shines in Web page creation. It's my program of choice whenever I want to create really professional-looking pages. (The only drawback is that not everyone owns it.)

FrontPage can create a new *Web site* (multiple pages, linked) with a wizard that walks you through each step. Then, you can customize the Web site by adding your own text, formatting, hyperlinks, and other objects.

One of the nicest features in FrontPage is *Themes*. Themes are preset combinations of backgrounds, formatting, fonts, and other elements that you can apply to your Web site at any time. To choose a different theme, open the **Format** menu, select **Theme**, and then pick a theme from the Themes dialog box.

The following steps walk you through the process of creating a new Web site with FrontPage and customizing it.

Publisher 2000, Too

If you happen to have it, Microsoft Publisher 2000 also creates very nice Web pages. It comes with some version of Microsoft Office 2000. Earlier versions of Publisher are not much good for creating Web pages.

No FrontPage Express?

If you have FrontPage installed on your PC, FrontPage Express may not appear to be installed, even if it was there prior to installing FrontPage. (Just as well, in my opinion! FrontPage is much better.) If you insist on using FrontPage Express, you can reinstall it from the Windows 98 CD or download the latest version from Microsoft's Web site.

Creating a New Web Site with FrontPage

1. Start FrontPage from the **Start** menu.

2. Open the **File** menu, point to **New**, and click **Web**.

3. Select one of the wizards from the list that appears, and click **OK**. For example, for your family Web site, you might choose **Personal Web**.

   Depending on which wizard you choose, you might need to work through some more dialog boxes, selecting which pages you want to include. Do so as needed.

4. When the wizard is finished, the pages appear in FrontPage, ready for your customization. See Figure 22.3.

FIGURE 22.3
A personal Web page created with a FrontPage Wizard, ready for customization.

(1) To view a different page in the site, double-click one.

(2) Use the Preview tab to see how the page will look in Internet Explorer.

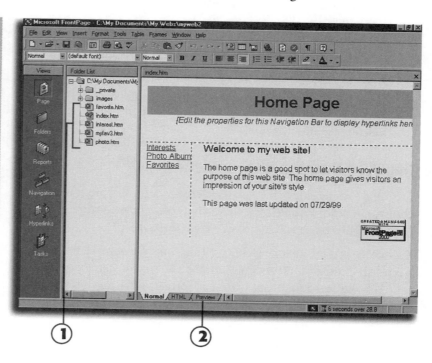

5. Replace all the sample text on each page with your own text. Double-click a page in the tree to switch to it.

6. Do any of the following to dress up a particular page:

   - Format the text using the formatting tools on the Formatting toolbar, the same as in any word processor.

   - Insert hyperlinks with the **Hyperlink** command on the **Insert** menu or the **Hyperlink** button 🖱 on the toolbar.

   - Change the theme (the colors, fonts, and overall look) with the **Theme** command on the **Format** menu.

7. Save your work.

SEE ALSO

➤ *To save your work directly to the Web server, see page 398.*

Creating Web Pages with Word

Whereas FrontPage creates Web pages exclusively, Microsoft Word is a more general-purpose tool. This word processor can save any document in Web format, converting it instantly for use on the Web; and Word 2000 can also create a group of linked Web pages (that is, an entire Web site).

In the following steps, I'll show you how to convert an existing Word document to a Web page. (This works in both Word 97 and Word 2000.) Following that, I'll show you how to create a new Web site from scratch with Word 2000.

Saving a Word Document in Web Format

1. Open the document in Word.

2. Open the **File** menu and click **Save as Web Page**. A special Save As dialog box opens with some additional controls. See Figure 22.4.

3. Click the **Change Title** button and type a title for the page. Then, click **OK**.

   This text will appear in the title bar in the Web browser when readers view the page.

4. Type a filename in the **File name** box.

5. Change the save location if desired. (To save directly to a Web server, see "Publishing Finished Pages to a Server" later in this chapter.)

6. Click **Save**.

Other Activities

You can do so much more with FrontPage than can be covered here! Explore all the menus and toolbars, and you will find commands for inserting graphics, creating frames, and lots more.

393

FIGURE 22.4
When saving as a Web page, you need to specify a page title as well as a filename.

① Click here to change the title.

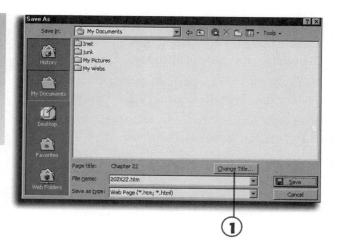

The above procedure is great for converting existing documents for use on the Web, but if you want a Web page (or Web site) designed specifically for Web use, from the bottom up, you should use the following procedure in Word instead.

You can create single Web pages in Word 2000 using any of its individual-page templates, or you can work through the Web Page Wizard to create a multipage site with links among the pages.

Creating a New Web Site with Word 2000

1. Open the **File** menu and click **New**.

2. Click the **Web Pages** tab.

3. To create a single Web page, click one of the page templates (such as **Column with Contents**).

   or

   To create a multipage site, click **Web Page Wizard**.

4. Click **OK**.

5. If you chose Web Page Wizard in step 3, work through the wizard, specifying what type of site you want to create. Here are some tips:

   • The Web site title will appear in the title bar when pages are viewed in a browser.

- Choose a Web site location on your hard disk, and then later transfer the pages to your Web server. That way, you will not have to be online every time you want to save your work as you construct the site.

- On the screen where you add pages to the site (Figure 22.5), add all the pages that you think you will need. By adding them this way, you ensure that they will be linked to the others.

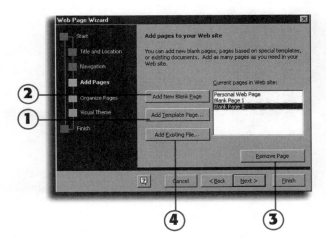

FIGURE 22.5
Add more pages as needed to your Web site.

1. Click here to add a page based on one of the Web templates.

2. Click here to add a blank page.

3. Click an existing page and click Remove Page to remove it.

4. nclude an existing HTML file in the Web with this button.

- On the screen where you arrange or rename the pages, assign meaningful names to each page by clicking it and clicking **Rename**. (Blank Page 1 and Blank Page 2 are not terribly meaningful.)

- When you are asked to choose a visual theme, click **Browse Themes** to see previews of each one. You may need to click **Install** in the box that appears to install a particular theme.

6. When the wizard has finished, a list of sample pages appears in the View bar, as shown in Figure 22.6. Customize the pages with your own content.

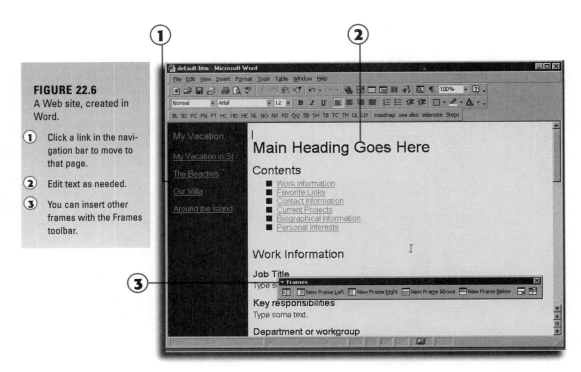

FIGURE 22.6
A Web site, created in Word.

① Click a link in the navigation bar to move to that page.

② Edit text as needed.

③ You can insert other frames with the Frames toolbar.

You can do almost anything to a Web site in Word that you can do to a regular Word document: change fonts, change alignments, create lists, and so on.

SEE ALSO

➤ *For more information about formatting text in a word processor, see page 68.*

Creating Web Pages with FrontPage Express

No FrontPage Express?

If you don't have FrontPage Express (it should be on the **Programs\Accessories\Internet Tools** menu if it's there), you can download it from Microsoft's Web site. Choose **Windows Update** from the top of the **Start** menu and select **FrontPage Express** as an update to download.

If you don't have FrontPage or Word, you can create Web pages with FrontPage Express. Warning: This is a much simpler program than the other two and not as intuitive to use. There isn't as much help for beginners as with Word and FrontPage, and no wizards or themes are available.

Start FrontPage Express and type the text for your Web page as if you were using a word processor. Choose styles for each paragraph from the **Styles** drop-down list; this helps format a particular line in a way that the browser will understand. For example, if you have a major heading, choose the **Heading 1** style for it. See Figure 22.7.

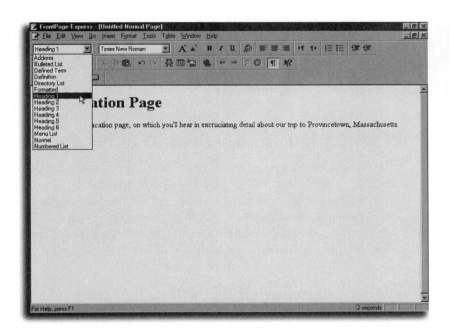

FIGURE 22.7
Select a style for each paragraph of text from the **Styles** list.

FrontPage Express has three toolbars. The top one is the Format toolbar. It contains formatting tools, such as the Styles list (see Figure 22.7), the Font list, buttons for bold, italic, and underline, and others.

The second is the Standard toolbar. It contains the standard Open, Save, and Print buttons, and buttons that insert graphics and hyperlinks.

The third is the Forms toolbar. It contains controls you can use to create online forms. (If you want to create online forms, however, do yourself a favor and get a more powerful program, such as FrontPage!)

Other Web Page Creation Programs

The three programs I've reviewed in this chapter are certainly not the only ones you can use. Many good Web page creation programs are available, both shareware and commercial. The following are a few of the more popular ones:

- Hot Dog Pro (shareware)
- EZ-HTML Edit for Windows (shareware)

- Adobe PageMill (commercial)
- HomeSite (commercial)
- Lotus Domino (commercial)
- Visual Page (commercial)

Publishing Finished Pages to a Server

To make your Web pages available on the Internet, you must copy them to a *Web server*. A Web server is a computer that is connected to the Internet full-time so that others can see the pages on it whenever they like. You can save the Web pages directly to your Web server as you create them, but you probably will want to wait until they are perfected before making them public.

Understanding Internet Addresses

The *address* is the location, or *path*, to which you save or copy a file or folder. Your hard disk has its own addresses for each file—for example, C:\My Documents\memo.doc.

A file on an Internet server has two addresses that both refer to the same location. One is its *Web address*, and the other is its *FTP address*. These are simply two ways of accessing the server. Web browsers use web addresses, and FTP addresses are used by FTP programs. For example, the Web address of a file might be

http://members.iquest.net/~fwempen/vacation.html

and the FTP address for the same file might be

ftp://ftp.iquest.net/members/1033/fw/fwempen/public_html/
vacation.html

The Web address is the one you will publicize; readers will use it to visit your page. Depending on the program you use to transfer the files, you may be able to use either the Web address or the FTP address to transfer the files to the server.

You need to find out from your ISP what Web and FTP addresses to use for your server. If you don't store the Web files in the right folder on the server, they might not be available to the public.

Personal Web Server

If you want to serve your pages to an intranet (a Web-based network inside your company) or set up a test environment before you publish your pages to your ISP's server, you may want to investigate the Microsoft Personal Web Server. It comes free with Windows 98, but it is not installed by default.

To install it, insert your Windows 98 CD and choose **Run** from the **Start** menu. In the Run box, type **x:\add-ons\pws\setup.exe**. (Substitute your CD-ROM letter for x.) Then, click **OK** and follow the directions to set it up.

FTP

FTP stands for *File Transfer Protocol*. It's a method of downloading and uploading files that predates the Web. It's a very quick, efficient means of transferring files, and it used to be very popular until the Web's popularity explosion.

Transferring Files with Web Folders

If you have created your page(s) in FrontPage 2000 or Word 2000, you can take advantage of a new feature in these programs—Web folders—to transfer the files to the server. This technique uses the Web address, so you do not have to bother with FTP.

Transferring Files to a Server Using Web Folders

1. In FrontPage 2000 or Word 2000, open the Web site to transfer.

2. Open the **File** menu and choose **Save as Web Page**.

3. Click the **Web Folders** button.

4. If you are saving to an existing Web folder, double-click the folder to open it.

   or

   If you need to create a new Web folder to save in, do the following:

   - Click the **Create New Folder** button . The Add Web Folder Wizard runs.

   - Type the Web address of the location to add (for example, `http://www.something.com/foldername`), as shown in Figure 22.8. Then, click **Next**.

FIGURE 22.8
Create a new Web folder in the specified location.

   - If prompted, enter a username and password for the site. Then, choose **Next**.

   - If you wish to change the name of the Web folder, type the new name into the box.

   - Choose **Finish**.

5. Choose **Save**.

> **Not Available?**
>
> If you see a message that the server cannot connect to the location, even though you know the address is correct, try one of the other methods. Your server may not support Web-based uploading, or some other problem may exist. Try the FTP method or the Web Publishing Wizard.

Transferring Files with FrontPage Express

FrontPage Express has its own Save As dialog box with a Page Location box. In it, you can type the Web address at which you want to save the file. See Figure 22.9. If prompted for a username and password, enter them, and the Web Publishing Wizard runs. You'll learn about the wizard later in this chapter.

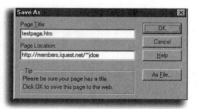

FIGURE 22.9
FrontPage Express allows you to transfer files to a Web address.

Transferring Files with FTP Locations

In most Microsoft applications (FrontPage, Word, and so on, versions 97 and later), you can save a file to an FTP location directly from the Save As dialog box. (This may work in other programs too; check it out.) This method is not quite as easy as the Web Folders method you learned about earlier, but it makes a good fallback if you can't make the Web Folders method work for some reason. (Another good fallback is the Web Publishing Wizard covered in the next section.)

Saving to an FTP Location

1. Open the Web site or page in the program in which you created it (Microsoft Word, FrontPage, and so on).

2. Open the **File** menu and choose **Save as Web Page**.

3. To work with an existing FTP location, skip to step 8.

   Or, to add a new FTP location, open the **Save in** drop-down list and choose **Add/Modify FTP Locations**.

4. Type the FTP site's address in the **Name of FTP site** box.

   Do *not* include anything after the first slash (/). (If you do, you will get an error message and the address won't work.) For example, if the address you were given is
   `ftp.iquest.net/fw/fwempen`, you would type `ftp.iquest.net` here.

5. If you must log in (very likely), click the **User** button and type your username. Then, type your password in the **Password** box. See Figure 22.10.

FIGURE 22.10
Set up a new FTP location.

6. Click the **Add** button.

7. Click **OK**. The new FTP location appears on the list.

8. Double-click the FTP location to connect to it.

9. Using the path you were given, navigate to the folder in which you are supposed to save your files.

10. Make sure the file name in the **File name** box is as you want it.

11. Click **Save**.

Transferring Files with the Web Publishing Wizard

The Web Publishing Wizard is a bit more out of the way than the other methods, but it is also foolproof and thorough. It walks you through the transfer step-by-step, allowing for any quirks or peculiarities of your server. It's also the method of choice if you don't have FrontPage, Word, or any of those other fancy programs that enable you to do a more direct transfer. (Remember, when you save with FrontPage Express, the Web Publishing Wizard kicks in to help.)

One at a Time

The Web Publishing Wizard transfers a single file or a single folder each time you use it, so you may want to put all the files to be transferred into a folder before you transfer them; that way you can do them all at once.

Using the Web Publishing Wizard to Transfer Files

1. Click **Start**, point to **Programs**, point to **Accessories**, point to **Internet Tools**, and click **Web Publishing Wizard**.

   If the Web Publishing Wizard is not there, install it using **Add/Remove Programs** (see Chapter 8).

2. Click **Next** to begin.

3. Click the **Browse Folders** or **Browse Files** button and locate the file or folder you want to transfer. Then, click **Open** to accept it, and then click **Next**.

4. Type a descriptive name for the Web server that you will recognize later. Then, click **Next**.

5. Type the Web address into the URL or Internet address box. Then, click **Next**.

6. If prompted, enter your username and password and click **OK**.

7. Click **Finish**. The Web Publishing Wizard transfers the file or folder to the server.

8. When a message appears that the transfer was successful, click **OK**.

SEE ALSO

➤ *To install the Web Publishing Wizard, see page 140.*

Advanced?

If the Web Publishing Wizard has not worked for you in the past, you may wish to click the **Advanced** button instead of **Next** in step 4. This brings up a drop-down list of connection methods; ask your ISP which one you should use.

part

V

MAINTENANCE AND PROBLEM-SOLVING

Optimizing Your Computer

Checking for Disk Errors

Sometimes drives get errors on them, and those errors can affect your system's performance. (See the next section, "Understanding Disk Errors," for a technical explanation of these errors.) The primary cause of these errors is abnormal program termination—in other words, shutting off the computer's power or restarting the system while it is in use. (Unexpected shutdowns aren't always your fault, of course; sometimes you'll have a power outage, or your computer will lock up.) These errors sometimes manifest themselves in odd ways—I have seen these disk errors cause everything from missing files to out-of-memory errors. Fortunately, there is a cure: ScanDisk, which is discussed later in this chapter.

Understanding Disk Errors

Before I show you how to use ScanDisk, you might want to learn a bit about these errors that ScanDisk is looking for and fixing. (Feel free to skip this section if you're not interested.)

Think of your hard disk as a grid of little compartments, like a wall of post-office boxes. Each compartment holds a piece of data, and each compartment has a unique address. Your computer maintains a big chart that identifies the contents of each compartment; it's called the File Allocation Table (FAT). The FAT is so important that your system maintains two identical copies of it in case one gets damaged.

When the FAT copies get out of sync with each other, or when the actual content of the disk gets out of sync with the FAT, a disk error occurs. The kinds of disk errors you might encounter include the following:

- A file's size being reported by the FAT does not match its size on the disk. (This is called an *allocation error*.) Allocation errors can cause the file to not open correctly because the FAT may not completely retrieve the file from all its address compartments.

- An address contains data, but the FAT does not know to which file the data belongs. (This is a *lost cluster* error.) This data may be important and belong to a file, but it also might just be junk that should have been deleted.

- A conflict in the FAT keeps the system from knowing to which of two files an address belongs. (The files involved in the dispute are *cross-linked*.) Of course, the data rightfully belongs to only one of the files, so when the wrongful owner is opened, it becomes corrupted because it contains data not its own. If that owner is a program file, the inappropriate data may prevent it from running properly in the future.

- The copies of the FAT do not agree because one of them has been damaged or is in error. This situation can happen if the computer loses power in the middle of a change being made in the FAT, and it can result in a file not appearing on a file list that you know should be there.

- A physical error on the disk causes it to be unreadable/ unwritable at a certain address. Whatever was stored there is probably lost. This situation can happen when you bump or jostle your computer's case while the computer is on. The head that reads the hard disk is like a needle on a phonograph, and the needle can come crashing down, scratching the hard disk at whatever address it happens to be at when the trauma occurs. You can also have physical errors on a hard disk that is slowly going bad or "dying."

Running ScanDisk

Your system has both a DOS and a Windows version of ScanDisk installed.

The DOS version runs outside the Windows environment. When you ran Windows Setup, the DOS version of ScanDisk checked your disk to make sure no errors existed. The DOS version also runs automatically the next time you start your PC whenever you have turned off the computer without shutting it down properly.

You will most often use the Windows version of ScanDisk, however. I run ScanDisk weekly to make sure my system does not have any errors. (Left uncorrected, errors can tend to cause other errors, creating a snowball effect.)

Checking for Errors with ScanDisk

1. Click **Start**, point to **Programs**, point to **Accessories**, point to **System Tools**, and click **ScanDisk**.

2. Click the drive you want to check (for example, **C:**). See Figure 23.1.

FIGURE 23.1
Choose the drive, the level of testing, and whether to fix errors automatically.

Advanced Options

For those who are techie enough to want the testing done a certain way, there are advanced options. Click the **Advanced** button to see and set them. These settings include which kinds of errors to look for, where to store the log file that lists the problems found, and how to correct the problems.

3. Choose **Standard** or **Thorough**.

   Standard checks for all errors except those on the physical surface of the disk; it is suitable for daily or weekly checks.

   Thorough checks for all errors including physical surface ones. Use this if you have been getting `Data error reading` error messages, if you have bumped or jostled the PC while it was running, or if it has been a month since your last thorough check.

4. To correct errors automatically, select the **Automatically fix errors** check box.

5. Click **Start**. The testing begins.

6. If you did not choose to correct errors automatically, and if ScanDisk finds an error, it reports the error in a dialog box. Click **Fix It** to continue.

7. When the testing is finished, a summary box appears. Click **Close** to close it.

8. Check any other hard disks on your system (if you have any). Then, click **Close** to close ScanDisk when finished.

Don't use your computer for anything else while ScanDisk is running; if the drive contents change, ScanDisk has to start over. If ScanDisk has trouble finishing because it continually starts over, even when you aren't doing anything, try some of the following to shut off programs that may be running in the background:

- Close all running programs that appear on the taskbar.
- Close all programs in the System tray (as explained in Chapter 3, "Running Programs").
- If you have Microsoft Office installed, Find Fast may be running. This utility indexes the files you use for faster access to them, but it can cause ScanDisk to restart repeatedly. To shut it down temporarily, double-click **Find Fast** in the Control Panel, and then open the **I**ndex menu and choose **P**ause Indexing.

SEE ALSO
➤ *To exit a program in the System tray, see page 64.*

Keep or Discard

If ScanDisk finds lost clusters, it asks you whether to keep or discard the data. I almost always choose **Discard**. Any kept data will not be in a recognizable form and won't be useful except perhaps to a data recovery specialist.

Using the Defragmenter

Earlier in this chapter, I explained how your disk is arranged into compartments, each holding a piece of data and each with a unique address. The storage system on your hard disk is not sequential, which is why the FAT has such a big job of keeping it organized. For example, suppose you had a word processing document that took up 18 compartments (called *clusters*) on the disk. Those clusters are not necessarily adjacent to each other; they may be scattered all over the disk. The FAT keeps a record of which 18 clusters that file uses, and when you open the file, the disk's read/write head hops around gathering up the pieces so they can be assembled into a file in your word processor.

When a file is not stored in adjacent compartments, it's considered *fragmented*. As you can imagine, hopping all over the disk to pick up the fragments takes time, which is why fragmentation slows down your system's performance. Compared to an unfragmented drive, a fragmented drive needs more time to retrieve a file (for example, when you issue the command in your word processor to open a document), and it sometimes takes longer to save a file, too.

How does fragmentation occur? When your hard disk is empty, files are written to it in sequential clusters. Suppose, for example, that you saved a word processing file that used 18 clusters. Then, perhaps you installed a new program. The new files are written right next to your word processing file. Now, you reopen the word processing file and type more pages, and it ends up needing a total of 20 clusters. No adjacent clusters are available next to the original 18, so the additional two are taken at another location. Over time, your file may be split into many locations over the disk.

When you *defragment*, a special program rearranges the content of your hard disk so that all files are stored in sequential clusters. That way, when the files are read, the disk read/write head reads from a single location rather than having to hop around, so it is able to read faster. Therefore, for best performance, you should defragment your drive regularly (say, once a month). This procedure won't turn an old PC into a powerhouse, but it may result in a modest speedup.

Defragmenting Your Hard Disk

As with ScanDisk, you can use a Windows utility to defragment your drive. You will want to use this procedure for each of your hard drives at least monthly.

You can also defragment removable drives of all types, but it is less critical to do so with those drives because their access time is rather slow already, and defragmenting will not help appreciably.

Defragmenting takes a long time, so you may want to begin it before you go to bed or out for the evening and let it run while you are away from the PC. Or, you can use the Task Scheduler to schedule it to run some other time, as you will learn at the end of this chapter.

Defragmenting a Disk

1. Click **Start**, point to **Programs**, point to **Accessories**, point to **System Tools**, and click **Disk Defragmenter**. The Select Drive box appears, asking which drive you want to defragment.

2. Choose your hard disk from the list.

3. Click **OK**.

4. Wait for the drive to be defragmented. Click the **Show Details** button if you would like to watch the process (see Figure 23.2).

Wait!

Don't use the PC for other things while it is running; any change to the disk forces the process to start over. See the notes at the end of the previous ScanDisk section for some tips on shutting down running programs if the defragmenter restarts continually and will not finish.

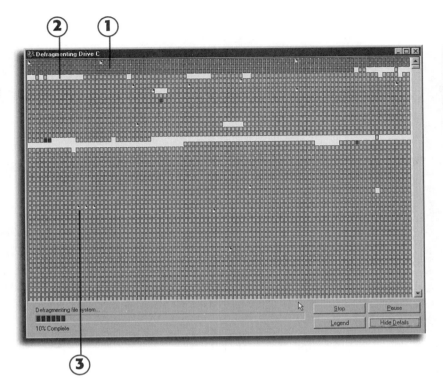

FIGURE 23.2
Choosing **Show Details** enables you to see a graphical representation of the defragmenting process.

(1) Each square represents a cluster.

(2) Defragmenting fills in these gaps.

(3) Squares like this represent unmovable files.

5. When the defragmentation is complete, click **Yes** to exit the defragmenter.

SEE ALSO

➤ *To schedule tasks such as defragmenting to run at a certain time, see page 421.*

Using Disk Cleanup

Disk Cleanup helps identify and remove files that you don't need on your hard disk. This gives you more room to store the files that you *do* want to keep, and to install new programs. It also makes your Start menu and desktop more tidy by removing shortcuts that no longer point to a working program. I run Disk Cleanup once a month on my system.

Running Disk Cleanup

1. Click **Start**, point to **Programs**, point to **Accessories**, point to **System Tools**, and click **Disk Cleanup**.

2. Select the drive you want to clean up, and then click **OK**.

3. Wait a few moments for Disk Cleanup to analyze your system. A report appears in a Disk Cleanup window, as shown in Figure 23.3.

FIGURE 23.3
Disk Cleanup reports which files could be deleted.

(1) Description of the selected category

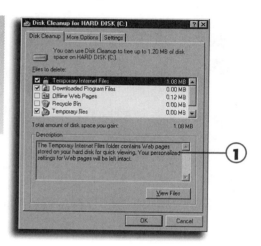

4. Check each category that you want to delete from the list (see Figure 23.3) and then click the **View Files** button. (Close the file-viewing window after looking at the files.)

5. If you decide that you would like to delete the files in a category, make sure a check mark appears in the check box next to that category.

6. Click **OK** after selecting or deselecting each category, as desired. A warning box appears.

7. Click **Yes** to confirm. The files are deleted, and the Disk Cleanup dialog box closes.

Disk Cleanup also has some additional options you can use to remove more files. On the **More Options** tab (see Figure 23.4).

- Click **Clean Up** under **Windows components** to open the **Windows Setup** tab of the Add/Remove Programs Properties box, from which you can remove Windows components as you learned in Chapter 8, "Installing New Programs."

Which Files?

As you might imagine, Step 5 is the critical one in this procedure. If you are not short on disk space, I recommend that you stick with only the categories that are marked by default for your cleanup operation.

- Click **Clean Up** under **Installed programs** to open the **Install/Uninstall** tab of the Add/Remove Programs Properties box. From there, you can remove installed programs, as you learned in Chapter 8.

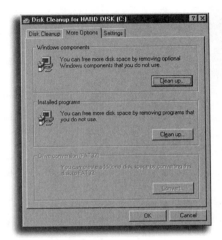

FIGURE 23.4
Other options you can set for Disk Cleanup.

On the Settings tab, you can select or deselect the check box (there's only one!) to automatically run Disk Cleanup when the free space on the drive gets low. This option is on by default.

SEE ALSO

➤ *To add or remove Windows components, see page 140.*

➤ *To remove installed programs, see page 148.*

Compressing Your Disk to Increase Capacity

Is your hard disk full? You have two choices: You can buy a new one (they are very cheap right now!) or you can stave off that day by using DriveSpace, a disk compression program.

How Disk Compression Works

Hard disks store data reliably, but there is often lots of wasted space between files. DriveSpace removes the wasted space in the disk storage system by storing the files using a different filing method so that your old disk can store more data.

DriveSpace essentially fools your system into thinking that a file is a disk, and it puts your files from the hard disk into that disk-like file. Because it's really a file, it isn't constrained by the inefficient filing system on a real disk, so you can store your hard disk content more efficiently.

Suppose your hard disk is drive C. DriveSpace creates a big file on C and calls it H. Windows treats this file like an extra hard disk. DriveSpace moves your files from C to H, gradually increasing the size of H until H takes up almost all the space on C. So now, this massive file is consuming drive C, and within that file is drive H and all the files that used to be on C.

All your programs expect to be on C. If they're on a drive called H, they might not work properly. So DriveSpace swaps the letters—your original C drive is renamed H and the new H drive is called C. Now, all the programs think they are on C. This process is completely automatic; you don't have to swap anything yourself.

DriveSpace approximately doubles the capacity of your current hard disk while slightly degrading its performance. (See the following note if you're curious about the mechanics of it.) The trade-off is that your hard disk may work a bit more slowly and that utility programs such as ScanDisk and Disk Defragmenter will take at least twice as long to run.

Before you use DriveSpace, you should back up any important files onto floppy disks. DriveSpace is fairly reliable, but not 100% safe; disk problems have been known to occur occasionally during compression. Better to be safe than sorry.

Compressing a Disk with DriveSpace

1. Click **Start**, point to **Programs**, point to **Accessories**, point to **System Tools**, and click **DriveSpace**. A dialog box lists the drives on your system (see Figure 23.5).
2. Click the drive you want to compress.
3. Open the **Drive** menu and click **Compress**.
4. Follow the self-explanatory prompts to finish the process.

After you have compressed a drive, you can use the **Compression Agent** program (also on the System Tools menu) to control the compressed drive. For example, you can use it to specify some files for additional compression or to make certain other files are uncompressed for faster access.

You can also manage your compressed drives by revisiting the DriveSpace window (Figure 23.5) after the compression has taken place. From there you can resize a compressed drive, change its drive letter, uncompress it, and more.

SEE ALSO

➤ *To back up important files, see page 426.*
➤ *To restore a backup, see page 426.*

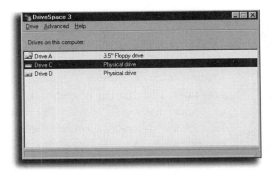

Uncompressing a Drive

I have had more system
problems when uncom-
pressing a drive than when
compressing one. Several
times, I have lost data
when uncompressing a
drive, and once my whole
hard disk was wiped out.
Therefore, you should be
sure to back up everything
first before you uncompress
a drive.

Converting to a 32-Bit File System

If you have upgraded your system to Windows 98 from an earlier
version of Windows and you have a very large, nearly full hard disk,
you may be able to get some benefit from converting your file system from 16-bit to 32-bit with a free utility that comes with
Windows 98. I won't get too technical about this, but basically a
32-bit file system is more efficient and eliminates some of the wasted
space on your hard disk so it can store more. You won't see as dra-
matic an improvement in the amount of free space with the conversion as you would with DriveSpace (covered in the previous section).
However, converting to a 32-bit file system is actually *good* for your
system and makes it run better, whereas using DriveSpace slows it
down.

To run the converter, click **Start**, point to **Programs**, point to
Accessories, point to **System Tools**, and click **Drive Converter
(FAT32)**. Then, follow the self-explanatory prompts to perform the
conversion.

Other Ways to Improve Performance

Windows 98 is a great operating system, but it requires quite a bit of
system resources. If you have an old or slow computer, try some of
the following to see if you can't eke out a bit more speed.

Keep the Display Simple

Windows 98 operates at peak speed when you are using a 32-bit video driver (in other words, a driver file designed to work with your specific video card under Windows 98) and when you use only the resolution and number of colors you need. For people with 14-inch monitors, that would be 640×480 resolution and 256 colors. For 15-inch and 17-inch monitors, the most you would want to use if you're looking for extra speed is 800×600 resolution and 256 colors. (This is not to say that other video resolutions and numbers of colors don't look great and have practical uses, but we're talking about wringing maximum speed out of your existing hardware right now.)

SEE ALSO

➤ *To check and change the video driver, see page 154.*

➤ *To change the video resolution and number of colors, see page 161.*

Check for Compatibility Mode

If you have certain DOS-mode programs loaded in your startup files when you install Windows 98, Windows runs in a special DOS-compatibility mode so that those programs will continue to function. Perhaps you don't need those programs anymore, but Windows has no way of knowing. DOS-compatibility mode can make Windows run much slower than normal.

To find out whether your system is running in DOS-compatibility mode, use the following procedure.

Checking for DOS-Compatibility Mode

1. Right-click **My Computer** and choose **Properties**.

2. Click the **Performance** tab. It should say Your system is configured for optimal performance, as shown in Figure 23.6. If it doesn't, you will see an explanation about what is forcing the system to run in DOS-compatibility mode.

3. Make a note of the recommended change, and change your startup files accordingly (by editing Autoexec.bat and/or Config.sys).

4. Restart the computer and return to the Performance tab to see if it now says your system is optimally configured. If it doesn't, repeat Step 3.

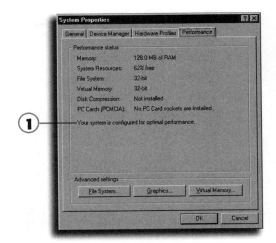

FIGURE 23.6
Check here for
compatibility-mode
issues.

① This message indicates
the system is not in
DOS-compatibility
mode.

Run Sysedit

If you need to edit `Autoexec.bat` or `Config.sys`, the easiest way is to
use a utility called Sysedit. It's like Notepad, except it automatically
opens several important Windows files. To run it, follow these steps.

Running Sysedit

1. Open the **Start** menu and click **Run**.

2. Type **Sysedit**.

3. Click **OK**. The System Configuration Editor window appears
   (see Figure 23.7).

4. Edit your startup files as needed.

5. Close the System Configuration Editor window, saving your
   changes.

6. Restart Windows.

Tuning System Performance Settings

The following steps outline a few nit-picking settings you can change
that will possibly speed up your system's performance a little.

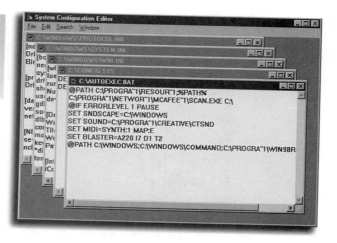

FIGURE 23.7
Edit Config.sys and
Autoexec.bat here as
needed.

Fine-Tuning Your System Performance

1. Right-click **My Computer** and choose **Properties**.
2. Click the **Performance** tab.
3. Click the **File System** button. A File System Properties dialog box appears.
4. On the **Hard Disk** tab (see Figure 23.8), open the **Typical role of this computer** drop-down list and choose **Network Server**.

   Don't worry if the computer isn't really a network server; this option merely sets the disk buffer settings to maximum.

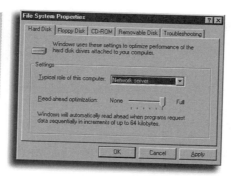

FIGURE 23.8
Maximize the disk buffer
by setting the machine
role to Network Server.

5. Make sure the **Read-ahead optimization** slider bar is set to **Full**.
6. On the **CD-ROM** tab, make sure the **Supplemental cache size** slider bar is set to **Large**.

7. Open the **Optimize access pattern for** drop-down list and select the appropriate setting for your CD-ROM drive's speed.

8. On the **Troubleshooting** tab, make sure that no check boxes are marked, unless you have previously marked one of them to eliminate a problem with your system.

9. Click **OK** to close the dialog box.

10. Click the **Graphics** button.

11. Make sure the **Hardware acceleration** slider bar is set to **Full** (unless you have set it lower for a reason). Then, click **OK**.

12. Click the **Virtual Memory** button.

13. Make sure the **Let Windows manage my virtual memory settings** option button is selected; then, click **OK**.

14. Click **Close** to apply your changes.

15. If prompted, click **Yes** to restart your system.

Updating Windows 98 with Windows Update

Windows Update helps you keep your copy of Windows 98 current. It compares the drivers and installed programs on your PC with a master list of the latest items available at the Microsoft Web site and suggests downloads that can bring your system up-to-date.

Running Windows Update

1. Open the **Start** menu and click **Windows Update**. Internet Explorer opens and connects to the Microsoft Web site.

2. Click **Product Updates**.

3. If this is the first time you have used Microsoft Update, a security warning appears, asking whether you want to install and run Microsoft Active Setup. Click **Yes**.

4. Wait for Windows Update to check your system and for the recommended updates to appear. See Figure 23.9.

Registered Users Only

To use Windows Update, you must have registered your copy of Windows 98 (or have used the workaround I explained in Chapter 11 in the sidebar "Reregister? Not Necessarily").

Windows Update also requires an Internet connection; if you don't have one, skip this or go to Chapter 17, "Setting Up Online Connectivity," to get set up.

FIGURE 23.9
Windows Update recommends these downloads to update my system.

5. Place a check mark next to the ones you want.

6. Click **Download**. A list of the programs you have chosen appears.

7. Click **Start Download**.

8. Depending on what you chose, a licensing agreement box may appear. If so, click **Yes** to continue.

9. Wait for the downloads to transfer and install themselves. You will see a confirmation page in Internet Explorer when they are finished.

10. Depending on the download, you may be prompted to restart your PC. Click **Yes**.

SEE ALSO

➤ To register your copy of Windows, see page 35.

➤ To set up an Internet connection, see page 288.

Scheduling Maintenance Tasks

Some of the tools you learned about in this chapter (most notably ScanDisk and Disk Defragmenter) take a long time to run and should be run on a regular schedule. Windows 98's Task Scheduler can be set up to make such programs run when you are not home or when you are sleeping, so that their running does not interfere with your computing productivity.

You can set up the maintenance using either Express or Custom modes. Express is very easy and great for beginners; Custom enables you to specify when and how often each individual program will run.

Express Scheduling Maintenance Tasks

1. Click **Start**, point to **Programs**, point to **Accessories**, point to **System Tools**, and click **Maintenance Wizard**.

2. Choose **Express** and then click **Next**.

3. Choose when you want the maintenance to run: **Nights**, **Days**, or **Evenings**. Then, click **Next**.

4. (Optional) To run all the scheduled tasks for the first time right now, mark the **When I click Finish, perform each scheduled task for the first time** check box.

5. Click **Finish**.

Custom Scheduling Maintenance Tasks

1. Click **Start**, point to **Programs**, point to **Accessories**, point to **System Tools**, and click **Maintenance Wizard**.

2. Choose **Custom** and then, click **Next**.

3. Choose when you want the maintenance to run: **Nights**, **Days**, **Evenings**, or **Custom**. Then, click **Next**.

4. A list appears of programs that start when Windows starts. Deselect the check box next to any of them that you want to disable from starting automatically. See Figure 23.10. Then, click **Next**.

FIGURE 23.10
You can prevent any of the programs from starting automatically at Startup.

5. To place Disk Defragmenter on the maintenance schedule, click **Yes, defragment my hard disk regularly**. Then, do the following:

   • Click **Reschedule** to specify when it should run.

   • Click **Settings** to change the default settings for the program.

   • Click **Next** when you've finished configuring the Disk Defragmenter.

6. To place ScanDisk on the maintenance schedule, click **Yes, scan my hard disk for errors regularly**. Then, set its schedule and settings the same as you did for Disk Defragmenter in Step 5. Click **Next** when finished.

7. To place Disk Cleanup on the maintenance schedule, click **Yes, delete unnecessary files regularly**. Then, configure its settings and click **Next**.

8. (Optional) To run all the scheduled tasks for the first time right now, mark the **When I click Finish, perform each scheduled task for the first time** check box.

9. Click **Finish**.

Adding a Maintenance Task

The Task Scheduler in Windows 98 can be modified to run other programs at regular intervals, too. For example, in Chapter 24, "Safeguarding Your System," you will learn about backup programs; you might want your backup program to run every night (or once a week).

To open the Scheduled Tasks window, double-click the **Task Scheduler** icon  in the System tray. Then, use the **Add Scheduled Task** Wizard to create a new task.

Scheduling a New Task

1. Double-click the **Task Scheduler** icon in the System tray.

2. Double-click **Add Scheduled Task**. The Scheduled Task Wizard opens.

3. Click **Next** to begin.

4. A list of programs installed on your system appears, as shown in Figure 23.11. Click the one you want to schedule, and click **Next**.

FIGURE 23.11
Select the program to schedule.

5. Type a name for the scheduled task (or leave the default name).

6. Choose an interval at which to schedule (Daily, Weekly, and so on). Then, click **Next**.

7. Set the controls that appear based on the interval you chose in Step 6. For example, if you chose Weekly, you would work with the controls shown in Figure 23.12. Click **Next** when finished.

8. (Optional) To set advanced properties for the scheduled item, select the **Open advanced properties for this task when I click Finish** check box.

9. Click **Finish**.

10. If you marked the check box in Step 8, set any additional properties for the item in the box that appears on the **Settings** tab. Then, click **OK**.

FIGURE 23.12
Specify details for the chosen interval.

chapter 24

Safeguarding Your System

Backing Up Your Files •

Restoring a Backup •

Protecting Your PC from Viruses •

How Data Gets Lost

Hard disks are fairly reliable in terms of storage. When you save something to a hard disk, it usually stays there intact. However, the following exceptions may occur:

- Disk errors, which you learned about in Chapter 23, can corrupt individual files, and the damage can spread to other files if you do not run ScanDisk to fix it.

- Physical trauma to the hard disk while it is operating (such as the PC falling off a table or being kicked) can damage areas of the disk, resulting in whatever data was in that spot becoming unreadable.

- Computer viruses can wipe out the FAT, so that although your data is still on the hard disk, you can't access it. Some viruses can even erase the hard disk itself.

- A mechanical failure in the hard disk mechanism can cause the hard disk not to read or write at all; therefore, you can't access your data even though it's still there.

If the lost data is critical, you might want to employ a professional data recovery service. This is not cheap, however, so it's *much* better to prepare for disaster ahead of time by making backup copies of your important files.

SEE ALSO

➤ *To correct disk errors with ScanDisk, see page 406.*

Backing Up and Restoring Files

Backing up your files need not be a big production. If you have a few important data files (such as word processing documents or databases), you can copy them to a floppy disk, to a zip disk or other removable media, or to a network location periodically. See Chapter 5, "Managing Files and Folders," to recall how to copy files. If you ever need the copies, simply copy them back to your hard disk.

If you have a lot of files to back up, however, you may wish to use a backup program. Such programs provide two benefits:

- They compress the files as they back them up so that more files can fit on a disk.

- They remember lists of files to be backed up so that you don't have to select each file individually each time you back up.

Because backed-up files are compressed for storage, you can't use them directly from the backup disk. You must run a Restore program to uncompress them and copy them back to your hard disk. I'll talk about restoring later in this chapter.

Which backup program should you use? Well, unless your backup needs are heavy duty (for example, backing up a network server for a company), just about any backup program will suffice. Windows 98 comes with a utility called Microsoft Backup that should work nicely for most people. In addition, if you have a zip or JAZ drive, or some other brand of removable large-capacity storage, that drive may have come with software you can use to back up your files. For example, my zip drive came with a program called One-Step Backup that copies the files I specify to a zip disk every day at a certain time.

In this chapter, I will focus on Microsoft Backup because it comes with Windows 98. Feel free to use a different program.

SEE ALSO
➤ *To add Windows components (such as Backup), see page 140.*
➤ *To copy files, see page 90.*
➤ *To schedule programs to run at certain times, see page 422.*

Backing Up with Microsoft Backup

To run Microsoft Backup, click **Start**, point to **Programs**, point to **Accessories**, point to **System Tools**, and click **Backup**. The first time you run it, Windows will check for *backup devices*. These are devices such as tape backup units that are specifically designed for doing backups. If it doesn't find any, a message appears to that effect, offering to run the New Hardware Wizard to configure one. If you don't have such a device, click **No**. Then the program opens, and you can proceed to one of the next sections.

Install It

Microsoft Backup may not be installed by default in Windows 98. You can install it on the Windows Setup tab of the Add/Remove Programs dialog box, the same as you did in Chapter 8, "Installing New Programs."

You can back up to any drive, a floppy, a hard disk, a network hard disk, a removable hard disk, and so on. If you have a high-capacity removable media drive, such as a zip or JAZ drive, I recommend using that. (You will need enough blank cartridges for it to contain the files you want to back up, of course. Prepare these beforehand, deleting any existing files from them.)

When you start Microsoft Backup, a dialog box prompts you for an action (see Figure 24.1). This dialog box appears each time you start the program, and it appears only at startup; if you close it (by clicking **Close**) you must restart the program to see it again.

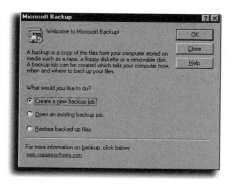

Click **Create a new backup job** and then click **OK**. If the dialog box has been closed or does not appear, open the **Tools** menu and choose **Backup Wizard**. Either way, the Backup Wizard starts. You can use it to do a complete backup of your entire system or to back up selected files.

Which is better? It depends. If you are backing up to floppy disks, or some other less efficient medium, the less you back up the better; back up only files that you cannot replace by reinstalling your programs. If you are backing up to a high-capacity medium such as a JAZ drive, you might prefer the relative ease (and peace of mind in not worrying that you have forgotten a file) of backing up everything.

Personally, I never back up the whole system because it would waste my time and my disks. Most of my hard disk is consumed by programs that I own the CDs for, and I could reinstall those programs easily if I had to. Besides, I back up to zip disks, which hold 100MB apiece. My hard disk holds 6G, so I would need 60 zip disks to back up the whole thing. They cost about $10 apiece, and I surely don't have $600 to spare for them! So I back up only my data files. I keep all the data files in a common folder (organized in subfolders within it), so I back up only that folder.

I'll run though both methods (full and partial) in the following sets of Steps.

Backing Up Your Whole System

1. From the Backup Wizard's first screen, leave **Back up My Computer** selected and click **Next**.

2. On the What to Back Up screen, leave **All selected files** selected and click **Next**.

3. Enter a destination and a name for the backup file. (See Figure 24.2). Click the **Browse** button to browse for a location, if needed. Then, click **Next**.

   For example, in Figure 24.2, I have chosen my zip drive (D:). You can use the filename `MyBackup.qic`, or you can specify a different name for the backup file, such as the current date or your name.

4. On the **How to Back Up** screen, select or deselect these check boxes as desired. Then, click **Next**.

   - **Compare original and backup files to verify data was successfully backed up.** This option checks each file after backup to make sure it was backed up correctly. It makes the backup take longer, but it may be worthwhile if you are backing up extremely important files.

   - **Compress the backup data to save space.** This option compresses each backed-up file so that the backup fits on fewer disks. It also makes the backup slower to restore, however (if and when you need to do that).

5. Type a name for this backup job. (For example, I might use **Complete** and today's date.)

6. Click **Start**.

Incremental Backups Later

The other option in Step 2, **New and changed files**, will be useful when you're running another backup in the future. It backs up only the files that have changed since the previous backup. (That's called an *incremental backup.*) You will probably want to do a full backup at least once a month, however, because to restore from an incremental backup, you must have every disk from the original and all incremental sets handy, and you will probably want to reuse disks.

The Archive Attribute

Previously, in Chapter 5, I explained about file attributes such as Read-Only, System, Hidden, and Archive. Backup programs turn the Archive attribute off when they back up a file; the Archive attribute turns itself back on again when a file is changed. That way, you (and the Backup program) can tell which files need to be backed up if you chose **New and changed files** in Step 2.

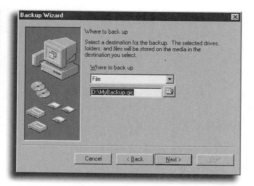

FIGURE 24.2
Select a name and a destination for the backup file. All the backed up files will be stored in that location.

7. Wait for the backup to finish. A Backup Progress window appears as the backup is happening (see Figure 24.3).

   When prompted, insert blank media (your disk) into the drive you are using and click **OK** to continue.

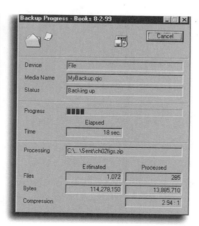

FIGURE 24.3
This Backup Progress screen reports the status of the backup as it occurs.

8. When the backup has finished, click **OK** to close the message box that reports this.

9. Click **OK** to close the Backup Progress window.

10. Exit from Microsoft Backup.

Backing Up Selected Files

1. From the Backup Wizard's first screen, choose **Back up selected files, folders and drives** and click **Next**.

2. An Explorer-like window appears, in which you can select the files you want (Figure 24.4). Do any of the following to select files:

   • To select an entire drive, place a check mark beside it.

   • To open a list of folders, click a plus sign. (A plus sign means subfolders are beneath that one.)

   • To select a folder or file, place a check mark next to it.

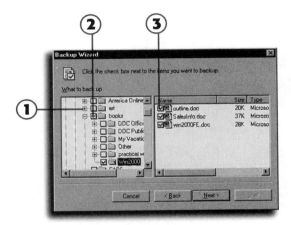

FIGURE 24.4
Choose the files you want to back up.

(1) Click a plus sign to expand a list.

(2) Select the entire folder.

(3) Select the file.

3. Click **Next**.

4. Go to the preceding procedure ("Backing Up Your Whole System") at Step 2 to complete the backup.

Restoring Files from a Backup

I hope you never have to restore files from a backup; I hope nothing bad ever happens to your PC that would necessitate it. But when you need a backup, it's awfully good to have it.

If something happens that wipes out your hard disk, you will first need to recover from that situation. You may need to install a new hard disk, reinstall Windows, and reinstall many of your applications. After that's done, make sure Microsoft Backup is installed, and then perform the following Steps to restore your data.

Quick Start

To quickly start Microsoft Backup, double-click the backup file (.qic) in a file listing for the first disk in the set.

Restoring a Backup

1. Insert the first disk of the backup set into your drive.

2. Start Microsoft Backup and choose **Restore backed up files** from the dialog box that appears. Then, click **OK** to begin.

3. Choose the restore destination (that is, where the backed up files are currently stored), and then, click **Next**.

4. A list of backup sets on the disk appears. If more than one is listed, select the one you want and then, click **OK**.

5. If you see a message about the set continuing on another disk, asking whether you want to continue logging, click **Yes**.

6. If you see a message to insert the next disk in the set, do so.

7. On the Restore Wizard screen that appears, select the file(s) you want to restore, the same as you selected files to include in the backup initially. See Figure 24.5.

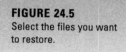

FIGURE 24.5
Select the files you want to restore.

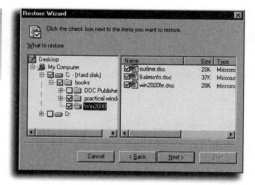

8. Click **Next**.

9. On the Where to Restore screen, choose **Original Location** or **Alternate Location**. If you choose the latter, specify a location when prompted. Then, click **Next**.

10. On the How to Restore screen, choose what to do if a file of the same name already exists in that location. Then, click **Next**.

11. Click **Start**.

12. If you see a Required Media box, click **OK**.

13. As prompted, insert disks and click **OK**. If you see any warnings or errors during the Restore, click **OK** to move past them and to continue with the Restore operation.

14. At the Operation Completed box, click **OK**.

15. Click **OK** to close the Restore Progress box.

16. Exit from Microsoft Backup.

SEE ALSO
➤ *To create a boot disk, see page 105.*

Protecting Your PC from Viruses

Computer viruses can wipe out your hard disk's contents, and in some rare cases even cause hardware damage. (A recent virus, for example, wiped out the computer's BIOS information, rendering it unusable.) That's the worst case. Many other less-devastating viruses exist, too, which corrupt individual files, play pranks, or merely attach copies of themselves to other files.

Many other types of viruses exist as well. Word macro viruses, for instance, infect Microsoft Word files and cause problems in Word (for example, one such virus forces every new document you create to be saved as a template).

> **Trojan Horses**
> Remember the old legend of the Trojan Horse? It appeared to be a gift, but it was actually filled with enemy soldiers. A type of computer virus called a *Trojan horse* does the same thing. It appears to be a useful program, but running it triggers something bad (such as file deletion) on the PC on which it runs.

How Do Viruses Infect a PC?

Viruses get into a PC in one of the following ways:

- Booting from an infected startup disk (floppy, hard disk, and so on)
- Running a program containing a virus
- Opening a Word or Excel file containing a macro that contains a virus

You *cannot* get a virus from reading an email message (unless it has a program attached to it that you run). You also cannot get a virus from surfing the Web or reading newsgroups (again, unless you download and run a program as part of that activity).

Generally speaking, viruses cannot infect data files; they infect only program files and the boot sectors of disks. An exception to this is if a data file (such as a Word document) contains an infected *macro* (which is, essentially, a mini-program); opening that data file and allowing the macro to run can infect your PC. This doesn't mean, however, that a virus cannot *harm* data files. A virus can wipe out an entire hard disk, data files and all. It simply cannot be *spread* through them (except via macros). In the following section I'll outline some ways to avoid virus infections.

How Can I Prevent Virus Infection?

To check for viruses and to prevent new ones from infecting your PC, you need an antivirus program. Windows 98 does not come with any virus protection per se. However, the Windows 98 Plus Pack comes with McAfee Anti-Virus, a very good virus-protection program. Another popular program is Norton Anti-Virus. I strongly urge you to get one of these programs and leave it running at all times, especially if you use the Internet a lot. You can download free trials from these locations:

McAfee Anti-Virus

http://www.mcaffee.com/

Norton Anti-Virus

http://www.symantec.com

You can prevent a lot of virus infection risk, however, just by being aware. It's like walking down a city street at night; you need to be alert to possible dangers and not engage in risky behavior. The following are some tips:

- In Internet Explorer, make sure your security levels are set to at least Medium for the Internet Zone. See Chapter 18, "Exploring the Web."

- Do not open attachments or run programs that you receive with email from unknown senders.

- If in doubt about an attachment, check it with your antivirus program before opening it.

- Download updates for your antivirus software from the company's Web site at least monthly. If you read about a new virus in the news, download an update immediately.

- If you open a Word or Excel file and see a message that it contains macros, asking whether you want to enable them, choose **Disable**. Then, open the **Tools** menu and click **Macros** and take a look at the macros in the file to see whether there are any suspicious-looking ones.

- Check in your BIOS setup program to see whether a boot sector protection exists that you can turn on. This prevents a program from writing to that critical startup area of your hard disk.

- If you accidentally start up the PC with an untested floppy disk in the drive, and you receive a message saying to remove it and press a key to continue, remove it and press **Ctrl+Alt+Del** to completely restart the boot process. This prevents any boot sector viruses that might have been on that floppy from infecting your PC.

- Use your anti-virus program to make an emergency startup disk, and then write-protect it. In the event of a virus infection, start your PC using that disk and follow its onscreen instructions.

SEE ALSO

➤ *To set Internet Explorer's security level, see page 324.*

➤ *To work with a PC's BIOS, see page 203.*

➤ *To use Internet Explorer, see page 302.*

➤ *To receive email with attachments, see page 350.*

chapter 25

Troubleshooting Problems

Startup Problems •

Windows Problems •

Problems with a Device •

Problems with a Program •

Troubleshooting Startup and Shutdown Problems

The following sections deal with problems that occur when you are starting up, restarting, or shutting down your PC.

Restarting a PC That Won't Restart Normally

Back in Chapter 1, "Windows Basics," you learned how to restart Windows. But sometimes Windows refuses to restart normally, and you must shut things down in a more "forceful" way to terminate whatever program has locked up. The following steps show how to do this.

Restarting a PC That Won't Restart Normally

1. Press **Ctrl+Alt+Del**. The Close Program dialog box appears.

2. Look for a program on the list that says Not responding next to it, and click that program.

   If you don't see one, skip to Step 7.

3. Click **End Task**.

4. Wait for the computer to restart (up to one minute).

5. If the computer will not restart, repeat Steps 1 through 4.

6. If the computer still will not restart, press **Ctrl+Alt+Del** again to reopen the Close Program dialog box.

7. Click the **Shut Down** button.

   This shuts down the computer rather than restarting it.

8. If the computer will not shut down using Step 6, turn off its power. Wait a few seconds before turning it back on.

   This is a last resort, because such an ungraceful shutdown can cause problems, but if none of the preceding steps worked, it is your only recourse.

If you are forced to shut down the PC by turning off its power before Windows says it is safe to do so, it may cause disk errors. When you restart the PC, ScanDisk will probably run and check for these errors. If ScanDisk doesn't run, you can run it yourself to check for errors; see Chapter 23.

SEE ALSO

➤ *To restart Windows normally, see page 29.*

➤ *To run ScanDisk, see page 407.*

Troubleshooting Missing File Error Messages at Startup

If you see an error message (usually gray on a black screen) at startup that tells you files are missing, one of the following is probably true:

- The files are actually missing.

- The files have been corrupted due to a disk error, which may or may not have already been repaired.

- Nothing is really wrong, but the computer has somehow gotten confused. (This is especially true if the missing file is HIMEM.SYS.)

Because you can't be sure which of the previous is the case, use the following procedure to troubleshoot.

Starting Up with a Missing File Error Message

1. Turn the computer's power off. Wait five seconds, and then turn it on again.

2. If you still see the same error message, jot down the file name on paper.

3. Press any key to continue loading Windows.

    If Windows won't load, see "Starting the PC in Safe Mode" later in this chapter. If that doesn't work, go to "Booting from a Startup Disk."

4. When Windows finishes loading, run ScanDisk.

5. If ScanDisk found and corrected any errors, restart the PC. Do you still get the same error message?

6. If you still get the error at startup, use Find to locate the file on your PC, if possible.

    If you can find where it is (even if it's corrupted), you will know where to put the fresh copy you are going to extract in the next step.

7. Extract a fresh copy of the file from the Windows 98 CD-ROM.

   See "Extracting a File from a CAB" later in this chapter for help. If you aren't sure where to put it, place two copies: one in \Windows and one in \Windows\System.

8. Restart the PC again. If you still get the error, refer to "Checking System Files" later in this chapter.

Troubleshooting Registry Errors at Startup

The Windows Registry is the repository of settings and controls that tell Windows 98 how to operate. The Registry includes everything from which programs are installed to which colors you have chosen for your color scheme. If this important file becomes corrupted, Windows may not start.

To correct registry errors, use the program Scanreg.exe at the MS-DOS prompt. (You can't do this from inside Windows; you must start the PC in MS-DOS mode.) Use the following steps.

Repairing the Registry with the Registry Checker

Not Restored?

If you use the /restore switch and see a message that the Registry was not restored, perhaps a third-party program (such as Norton Unerase) has the drive's disk access locked. To work around this, step through the startup routine using step-by-step prompting from the Startup Menu and choose **N** for every prompt except the one that loads HIMEM.SYS. Then, when the command prompt reappears, try **scanreg /restore** again.

1. Restart the computer. Press and hold down the **Ctrl** key until the Startup menu appears.

2. Choose **Command prompt only**.

3. At the command prompt, do one of the following:

   • Type **scanreg /restore** and press **Enter**. (It is customary to use a space before the slash.) Use this if you got the error immediately after installing a new program or device, and you want to put the registry back the way it was. This replaces the current Registry with the most recent backup of it.

   • Type **scanreg /fix** and press **Enter**. Use this if you have *not* just installed something new, and you want to fix the existing copy of the Registry rather than going back to the last backup.

4. After the Registry Checker finishes repairing the Registry, press **Enter**.

5. At the command prompt, type **scanreg /opt** and press **Enter**.

   The /opt switch causes the Registry Checker to optimize the registry by removing unused space.

6. Restart your PC.

Sometimes Windows can detect a registry problem itself and correct it by copying the most recent registry backup. You may see a message such as this:

You have restored a good registry. Windows found an error in your system files and restored a recent backup of the files to fix the problem.

If you see that, restart your PC, and the problem should have corrected itself. If it doesn't, running Scanreg.exe with the /fix switch should clear up the problem.

Starting a PC in Safe Mode

Safe mode is a special troubleshooting mode that you can use to fix problems with Windows 98 that prevent it from starting normally. For example, perhaps you have inadvertently installed the wrong video driver—one that scrambles your display. You can use Safe mode to start Windows 98 in plain VGA mode and then make the driver change and restart normally.

If Windows 98 fails to start, the next time you attempt a startup the Startup menu appears (see Figure 25.1). If the Startup menu does not appear automatically, you can force it to appear by holding down the **Ctrl** key as the computer boots. (You can also press **F8** when you see the message Starting Windows 98, but that message flashes by quickly and it's easy to miss it.) From the Startup menu, you can choose **Safe mode** (option 3).

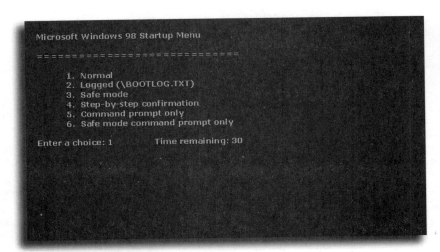

FIGURE 25.1
The Startup menu, from which you can choose Safe mode.

Safe mode starts Windows in a bare-bones state, with a generic driver for the essential components such as video, mouse, and keyboard. It does not load any programs that normally load at startup, or any drivers for "unnecessary" hardware such as scanners. As you can see in Figure 25.2, the words "Safe mode" appear in each corner so that you remember that you are not in regular Windows 98.

FIGURE 25.2
Safe mode enables you to start Windows when it won't start normally.

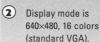 Safe mode indicators in corners.

② Display mode is 640×480, 16 colors (standard VGA).

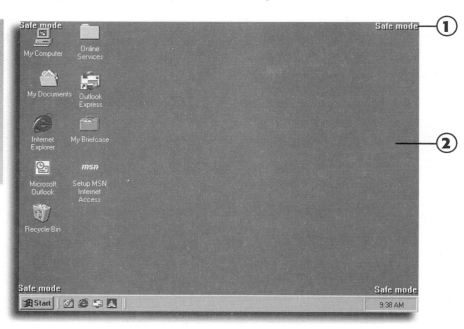

Usually when Windows will not start normally, an error message appears giving you a hint as to why. If the problem is a certain program or device, correct the problem as described later in this chapter in the sections "Troubleshooting Problems with a Device" and "Troubleshooting Problems with a Program."

SEE ALSO
➤ *To work with display modes, see page 161.*

Booting from a Startup Disk

If Windows will not start and none of the solutions I've given you so far have worked, you may need to start it using your Windows 98 startup disk. (Remember, you made one in Chapter 5.) If you don't have a startup disk, you can make one on another Windows 98 PC if one is available. (Ask around!)

The startup disk not only contains files that start your PC, but it also contains many helpful utilities you can run from the command prompt. So many of them are available, in fact, that they don't all fit on a single floppy; they have been compressed to fit. You can't use them in their compressed state.

When you start your PC with the startup disk, it creates a RAM disk (a virtual hard disk made from extra memory), and decompresses the utilities there. When working with a PC that has been started with the startup disk, you will have an additional drive letter available, and that drive will contain the utility programs.

Starting a PC with a Startup Disk

1. Place the startup disk in the PC's floppy drive and turn it on. You will see a menu like the one in Figure 25.3.

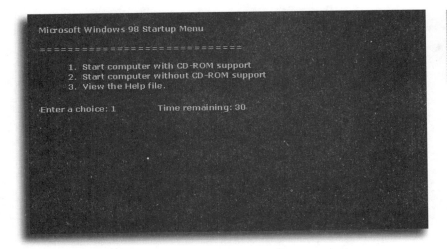

FIGURE 25.3
Choose whether to load CD-ROM support.

2. If you think you will need CD-ROM access to fix the problem, press **1**. Otherwise press **2**. (If in doubt, press **1**.)

3. Wait for the startup disk to finish loading drivers and decompressing files. The A:\> prompt appears when it is finished.

4. Do either of the following, as needed:

- Copy whatever files are needed from your CD or other disks to get Windows working again. (You may need to get some expert help with this.) Then, restart the PC and cross your fingers!

- Use the utilities on the RAM drive to check and rebuild your system. See "Recovering from a Complete PC Failure" next for details.

Recovering from a Complete PC Failure

If you are reading this section, I'll assume that the worst has happened—your hard disk has failed and you've had to replace it, or a virus has wiped out its contents, or for some other reason you need to rebuild from square one. You have just booted from your startup disk (see the preceding section), and now a cursor is blinking at you from an A:>\ prompt. What next?

First, can you access your old hard disk at all? If so, copy off any essential data files onto floppy disks.

If you have already installed a new hard disk, you should make sure your BIOS detects it properly, and then partition and format it. You should reformat your old hard disk if your disaster was due to virus infection.

To partition a drive, use the FDISK command, which is on your startup disk (A:). Partitioning the drive sets up the drive in one or more chunks, and each chunk can be formatted as a separate drive letter. You should not need to partition your drive unless you just installed a brand-new hard disk.

You can partition a physical drive into one or more *logical* drives, which are separate drive letters. Depending on your system's BIOS limitations, you may need to break up an extremely large drive into chunks of about 2 gigabytes apiece. FDISK will help you with this, suggesting the appropriate maximum size for the primary partition and helping you create additional partitions (*extended* partitions) from the remaining space.

Repartitioning an Old Drive

If you have an old hard disk that you need to reformat anyway, and you are unhappy with its current partitions, now is the time to repartition it! For example, suppose you had a 2GB drive. Under your old operating system that you originally bought with the PC, you were limited to hard disks of 512MB in size, so your 2GB drive is broken into four logical drives.

Now that you are using Windows 98, which supports larger drives, you could delete all those partitions and create one large one, so you could have a single drive of 2GB. Repartitioning wipes out everything on a drive, so you would not normally be doing this, but because you have to reinstall everything anyway, you can take advantage of the situation and set up your partitions the way you have always wanted them.

Partitioning a Drive

1. At the command prompt, type **FDISK** and press **Enter**.

2. At the message about enabling large disk support, type **Y**.

3. Choose option 4 to display existing partition information for the drive.

4. Do one of the following:

   - If you see partition information that indicates that drive C is partition 1, the drive has already been partitioned. Press **Esc** to return to the FDISK main menu and then press **Esc** again to exit FDISK. Then, go on to the next procedure, "Formatting a Drive."

   - If you see a message that no partitions exist, press **Esc** if needed to clear that message. Then, continue to the next step.

5. Type **1** to choose Create Primary DOS Partition, and then press **Enter**.

   If you see the message **Primary DOS partition already exists**, press **Esc** twice to exit from FDISK. Otherwise, FDISK checks the disk and creates the partition and this message appears:

   ```
   Do you wish to use the maximum available size for a Primary
   DOS partition and make the partition active (Y/N)?
   ```

6. Type **Y** and press **Enter**. FDISK verifies the partition. Then, you see this message:

   ```
   You MUST restart your system for your changes to take
   effect. Any drives you have created or changed must be for-
   matted AFTER you restart.
   ```

7. Press **Esc** to exit FDISK.

8. Restart your PC again using the startup disk.

After you partition and reboot, you must format each partition. To do so, change to the RAM drive and then type **FORMAT** and the drive letter to be formatted. For example, to format the C: drive, type **FORMAT C:**. To make the drive bootable, add an /S switch at the end: **FORMAT C: /S**.

Partitioning

Partitioning prepares the drive for use by dividing up its big physical surface into one or more logical compartments. Each of these will have its own drive letter. If you can, it's usually best to make the drive one big, single partition, unless you have a reason for needing multiple drive letters.

Large Disk Support

Choosing **Y** in Step 2 enables 32-bit file system support, which is more efficient and modern; choosing **N** forces the drive to use the 16-bit file system for backward compatibility.

Do not confuse 16- and 32-bit file systems with 16- and 32-bit programs. The file system is the underlying structure that determines how your disk stores files. It doesn't have anything to do with the individual programs or how they run.

Out with the Old

If your old drive has partitions and you want to change them, press **Esc** and then use option 3 to delete all existing partitions.

After formatting, check each drive to make sure it is readable from the prompt. Switch to the drive by typing its letter and a colon and pressing **Enter**. Then, type **DIR** and press **Enter**. Because the drive is empty, a File not found message appears. That's good—it means the drive is formatted and usable.

After partitioning and formatting, you can install Windows on the drive. Refer to Appendix A.

Startup Troubleshooting Tips

If your PC still won't start, here are a few last-ditch things to look at or try.

Blank Screen

If you don't see anything at all onscreen, and you hear nothing, not even a fan, the computer is not getting power, or the power supply is defective.

- Is the computer plugged into an electrical outlet? Does that outlet have power? Sometimes a light switch that you would not expect can turn the power on/off for an outlet.
- If the computer is plugged into a power strip, is that power strip's switch on?
- Is the power cable plugged firmly into the back of the PC?

If the screen is blank and you hear nothing except the power supply fan (no disk activity), something is wrong with either the motherboard or the processor, or the video card is not installed correctly.

If you see a blank screen and hear a series of beeps, the memory is not installed correctly or is defective, or some kind of motherboard error exists.

If you see a blank screen, hear a single beep, and see or hear some disk activity, the computer is starting normally, but the monitor isn't showing it. Try to figure out where the disconnect is between the monitor and the computer.

- Is the monitor getting power? Check to make sure it is plugged in and turned on. A light should illuminate on its front when it has power.

- Is the light on the front of the monitor solid green? That's good. If it's amber or blinking, the monitor is in Standby mode, which could indicate one of two things:
  - The monitor is fine but is not receiving any signal from the computer.
  - The monitor has set itself in Standby mode and needs to be awakened. Try pressing the buttons on the front of the monitor to see whether any of them will wake it up.
- Are the monitor contrast and brightness controls set appropriately?
- Is the monitor firmly plugged into the video card?
- Has the video card come dislodged from the motherboard inside the PC case?

Can't Boot from a Floppy

If you try to boot from a floppy but the system keeps asking you to insert a bootable floppy and press Enter, your BIOS program may not be aware of the floppy drive, or the BIOS may have been set up so that it doesn't boot from the floppy drive (or doesn't boot from it first).

Enter the BIOS setup program and confirm that the floppy drive is set up there. Then, check the boot sequence in the BIOS setup program. This command is probably in the Advanced section of the BIOS options. Make sure that the first boot device is set to A: (or Floppy) and that the second is set to C: (or IDE-0). Then exit the BIOS program, saving your changes. If this problem persists, you may have a bad floppy drive or floppy cable.

Hard Disk Not Bootable

If you see a message such as No Operating System or No Command Processor, or something prompting you to insert a disk with startup files, your hard disk does not contain the startup files needed to start the PC. Perhaps a virus has erased them, or perhaps you have accidentally deleted them yourself.

Boot from a floppy (your Windows startup disk works fine for this). If the computer starts and you see the A:\> prompt, try switching to C: by typing **C:** and pressing **Enter**. If you can get to a C:\> prompt like that, you know that the hard disk is partitioned and formatted and merely needs to have the system files re-transferred. On the other hand, if you see Invalid Drive Specification or something about the drive not being readable, you will need to reformat it, as explained earlier in this chapter.

To transfer the system files to the hard disk from your bootable floppy, type **SYS C:** at the A:\> prompt and press **Enter**. This copies the system files to your C: drive. When you see the message **System Transferred**, you know it's finished. Then, remove the floppy from the drive and restart your PC.

Troubleshooting Problems with Windows

In this section, I'll talk about those times when Windows starts but doesn't work correctly. Perhaps it locks up frequently or gives you error messages when you try to do anything.

The problem could be any of the following:

- You have used Windows Update to update your copy of Windows 98, and something about the update is causing the problem.

- Somehow one or more of the Windows system files have become corrupted, damaged, or deleted.

- The Registry has become corrupted or damaged, or invalid information has been written to it.

- A specific program you have installed is causing Windows in general to malfunction.

First things first: What have you done recently that changed your system? Whatever it was, try to undo it. If you have recently used Windows Update, remove the update as described in the following section, "Removing a Windows Update." If you have recently installed a new program, uninstall it (see Chapter 8).

Next, do you see any error messages about particular files causing a problem? If so, jot down the names of the files and try extracting fresh copies of them from the Windows 98 CD. See "Extracting a File from a CAB" later in this chapter for details.

If you can't think of what might have caused the problem, you might try running a general check of your system files, as described in "Checking System Files" later in this chapter.

Finally, if nothing else works, try reinstalling Windows 98. See Appendix A.

SEE ALSO

➤ *To remove an installed program, see page 148.*

➤ *To reinstall Windows 98, see page 470.*

Removing a Windows Update

To remove an update, revisit the Windows Update Web page (see Chapter 23, "Optimizing Your Computer") and choose **Show Installed Updates**. This changes the list of updates to include the ones you already have (see Figure 25.4). To reinstall one, reselect it. Some updates have an Uninstall button next to them; for these, you can click it to uninstall the update.

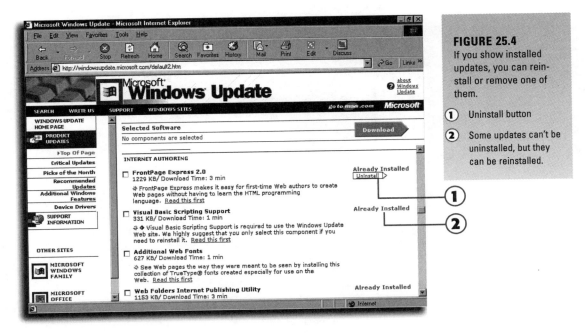

FIGURE 25.4
If you show installed updates, you can reinstall or remove one of them.

① Uninstall button

② Some updates can't be uninstalled, but they can be reinstalled.

You can also uninstall Windows updates even if you can't connect to the Internet. To do so, open System Information (as explained in the following section) and choose **Tools** and then **Update Wizard Uninstall**.

SEE ALSO

➤ *For more information about Windows Update, see page 419.*

Running System Information Utilities

System Information is a great utility in Windows 98 that provides detailed information about your system. Start it from the **Start** menu by choosing **Programs**, then **Accessories**, and then **System Tools**, and clicking **System Information**.

You can use System Information to troubleshoot a variety of device problems (which you'll learn about later in this chapter), but it also contains a Tools menu with several important utilities on it. See Figure 25.5. In the following sections, I'll outline some of these tools that can help fix Windows problems.

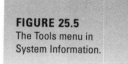

FIGURE 25.5
The Tools menu in System Information.

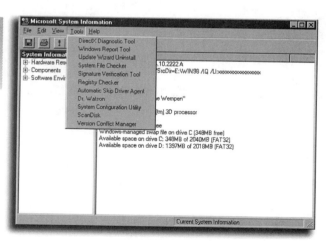

Extracting a File from a CAB Archive

If you think that a certain system file may be corrupted (for example, if you frequently see error messages referring to it), try extracting a fresh copy of it from the Windows 98 CD-ROM.

Windows files are stored in compressed archives in the Windows 98 CD-ROM. These archive files have the extension CAB. (It's short for "cabinet.") To extract a needed file from one of these CAB files, follow these steps.

Extracting a File from a CAB

1. Start **System Information** if it is not already running. (Open the **Start** menu, point to **Programs**, point to **Accessories**, point to **System Tools**, and click **System Information**).

2. Open the **Tools** menu and click **System File Checker**.

3. Choose **Extract one file from installation disk**.

4. Type the name of the file in the text box.

5. Click the **Start** button. The Extract File dialog box opens.

6. Type the path to the CAB file in the **Restore from** box, or click the **Browse** button to locate it.

7. Type the location where you want to place the file in the **Save file in** box, or click the **Browse** button to locate it.

8. Click **OK**.

9. When a message appears that the file has been successfully extracted, click **OK**.

Checking System Files

If you do not know which Windows file is causing the problem, you may want to check them all. The following procedure compares each of the system files to the versions on the Windows 98 CD-ROM and offers to replace the existing ones with fresh copies of the originals.

Reinstalling Altered System Files

1. Start **System Information** if it is not already running. (Open the **Start** menu, point to **Programs**, point to **Accessories**, point to **System Tools**, and click **System Information**).

2. Open the **Tools** menu and choose **System File Checker**.

3. Choose **Scan for altered files**.

4. Click **Start**.

5. Wait for the program to scan for altered files. When it finds one, a window appears informing you.

If It Ain't Broke...

Don't use the System File Checker to replace all altered files unless you are having a problem, because some of those files might have been altered for a good reason that the program doesn't recognize. Replacing altered files with the following procedure can potentially introduce problems of its own. (If you are having problems anyway, however, it's a risk worth taking.)

6. If an altered file is found, click **Yes** to replace it.

7. When a message appears that the scan is finished, click **OK**.

8. If prompted to restart your computer, click **Yes**.

Checking the Registry

You saw earlier in the chapter how to fix the Windows Registry from the command prompt when you can't start Windows. But you can also check and correct smaller registry problems from within Windows.

Checking the Registry from Windows

1. Start **System Information** if it is not already running. (Open the **Start** menu, point to **Programs**, point to **Accessories**, point to **System Tools**, and click **System Information**).

2. Open the **Tools** menu and choose **Registry Checker**. The checker runs, looking for errors. If it finds any, it offers to fix them.

3. After checking for errors, the Registry Checker offers to back up the system registry. Choose **Yes** or **No**.

4. If prompted to restart your computer, click **Yes**.

Disabling a Program that Loads at Startup

The System Configuration Utility helps you manage the contents of your startup files and control which programs load at startup, too. If you are having a Windows problem because of a program that loads at startup, you can disable that program from starting automatically with the following procedure.

Disabling Startup Programs

1. Start System Information if it is not already running. (Open the **Start** menu, point to **Programs**, point to **Accessories**, point to **System Tools**, and click **System Information**.)

2. Open the **Tools** menu and click **System Configuration Utility**.

3. Click the **Startup** tab. A list of programs that currently load at startup appears. See Figure 25.6.

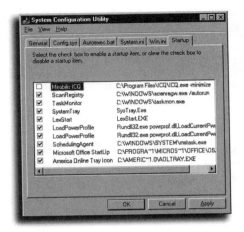

4. Remove the check mark next to any program that you do not
   want to load at startup.

5. Click **OK**.

6. If prompted to restart your computer, click **Yes**.

Troubleshooting Problems with a Device

Perhaps Windows itself works okay, but a particular piece of hardware is giving you fits. Maybe it doesn't work at all, or maybe it
works sporadically or poorly in general. In this section, I'll help you
figure out why and explain how to fix it.

Here's the general outline for troubleshooting a device:

1. Make sure that Windows knows the device is installed.

2. Make sure no resource conflicts exist.

3. Run diagnostic tests for the device, if available.

The following sections explain how to do each of those things.

Checking a Device in Device Manager

If a device isn't functioning, your first stop should be Device
Manager. It can tell you whether Windows sees the device and
whether resource conflicts exist that might prevent it from working.

**Other System
Information Utilities**

Lots of other utilities are
available on the Tools
menu in System
Information, as you can see
from Figure 25.5; you may
want to explore some of
these on your own.

Locating a Device in Device Manager

1. Right-click the **My Computer** icon on the desktop and choose **Properties**.

2. Click the **Device Manager** tab.

3. Locate the device on the list. Click the plus sign next to a device type to expand the list as needed. See Figure 25.7.

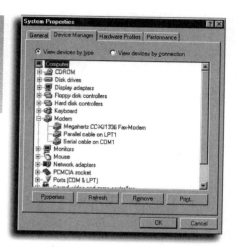

If the device appears in the right category on the Device Manager listing, and no special symbols are shown next to it, the device is probably installed correctly.

If a yellow circle with an exclamation point appears next to the device, the device has a resource conflict. See "Fixing a Resource Conflict" later in this chapter.

If a device has a red X next to it, the device has been disabled, either in Windows or in the BIOS program. Double-click the device to open its properties, and then make sure the **Disable in this hardware profile** check box is not marked. Then, check in your BIOS setup to make sure the device has not been disabled. Most BIOS programs allow you to enable or disable serial and parallel ports, for example.

If the device is not on the list, look for an Other Device entry. If the device appears there, you need to reinstall the drivers for it or run its setup program again. See "Setting Up Device Drivers in Windows" in Chapter 11, "Installing Hardware."

Fixing a Device Seen as "Other Device"

If the device is in the Other Device category instead of the one it is supposed to be in, Windows has partially detected the device but can't figure out what kind of device it is. You can help it by running the device's setup program that came with it or by installing updated drivers for it.

SEE ALSO

➤ *To install updated drivers for a device, see page 211.*

Fixing a Resource Conflict

If you find a yellow circle and exclamation point next to a device, a *resource conflict* exists.

First, let me explain what I mean by resources. Each device that communicates directly with the processor has a base address and an *interrupt request* (*IRQ*) number. The base address is a hexadecimal code that refers to the memory location in which the device's information is contained. For example, COM1's base address is usually 2F8H, and COM2's is usually 3F8H. Each device (including each COM port) must have its own unique base address.

IRQs are communication lines between the device and the processor, and most systems have 16 of them (0 through 15). Generally speaking, each device has its own, but some devices share a single IRQ (such as some COM ports). The term *resource* refers generically to either the IRQ or the base address.

Windows dynamically assigns base addresses and IRQs to devices through Plug and Play each time you start the PC. However, some devices are quirky and will work only with certain settings, and other devices are not Plug-and-Play compatible. Still others may require you to set jumpers on the circuit board to permanently select certain IRQs or addresses, and those settings may conflict with the automatically assigned settings Windows has chosen. Thus, sometimes you may need to set a device's resource allocation manually, bypassing Plug and Play.

Manually Assigning Resources to a Device

1. Locate the device in Device Manager (see the preceding section) and double-click it. Its Properties box appears.

2. Click the **Resources** tab.

3. Check the Conflicting Device list. If a conflict is listed, note whether it is an Input/Output Range conflict or an IRQ conflict. For example, in Figure 25.8, the problem is an IRQ.

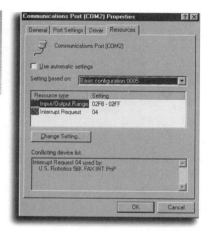

FIGURE 25.8
This device has a resource conflict with another device.

4. Deselect the **Use automatic settings** check box.

5. Open the **Settings based on** drop-down list and choose a different configuration. Keep trying different configurations until you find one that reports No conflicts in the Conflicting Device list.

6. Click **OK** to close the dialog box.

Running Diagnostic Tests on the Hardware

Some devices come with their own software that can run tests. (Sound cards, for example, typically come with such programs.) Consult the documentation for the device to see if such a utility is available.

You can test a modem's operation directly from the Modem Properties in the Control Panel, as you learned in Chapter 17, "Setting Up Online Connectivity."

SEE ALSO

➤ To test a modem, see page 286.

Troubleshooting Advice for Specific Devices

The following sections contain some extra tips I have picked up over the years in troubleshooting three types of devices that give users more grief than any others: video cards, modems, and sound cards.

Checking Video Devices

If the monitor's display looks scrambled from the moment you turn it on (not just in Windows), the monitor is broken. You need a new one. (They are very expensive to repair, and new monitors are fairly cheap.)

If the monitor's display looks scrambled in Windows only, you need a different video driver. Use Safe mode (explained earlier in this chapter) to restart the PC, and then change the video driver.

If the image doesn't fill the entire monitor or is off-center, your monitor's image controls need to be adjusted. Refer to its manual to find out how.

If the display flickers noticeably, the refresh rate is too low.

If pictures don't look very good, change to a greater color depth.

SEE ALSO
➤ *To change the video driver, see page 154.*

➤ *To change the refresh rate, see page 164.*

➤ *To change the color depth, see page 161.*

Checking Modems

If the modem appears to dial and connect, but it keeps making staticky noises and beeping until the remote modem finally hangs up, your modem is not set up correctly in Windows (perhaps Windows has detected it as the wrong make or model), or the telephone wiring connection is very poor quality.

If the modem won't stay connected to your ISP (especially if you use America Online as your provider), perhaps the setup string that the program is sending is inappropriate for that modem. Different modems require different setup strings in the form of *Hayes commands.* Each setup string begins with AT (attention), followed by a series of two-character codes (the Hayes commands) that turn on or

---

No Suitable Configurations

In rare cases, all the configurations on the list (in Step 5) have a conflict. If you face this situation, you can try changing the Interrupt Request (IRQ) and the Input/Output Range separately. Keep choosing configurations until you find one with only one conflict. Make a note of which type it is. Then, click the matching line in the Resource Settings list. Next, click **Change Setting**. One of two things may happen: You may see a message that the setting cannot be modified, or you may see a box containing alternate settings. If you see the latter, try a different setting. Repeat this procedure until you find a setting that produces no conflicts.

If Windows 98 tells you that the setting cannot be modified, try this: In the Conflicting Device list, note the device that is the other half of the conflict. Then, try modifying the settings for that device so that it no longer conflicts.

Another possible remedy is to go into your BIOS program and disable one of your COM ports that you are not using, freeing up an IRQ and address that one of the devices might be able to use.

off certain modem features. When you install a communication program such as America Online, it asks what kind of modem you have. This is important because the America Online software knows what strings to send to what modems. If you tell it that you have the wrong type of modem, it will send the wrong string. Even though it may be able to connect briefly, it won't be able to stay connected. Call America Online's technical support for help.

If there is no dial tone but the modem appears to be installed right, perhaps you do not have a working telephone line plugged into the correct jack on the modem. You should see two jacks on the modem; one for the incoming line and one for the outgoing phone. Make sure you have the phone line plugged into the incoming one. If they are not labeled, switch the lines and try again. If that doesn't help, try plugging a telephone directly into the line that is feeding into the modem. Do you hear a dial tone? If not, your phone line is the problem.

If you still keep getting a No Dial Tone message when trying to dial out, you may have a resource conflict.

Checking Sound Cards

If you aren't getting sound, you need to figure out whether the sound card isn't working at all or only in certain programs. Ask yourself the following questions:

- Do you have speakers plugged into the sound card?
- If the speakers have a power switch, is it on?
- Are the speakers plugged into an electrical outlet if they run on AC power?
- Have you installed the driver software that came with the sound card? Most sound cards won't work unless you do so.
- Have you run the diagnostic program that came with the sound card?

If the sound card does not work at all, even in its own diagnostic program, it is either defective or improperly installed. If the diagnostic program acts like everything is fine, but you don't hear anything, probably something is wrong with your speakers.

If Windows appears to have the sound card set up correctly (in Device Manager), but you don't hear anything, perhaps the volume is set too low. If you have a speaker icon in your System tray, double-click it and make sure that the volume is not muted nor turned down all the way.

Troubleshooting Problems with a Program

Program problems fall into these categories, generally speaking:

- You can't figure out how to run the program.
- The program won't start.
- The program locks up while running.

Unfortunately, I can't help you with that first one, but in the following sections I'll help you troubleshoot startup and lockup problems with individual programs.

Determining Why a Program Won't Start

If you are trying to start the program from the Start menu and nothing happens, perhaps the shortcut there no longer points to the program. Recall that the programs listed on the Start menu are only shortcuts; the real programs are stored on your hard disk. Using Windows Explorer, try to locate the file that starts the program, and double-click it there. If the program runs that way, you need to change the shortcut on your Start menu. (See Chapter 7, "Organizing Your Programs.")

If the program appears to start but then its window vanishes, or if you get an error message, try restarting Windows and giving the program another try. If a problem still occurs, remove and reinstall the program.

SEE ALSO

➤ *To modify the Start menu's programs, see page 124.*

➤ *To uninstall a program, see page 148.*

➤ *To install a program, see page 142.*

Exiting a Malfunctioning Program

If a program has stopped responding to commands, you won't be able to exit from it normally. Don't panic when this sort of thing happens; it's an expected part of computing. Exit the program using the following steps and then restart your PC (as explained in Chapter 1, "Windows Basics").

Exiting a Program That Has Stopped Responding

1. Press **Ctrl+Alt+Del**. The Close Programs dialog box opens.

2. Select the malfunctioning program from the list. It may say (Not Responding) next to it, but it might not.

3. Wait several seconds while Windows attempts to shut the program down.

4. If a dialog box appears, asking whether you want to Wait or End Task, click **End Task**.

5. Restart your PC.

You should always restart your PC after shutting down a problem program because whatever caused it to malfunction may also cause problems with other programs. By restarting, you flush the problem out of the computer's memory (in most cases).

SEE ALSO

➤ *To restart your computer, see page 29.*

➤ *To check your hard disk for errors that could be causing program malfunctions, see page 406.*

➤ *To troubleshoot continued problems running a program, see page 459.*

Fixing a Program That Locks Up Frequently

The best way to fix a problem that frequently locks up is to uninstall the program and then reinstall it.

If that doesn't solve the problem, perhaps the program has a conflict with one of your devices (or maybe just one of the drivers for one of the devices). Try visiting the manufacturer's Web sites for each of your devices to see whether driver updates are available. Then, visit the Web site for the program manufacturer to see if the problem you are experiencing is a known bug and whether a workaround is available.

Configuring DOS-Based Programs

Almost all programs you buy today are designed for Windows, but you may run into the occasional older program (probably a game) designed to run under DOS. Such programs sometimes work fine under Windows, and sometimes they don't work at all. You just never know until you try them.

Setting Up a DOS-Based Program

The following steps show how to set up a DOS-based program to run under Windows 98. It's an optimistic procedure, which depends on everything working as it should. Try this first, and resort to the procedures later in this chapter only if this doesn't work.

Installing a DOS-Based Program

1. Insert the CD or the floppy for the program.

2. Browse the file listing for the program and locate the setup program (usually Setup or Install). Then, double-click it.

3. If the installation program appears in a pinched-looking window rather than full-screen, press **Alt+Enter** to make it fill the entire screen.

4. Follow the prompts to complete the installation.

   If you are not sure what to pick for an option, stick with the default.

   If the program asks whether it should detect your sound or video, choose **Yes**.

   If the program asks whether you want it to be set up to be launched from within Windows, choose **Yes**.

   If the program wants to modify your setup files (Config.sys and Autoexec.bat), choose **No**.

5. When the program is finished, if you see a DOS prompt, type **exit** and press **Enter**.

6. If the setup program told you to restart your computer, do so.

7. Browse your disk's file listing and locate the folder where the new program was installed.

Which File Runs the Program?

If you see a file that ends in .pif, use that file to run the program. PIF files are shortcuts to DOS applications that include special running instructions that help them run better under Windows. If a DOS program comes with a PIF file, you should use it.

If you see a .bat file, use that. If no .pif or .bat files are present, look for a .com or .exe file with a name similar to the program name.

8. Locate the file that runs the new program and double-click it. The documentation that came with the program should tell you which file to use; see the following note for help with this.

9. After you're sure the program works, create a shortcut for it on your desktop or on your Start menu.

SEE ALSO

➤ *To create program shortcuts, see page 147.*

Troubleshooting DOS Program Operation

If a DOS-based program doesn't work using the preceding setup routine, you will probably need to make some changes to its properties.

When you make changes to the properties for a DOS program, Windows creates a separate shortcut (with a PIF extension) to hold those changes. You then use the PIF file to run the program.

What changes should you make? Well, the best place to start is the Windows Help system's MS-DOS Programs Troubleshooter. To locate it, from the **Start** menu choose **Help**, click the **Index** tab, look up **MS-DOS Programs**, and then click **Troubleshooting**. Then, click the **Click here** link and use the controls that appear in the right pane to walk through the troubleshooter. See Figure 25.9.

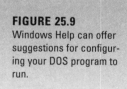

FIGURE 25.9
Windows Help can offer suggestions for configuring your DOS program to run.

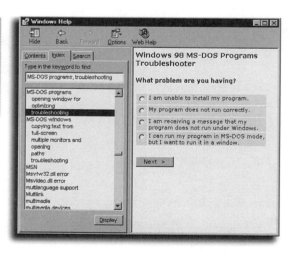

To display the Properties box for the program, right-click it and choose **Properties**. Notice that the Properties box for a DOS-based program or a PIF file has more tabs than a regular (Windows) program. Some of the most common changes to make to properties for MS-DOS programs include the following:

- If the program starts with the window squashed (that is, not full screen), you can switch it to full screen with **Alt+Enter**. But if you set the Usage setting on the **Screen** tab to **Full Screen**, it will always start full screen.

- If your DOS program locks up every time your screen saver kicks in, deselect the **Allow Screen Saver** check box on the **Misc** tab.

- Some DOS programs have their own shortcut key combinations that you may be accustomed to using. If these key combinations conflict with Windows' own, the Windows ones take precedence. To make the DOS application's shortcut key combinations dominant, deselect any of the check boxes in the **Windows Shortcut Keys** area on the **Misc** tab. See Figure 25.10.

FIGURE 25.10
Override any Windows-reserved shortcut keys here.

- Some older programs require you to type switches or parameters after the command to run them at the DOS prompt. To execute those extra instructions every time the program runs, enter the extra text on the **Cmd** line on the **Program** tab. See Figure 25.11.

FIGURE 25.11
Enter any extra parameters, switches, or other commands for the program.

- The Close on Exit check box (see Figure 25.11) determines whether the DOS window closes when you exit the program. Usually this is a good thing, but if you are trying to troubleshoot why a program isn't working under Windows, you may want to read any error messages that appear before the program terminates. In such cases you could deselect this check box so that the DOS window with the error messages remains onscreen until you type **exit**.

- If the program will not run from Windows and you have tried everything, you may need to run it in MS-DOS mode. This restarts the PC each time you run the program so that the Windows interface isn't even loaded. When you exit the program, the PC restarts again and reloads Windows 98. To set this up, on the **Program** tab, click the **Advanced** button to see the Advanced Program Settings dialog box. Then, click the **MS-DOS Mode** check box to turn it on.

- Some programs running in MS-DOS mode require special additions or subtractions to the computer's startup files. You can set these up by clicking **Specify a New MS-DOS configuration** in the Advanced Program Settings dialog box (see Figure 25.12) and entering the custom `Autoexec.bat` and `Config.sys` files in the boxes provided.

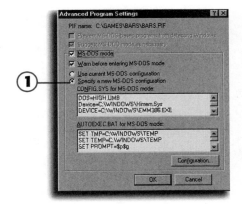

FIGURE 25.12
You can turn on MS-DOS mode so that the DOS program can run without Windows being loaded.

① You can customize the startup files that are used when the PC starts in MS-DOS mode to run this program.

SEE ALSO

➤ *To run programs with the **Run** command, see page 52.*

part

VI

APPENDIXES

Appendix

A

Installing Windows 98

Upgrading from a Previous Version •

Starting Setup on a New PC •

Troubleshooting Common Problems •

Upgrading from a Previous Version of Windows

If you have Windows 95 or the original edition of Windows 98, a message appears when you insert the Windows 98 Second Edition CD into your drive. It reports that the version on the CD is more recent and asks whether you want to upgrade. Click **Yes**, and you're on your way; just follow the prompts. Make sure that any antivirus software is disabled before you upgrade; sometimes, such software can interfere with the setup process.

When you upgrade over an earlier version, Windows keeps all the same settings as before. The Setup program does not ask about your preferences, your desired accessories, your time zone, or any other details because it picks them up from your current system.

A typical upgrade from Windows 98 requires approximately 195MB of free hard disk space, but it may range between 120MB to 295MB, depending on your system configuration and the options you choose to install. If you don't have enough disk space, delete some files or uninstall some programs before you run Setup.

Video Incompatibilities with Setup

If you have the Number Nine Imagine 128 Display Adapter or the STB Velocity 128 3D AGP (Nvidia Riva 128), you should run Setup from MS-DOS or change your display driver to VGA first (see Chapter 9, "Customizing the Screen Appearance"). To run Setup from DOS, restart the computer in MS-DOS mode. Then, change to the CD-ROM drive at the DOS prompt (by typing its drive letter and a colon) and type **Setup**.

Starting the Windows 98 Setup Program on a New PC

The main challenge in installing Windows 98 on a new PC is getting started. Windows 98 comes on CD-ROM, but a PC with a totally blank (possibly unformatted) hard disk does not have the CD-ROM drivers set to load at startup. The following sections cover what to do in various scenarios, ranging from ideal to nightmarish.

If You Have a Floppy That Came with Windows 98

If Windows 98 came with a floppy disk in addition to the CD, place it in the floppy drive and restart the PC. Then, follow the instructions onscreen.

If You Have a Formatted, Bootable Hard Disk

If you can boot from your hard disk to a DOS prompt (that is, if you turn the computer on and you see a black screen with a gray text prompt such as c:\>), do the following:

Running Windows Setup from a DOS Prompt

1. Place the Windows 98 CD into the CD-ROM drive.

2. Type the CD-ROM drive letter and a colon (for example, **E:**).

3. Press **Enter**.

4. Type **Setup** and press **Enter**.

If you see the message Invalid drive specification at Step 2, the CD-ROM drivers have not been loaded. Locate the disk that came with the CD-ROM drive and run the installation program on it to install the CD drivers. Then, reboot the computer and try the above steps again.

If You Have a Bootable Disk Created in Windows 98

If you previously had Windows 98 installed, you may have created an emergency disk (as described in Chapter 5 of this book, in the section "Creating a System Diskette"). If so, you can boot from that.

Starting the PC from a Windows Emergency Disk

1. Insert the bootable emergency disk in the floppy drive and turn the PC on.

2. When prompted, choose **Start the Computer with CD-ROM Support**.

3. Place the Windows 98 CD into the CD-ROM drive.

4. At the DOS prompt, type the CD drive letter and a colon (such as **E:**).

5. Press **Enter**.

6. Type **Setup** and press **Enter**.

If You Have Another PC with Windows 98 Installed

If you or a friend has Windows 98 on another PC, use that PC to make a startup disk (see Chapter 5), and then follow the steps in the preceding section.

What Else Can I Try?

We're heading toward the bottom of the barrel, folks. It starts to get complicated if you don't have the resources needed for any of the preceding scenarios. I strongly suggest that you try to get someone else who has Windows 98 to make a startup disk for you so that you don't have to go through any of the following rigmarole.

To start the Windows 98 Setup program, you need to do two things:

1. Start the PC.
2. Load the CD-ROM drivers so that you can access the CD, or copy all the files from the CD to a drive that the PC can read from.

To start the PC, you need any bootable disk. It can be an old DOS disk—just about anything. You can make a bootable disk from any computer by typing **SYS A:** at the DOS prompt.

The CD-ROM drivers load only at startup, so you must include them in the Config.sys and Autoexec.bat files on whatever disk you are starting up from. That means you will need a text editing program (such as Notepad in Windows or Edit in DOS). In Config.sys, you need a DEVICE= line that points to the CD-ROM driver. You can copy the driver file to the boot disk so it is available. It might look something like the following:

```
DEVICE=A:\MYCDROM.SYS /D:CDROM1
```

if the file is called MYCDROM.SYS and it is located on your floppy (A:) drive.

In the Autoexec.bat file, you will need a pointer to the file MSCDEX.EXE, something like this:

```
A:\MSCDEX.EXE /D:CDROM1
```

Common Installation Problems

After you get it started, the Windows 98 Setup program works fairly well. But in case you run into problems, here are some ideas for solving them.

Missing Files

As you are installing, you may see a message that the Setup program cannot locate a particular file on the CD. Sometimes, just clicking **OK** to let it try again is enough to jolt things back into working order.

If that doesn't work, and you are upgrading from a previous version, you might try pointing the Setup program to your `C:\Windows` folder or `C:\Windows\System` to see if an earlier version of the file is there and will suffice.

If that still doesn't work, I would (reluctantly) choose **Skip File**. The file might not be crucial, so it's possible that the Setup program can continue without it.

Prompt for Driver Disk

As Windows is detecting your hardware, it may ask you for a setup disk for a particular device. Dig through the disks that came with your PC and find/insert the one it wants.

Using the disk that came with the device is usually the best choice because the drivers on that disk are specifically designed to work with that particular model. However, if the device is old (more than a year, as an estimate), and if Windows 98 provides a driver for that exact make and model, you should use that instead.

After Windows 98 has finished installing, you can go to the device manufacturer's Web site and download newer drivers for it if desired.

More Setup Help

Read the file `Setup.txt` on the Windows 98 CD using any text editor; it provides detailed assistance for getting CD-ROM drivers to work.

Disable BIOS Shadowing

If you have continual problems installing Windows 98 on a PC, and you can't make it work using any of the methods here, try going into the BIOS setup (see Chapter 11, "Installing Hardware") and disabling the BIOS Shadowing feature.

Mysterious Error Messages

If you have Internet access on another PC, go to http://
www.fixwindows.com/howto/98error.htm, where there is a wonderful
list of Windows 98 Setup error messages along with explanations of
what each one means. (Tip: The solution provided to a lot of the
error messages is "Install from the DOS prompt." Doing so avoids a
multitude of annoying setup problems.)

Blue-Screen Error Reading CD

If you see a blue screen with white writing that tells you it can't read
the CD-ROM, take out the CD and clean it with a soft, lint-free
cloth, removing any fingerprints and dust specks. Then, try it again.
If that doesn't solve the problem, you either have a defective
CD-ROM (return it for a refund) or a defective CD-ROM drive
(contact your PC manufacturer).

Windows Information Online

Windows Software Available for
Download •

Windows Troubleshooting Help •

Windows News and Reviews •

Windows 98 USENET Newsgroups •

Sources of Windows Software

Top Picks

Shareware.com

`http://www.shareware.com`

This site does not store most of the files directly on its server; instead it provides links to FTP servers all over the world from which you can download the programs. This is nice because if one site isn't working right, you can try another site without having to go to a completely different search.

Dave Central Shareware Archive

`http://www.davecentral.com`

I'm not sure who Dave is, but his software archive is great. You'll find software here both for Windows and Linux (another operating system). Dave also provides software recommendations and a "pick of the week."

Download.com

`http://www.download.com`

This site is run by the information powerhouse CNET, so you know it has to be good. It includes software both for PCs and Mac. Not all the software for PCs here is for Windows necessarily, so choose carefully. You can run DOS-based programs under Windows (See Chapter 25, "Troubleshooting Problems"), but it's easier to stick with Windows programs.

FilePile

`http://filepile.com/nc/start`

A searchable archive with more than a million programs in it. Just type the keywords for what you want and click **Start File Search**, and you're on your way.

ZD Net Software Library

http://www.zdnet.com/swlib/

ZD stands for Ziff-Davis, a publisher of computer magazines (among other things). This site features reviews, lots of downloads, a searchable index, and links to articles in the Ziff-Davis magazines (surprise!).

Other Sites

Albert's Ambry

http://www.alberts.com/

Clicked.com Top 20 Shareware Gallery

http://www.clicked.com/shareware/index.html

Completely Free Software.com

http://www.completelyfreesoftware.com/

Daily Double Download

http://www3.zdnet.com/yil/content/depts/doubledl/dlcurrent/
dlcurrent.html

Download.net

http://www.download.net/

File Mine

http://www.filemine.com/

FileDudes

http://www.filedudes.com/

Filez

http://www.filez.com/

Garbo Anonymous FTP Archive

http://garbo.uwasa.fi/

Jumbo! Download Network

http://www.jumbo.com/

Pass the Shareware

http://www.passtheshareware.com/

Shareware Central

http://www.q-d.com/swc.htm

SOFTSEEK.com

http://www.softseek.com/

WinPlanet

http://www.winplanet.com/

Washington University Data Archive

http://wuarchive.wustl.edu/

Places to Get Troubleshooting Assistance

Top Picks

FixWindows.com

http://www.fixwindows.com/

This site is devoted to fixing Windows problems. You'll find a wealth of troubleshooting ideas and information, as well as step-by-step how-tos, downloadable drivers and patches, and links to shareware. Also check out the troubleshooting flowcharts for Windows 98 at http://www.fixwindows.com/charts/98/win98cht.htm.

Microsoft—Personal Online Support

http://support.microsoft.com/support/default.asp

Your link to the vast libraries of information about various Windows products, including Windows 98 and virtually every other product

Microsoft has ever made. This site is always my first stop if I can't find something I need to know in the Help system in Windows.

Troubleshooters.com

http://www.troubleshooters.com/twin98.htm

This link points to the Windows 98 information on the site; the site itself is much larger. A wealth of information is available here for the intermediate to advanced user.

WinDrivers.com

http://www.windrivers.com/

Wondering if an updated driver is available for one of your devices? Find it and download it here. Quite a bit of troubleshooting data is also available.

Other Sites

24-Hour Support.com

http://www.24hoursupport.com/

A Troubleshooting Guide to Windows 98

http://members.aol.com/Knows98/index.htm

Help! Channel from ZD Net

http://www.zdnet.com/zdhelp/

Troubleshooting Microsoft Windows

http://www.windowsgalore.com/windows.95/

Windows Annoyances

http://www.annoyances.org/win98/

Windows News and Reviews

Top Picks

Hardware Central

http://www.hardwarecentral.com/

Reviews the latest hardware upgrades that you might want to buy for your PC. (This site is part of a larger site, My Desktop, at http://www.mydesktop.com.)

Windows 98.org

http://www.windows98.org/main.html

A very content-rich and nice-looking site devoted to Windows 98, including downloads, articles, opinions, and a discussion area.

WinPlanet

http://www.winplanet.com/

News, information, opinions, and downloads specifically about Microsoft Windows; you may spend more time here than you intended to reading the articles. Also, click the Tech Support link on the navigation menu to visit VirtualDr, a troubleshooting discussion area. (WinPlanet is also part of My Desktop, at http://www.mydesktop.com.)

Windows Galore: Windows 98 Tips and Tricks

http://www.windowsgalore.com/windows.98/index.htm

Tons of information here about troubleshooting, customizing, tweaking, and otherwise fiddling with Windows 98. Learn about "Easter eggs" (hidden programs that appear when you press certain key combinations), get information for changing passwords and removing viruses, and more.

Other Sites

Bob Cerelli's Windows Page

`http://www.halcyon.com/cerelli/`

PC Computing: Windows 98

`http://www.zdnet.com/pccomp/features/windows98/welcome.html`

Windows 98 Megasite

`http://www.winmag.com/win98/`

Windows Help-Net Windows 98 Tips and Tricks

`http://www.windows-help.net/windows98/`

Winfo Central

`http://winfocentral.com/`

USENET Newsgroups that Discuss Windows 98

You can read newsgroups such as these using Microsoft Outlook Express or any other news reader program. See Chapter 21, "Participating In Online Discussions," for details. In addition to these groups, your news server may carry others, too.

```
alt.windows98

alt.win98

comp.os.ms-windows.apps.compatibility.win95

comp.os.ms-windows.apps.utilities.win95

comp.os.ms-windows.networking.win95

comp.os.ms-windows.setup.win95

comp.os.ms-windows.win95.misc
```

Group Not There?

Not all news servers carry all the newsgroups listed here. To read a newsgroup that your news server doesn't carry, visit DejaNews (`http://www.dejanews.com`); this Web site lets you browse—and even post to—almost every newsgroup on the planet.

comp.os.ms-windows.win95.moderated

comp.os.ms-windows.win95.setup

microsoft.public.internetexplorer.win95

microsoft.public.win95

microsoft.public.win95.dialupnetworking

microsoft.public.win95.filediskmanagement

microsoft.public.win95.msdosapps

microsoft.public.win95.multimedia

microsoft.public.win95.networking

microsoft.public.win95.printingfontsvideo

microsoft.public.win95.setup

Appendix

C

Accessibility Tools

Installing Accessibility Tools and
Options

Running the Accessibility Wizard

Overview of Accessibility Features

Enabling or Disabling Options

Installing the Accessibility Tools and Options

The Accessibility features are broken down into two groups: Tools and Options.

- **Tools.** The Accessibility Wizard and the Magnifier, both of which can be run from the Start menu (in the Programs\Accessories\Accessibility folder).
- **Options.** The Accessibility settings you can change from the Control Panel.

Neither group's features are installed by default, however. To install them, use the Adding and Removing Windows Components procedure in Chapter 8, "Installing New Programs." Go ahead and install both.

SEE ALSO

➤ *To add or remove windows components, see page 140.*

Running the Accessibility Wizard

The Accessibility Wizard configures Windows 98 to use the accessibility features that you need for your special situation. It is a great time-saver—if you run it, you won't have to configure the individual options separately.

To run the Accessibility Wizard, click **Start**, point to **Programs**, point to **Accessories**, point to **Accessibility**, and click **Accessibility Wizard**. Then, follow the prompts onscreen. For example, the first screen of the Wizard, shown in Figure C.1, asks which of the lines you can read. Click the smallest line of text that you can comfortably see, and then click **Next** to go on to the next screen.

Each of the settings that the Accessibility Wizard changes can also be changed manually, as you will see later in this appendix.

FIGURE C.1
The wizard asks questions about your abilities; click the appropriate responses.

① A blue box surrounds the current selection.

Using the Magnifier

The Magnifier blows up whatever the mouse pointer touches in a pane at the top of the screen. For example, in Figure C.2, the pointer is in the Magnifier Settings dialog box, and the check boxes it hovers over appear magnified. To turn on the Magnifier, click the **Start** button, point to **Programs**, point to **Accessories**, point to **Accessibility**, and click **Magnifier**.

Startup
Add a shortcut to the Startup menu (on the Start menu) to make it load automatically each time you start Windows. See Chapter 7, "Organizing Your Programs."

FIGURE C.2
The Magnifier at work.

① Magnified area

② Click Exit to turn the Magnifier off.

The Magnifier Settings box remains onscreen as you work. To turn off the Magnifier, click **Exit**. To close the Magnifier Settings and leave the feature on, click **OK**.

SEE ALSO
➤ *To choose which programs load at startup, see page 137.*

Introducing the Accessibility Options

In the **Control Panel**, double-click **Accessibility**, and the Accessibility Properties box opens. Here, you can set each of the individual accessibility features that the Accessibility Wizard configures automatically.

Many of these features have two things you can set: First, a check box turns the feature off or on. Then, a Settings button opens a dialog box with which you can configure that feature.

Reviewing the Keyboard Options

Set any of these keyboard options as needed to control how the keyboard works:

- **StickyKeys.** This feature treats Ctrl, Shift, and Alt as toggles, so that each time you press them, they toggle between Off and On. That way, you can issue key combinations (such as Alt+F) without having to press two keys simultaneously.

- **FilterKeys.** This sets Windows to ignore brief or repeated keystrokes that might occur if a mobility impairment makes it difficult for you to type.

- **ToggleKeys.** This plays sounds when you press the Caps Lock, Num Lock, or Scroll Lock, so that you will notice when you have pressed them.

Setting the Settings

After turning a particular feature on, don't forget to click its **Settings** button to find out how to use the feature and to fine-tune it. For example, the Settings for StickyKeys box appears in Figure C.3.

FIGURE C.3
Each option has its own settings.

Reviewing the Sound Options

These features provide visual cues for deaf or hard-of-hearing users when a sound is played.

- **SoundSentry.** With this on, Windows generates a visual warning onscreen whenever the system makes a sound.
- **ShowSounds.** This turns on "closed captioning" when available in certain programs so that you can read the speech or sounds being generated.

Reviewing the Display Option

Only one feature is here: High Contrast. Use this if you want Windows to use colors and fonts designed for easy reading. This can be very helpful if you have a visual impairment but are not completely blind.

Reviewing the Mouse Option

Only one feature is here, as well: MouseKeys. With this feature on, you can use the arrow keys on the numeric keypad to move the mouse. This works great for those with a mobility impairment that makes it difficult to control a mouse.

Other Display Settings

You can also use the Display Properties (from the Control Panel) to choose a color scheme with high contrast or to choose to use larger fonts in general.

Other Mouse Settings

You can also use the Mouse properties in the Control Panel to choose a different pointer size and/or to use Mouse Trails. A larger pointer and mouse trails can really make the mouse pointer more visible onscreen. You'll find more about mouse settings in Chapter 10, "Customizing System Settings."

Reviewing the General Options

The General tab's settings help you control how the accessibility features work in general:

- **Automatic reset.** This turns off accessibility features after the PC has been idle for a set number of minutes. (This does not turn the feature's check box off in the Accessibility Options; it merely suspends the feature temporarily.)

- **Notification.** This plays sounds and/or warning messages when an accessibility feature is being turned off or on.

- **SerialKey devices.** This enables support for special devices that allow alternative keyboard and mouse access designed for handicapped individuals.

GLOSSARY

Active controls   Utilities or display windows that are dynamically updated with Internet content. See *Active desktop*.

Active desktop   A feature in Windows that enables you to place active controls directly on the desktop.

Active window   The window that is being displayed or used at the moment.

Adapter   Generically, this can refer to any card in a motherboard slot, but it usually refers to the video card.

Address   The location, or *path*, to which you save or from which you open a file or folder.

Allocation error   An error in which the file's size being reported by the FAT does not match its size on the disk.

America Online   A popular online service and Internet provider.

Application   A computer program that helps you accomplish some task or activity.

Archive attribute   An attribute for a file that indicates it has been changed since it has been backed up.

AUTOEXEC.BAT   A startup file that processes its batch of commands whenever the computer starts.

BIOS   Stands for basic input/output system. An automatically executed startup routine that runs certain tests and checks for installed hardware. The BIOS program is stored on a Read-Only Memory (ROM) chip mounted on the motherboard.

BIOS setup program   A built-in program in a PC that enables you to configure the PC's base-level settings.

Bitmap   An image made up of colored dots, such as a photo or a scanned drawing. Also called a *raster graphic*. Compare to *vector graphic*. Can also refer to a specific graphics format (.bmp).

Boot   To start up a computer.

Boot disk   A disk (hard or floppy) that contains the startup files needed to boot a computer.

Briefcase   A special folder on the Windows desktop that helps synchronize files between two computers.

Browser   A program that enables you to browse the World Wide Web. See *Web browser*.

CAB file   Short for *cabinet file*. A compressed archive of files; part of the Windows 98 setup.

Card   A circuit board that you plug into a slot on the motherboard to add hardware capability. Can also refer to a *PCMCIA card*.

Cascade   To arrange open windows so that the windows overlap with each title bar visible in an orderly, cascading alignment. Compare to *Tile*.

Channel bar   An active control that lists channels you can view on the Internet. The Channel bar came with Internet Explorer 4.0 and Windows 98, but not with Windows 98 Second Edition.

Channels   Internet content similar to Web pages, but viewed in a special browser window.

Character repeat   Holding down a key on the keyboard so that it types continuously onscreen.

Classic style   A desktop operation mode for Windows 98 in which most items work as they did in Windows 95. Compare to *Web style*.

Click   To press and release the left mouse button once.

Clipboard   A holding area for Windows programs, used to transfer and copy data.

Close button   The X button in the top-right corner of a window, which can be used to close the window.

Cluster   A small physical section of a disk. An organization unit by which files are stored.

CMOS   Stands for Complementary Metal Oxide Semiconductor. A microchip on the motherboard that stores the BIOS setting changes you make with the BIOS setup program.

Color depth   The number of colors that make up the display in a particular video display mode. 256 colors (8-bit) is a common color depth.

Compression   A method of making a file fit into a smaller amount of disk space by storing it more compactly. Two kinds of compression are *file compression* and *disk compression*.

CONFIG.SYS   A startup file that lists the drivers and system settings the PC should load when it starts.

Cross-linked files   An error in which a conflict in the FAT keeps the system from knowing to which of two files an address belongs.

Defragment   To reorder the data on a disk so that all files are stored contiguously rather than in multiple noncontiguous pieces.

Desktop   The colored background behind the icons and menus on the Windows screen. Can also refer generically to the background and all icons on it.

Device driver   See *Driver*.

Digital camera   A camera that saves images in electronic format and feeds them into your PC instead of putting the images on conventional film.

Digitize   To scan an image or record it with a digital camera so that it becomes a computer file.

Directory   An older, MS-DOS name for *folder*.

Disk compression   A compression method that compresses an entire disk. The DriveSpace program in Windows is a disk compression program. Compare to a *file compression* program.

Document   A data file containing primarily text, such as a word processing document. Can also refer generically to any data file.

DOS   Stands for Disk Operating System. For many years, the definitive operating system for PCs. The most popular brand was MS-DOS. Newer systems that use Windows 95 or 98 do not rely on a DOS user interface.

Double-click   To press and release the left mouse button twice quickly in succession.

DoubleSpace   A version of DriveSpace that came with MS-DOS version 6.20.

Download   To transfer a file from an Internet location to your own PC.

Drag   To click and hold down the left mouse button while moving the mouse. Dragging moves whatever was pointed at.

Drag and drop   An editing technique whereby you can drag text, an icon, or some other object to move it.

Driver   A file containing instructions that helps Windows interact with a particular hardware device.

DriveSpace   A program that compresses your hard disk so you can store more files on it.

DVD drive   Stands for Digital Versatile Disk (or Digital Video Disk). A type of super CD-ROM drive that can read DVD disks holding as much as 8.5 gigabytes on each side. DVD drives can also function as regular CD-ROM drives.

Email   Short for electronic mail. A message sent or received over the Internet.

Explorer   Can refer to *Windows Explorer*—a file management tool, or *Internet Explorer*—a Web browser.

Extension   See *File extension*.

FAT   Stands for File Allocation Table. A system chart stored on your hard disk that keeps track of which files are using which physical spots on the disk.

491

File compression   A method of compressing an individual file so that it takes up less space on your disk. Programs such as PKZip are file compression programs.

File extension   The code following the period in a file's name that indicates what type of file it is.

Folder   An organizing unit into which files can be placed on a disk.

Fonts   Typefaces that you can use onscreen and in printed documents.

Fragment   A part of a file that is stored noncontiguously with the rest of the file. File fragmentation slows down system performance; see *defragment*.

Freeware   Software that may be freely distributed without charge but that may not be modified without the owner's consent. Compare to *shareware* and *public domain*.

FTP   Stands for File Transfer Protocol, a method of transferring files between computers on the Internet.

FTP address   The address needed to access a particular computer on the Internet via FTP. FTP addresses generally begin with ftp://.

Gigabyte   Approximately one billion bytes. Abbreviated as GB or G.

Graphical User Interface (GUI)   A computer interface that relies on graphics rather than text. Windows 98 is a GUI; MS-DOS is not.

HTML   Stands for Hypertext Markup Language, the programming language in which Web pages are written.

Hyperlink   An active link to another Web page or address, typically underlined. Click a hyperlink to jump to the specified document, page, or other destination.

Incremental backup   A backup that backs up only the files that have changed since the previous backup.

Internet   A vast interconnected network of computer networks all over the world.

Internet Explorer   The Web browser program that comes with Windows 98.

Interrupt request   See *IRQ*.

IRQ   A path from the processor to a device on the motherboard. Each system has 16 IRQs (0 through 15), and each device should be assigned its own IRQ.

Kilobyte   1,024 bytes of data or storage space. Abbreviated KB or K.

LAN   Stands for Local Area Network, a network confined to a small area such as a single building.

Lost cluster   An error in which an address contains data, but the FAT does not know to which file the data belongs.

Macro   A recorded set of keystrokes or mouse actions that you can play back later to save yourself time performing repetitive tasks.

Maximize   To expand a window to fill the entire screen.

Megabyte   Approximately one million bytes of data or storage space. Abbreviated MB or M.

Message header   The area of an email message containing the sender, the receiver, the subject, date, and time, and other details.

MIDI   Musical Instrument Digital Interface. A format that allows communication of musical data between devices, such as computers and synthesizers.

Minimize   To shrink a window so that it does not appear onscreen except for a button for it on the taskbar.

Modem   *Mo*Dulator *Dem*odulator. A device that allows computers to send and receive data through phone lines by converting it to audio and back.

Multimedia   An activity involving more than one medium, such as a game that includes both visuals and sounds. Can also refer to certain hardware components that make such activities possible (sound cards, CD-ROM drives, speakers, and so on).

Multitasking   To perform more than one task at once.

My Computer   A window containing icons for each drive on your system, along with several other special-purpose icons (such as for dial-up networking and printers).

Net   See *Internet*.

Netscape Navigator   A competitor Web browser to Internet Explorer.

Network   A group of computers connected, usually with cabling and network interface cards (NICs) or through the Internet. One popular type is a Local Area Network, or *LAN*.

Network Neighborhood   An icon on the Windows desktop that opens a window in which you can browse your LAN.

Newsgroup   A public area online where people can post and read messages on a particular subject using a news-reader program (such as Outlook Express).

Operating system (OS)   The software that starts and runs your computer. Windows 98 is an operating system.

Paint   A simple graphics program that comes free with Windows 98.

Parallel port   A port that sends several bits of data at once (that is, in parallel). Most printers run on a parallel port, as do some scanners. Compare to *Serial port*.

Partition   To prepare a hard disk for formatting by assigning drive letters to one or more sections of it.

Path   The full location of a folder, file, or other object. For example, `C:\Windows\System` is the path to many of the files that run Windows 98.

PCMCIA card   A credit-card-sized hardware device that plugs into a laptop computer, providing additional functionality. PCMCIA stands for Personal Computer Memory Card International Association, the group that developed the standard by which it operates.

Plug and Play   A method of identifying and configuring new hardware in Windows 95/98. If your motherboard and the new device are both Plug-and-Play-compatible, Windows detects and configures them automatically when you add your upgrade components.

Pointer scheme   The set of default pointers for various tasks and situations.

Pointer speed   The distance that the pointer moves onscreen when you move the mouse a certain amount.

Pointer trails   A feature you can turn on in Windows in which the mouse pointer leaves "trails" wherever it moves so that you can see it moving more easily. Great to help locate the cursor for someone with a visual impairment.

Program   A set of instructions for a computer to execute. Sometimes called an *application*.

Public domain   Software that is free to distribute and free to modify. The original owner has given up all rights to it. Compare to *freeware*.

Quick Launch toolbar   The group of icons to the right of the Start button that provides quick access to several popular Windows 98 tools.

RAM   Random Access Memory. The main memory that holds the programs and data currently being used.

Raster graphic   See *bitmap*.

Recycle Bin   An icon on the desktop that opens a window of files you have deleted. You can undelete to restore deleted files to their original locations.

Refresh rate   The speed at which the display on your monitor is repainted or "refreshed". Higher refresh rates mean less flicker.

Registry   A file containing all the settings, preferences, installed program information, and other data about your copy of Windows 98.

Repeat delay   The delay between when you hold down a key and when *character repeat* starts.

Repeat rate   The speed at which *character repeat* occurs.

Resolution   The number of pixels that make up a display. Common resolutions are 640×480 (which is standard VGA) and 800×600.

Resource conflict   A situation in which two or more devices on a system are trying to use the same base address or IRQ.

Resources   See *system resources*.

Restore   To change a maximized window so that it is no longer maximized. Also, to undelete files from the Recycle Bin. Also, to copy files from a backup back to the original locations from which they were backed up.

Right-click   To press and release the right mouse button once.

Right-click menu   See *Shortcut menu*.

ROM   Stands for Read-Only Memory. A small amount of non-volatile memory (that is, it doesn't blank out when you shut off the PC) that stores important startup information for your PC.

Safe mode   A Windows operation mode in which generic drivers are loaded to enable the PC to start when it otherwise would not because of a system problem. Safe mode is for troubleshooting; you would not want to do normal work in Safe mode.

Scandisk   A utility program that checks a disk for errors.

Scanner   A device for digitizing pictures so that you can use them in your computer. Some scanners also come with optical character recognition (OCR) software, which allows you to scan text and then translate the picture of the text into real text in a word processor.

Serial port   A port that sends data one bit at a time (that is, serially). You can plug external modems, mice, and many other types of devices into a serial port. Compare to *parallel port*.

Shareware   Software that is freely distributed in trial form; users are honor-bound to pay for it if they like it and continue to use it. Compare to *freeware*.

Shortcut   An icon or menu item that points to a file. The shortcut is not the original, so deleting the shortcut does nothing to the original.

Shortcut keys   Key combinations you can press instead of issuing certain commands. For example, Ctrl+C is a shortcut for opening the Edit menu and choosing Copy in most programs.

Shortcut menu   A menu that appears when you right-click an object.

Source code   The programming script behind a macro, a program, or a Web page.

Start menu   The menu that appears when you click the Start button.

Status bar   The bar at the bottom of a window that reports messages, amounts, or other data.

Subscribe   To add a newsgroup to the list of newsgroups you want to monitor. Or, for an email newsletter or discussion group, to sign up to receive it.

Swap file   A portion of the hard disk set aside to be used as a temporary holding tank for information that won't fit in the computer's memory as it operates.

System event   Any activity that Windows controls, such as opening a window, closing a window, exiting Windows, and so on.

System resources   Generically, this means the memory available for running the operating system and your programs. In Windows, it also includes virtual memory created with a swap file.

System tray   The area in the bottom-right corner of the Windows screen, in which icons for programs running in the background appear.

Taskbar   The bar at the bottom of the screen, showing buttons for each open window or running program.

Temporary file   A file that Windows or some other program creates to hold data as it calculates; it deletes the file automatically when it is finished with it.

Theme   A collection of settings you can apply as a whole. There are mouse themes, sound themes, desktop themes, and themes in applications such as FrontPage.

Tile   To arrange windows so that each window fits onscreen and none overlap. Compare to *Cascade*.

Toggle   To turn a feature on or off.

Trojan horse   A type of computer virus that masquerades as a useful program but that does damage to your system.

URL   Stands for Uniform Resource Locator. Synonymous with Web address.

Upload   To transfer a file from your own PC to another computer through the Internet or a communication program.

Vector graphic   A graphic created with mathematical formulas rather than with individual dots. Compare to *Bitmap*.

Video driver   A file that tells your operating system (Windows 98) how to work with your video card.

Virus   A destructive piece of programming that attaches itself to useful files and spreads from computer to computer, infecting more files and often causing damage.

Wallpaper   A graphical image placed on the desktop for decoration.

Web   See *World Wide Web*.

Web address   The address by which you access a Web page. Most Web addresses begin with `http://`. Also called URL.

Web browser   A program designed to view Web pages.

Web page   A file created in the HTML programming language that can be made available on a Web server and viewed with a Web browser.

Web server   A computer connected to the Internet full-time which "serves up" Web pages to other computers on the Internet that request access to them.

Web site   A collection of Web pages tied together with hyperlinks and organized around a common subject (usually all created by the same company or individual).

Web style   An operating mode in Windows 98 that makes the desktop and all windows more like a Web page.

Windows Explorer   A program in Windows 98 that helps you view and manage files.

Wizard   A series of dialog boxes that help you accomplish an otherwise-tricky task by asking you a series of questions.

Word   A powerful word processing program that you can purchase separately from Windows 98. It can also be purchased as part of the Microsoft Office suite.

Wordpad   A simple word processing program that comes free with Windows 98.

World Wide Web   An interconnected network of Web pages available on the Internet.

Zip file   A compressed archive of files in the ZIP format. Many programs you download from the Internet come this way. You must unzip them using a utility such as WinZip.

INDEX

Symbols

3D mouse pointers, 188

16-bit file systems, 445

24-Hour Support.com, 479

32-bit file systems, 415, 445

A

accessibility features
  Accessibility Wizard, 484
  audio, 487
  display, 487
  general options, 488
  keyboards, 486
  Magnifier, 485-486
  mouse, 487

Accessibility Wizard, 484

accessories. *See* programs

active controls. *See* Web Style Desktop

Active Desktop. *See* Web Style Desktop

adapters. *See* video

Add New Hardware Wizard, 204-207

Add Printer Wizard, 207, 210

Add Scheduled Task Wizard, 423

Add/Remove Programs utility, installing/ uninstalling
  Desktop themes, 178-179
  from CD-ROM disks, 143
  ICS (Internet Connection Sharing), 261-262
  My Briefcase, 277
  Microsoft Backup, 427
  Microsoft Chat, 379
  new programs, 142-143, 149-151
  Windows 98 compo-nents, 140-142

adding. *See* installing

Address Book
  email addresses
    adding, 359-361
    deleting, 362
    editing, 362
    printing, 362
    selecting, 361-362
  Internet, 398
  toolbar, 114
  Web pages, 306

Address Taskbar toolbar, 133

Adobe PageMill, Web pages, 398

Adobe Photoshop, 72

alarms for power manage-ment, 272-274

Albert's Ambry (share-ware programs), 477

Altavista search engine, 318

animated hourglass mouse pointers, 188

annotating graphics, Imaging, 73-75

applications. *See* pro-grams; utilities

Archive attribute, 100, 429

arranging. *See* sorting

arrow mouse pointer, 10

artwork. *See* graphics

attachments, email mes-sages
  reading/saving, 350-352
  sending, 364-365

attributes, files/folders
  Archive, 429
  changing, 100-101
  setting, 99-100
  viewing, 101

audio
  accessibility options, 487
  Desktop themes, 178-179
  multimedia settings, 190-191

What's This? Arrow, 10
Windows standard, 188
*Windows standard, plus
large and extra-large,
188*
properties, 185-186
*changing double-click
speed, 187*
*changing pointer speed,
187-188*
*pointer schemes,
188-189*
*switching buttons,
186-187*
Mouse Trails feature, 487
MouseKeys feature, 487
moving
files/folders, 90-91
Clipboard, 93-94
drag and drop, 91-93
text, 56-57
windows, 19-20
multimedia
programs. *See also* audio
programs
Media Player, 80-81
video programs, 80
settings, 189
audio, 190-191
*CD-ROM music,
193-194*
MIDI ( ), 192-193
video, 190-192
**multiuser operations
(Windows 98), 232**
User Profiles
disabling, 238-239
enabling, 232-234
global, 237-238

users
adding, 234-235
changing settings, 237
deleting, 236
switching between, 236
**Musical Instrument
Digital Interface.** *See*
**MIDI (Musical
Instrument Digital
Interface)**
My Briefcase files
copying
with disks, 277-279
on networks, 279
synchronizing
from disks, 279-281
from networks, 281
My Computer
drives/folders, 88
files/folders
managing, 84
*moving/copying with
drag and drop, 92-93*
**My Documents,
file/folders**
managing, 85-86
moving/copying with
drag and drop, 92-93

N

naming
Desktop shortcuts,
renaming, 130-131
files/folders, 98-99
rules, 59
navigating
drives/folders, 87
programs, 53-54

**Netscape Navigator,
302-304**
**Network Interface Card
(NIC), 253**
Network Neighborhood
file/folders
managing, 85
*moving/copying with
drag and drop, 92-93*
sharing, 245-247
mapping drives, 247-249
networks
client drivers, 253
components, installing,
253-255
direct cable connection,
255-256
files, My Briefcase
copying, 279
synchronizing, 281
finding computers,
249-250
null modem cables, 255
passwords, 240
peer-to-peer, 244
printers, 226, 228
installing, 209-210
protocols, 253
resources, 244
server-driven, 244
sharing
devices, 252-253
*disabling for Internet
connectivity, 289*
*drives by mapping,
247-249*
files, 251
*files via Network
Neighborhood,
245-247*
folders, 252-253
printers, 249-251
shortcuts to drives, 247

X-Z

Yahoo! search engine, 317-318

ZD Net Software Library, 477

ZIP disks. *See also* **boot disks, CD-ROM disks, floppy disks, hard disks, Jaz disks**
    downloading files, 144-147
     formatting, 107